To Colin with

Christ

Ju   n.

CAMP 020

MI5 and the Nazi Spies

The Official History of
MI5's Wartime Interrogation Centre

Introduced and edited
by Oliver Hoare

PUBLIC RECORD OFFICE

Public Record Office
Richmond
Surrey
TW9 4DU

© Crown Copyright 2000
Introduction © Oliver Hoare 2000

ISBN 1 903365 08 2

A catalogue card for this book
is available from the British Library

DEDICATION
For Georgia

Front of jacket:
Image from morale-raising Ministry of Information
wartime poster (PRO, INF 3/126).

Back of jacket:
Lieutenant-Colonel R.W.G. Stephens (Imperial War Museum, HU 66769);
Golenko, Vera Erichsen, Lindemans and Schellenberg (PRO, KV 4/13).

Printed by Bath Press Ltd, Bath

Contents

Terms and Abbreviations   vi

Introduction by Oliver Hoare   1

A Digest of Ham by Lieutenant-Colonel R.W.G. Stephens   31

Volume One: A Digest of Ham   31

Part I:	A Digest of Ham	33
	The Disruption of the NSDAP in the UK	34
	The "Phoney War"	35
	General Internment	39
Part II:	Ham 1940 to D-Day 1944	40
	The First Phase at Ham	42
	The Reserve Camp, Huntercombe,	
	or Camp 020R	46
	The Second Phase at Ham	47
Part III:	Ham – From Defence to Attack – D-Day	
	to the End	59
	(a) Agents operating before D-Day	60
	(b) Line Runners	61
	(c) "Stay-Behind" Network	67
	(d) Agents from Autonomous	
	Movements	67
	(e) Traitors from the Resistance	
	Movement	68
	(f) Saboteurs, "Bunker" and other	
	Agents	70
	The Forward Unit at Diest	71
Part IV:	Ham – Normal C.I. from D-Day to the End	73
Part V:	CSDIC (WEA) in Germany	82
	(a) Historical cases	83
	(i) The Last Days of Hitler	83
	(ii) The Liberation of Mussolini	
	in September 1943	87
	(iii) Other historical cases	92

(b) Scientific and technical issues   94
(c) Subversive movements   95
(d) Counter-espionage in the British
     Zone   97

Part VI: Envoi   103

Part VII: On the Interrogation of Spies   105
           The Nature of the Spy   105
           Characteristics of an Interrogator   107
           The Objective   109
           The Network of Investigation   113
           On the conduct of a C.I. investigation 114
           (a) Preliminaries   114
           (b) The Plan   117
           (c) The first vital interview   117
           On Special Devices   119
           (a) The use of "M" and Indirect
                Interrogation   119
           (b) The Stool Pigeon   122
           (c) The Cross-ruff   124
           (d) Confrontation   124
           (e) Assessors   125
           (f) The Legend of Cell Fourteen   126
           (g) The Technique of
                "Blow Hot – Blow Cold"   127
           (h) The Cover Story   128
           (i) "Sympathy Men"   129
           (j) Interrogation of the Wrong
                Prisoner   130
           (k) Faking of Newspapers   130
           (l) Exploitation of
                Rank-consciousness   130
           (m) Drink   130

Volume Two: Case Histories   133

Volume Three: Case Histories (Concluded)   301

Appendix   367

Index   370

Publisher's Note

This publication reproduces A *Digest of Ham*, written by Lieutenant-Colonel R.W.G. Stephens, the Commandant of Camp 020. The original files KV 4/13, KV 4/14 and KV 4/15 may be consulted at the Public Record Office, Kew. The symbol [...] is used where material from the original documents has been retained under section 3(4) of the Public Records Act 1958. In instances where [...] signifies agents' names that were originally retained for their own protection – but which are now in the public domain – their codenames, where known, have been inserted in square brackets. The introduction and index are modern additions.

Acknowledgements

I am indebted to the following people: Chris Doutney and Anne Kilminster for commissioning this book; Paul Sinnott, Sheila Knight and Peter Leek for all their hard work in preparing it for publication; members of the Security Service; Mrs Ward-Thomas and Mrs Williams, who kindly agreed to be interviewed; John 'Mr Latchmere' Morgan for showing me round Latchmere Resettlement Prison; Roy C. Nesbit for getting me started; G.T. Zwanenburgh, KON, MBE and Georges Van Acker for information on Karl Gartenfelt. The following I would like to thank for inspiration and encouragement: Prof. Christopher Andrew, Prof. Michael Dockrill, Prof. Andrew Lambert and Mark Seaman. I would like to thank all my PRO colleagues, but a special mention must go to Dr John Fisher, William Spencer, Dr Tracy Borman, Hugh Alexander and Maura Davies. I am also indebted to John Cox for his meticulous proofreading and to Lisa Kenwright of Indexing Specialists for compiling the index. For general moral support, thanks go to Ben Quinn, Hugh Byrne, Charles Hoare, George Staines and Jane Cox.

Terms and Abbreviations

001 – Camp 001, HM Prison Dartmoor
020 – Camp 020, Latchmere House, Ham Common (also known as B.1.E)
Abwehr – German Secret Service
AO – Auslands Organization (foreign groups of the Nazi Party)
B1A – Special Agents Section of B Branch (Espionage), MI5
BUF – British Union of Fascists
'C' or CSS – Head of the Secret Intelligence Service (MI6)
CI – Criminal investigation
CID – Criminal Investigation Department *or* Committee of Imperial Defence
CSDIC – Combined Services Detailed Interrogation Centre
CSDIC (WEA) – Combined Services Detailed Interrogation Centre (Western
    European Area)
DAF – German Labour Front
DDG – Deputy Director General. In this document it refers to DDG of MI5,
    Brigadier O.A. ('Jasper') Harker.
DG – Director General. In this document it refers to the DG of MI5, either Vernon
    Kell (1909–1940) or David Petrie (1940–1946).
FAK – Frontaufklärungs Kommandos
FAT – Frontaufklärungs Truppen
FBI – Federal Bureau of Investigation
FSP – Field Security Police
GC & CS – Government Code and Cipher School
GIS – German Intelligence Service
GSS – German Secret Service
HUMINT – Human intelligence, general term for intelligence gathered via
    interrogation or in person, as opposed to SIGINT (signals intelligence).
IO – Intelligence Officer
ISK – Intelligence Service Knox
ISOS – Intelligence Service Oliver Strachey (a general term used for decrypts of
    German Abwehr, SD and RSHA intelligence messages)
ISTOC – Intelligence gained from an SIS source at the German Embassy,
    Stockholm
JIC – Joint Intelligence Committee
KO – Kriegsorganisation (foreign stations of the Abwehr)
LRC – London Reception Centre
MI1 – Directorate of Military Intelligence
MI3 – German Section, Military Intelligence
MI5 – Imperial Security Service, also known as Security Service
MI6 – Secret Intelligence Service
MI8 – Radio Security Service (RSS)
MI9 – Escape and Evasion
MI11 – Field Security Police (FSP)
MI19 – Combined Services Detailed Interrogation Centre (CSDIC)
MO – Medical Officer
M/V – Motor vessel

NID – Naval Intelligence Division

NSDAP – National Sozialistische Deutsche Arbeiter Partei

OKW – Oberkommando der Wehrmacht, High Command of the German Army

OSS – Office of Strategic Studies

POW or PW – Prisoners of War (PW is used throughout this document)

PPF – Parti Populaire Français (French collaborationist group)

PWIS – Prisoner of War Intelligence Services

RIS – Russian Intelligence Service

RPS – Royal Patriotic School (see LRC)

RSHA – Reichssicherheitshautamt, Nazi Party Security Agency

SD – Sicherheitsdeinst, Nazi Security Service

SEALION, Operation – Planned German invasion of Britain, 1940

SHAEF – Supreme Headquarters Allied Expeditionary Force

SIGINT – Signals Intelligence

SIS – Secret Intelligence Service, also know as MI6

SNUFFBOX – Operation by British Intelligence to wipe out Fascist movements in Britain on the outbreak of war

SOE – Special Operations Executive

S/W – Secret writing

ULTRA – Intercepted wireless traffic of high-grade ciphers of whatever source, German, Italian or Japanese. In the US it was also referred to as MAGIC.

W Board – Wireless Board, controlling body of the Double Cross Committee

WT – Wireless Telegraphy

WX – Camp WX, Isle of Man

Y – The intercepted wireless traffic in low- and medium-grade codes and ciphers (see ULTRA)

YP – 'Yellow Peril', administrative system adopted at Camp 020 whereby important information was printed on easily identifiable bright-yellow paper.

XX – Double Cross Committee, also known as the Twenty Committee as the symbol XX makes the number twenty in Roman numerals. Can also refer to Double Cross agents.

Lieutenant-Colonel R.W.G. Stephens, the formidable Commandant of
Camp 020 and author of *A Digest of Ham*. (Imperial War Museum, HU 66769)

Introduction

'The story of Ham is stranger than fiction: indeed, as a work of fiction it would violate the probabilities.'

What follows in the succeeding pages is a most extraordinary document. It is extraordinary not only for its content, but also because of its author and the style in which it is couched. Although the creator's name appears nowhere on the original manuscript, it is undoubtedly the work of that MI5 extrovert Colonel 'Tin Eye' Stephens.[1] 'Tin Eye' was the fierce and uncompromising Camp Commandant of MI5's wartime interrogation and holding centre for enemy agents. The document reproduced here is MI5's secret official history of that spy prison, ominously known as Camp 020.

On 16 September 1999 Britain's Security Service, MI5, released a number of its files to the Public Record Office (PRO), Britain's national archive. This was the third such release in as many years and consisted largely of personal files on Nazi agents and policy files relating to counter-espionage activities of the Second World War, including the history of Camp 020.[2] The Security Service's move towards greater openness began on 18 November 1997 when it took an unprecedented step for such a secret organization and, for the first time, released some of its historical files. Inevitably historians have viewed this openness with some scepticism, and the Security Service has since been accused of waging a 'charm offensive'.[3] Whilst there is undoubtedly some truth in this allegation, further releases have taken place and will continue to do so as the Security Service brings itself in line with other Whitehall departments. To date there have been five separate releases, and currently over 500 Security Service files are now available for consultation at the PRO.[4] These documents relate almost exclusively to British counter-intelligence activities during the two World Wars; most peacetime activities of MI5 are still considered too sensitive for release, although it has been agreed that the interwar papers will be released once all the wartime documents have been transferred to the PRO. This openness has of course fed the huge appetite for 'spy stories' that exists amongst the media and the general public alike. As a result, all MI5's document releases have enjoyed extensive press coverage. However, the history reproduced here seems to have slipped into the public domain with relative anonymity – which may perhaps be attributed to the file's somewhat esoteric original title, *A Digest of Ham*. This stomach-churning witticism, redolent of Tin Eye's literary approach, refers to Camp 020's location near Ham Common in the London Borough of Richmond. The media have ignored this particular file, preferring to pay greater attention to more salacious or higher profile case files, such as the First World War seductress Mata Hari, the fascist renegade Lord Haw-Haw and the literary Nazi collaborator P.G.Wodehouse.[5] However, the history of Ham is no less sensationalist, with tales of intrigue, fraud, blackmail, interrogation, theft, drugs, perverts, playboys, prostitutes, violence, sabotage, double agents and, of course, espionage. Whilst 'Tin Eye' Stephens' version of events reads more like a Bulldog Drummond novel[6] than an official history, it does provide a good deal of historical analysis of interrogation and 'turning' techniques. It was these two developments that yielded large quantities of human intelligence (HUMINT) and crucially led to the creation of the fantastically successful Double Cross system (see p.22).

The original document is divided into three separate files, with the PRO designations KV 4/13, KV 4/14 and KV 4/15. Due to the length, particularly of the latter volumes, editing of the less salient case studies has been necessary. The first volume (KV 4/13) has been reproduced in its entirety with the exception of a 54-page interim interrogation report on the husband-and-wife case of Joseph and Mathilde Gobin. This case was included by Stephens by way of example to bring out particular lessons of interrogation, but these aspects and the story of the Gobins are covered more succinctly elsewhere in the document. Volume One is perhaps the most revealing and enlightening section, as it deals with interrogation techniques, trends in enemy espionage and the various phases in Camp 020's development, such as the establishment of a reserve Camp at Huntercombe (Camp 020R)[7] and forward Camps at Diest, near Brussels, and Bad Nenndorf, near Hanover. That Stephens considered Volume One to be a 'digest' is apparent from the document's original title, but he also uses this section as a vehicle for his own 'message'. Although certainly outside Stephens' remit, the first volume, particularly the section entitled 'Envoi', is used to assert his own views and justifications for the continuation of the British Secret Service as a whole. Warning of the nuclear hazards of the postwar era, Stephens accurately anticipates the Cold War scenario, clearly identifying where the dangers lie.

> The stark reality is that the security lies in the atom bomb, and it is the responsibility of the Intelligence Service to know how best it can be used for us, and on the instant, when and where it is to be used against us . . . the Colossus astride Europe is Russia. And that ally is spying upon us in a large, a very large way.[8] (1946)

Stephens remarks that Volumes Two and Three are 'pure intelligence' and really meant for a 'student with leisure'.[9] However, strictly speaking the case studies are not 'pure intelligence', but rather summaries of the more interesting cases investigated by Stephens and his staff. They include brief details of how agents were 'broken' and what the intelligence yield was. Stephens listed over 200 separate cases, in which some 350 individuals are mentioned.[10] As a whole the case histories are lengthy, but each individual case is concise and adorned with flashes of Stephens' outspoken and in places perhaps unconscious wit, which makes for entertaining reading. The case studies are generally in chronological order, starting with the incompetent 'invasion' spies of 1940 and ending with the spymasters and stay-behind agents who were picked up by the advancing Allies.

The origins of Stephens' history

Towards the end of the Second World War the Director General of the Security Service, Sir David Petrie, instructed his head of research, John 'Jack' Curry, to write a history of the Service. The 'Curry history', as it became known, was for MI5 eyes only and intended strictly for internal consumption. The Curry history was stored in the vaults of the invaluable MI5 registry for over 50 years, until 1999 when it was transferred to the Public Record Office.[11] The original title, *The Security Service: Its Problems and Organisational Adjustments 1908-1945*, suggests that Curry's intention was to highlight the difficulties experienced by the Service, rather than to document its wartime successes, however considerable they were. The purpose was to aid future MI5 directors in the event of a war, and as such the Curry history focused on the requirements needed to put the service on a war footing. To aid Curry in his task the DG ordered each of the divisional heads to review the work of their department, identify significant areas of interest and appoint a suitable officer to produce a rough draft of their findings for inclusion into the overall history. For subsection B.1.E (Camp 020), Lieutenant-Colonel G. Sampson was charged with this task. Sampson was well placed to write such an account; he had served for the duration of the war alongside Major R. Short as Assistant Commandant at Camp 020 and had in fact served at Ham longer than

Lieutenant-Colonel G. Sampson, assistant commandant and initial author of the history of Camp 020. (Imperial War Museum, HU 66757)

Major R. Short, assistant commandant and assistant author. Short accompanied Stephens to Diest and then Bad Nenndorf. After the War, Short gave evidence against Stephens during a Court Martial for ill-treatment of prisoners. Stephens was cleared of all charges, and Short's own reputation became tarnished. (Imperial War Museum, HU 66758)

anyone else, including Stephens. Before Stephens took over on 10 July 1940 as Camp Commandant, Sampson had been at Ham for some time to supervise the building work that transformed Latchmere House from an old First World War military hospital into a modern interrogation centre. On 22 June 1945 Sampson sent a preliminary draft of the Camp 020 history to 'Jack' Curry, which had previously been seen and approved by Colonel Stephens. On 21 September Sampson duly submitted to the Deputy Director General of MI5, Brigadier O.A. ('Jasper') Harker, what he thought was to be the final draft: a succinct version of 'no more than a hundred pages', as he had been instructed.[12] A copy of the 'final' version was again sent to Colonel Stephens for comment, although on this occasion no approval was forthcoming. In a letter to Harker in March 1946, some six months after Sampson had submitted his 'final' draft, Stephens apparently had a change of heart and announced his frank disappointment at Sampson's attempt – 'It is uneven, does not cover the ground and is tedious reading'. During the six months that had elapsed prior to this correspondence, Sampson had left the Security Service, putting his extensive linguistic skills to use at the United Nations. Due to this fact, Stephens suggested that, with the assistance of Major R. Short, he himself should re-cast the whole history from scratch, having already tried and failed to strengthen the existing Sampson report.[13] To aid in this self-appointed task, Stephens requested a sneak preview of the Curry history, which by this stage had just been completed. Petrie, however, had similar objections to the bulky Curry history and was unwilling to make it available to Stephens.[14] Since the Curry history was already complete, although in a form unacceptable to Petrie, it is apparent that the achievements of 020 and its associated camps were regarded so highly by the DDG that a separate history, independent of Curry's, was required. On 3 April 1946 Harker gave Stephens his, and the DG's, full approval to go ahead with the rewrite, emphasizing the significance and value of Stephens' work and experience:

> As you know I regard the work of 020 to have been of such vital importance to the Organisation [MI5] that it is essential that any future D.G., who may have to start a similar show, should have the full benefit of all your experience.[15]

At the time of writing, Stephens was head of No. 74 CSDIC (also known as Bad Nenndorf) in Germany; and he did not seem overly pleased with the end result, admitting in the editor's note that he was 'very busy at the time' and that the document did not 'recapture the strain of those anxious years'.[16] By now the history had been written three times, and it suffered from the same defect as the Curry history – an excessive amount of material. The Sampson draft had only run to 109 pages, but the rewrite extended to some 450 pages. Even assuming that Stephens began work on the history immediately he got word from the DG (April 1946) and taking into account Major Short's help, the document was compiled quite hastily. If one compares the initial Sampson draft with Volume One of Stephens' variant, it is clear that it is more or less a direct rewrite, although it is obviously heavily 'sauced' with Stephens' overbearing style. The supplementary volumes of case histories, on the other hand, which made up the bulk of the additions to the history, were written completely from scratch. Even so, as already indicated, the case histories were hardly 'pure' or raw intelligence, as Stephens suggested, but a distillation of material culled largely from MI5 personal files and from Stephens' memory.[17]

MI5 maintained personal files on practically all known or suspected enemy intelligence agents and officers. Over 300 of these personal files are now available at the PRO.[18] The mass of detail contained in these files is quite astonishing: they include photographs, censored letters, recorded conversations, lists of associates, sketches of residences, interrogation reports, confessions, preparation papers for prosecution and extracts from SIS and double agent reports, as well as information gleaned from 'Most Secret Sources' (intercepted wireless signals, known as ULTRA). The sum and substance of these files is to be found in the detailed interrogation report – also referred to as the 'Camp 020: Main Report' or 'Interim Report' – included in most of the personal files. Often several hundred pages long, the 020 Main Report describes, in chilling detail, all aspects of the agent's life and work. In some cases the report extends, literally, from the agent's childhood to execution. Whilst Stephens used these in-depth reports to compile the case histories, he also relied heavily on what was referred to as 'Yellow Perils' or 'YPs'. The name 'Yellow

Peril' was coined, unsurprisingly, by Stephens and referred to an administrative procedure that he himself had devised. This very simple and effective method consisted of printing any important summary of information on bright-yellow paper.[19] Once a YP was placed amongst the routine white paper of the personal files it would stand out prominently, thus facilitating easy access and quick reference. The pride 'Tin Eye' took in this innovation was almost as deep as his loathing of the spy.

> If character can be expressed in colour, yellow is probably the most fitting shade for the average spy. But the renowned Yellow Peril of Ham was not developed out of any such fancy . . . . YP's sent out from Camp 020 became something more than mere official documents. Personalities were their subject as much as stark facts; the personality became their keynote. It became the wont of the Commandant to preface each report on despatch from Ham with a concise and trenchant summary of a commentary of the case. Soon the Yellow Peril had won fame as well as attention.[20]

For anyone researching the personal files, the 'Yellow Perils' are still a very useful aid, providing quick access to the required information. And if written by Stephens, they provide some light entertainment, too. It is also worth noting that the case studies in Volumes Two and Three of this document serve as a very useful summary guide to many of the personal files held at the PRO.[21]

Stephens and the establishment of Ham

As the reader may have already grasped, the story of Camp 020 is inextricably linked to one man in particular – Lieutenant-Colonel Robin William George Stephens. Stephens was undoubtedly a larger-than-life character, and even within MI5 he was considered something of an extroverted oddball. He had a fearsome reputation as a temperamental authoritarian and, although popularly known throughout the service as 'Tin Eye', this familiarity did not necessarily extend to his presence. It is unclear how exactly the nickname was coined, although it may be safe to assume that it referred to the steely glare that emanated from behind Stephens' ever-present monocle. Sharp and immaculate in his dress, Stephens' physical appearance was more reminiscent of a stereotypical Gestapo officer (see photograph on page viii). His staff at Camp 020 confirm that his temper was short when dealing with those he saw as working for the enemy, and he did not suffer those he regarded as fools gladly. However, his intimidating manner and appearance were largely an act put on for interrogration purposes. His immediate staff thought fondly of him, and his personal secretary once said he was 'the kindest boss she had ever worked for'. He was also known as a generous host, the monthly mess parties being remembered for good food and copious amounts of drink.[22] Stephens' abhorrence of the enemy was above the norm and tended to verge on the obsessive. This sentiment was instilled into his staff and was something he considered a paramount prerequisite for any interrogator: 'First and foremost there must be certain inherent qualities. There must be an implacable hatred of the enemy.'[23] Stephens' animosity appears to have been as wide as it was deep (his apparent xenophobia was fair in that it extended equally to all creeds and races):

'. . . both men were abnormally intelligent for Icelanders, but still not over-intelligent . . .'[24]

'Because he was a good Frenchman, he accepted the German's money'[25]

'Italy is a country peopled by undersized, posturing folk'[26]

'Of all the obstinate, stubborn, immoral and immutable Spaniards Juan Gorez de Lecube was incontestably the most mulish'[27]

One must, however, tread carefully. Stephens was not only a product of his time, but he seemed to take great delight in expounding derogatory comments and making sweeping overstatements for pure impact and entertainment value. Despite what might be interpreted as racist comments, it would seem that Stephens was more astute than this type of language might suggest. When assessing the 'Nature of the Spy', Stephens begins by provoking the reader with the suggestion that national characteristics may give some indication of a spy's motives. However, he coldly concludes that 'National Characteristics in spies are inconclusive . . . the interrogator must treat each spy as a very individual case for that matter, a very personal enemy.'[28]

After the War, while head of No. 74 CSDIC at the aptly named Bad Nenndorf, Stephens' reputation was put under further pressure when he faced Court Martial for claims of ill treatment and brutality. A Foreign Office memo summarized the charges put forward by Bad Nenndorf inmates:

(1) insufficient clothing; (2) intimidation by the guards; (3) mental and physical torture during the interrogations; (4) they were kept in solitary confinement for long periods with no exercise; (5) they were committed to punishment cells, not for any offence, but simply because the interrogator was not satisfied with their answers; (6) in the punishment cells, during the bitter winter, they were deprived of certain articles of clothing, had buckets of cold water thrown into the cell and were forced to scrub the cell floor for long periods, and were assaulted and man-handled; (7) medical attention was grossly inadequate; (8) food was insufficient; (9) discharge of prisoners was unnecessarily delayed; (10) personal property of the prisoners were stolen.[29]

Stephens was in fact cleared of all charges, some of which were struck from the charge sheet on the first day of the proceedings.[30] In his singular manner, he gave his judgement on those who had accused him:

> Their motives are invariably foul, most of them are degenerates, most of them come diseased from V.D., many are chronic medical cases . . . they are pathological liars and the value of their Christian oath is therefore doubtful.[31]

However, it would seem that despite Stephens' reputation he appeared, at least on paper, to be the perfect officer and gentleman. Born to British parents in Alexandria on 23 June 1900, he was initially educated at the Lycée Français in Egypt. In 1912 the family returned to Britain, and the young Stephens finished his education at Dulwich College. At the age of 18 he joined the Royal Military Academy Woolwich, later transferring to Quetta Cadet College in India and finally joining the Indian Army, where he served in five campaigns on the North West Frontier, took part in the Mahbar Rebellion and was mentioned in despatches. Some time after the First World War Stephens appears to have been attached to the Indian Political Service, then later became a magistrate and an assistant Judge Advocate General in India. On 9 September 1939, at the age of 39, Stephens joined the Security Service with the rank of Captain. Field Marshal (later Lord) Birdwood, whom Stephens served under in India, acted as his sponsor and conducted the then obligatory introduction into the secret world of MI5. It would seem that Stephens was a typical MI5 recruit: he was part of the old boy network and had of course been in the armed services in India.[32] However, Stephens' past was sketchy in places and he had obviously been something of a rolling stone. His claimed knowledge of languages suggested that he had travelled extensively. With varying degrees of proficiency, he could speak, read and write Urdu, Arabic, Somali, Amharic, French, German and Italian. He had indeed travelled widely in Egypt, India, Arabia, the Persian Gulf, Abyssinia, French Somaliland, British Somaliland, Sudan, Germany, Italy, France, Greece, the Black Sea and Switzerland. In 1933, on return to England from India, Stephens became in some way connected with the courts at Lincoln's Inn. Although he was never to officially qualify as a lawyer, he did collaborate with Sir Harry Lushington Stephen on *A Digest of the Laws and Evidence in Courts Martial* (a title echoed in this document's original title, *A Digest of Ham*).[33] Stephens' writing skills were also employed during a spell in journalism, and it seems probable that it was during this period that Stephens developed his rather eccentric writing style. A brief statement on his Security Service application form mentions that he played a mysterious unofficial role in the Italian Abyssinian Crisis, earning him the Star of Abyssinia. Between 1937 and 1939, while based in Lincoln, he worked for the National Fitness Council for England. It is likely that it was also in Lincoln that he met his future wife, Joan Geraldine Pearson Dowling.

It is unclear what role or what training Stephens received on entering the Security Service, although he was soon to act as an interrogator at the Oratory

Schools. Along with the inimitable Dick White, Assistant Director of B Branch, Stephens was instrumental in pushing for the establishment of a dedicated interrogation camp.[34] The first documentary evidence of Stephens' work at the Security Service also happens to be the first reference to what was later to become Camp 020. In an undated memorandum (other sources would suggest it was 4 or 5 July 1940) to the newly formed Home Defence (Security) Executive, commonly known as the Swinton Committee, the then Captain Stephens, complained that he had been forced to interrogate suspected subversives in a variety of unsuitable and cramped accommodation.[35] These early interrogations – which included subversive British Nationals and then, after the outbreak of war, a large number of interned aliens – took place in a variety of makeshift interview rooms dotted around London, at venues such as Scotland Yard, Wandsworth and Holloway prisons, Cannon Row, Olympia and, in particular, the Oratory Schools. The last straw came when the interrogation of an internee by the name of Schutz was delayed because the interrogation rooms at the Oratory School, which doubled up as the officers' sleeping quarters, was occupied whilst an officer was having difficulties in changing his trousers.

The Swinton Committee sympathized with Stephens' plight, and the farcical 'trouser incident' may well have been the deciding factor in the Committee's decision to create a permanent interrogation camp. With Home Office approval and

A less 'terrifying aspect' of Colonel Stephens, seen here relaxing with his wife, Joan.

the necessary Treasury grant, it was agreed that the Office of Works should identify and equip a building suitable for the interrogation and holding of British subversives and enemy aliens who couldn't be classified as POWs. This centre was to be modelled on the POW camp at Cockfosters, which had been used for similar purposes. It was made clear that internees would only be held for purposes of interrogation and that the period could not extend for longer than two months. Once interrogation had been completed, the internees were to be returned to their original place of detention. MI5 had supreme command of the camp and, apart from a military guard for external security, it would be completely independent of the Armed Services. MI5 were required to supply interrogation and secretarial staff, while internal order would be maintained by prison warders made up from 'odds and sods' not needed or wanted by their own military units.[36] Whilst independent of the Services, the camp was to be run in a strict military fashion. Officers wore the service uniform of their origin, Stephens setting the standard by retaining his spotless Gurkha Rifles uniform.

Within a matter of days of Home Office approval, Latchmere House was selected as the most appropriate site. This rather plain Victorian mansion, built by a prosperous merchant, Joshua Field, was suitably located in the leafy suburbs of West London, near Ham Common.[37] It lay in its own grounds at the end of a secluded and wooded road. The house and accompanying grounds had originally been purchased by the War Office for use as a Military Hospital during the First World War for 'neurasthenic' officers recovering from shell shock.[38] As a result of

Exterior of Latchmere House in November 1940 – at the height of Operation LENA, in which the first wave of German clandestine agents tried to penetrate the UK. The operation failed miserably. The photograph shows the inner compound surrounded by barbed wire. (Imperial War Museum, HU 66759)

this medical capacity, Latchmere was already furnished with an annexe comprising some 30 rooms that were easily adapted for the detention of prisoners. Later these cells were installed with 'bugging' equipment known as 'M' devices, which were used for listening in on unsuspecting inmates. A number of outbuildings and Nissen huts were built for staff accommodation. The house itself was used largely for interrogation and administrative purposes. Although fairly remote, Latchmere was hidden from preying eyes by the erection of a tall wooden fence around the entire perimeter. The interior compound was similarly surrounded with double barbed wire. Secrecy and security were of course top priority, and passes were to be produced on entering and leaving, all names of staff and visitors being entered in a little book by the Military Police who manned the one and only exit. The few residents in the immediate vicinity were also vetted from time to time. Internally, security was equally tight: anyone wishing to pass from the inside to the outside, or vice versa, had to pass through at least four security checks.

Initially Sampson headed the operation, but this was only to oversee the building work. The new camp was simply referred to as 'Ham' or 'B.1.E' (a subsection of MI5's B Branch, Espionage); it was not until December 1941 that it received the military designation Camp 020. The classification 020 was adopted from a similar institution, Camp 001, the hospital wing of HM Prison Dartmoor, which was being used to house sensitive internees.[39] On 10 July 1940 'Tin Eye' Stephens and a small complement of staff took possession of Latchmere House and it associated grounds. By 27 July, the first inmates had arrived and Camp 020 was truly open for business.

'Spy fever'

As the Second World War loomed, an epidemic of 'spy fever' broke out in Britain. Having not learnt the lessons of the First World War, the British public was once again gripped by a so-called 'Fifth Column' panic. This paranoia was greatly exaggerated by the rapid fall of France and the Low Countries, and in particular with the invasions of Denmark and Norway. It was commonly perceived that hordes of German agents had been working behind the Western lines, assisting the Wehrmacht in their rapid advance over Europe. It was therefore logical to conclude that a similar operation was taking place in Britain. It was known from a highly placed SIS source[40] that there was a German plan to invade Britain, known as Operation SEALION, but there was certainly no such Fifth Column in Britain. Of the six German agents known to be working in Britain, four were picked up immediately war was declared; a Swedish woman was put under surveillance, then picked up in December when she applied for an exit permit to leave the country; and the sixth, a Welsh electrician named Arthur Owens, was 'turned' into a double agent, codename SNOW (see p.15).[41] However, with a spate of 'Fifth Column' articles in the press, it was not easy to allay the fears of an alarmist public, especially as some senior military officials seemed to vindicate such reports. General Ironside, Commander in Chief of the Home Forces, publicly announced that enemy agents were 'definitely preparing aerodromes in Britain'.[42] Other official sources were also guilty of alarmist views – including the Ministry of Information, which issued a leaflet proclaiming the precarious catch-22 scenario posed by a Fifth Column:

> There is a fifth column in Britain. Anyone who thinks that there isn't . . . has simply fallen in to the trap laid by the fifth column itself. *For the first job of the fifth column is to make people think that it does not exist.*[43]

During the early stages of the war, MI5 experienced rapid expansion that strained the organization almost to breaking point. According to the Curry history, at the end of 1938 MI5 totalled 133 staff and by the beginning of 1941 this number totalled 868 (634 were women). In the space of a year the staff numbers had grown by six and a half times, but the strain was exacerbated by new vetting requests from security-conscious government officials and by the flood of enquiries from the general public regarding spy scares. Although inundated by absurd accounts of enemy espionage, MI5 were obliged to investigate. A great deal of time and effort was taken up by these largely spurious reports – including accumulation of files on time-wasting subjects such as enemy signalling by the 'burning of trees, hedges and haystacks', suspect markings on telegraph poles and on the ground, the use of carrier pigeons for sending secret messages and, most alarming of all, the grave dangers posed by 'obscure pieces of paper'![44] By the end of the so-called 'Phoney War' the bureaucracy was becoming unmanageable. With the deluge of paper and confusion in the chain of command caused by such rapid growth, MI5 was coming close to collapse.

On top of these problems, MI5 was stretched further still by the controversial decision to intern all enemy aliens. In the latter part of May 1940 the War Cabinet debated the pros and cons of mass internment. Churchill was keen to go ahead, but the Home Secretary, Sir John Anderson, believed that general internment would put an unbearable exertion on the administrative machine. Whilst this must surely have been a concern for MI5, they continued to support the proposal for mass internment in order to curb the possibility that enemy agents were at large in Britain. The first function of the newly created Home Defence (Security) Executive was to discuss a paper commissioned by Churchill from the Chiefs of Staff on the problems that would arise if France fell out of the war. On 27 May the Executive recommended:

> ruthless action . . . to eliminate any chances of Fifth Column activities and internment of all enemy aliens and of subversive organisations, which the latter should be proscribed.[45]

As the Continent fell country by country into Nazi hands, the arguments for general interment gathered more and more credence. With Italy joining the fray on 11 June, the War Cabinet approved the final recommendations that all categories of aliens should be interned, with priority given to MI5's 'most wanted' list. At the height of internment (end of July 1940), it was estimated that 27,000 people, including 4,000 Italians, had been detained – most of whom were in fact anti-Nazi.

Reorganization of MI5 and ISOS

In May 1940 Churchill created the Home Defence (Security) Executive. This body later became known as the Security Executive and was often referred to as the Swinton Committee, after its head, former Air Secretary, Lord Swinton. It was the Prime Minister's vision that the Swinton Committee should smooth over the considerable 'overlaps and underlaps' of the various agencies dealing with counter-espionage and subversion. Churchill specifically charged Swinton to 'find out whether there is a fifth column in this country and if so to eliminate it'.[46] Swinton was highly critical of MI5's leadership, which had already come under review in May of that year from Lord Hankey. Hankey, a minister without portfolio, had undertaken an investigation of SIS that had been extended to include MI5 at the request of the Prime Minister, the Foreign Secretary and the Service Chiefs.[47] With mounting pressure on MI5 to deal with the perceived threat of a Fifth Column, something had to give, and on 10 June 1940 the 68-year-old veteran Director General, Vernon Kell, was dismissed, along with his long-time deputy, Eric Holt-Wilson. 'Jasper' Harker, head of B Branch, temporarily filled the post until November 1940, when Sir David Petrie took the helm. Petrie, who had been former head of the Delhi Intelligence Bureau, had also been critical of MI5's administration. Before taking the post of DG, Petrie had been called out of semi-retirement in Cairo to conduct a review. In addition to those of Hankey and Swinton, this was the third review of the service in under a year. Although Petrie was generally disparaging of MI5, suggesting that recruitment and administration procedures were outdated, he did recommend that Vernon Kell should not be deposed from the post of Director General.[48] However, by the time Petrie's report was submitted in February 1941, MI5's founding head had already been dismissed after 31 years of dedicated service.[49] At this point morale within the service was at very low ebb, and some senior officers even threatened resignation. However, Petrie was an able manager and began to breathe new life into a leadership that many believed had stagnated under Kell. Whilst Petrie was responsible for some significant administrative changes (especially within the registry, which had fallen into disarray and needed modernization), it should be noted that this 'breath of fresh air' coincided with and was to a large extent facilitated by a crucial breakthrough in signals intelligence, known as ISOS.

In August 1940 the Radio Security Service (RSS), also known as MI9, had succeeded in intercepting some Abwehr radio signals. By December the brilliant cryptographers of GC & CS based at Bletchley Park had broken the main hand cipher used to encrypt the Abwehr's secret radio messages. This signals intelligence became known as Intelligence Service Oliver Stachey (ISOS), after the section head at Bletchley Park. In December 1941 a further breakthrough was made when the machine cipher code was broken, and this intelligence became similarly known as Intelligence Service Knox (ISK), after the talented cryptographer 'Dilly' Knox. From this point on, MI5 were able to read all Abwehr signals traffic continuously throughout the war. The value of this signals intelligence not only had the greatest significance for MI5 for counter-espionage purposes and the identification of enemy agents but also confirmed the success of the Double Cross system (see p.22), which ultimately led to operational deception at a strategic level.[50]

From 'non-entities' to 'real' spies

In an attempt to meet the Prime Minister's demands, the Swinton Committee went on to consider all questions relating to Fifth Column activity, counter-espionage and counter-subversion. At the top of the list of subjects for discussion were 'arrangements for dealing with suspected enemy agents' and 'facilities for interrogation and detention'.[51] As already mentioned, this led to the establishment of Camp 020 in July 1940. Shortly afterwards, on 27 July, the first batch of internees arrived. This group numbered 27 men and consisted largely of British subversives (mainly members of the BUF) but also included a few enemy aliens resident in Britain, as well as a handful of foreign suspects who had been evacuated with the British at Dunkirk.[52] Stephens skates over this early period, briefly mentioning a few 'treacherous . . . shabby nonentities',[53] none of whom are referred to in the case histories. Whilst the establishment of Camp 020 and the incarceration of a few fascists allowed Swinton to report that something was being done to combat the Fifth Column, it proved a tactical error. Amongst these internees, the British claimed their rights as British citizens and appealed for wrongful imprisonment. This was worsened by the fact that Camp 020 had not yet been designated a place of detention by the Home Secretary under the Defence Regulations. With representations in Parliament, the existence and status of the Camp became publicly known. Whilst this publicity was unwelcome to the Security Service and led to requests by Protecting Powers and other bodies to inspect the camp, it did go some way to allay the public's anxiety over spy scares.[54] By October it had been decided to concentrate on the more serious cases, and by end of September all British subjects had been transferred to another institution, in Ascot.[55] With regard to the foreign element, it was quickly realized that they could not be lightly admitted on mere suspicion of spying, for if they proved innocent and were allowed to 'walk' the fate of other inmates and the methods of interrogation would surely be compromised. By November 1940, Camp 020 'had settled down to its proper role' and had become a permanent detention centre reserved entirely for enemy agents and those that were gravely suspected of being spies.[56]

In the latter part of 1940, as the Lüftwaffe and RAF fought out the Battle of Britain, the first 'real' spies began to arrive in Britain. They arrived via a variety of clandestine means – small boats, parachute, seaplanes, U-boats. This distinct initial group of agents was referred to as the 'Invasion Spies'. These unfortunate and badly trained individuals were under the impression that the Nazi invasion of Britain, Operation SEALION, was imminent and expected support from the invading troops. From September to November 1940, the Abwehr sent 21 agents to the UK for the purpose of reporting on British defence measures and general morale. Their secondary mission, once the proposed invasion was underway, was to mingle with the retreating enemy forces and report their movements by wireless. The plan, known as Operation LENA, was ill conceived and the agents were badly trained and in many cases working under duress. All were captured, apart from William Ter Braak who committed suicide (see p.23). Three became double agents and five were executed, the rest being interned for the duration of the war. The Abwehr and its associated espionage organizations never really recovered from this debacle.[57] By late 1940 MI5 had the basis of a Double Cross system in place and were also reading Abwehr signals, which made it almost impossible for German agents to penetrate the UK without interception.

The first 'Invasion Spies' arrived on the morning of 3 September 1940. Jose Walberg, Carl Meyer, Charles Van Der Kieboom and Sjoerd Pons (p.134) landed in two separate dinghies. The first landed near Dungeness, and the second a few miles along the coast, between Dymchurch and Rye. The whole group had been towed over in fishing boats by a German minesweeper; they then sailed closer to the coast, where they boarded the two dinghies and rowed to the shore. All four men were captured in a matter of hours, largely due to their own stupidity. They were also carrying false papers based on information sent by Britain's earliest wartime double agent, SNOW, and were thus easily identifiable. Three of them were executed, but Pons eluded the hangman's rope by convincing the Court that he had been blackmailed into working for the Germans.

Shortly after the first seaborne landing, the first parachute agent was dropped. Under the instruction of Abwehr spymaster Major Nikolaus Ritter, a small unit was created for clandestine parachute drops. The unit was headed by Hauptmann Karl Gartenfelt. Using specially painted Heinkel He111s and Ju88s, Gartenfelt would fly low over the English Channel to evade radar and then climb to an altitude of 20,000 feet. When nearing the drop zone, he would descend to 3,000 feet, throttle the engines and descend a further 2,500 feet to below 500 feet, then drop the poor Abwehr agents into the waiting arms of MI5.[58] The first parachute agent was Gösta Caroli, later known as double agent SUMMER; his arrival had been expected, again through agent SNOW (pp.137-41). Between January and July 1941 a further four parachute agents were dropped, as well as another dinghy party to Scotland; again all of them were caught, except for Ter Braak.

After the first spate of clandestine landings by parachute and small boats, the Germans gave up the idea almost entirely and turned to the only other method left to them, which was infiltration of agents through the guise of refugees. Unfortunately for the Abwehr, an MI5 reception awaited refugees, at the London Reception Centre, to ascertain their *bona fides*.

The London Reception Centre

By early summer 1940, with the collapse of France and the Low Countries, Britain began to experience a huge influx of refugees from the Continent. Under the Aliens Orders, enemy aliens were normally interned while non-enemy aliens had to convince MI5 and the immigration and Security Control officers that they had a good reason to be in Britain. Initially aliens were vetted in a very *ad hoc* fashion by 'examiners', known as B.24s, in improvised areas normally at the port of entry. The process that the examiners employed consisted of 'running a finger down a list of names to see if any "struck a chord" from memory'. Whilst the examiners tried to make the 'best of a very bad job', it was soon realized that such a procedure was simply not efficient or effective.[59] The solution was to create a central establishment for the specific purpose of processing refugees, and this took the form of the Victoria Royal Patriotic School, a large neo-Gothic mid-Victorian charity institution near Clapham Junction. Female refugees were to be housed in similar accommodation in a nearby building in Nightingale Lane. Section D4 of MI5, which dealt with travel control, instituted a directive that all aliens should be sent to the new reception centre. The only exception to this rule were travellers able to prove their *bona fides* unequivocally, such as military personnel, high-ranking allied officers, SIS and SOE accredited agents, and those in possession of diplomatic papers.[60] The Royal Patriotic School (RPS) opened for its new role on 10 January 1941; in October 1942, after extensive reorganization, it became known as the London Reception Centre or LRC. The influx of aliens processed at the LRC rose sharply from 155 in January to an average of 700 a month. As to be expected, there were many teething problems. Although the LRC came under Home Office control, it was run by the espionage section of MI5 (subsection B.1.D.). Dick White, head of B Division, was responsible for reforming procedures that brought about an effective administration. By the autumn of 1941 many of the difficulties had been ironed out, with the introduction of stricter discipline, a larger complement of examining staff and registry secretaries, and the creation of property, photographic and intelligence sections. These changes all helped to speed up the process and, in Dick White's words, greatly assisted the LRC in its main function of distinguishing between the 'sheep' and the 'goats' – i.e. genuine refugees, as opposed to suspected or enemy agents.[61]

The most significant innovation, however, was the reorganization of record keeping, in conjunction with a sound system of interrogation.[62] A card-indexing scheme was introduced to record the methods and routes used by enemy agents and by legitimate members of the Allied resistance movements. Gradually a great variety of useful information was built up, including enemy controls and regulations, living and travelling conditions, Gestapo interrogation techniques, and enemy penetrations of escape organizations.[63] MI5 and SIS of course maintained their own indexes of information, but the data that they provided was on suspected agents, whilst what was required for LRC was positive non-suspect data on persons that were 'pro-Allied' and whose appearance in an alien's testimony could prove his or her story. This unique body of knowledge became known as the Information Index and was invaluable in quickly establishing whether an alien was 'sheep', and therefore available for Allied service, or a 'goat' to be passed on to Camp 020 for further interrogation. The object of the LRC was not only to detect spies, undesirables and renegades, but also to be on the look-out for prospective recruits for Britain's other clandestine organizations. To this extent SIS and SOE maintained a presence at the LRC, although MI5 reserved the right to interview all comers first.[64]

It was estimated that 33,000 aliens were inspected at the LRC, and only three enemy agents with missions in Britain were known to have passed through undetected.[65] This success was facilitated by two crucial factors. The first of these was the effective control of individuals within the country, which meant that the clandestine landing of spies was an uneconomic project. The second was the strict control of individuals entering the country. The LRC formed a 'narrow bottleneck' through which all refugees passed, or at least all those that were not immediately able to prove they were genuine refugees. The enemy was aware of the existence of the LRC and briefed their agents accordingly, but it became increasingly difficult to construct a convincing story that was not checkable via the Information Index, and in any case the cover stories concocted by the Abwehr were often flimsy and poorly researched.

The whole process of the LRC was greatly facilitated by an informal and friendly ethos. Most interviews were one to one and conducted in a relaxed manner. Larger groups were initially dealt with by a short questionnaire. The accommodation was very simple, but adequate; and welfare officers were able to issue small sums of money and cigarettes, as provided by the Allied governments concerned. Recreations included dance bands, cinema shows, a football pitch and a croquet lawn. It was generally perceived by the staff that it was unnecessary to be heavy-handed, as 95 per cent of the refugees were not only totally honest but had genuinely faced great hardship to get to Britain. Secondly, it was discovered that in a cooperative atmosphere 'aliens would always divulge more readily and more fully all the information he may have in his possession, which even if innocent, may well have a bearing on other cases.'[66] Indeed, Lieutenant-Colonel Baxter, Head of B.1.D (LRC), stated that 'the importance of this psychological [friendly] approach in LRC work cannot be too strongly stressed'.[67] However, such an amenable approach did not extend to the dark confines of Camp 020. Once an alien was positively identified as an enemy agent or seriously suspected of being one, he or she would be quickly escorted from the LRC to Ham for a more thorough investigation.

Interrogation and treatment of prisoners

The main aim of Stephens and his staff was initially to establish the guilt of those unfortunate inmates who found themselves at 020; and secondly, to obtain as much valuable information about the enemy's intentions as possible. However, because Camp 020 was an entirely novel venture there was no manual or rule book for this type of work. During the First World War there had been interrogations of enemy agents, but in many cases they were designed solely to establish the guilt of the accused and obtain a confession with a view to prosecution. There was no permanent installation for such purposes, let alone anything on the scale of Camp 020. Therefore the development of interrogation rested largely on a process of trial and error. Due to the fact that there was no central pool of trained officers for this type of work, a large number of candidates from various sources were considered. The common recruiting practice within the clandestine services of using private channels and personal recommendations was employed on most occasions. The only quantifiable requirement for a post seemed to be a proficiency in languages; also, those who 'were widely travelled, had considerable experience of life . . . and showed themselves to be adaptable' proved to be suitable.[68] Many were rejected at the first interview, as were many of those who went on to serve the initial probationary period.[69] Stephens believed that there were two types of interrogator, the 'breaker' and the 'investigator'. The 'breaker' would establish the guilt by obtaining a written confession; the 'investigator' would then extract and report any relevant data. Stephens wrote: 'It is customary to say that a breaker is born and not made.' And since he often conducted the first and crucial interview, at which most 'breaks' were made, it is likely that he considered himself to be a 'born breaker'.[70]

On arrival at Camp 020 the prisoner was stripped and given a body search – which, after the discovery of secret-writing materials concealed in a false tooth, included a thorough dental search. Prison clothing would be issued, consisting of flannel trousers and a coat, and a six-inch diamond shape made from white cloth was sewn on a prominent part of the clothing. The prisoner was then put in a cell

Dr Harold Dearden, psychiatrist at Camp 020. Dearden often found himself at loggerheads with Colonel Stephens and in 1943 threatened to resign after an argument. Stephens grudgingly retracted his comments, but in the history poignantly remarks 'Strange people psychiatrists; even in war.' (Imperial War Museum, HU 66755)

alone. The officers dealing with the prisoner were under strict instructions not to talk to the prisoner or answer any questions that might be put to them. At the next stage, the prisoner's personal particulars were taken: name, date and place of birth, nationality, address, height, weight, etc. Dr Dearden would carry out a physical examination and a photograph would be taken, both in prison garb and in civilian clothing. The latter photo could be shown during interrogations without giving away the fact that the person was detained at 020. These photographs were also used for recognition purposes in the event of an escape. All personal property was confiscated and thoroughly checked for hidden equipment, especially secret-writing materials. It was normally paramount that the interrogation began immediately. In cases where it was not so urgent, a few days would be spent compiling all possible information known about the suspect, which would then be used to reinforce an image of omnipotence.

The first interview, however, was considered crucial for obtaining a 'break'. The prisoner would be marched into the interrogation room, where he would find a 'panel' of officers, often headed by the Commandant. A secretary would also be present to note down the proceedings on a stenograph. The suspect would remain standing throughout, while the interrogator fired questions and statements at the accused, often not leaving time for answers. The popular cliché propagated by 1970s 'cop shows' of the accused being allowed the comfort of a chair and a cigarette was not part of the routine. Stephens did not tolerate familiarity with the suspect, there was to be 'No chivalry. No gossip. No cigarettes . . . Figuratively, a spy in war should be at the point of a bayonet.' Later, when Stephens appeared at Court Martial after the war, he explained how the first interrogation should be conducted:

> It is a question of atmosphere . . . The Room is like a court and he is made to stand up and answer questions as before a judge . . . There is no question of searchlights being turned on the prisoner to extract truths.[71]

Perhaps surprisingly, considering Stephen's formidable reputation, the first and unbreakable rule to be instituted was that physical violence was not to be used under any circumstance. But this non-violent approach was not derived from a sense of rectitude: he explained that there was a purely functional reason to refrain from rough behaviour. 'Violence is taboo, for not only does it produce answers to please, but it lowers the standard of information.'[72] Moreover, terror tactics of this sort were of little use when trying to 'turn' an agent for Double Cross purposes. This non-violent ethos apparently pervaded the camp, as confirmed by some of the surviving secretarial staff:

> In fact the Commandant although a terrifying aspect, was a skilled interrogator who obtained results without recourse to assault and battery. Indeed it was the very basis of Camp 020 procedure that nobody raised a hand against a prisoner.[73]

During the early stages of 020, one serious incident involving violent behaviour did take place (see p.140). The visiting officer concerned, one Colonel Scotland, a senior Military Intelligence officer from the War Office, was quickly banned by Stephens from any further interrogations. There were further repercussions at a senior level: as a result of the 'deplorable incident', the Home Secretary, Herbert Morrison, suggested that 020 should come under civilian control. The DG, Petrie, then became involved, giving personal assurances that such an occurrence would never take place again, and control of Camp 020 was retained by MI5.[74]

However, whilst physical cruelty was absent from the interrogation room, refined psychological intimidation in a variety of forms brought effective results. Not surprisingly, the most effective technique was the threat of execution. If convicted for espionage under the Treachery Act, the sentence was death. Sixteen spies were executed during the war, fourteen of which came from Camp 020. Most were hanged, at either Wandsworth or Pentonville prison, and one was shot at the Tower of London (see p.156).[75] However, the vast majority were never prosecuted, much to the disgust of Stephens, and those that were executed became known as the 'Unlucky Sixteen'.[76] The event of an execution was greeted with mixed feelings by the staff at 020. Most thought the death penalty was deserved, and some literally jumped with joy; others believed it unnecessary.[77]

The threat of execution was also backed up by the impression that the British Secret Service was omnipotent and that the suspect might as well admit to what was already known. This was, of course, greatly facilitated by ISOS material. If a quick 'break' was not obtained at the first interview, a number of indirect techniques

Parachute agent Karl Richter (centre) returning to the spot where he had landed in Hertfordshire on 14 May 1941. He is accompanied by (left to right) Stephens, Lieutenant-Colonel G. Sampson, Major R. Short, Lieutenant-Colonel D.B. 'Stimmy' Stimson and Captain E. Goodacre. Richter was executed on 10 December 1941 under the Treachery Act. (Imperial War Museum, HU 66766)

were employed. Outside the interrogation room, stool pigeons, 'sympathy men' and 'bugging' devices were used to great effect. Prisoners could often be coaxed into a weak position over a prolonged period, then brought into interrogation at the crucial moment when they were at their lowest ebb and likely to break.

The legend of 'Cell Fourteen' was another powerful psychological tool. Highly reminiscent of George Orwell's Room 101 in the novel *1984*, 'Cell Fourteen' gained a sinister reputation. The cell had been a padded cell in the days when Latchmere House was a psychiatric institution, but had been converted and was now just like any other cell. This was purely a psychological contrivance that played on the prisoners' own worst fears, which they imagined would come to fruition in Cell Fourteen. Often used as a last resort, the interrogator would say 'you will now be taken to Cell Fourteen', at which point the prisoner would, more often than not, cave in. 'If it failed, then little hope remained of a break'; the success of this technique, as with many others, 'depended on the delivery, atmosphere, timing – last but not least upon the personality of the interrogator.'[78]

Many techniques were tried, some more productive than others. The use of drugs and alcohol to 'loosen the tongue' not only proved unreliable, but often led to a stiffening of resistance with the prisoner becoming more relaxed and self-confident. One method that did prove particularly valuable was the technique of 'blow hot – blow cold'. This technique will again no doubt be familiar to the fan of 1970s 'cop shows' as 'good cop, bad cop', but in reality it was Colonel Stephens and his staff who developed and refined this procedure. 'Blow hot – blow cold' was often employed on suspects who were considered more susceptible to a 'gentlemanly' approach. The first interview would be similar to that already described, but there would be no let-up and the suspect would be sent away without any opportunity to rebut accusations. Later, as if by chance, he would be approached by another officer, who offered to smooth things over providing he was willing to cooperate.

After prisoners had admitted to accusations of espionage, they generally unburdened themselves and were happy to cooperate fully. Many agreed not only to work for the Allies as double agents but also as stool pigeons and 'sympathy men' within the camp. For prisoners who were permanently detained, life was not unlike that of other general internees. It was fairly routine yet not uncomfortable; gardening facilities, a library and recreation rooms were provided; daily exercise was taken; and some prisoners were allowed to cook their own food. Rations were similar to those of British troops, although there tended to be more bread and less meat, and could be supplemented by vegetables grown by prisoners in five acres of land designated for the purpose. Camp 020 was not a POW camp, so treatment of prisoners was not subject to the Geneva Convention; nor was 020 listed by the Red Cross. For all intents and purposes, it was a civilian camp. It therefore came under Home Office regulations, and Home Office representatives made periodic visits. Throughout the war there were only three attempts at escape, all of which were unsuccessful. Similarly, suicide was infrequent. In fact there were only three serious attempts (see p.55) – although, despite the strict precautions taken to curb suicide, one Norwegian, Saetrang, managed to hang himself on the night of his arrival.

Diest and Bad Nenndorf

Before D-day, German espionage attempts to infiltrate Britain were confined to clandestine landings; thereafter the majority of agents attempted to enter the UK posing as refugees. However, the Abwehr failed to take advantage of the huge influx of refugees as a means to penetrate England in the summer of 1940, when it would have been relatively easy to do so; and later, when they switched to this tactic, Britain had already tightened up its travel controls and created the formidable LRC. Moreover, during the post-D-day period they again failed to take advantage of relaxed travel controls within England and concentrated all their efforts on the Continent with 'stay-behind networks' and 'line crossers'.[79] From D-day to the cessation of hostilities, Camp 020 began to receive 'shabby stay-behind agents' and 'frontlaufers'; the latter group would cross enemy lines and then return with tactical information, whilst the former would remain in place as the Allies advanced and reported back via wireless. The most significant stay-behind agent was the Dutch resistance leader turned informer Christian Lindemans, alias King Kong (see p.327-9). Other significant groupings during this operational stage were the French collaborationists (such as the PPF), the Francists and a number of anti-Bolshevists.[80]

Initially these new agents were sent to Ham via train or aeroplane, but this was a lengthy and awkward process. It was therefore quickly deemed necessary to create a forward interrogation centre. This took the form of Diest, alias 1 Det. CSDIC (UK); and then later Bad Nenndorf, alias CSDIC (WEA). Diest was formed in November 1944; 'it was a medieval sort of place . . . with dungeons and moats and excellently suited for the purpose'.[81] It was commanded by Stephens and run by a combination of 020 and MI19 staff. Diest continued to function until 30 September 1945, when it was absorbed by Bad Nenndorf. Nenndorf had been set up on 30 June 1945, and when Diest ceased to function Stephens took control. As the Western Allies made the final push eastward into Germany, a vanguard of espionage directors, spymasters and intelligence officers were progressively picked up. The most notable of these characters were Walter Schellenburg (p.365), personal assistant to Himmler and later deputy head of the SD (successor to the Abwehr), and Ernst Kaltenbrünner (p.363), successor to Heydrich as head of the RSHA, which included the Gestapo. Kaltenbrünner, however, was wanted at Nuremberg for war crimes and so remained partially 'unbroken', much to the regret of Stephens, who considered him to be 'a giant in evil' and a 'sycophantic thug'. Subsequently, Kaltenbrünner was executed for crimes against humanity. A vast amount of information was obtained from these career intelligence officers about elusive Abwehr and RSHA personalities, as well as interesting confirmations of previous conjectures.[82]

The Double Cross system

It was soon realized that once spies had been broken they could be exploited and 'turned' to work for the British as double agents. Vernon Kell had already established the essence of the Double Cross system during the First World War;

A picture showing Ernst Kaltenbrünner, head of the RSHA, after his execution. Kaltenbrünner was described by Stephens as 'a giant in evil, ruthless to a degree and bitter'. Much to Stephens' annoyance he was unable to fully 'break' Kaltenbrünner, who was required to testify at Nuremburg for War Crimes. (PRO, FO 371/56935)

but at that stage it lacked sophistication, and its full and devastating potential was not realized until the Second World War, when it became one of the greatest intelligence coups.[83] In the words of J.C. Masterman, chairman of the Twenty Committee (so called because 'XX', the symbol of the Double Crosses, was the Roman numeral for twenty) that ran Britain's double agents: 'By means of the double agent system *we actively ran and controlled the German espionage system in this country.*'[84] Whilst this staggering claim was largely correct, there were some negligible anomalies. A Dutch parachute agent, Englebertus Fukken, alias William Ter Braak, managed to remain at large from November 1940 to April 1941, longer than any other agent sent to Britain during the war. After running out of money and ideas, Fukken tragically committed suicide in an air-raid shelter in Cambridgeshire.[85] Although he was never at 020, Stephens includes him in the case histories. The Curry history reveals that there were also a number of German agents working in the 'neutral' Portuguese and Spanish embassies, outside MI5 control. Nevertheless, they were kept under close surveillance;[86] and one embassy

Engelbertus Fukken, alias William Ter Braak. The only agent to remain at large in Britain. Although he escaped the rigours of Camp 020, Fukken became desperate after running out of money and ideas. He shot himself with his Abwehr-issue pistol in a public air-raid shelter near Cambridge. (PRO, KV 2/114)

clerk, Rogerio Menezes, was arrested at the Portuguese Embassy and taken to Camp 020. The Menezes case proved a considerable coup for Stephens, as it led to the uncovering of 17 spymasters and their agents.[87] The one other case outside the MI5 'net' was Paul Georg Fidrmuc, codename OSTRO. In 1942 ISOS picked up 37 OSTRO messages, which gave the impression that a large international network of agents was at work, some of whom seemed to be based in England. It was clear from ISOS that OSTRO's intelligence was entirely false and obviously a figment of Fidrmuc's imagination.[88] However, in the run up to D-day OSTRO filed a report with the 'usual erroneous information', but by pure fluke suggested that the Allies were to make an assault on the Manche [Cherbourg] peninsula. On 19 occasions between April and October 1944, the Twenty Committee discussed what was to be done with OSTRO.[89] The Committee even considered 'doing away with him altogether', but this action was thwarted by 'C' (the head of SIS), who favoured bringing him across to the Allies' side. It remained the conclusion of MI5 that OSTRO's intelligence was 'based on newspaper reports, enhanced by a lively imagination'.[90] In 1946 American forces in Austria finally arrested OSTRO, but under interrogation he strongly maintained that he had three valuable sources, one in Paris, one in the Middle East and one in Britain. He was never held at Camp 020 or interviewed by Stephens, although a Mr Johnson, acting as MI5's agent (U.35), did interrogate him on a number of occasions, but to no avail.[91]

From its outset (2 January 1941), the ultimate aim of the XX Committee had been 'to mislead the enemy, and perhaps deflect his plans, by handing out false information'.[92] The Double Cross system was therefore carefully manoeuvred from what initially was a counter-espionage and defensive role to a more offensive attacking role. The culmination or high point came with a strategic deception concerning the D-day landings. GARBO, the greatest double agent of the war, convinced the Germans that the Allied invasion of Normandy was in fact a tactical diversion and that the real invasion would take place in the Pas de Calais area. This false information had the desired effect, and the crack 1st and 116th Panzer divisions were ordered to the Calais region instead of Normandy. This was a crucial moment: the Allied invasion was far from consolidated, and the effect of battle-hardened German reinforcements might well have tipped the balance and conceivably forced the Allies back into the sea altogether. GARBO's ruse, however, was so smooth that he continued to pass false information, particularly on V-weapon damage; and long after the war the Germans were still convinced that he had been working for the Nazi cause. Juan Pujol (GARBO's real name) was the only man during the war to receive both the German Iron Cross and an M.B.E. He was never interned at 020, nor was he 'turned'; he had volunteered his services, and after some altercation and proof of his *bona fides* he began work under MI5's skilled controller, Tomás Harris. Although Pujol was never at Camp 020, the existence, security and growth of the Double Cross system owed much to the ability of the camp's personnel.

Whilst Stephens' most immediate concern was to 'break' agents, the ultimate goal was to 'turn' them. Of course not all agents were suitable for such work, even if they offered their services or had been enticed by the prospect of Double Cross work in order to obtain a 'break'. However, the selection not only required a skilled eye, but there were certain basic prerequisites that applied, as Stephens makes clear:

> Firstly, that the whole story has been extracted; secondly, that the man will work under orders; and thirdly that the menace under which the enemy demands service is no longer real.[93]

Other considerations were also present. The capture of an agent could not be made public; and if anyone witnessed the arrest of an agent, the potential for Double Cross work could be compromised. No matter how slim the risk, the Twenty Committee could not allow the Abwehr to become aware of even one double agent, in case that brought down the whole fragile system.

Stephens appears to have been largely responsible for the initial selection of potential double agents, at least those emanating from 020. The process of 'turning' would take place during interrogation once a full 'break' had been made. If the case was viable, then the agent would be passed on to the Special Agents section (B1A), headed by Colonel Tommy Robertson. Roberston has been described as the 'real' architect of the Double Cross system, and it was under his skilful direction that the running of double agents took place.[94] It was immediately apparent to Robertson that there was an ever-present predicament with the Double Cross system, and that 'a balance was to be struck' between the risks involved in releasing true information to the enemy in order to retain their confidence. The ultimate aim was to perform a 'knockout blow' – which was, of course, delivered by GARBO.[95] Approximately 120 double agents were employed by MI5 during the war, though

Parachute agent Wulf Schmidt who was 'turned' to became a successful double agent. He was given the codename TATE, after the music-hall comedian Harry Tate. For this photograph he posed with the wireless that he used for sending messages back to the Abwehr, under MI5 control. (PRO, KV 2/62)

many of these were not developed and others were not of great importance. Eleven agents were successfully 'turned' at Camp 020, including some of the more notable agents, such as SUMMER (real name Gösta Caroli, pp.137-41), TATE (real name Wulf Schmidt, pp.138-41), G.W. (real name Gwilym Williams, pp.178-9), ZIG-ZAG (real name Edward Arnold Chapman, pp. 217-26), and MUTT and JEFF (real names John Moe and Tör Glad respectively, p.162). The names of these and other double agents were in most cases erased from the original document – indicated here by [...] – in order to protect them. But in some instances it has been possible to deduce their identity from other published sources, in which case their codename has been added in square brackets.[96]

Conclusions

Since 1972, with the publication of Masterman's *Double Cross System*, details of this fantastic subterfuge have been well documented – although the identities of most of the double agents are still officially unknown – and its contribution has been assessed and acknowledged. Similarly, the success of British wartime signals intelligence (SIGINT) has been well established, with scores of historical works, memoirs, novels and, most recently, film adaptations.[97] Some of those representations are less than historically accurate, but the proposition (first put forward by that eminent official historian of intelligence, Sir Harry Hinsley) that whilst SIGINT did not win the war alone it certainly shortened it remains an overriding theme in fiction and faction alike.[98] In comparison, however, the impact of Camp 020, Huntercombe (020R), Diest and Bad Nenndorf, and of the LRC and HUMINT generally, is still relatively undetermined. There is no doubt that the mass of information extracted by interview and interrogation was of supplementary value to ULTRA and probably confirmed much that was already known from SIGINT. However, Colonel Stephens implies that HUMINT, and specifically that extracted at 020, was of paramount importance and on a level with SIGINT:

> Ham became known as one of the two most important sources of information in the war, comparable in accuracy indeed to the other which was ISOS itself.[99]

Stephens was not one to understate his cause, so one must take care with this assertion, especially since Stephens is specifically referring to ISOS, the Abwehr signals intelligence, rather than ULTRA as a whole. Perhaps official MI5 historian 'Jack' Curry was more accurate when he stated that:

> ... the interrogation of known agents at Camp 020 or the LRC and the work of B.1.A. in dealing with the traffic of agents who were turned around, all combined to furnish complementary pieces of evidence without which the ISOS material by itself could not be fully understood or explained, and had a very limited practical value.[100]

Curry's point may easily be validated if one tries to read the raw ISOS decrypts, now available at the PRO (HW 19). This intelligence would make little sense without some knowledge of the Abwehr's order of battle, which was not known to MI5 until they succeeded in piecing it together from various interrogations held at Camp 020. In fact before the war MI5's knowledge of the Abwehr was extremely weak – so much so, that the name of the German espionage organization, the Amstgruppe Auslandsnachrichten und Abwehr and its head, Admiral Wilhelm Canaris, was unknown to them.[101]

In terms of espionage, there is little doubt that the information gleaned from ISOS was more valuable than that from 020, but they of course facilitated one another. In operational terms it is difficult to assess the value of HUMINT, or indeed to separate it from information gleaned from SIGINT. Distinguished intelligence scholars Hinsley, Howard and Andrew all agree that SIGINT, along with aerial photographic reconnaissance (PR), provided the two most useful and important sources of wartime intelligence.[102] But the significance of HUMINT during World War Two is something that still requires some clarification. Perhaps now that many previously retained records, including the one reproduced here and MI5's personal files, are in the public domain, a fuller assessment of the value of HUMINT can be undertaken.[103] Indeed, students wishing to pursue that course may find it helpful to use this rather odd history as a starting point for such a study and as a rough guide to the highly informative Security Service personal files. For the general reader, however, this is not a dry or tedious official history. Whilst this document was written to serve that function, it is quite clear that the author has written it to entertain, and it is simultaneously marred and embellished by Stephens' personal views and comments. His manner is all pervading, so much so that the whole document is imbued – as it would seem was Camp 020 – with the character of Colonel 'Tin Eye' Stephens. This, combined with an intriguing and dark subject matter, makes for the most compelling of any official history.

Notes

1 KV 4/8 Harker to Stephens 3 May 1946 – 'he [the DG] is quite in agreement with your proposal that you [Stephens] and the officers you mention should cooperate in recasting the whole history [of Camp 020]'.
2 Security Service material has been released to the public at the PRO on 18.11.97, 27.1.99, 16.9.99 and 19.5.00, and a further release has been scheduled for 08.11.00.
3 'The Charm Offensive: "The Coming Out of MI5" ', *Intelligence and National Security*, Vol.15, No.1, pp.183-90, Richard C. Thurlow (London: Frank Cass, 2000).
4 Most of them under the reference KV; there are also a number of Home Office files relating to the Security Service and Camp 020, largely in HO 213.
5 KV 2/1-2, Mata Hari; KV 2/74-75, P.G. Wodehouse; KV 2/245-250, William Joyce, alias Lord Haw-Haw, KV 2/245-250.
6 Created by Herman Cyril McNeile (pen name Sapper), the fictional character Hugh 'Bulldog' Drummond appeared in several novels, the first of them entitled *Bull-dog Drummond*. Bulldog was a hefty and apparently brainless British ex-army officer who foils the plans of Carl Peterson, an international crook. Colonel Stephens' literary style is very similar to that of McNeile.
7 During November 1940 Camp 020 became a casualty of the Blitz and sustained great material damage, though luckily only one inmate was killed. After another freak bomb attack, in January 1941, it was decided that an entire reserve camp should be built at Nuffield, in Oxfordshire. Although Huntercombe (Camp 020R) had the capacity of Ham, it was never really used to its full extent and tended to hold those agents that were no longer of use.
8 *Camp 020*, p.34.
9 *Camp 020*, p.32.
10 These have been edited down to 150 case studies, in which 186 individuals are mentioned.
11 'The Security Service: Its problems and Organisational Adjustments 1908–1945' (KV 4/1-3). This document has been published by the PRO as *The Security Service 1908–1945: The Official History*, with an introduction by Christopher Andrew (London: PRO Publications, 1999). Any further footnotes to this source will give the page number of the publication rather than the original document.
12 KV 4/8, p.2c, Sampson to Harker (DDG) 21 September 1945. Both drafts of Sampson's history are contained within KV 4/8.
13 Stephens to Harker, 28 March 1946 (KV 4/8, p.3a). Stephens requested Major R. Short to assist him in writing the history; the other officer mentioned in this letter has been blanked out, but is quite possibly Captain Goodacre.
14 Harker to Stephens, 3 April 1946 (KV 4/8, p.4a); and Petrie (DG) to Curry, 29 March 1946 (KV 4/1, p.26).
15 Harker to Stephens, 3 April 1946 (KV 4/8, p.4a).
16 *Camp 020*, p.32.
17 Ibid.
18 Personal files are found in PRO class KV 2.
19 Due to the passage of time, the 'Yellow Peril' papers now have a deeper orange appearance.
20 *Camp 020*, p.207.
21 The personal files are arranged by name and therefore quite easy to locate, although one must bear in mind that most agents had several pseudonyms.
22 Interview in May 2000 between the author and two Camp 020 secretarial staff, Mrs Ward-Thomas and Mrs Williams.

23 *Camp 020*, p.107.
24 *Camp 020*, p.295.
25 *Camp 020*, p.243.
26 KV 4/14, p.306.
27 *Camp 020*, p.205.
28 *Camp 020*, p.107.
29 FO 371/70830, paper CG 2671, 19 June 1948.
30 West, *MI5*, p.146.
31 FO 371/70830 paper CG 2290/G 'Evidence before the Court of Enquiry', p.5, June 1948.
32 Under the direction of Vernon Kell (DG 1909–1940) all MI5 recruits were introduced personally by family or friends connected with intelligence circles, many of which had served in India. The India Army List states that Stephens served in the 2nd King Edward's Own Gurkha Rifles from 1919 to 1931.
33 Sir Harry Lushington Stephen and R.W.G. Stephens, *A Digest of the Laws of Evidence in Courts Martial* (London: Macmillan).
34 Andrew, *The Security Service*, p.176. Dick White was a high-flying career intelligence officer who rose to become the only person to head both MI5 (1953–1956) and MI6 (1956–1968). In 1968 he was appointed as the first Intelligence Coordinator to the Cabinet, a post that was created specifically for him.
35 KV 4/8, p.1.
36 HO 45/26007, Proposed Interrogation Centre, 11.7.40.
37 Interview between the author and John 'Mister Latchmere' Morgan, Senior Officer, HMP Resettlement Prison Latchmere House.
38 KV 4/8, p.3.
39 West, *MI5*, p.144.
40 Paul Thümmel, a senior Abwehr official who was working as an SIS operative through Czech Intelligence. In 1940 he was SIS's best intelligence source. Christopher Andrew, *Secret Service: The Making of the British Intelligence Community* (London: Sceptre edition, 1986), p.647.
41 F.H. Hinsley and C.A.G. Simkins, *British Intelligence in the Second World War, Vol.4: Security and Counter Intelligence* (London: HMSO, 1990), p.41.
42 Andrew, *The Security Service*, p.11.
43 Andrew, *Secret Service*, p.667.
44 KV 4/28, 'Report on the Work of B3C in connection with suspected communications with enemy by light signalling'; KV 4/10, 'Report on the use of carrier pigeons by the German Intelligence Service 1940–41'; KV 4/11, 'Report on the operations of B3C in connection with suspected Fifth Column activities during the war 1939–1945'; KV 4/12, 'An investigation of markings on telegraph poles for suspected codes'.
45 Hinsley and Simkins, *British Intelligence, Vol.4*, p.52.
46 Andrew, *Secret Service*, p.668.
47 Hinsley and Simkins, *British Intelligence, Vol.4*, p.39.
48 KV 4/88, 'Director General's Report on the Security Services, February 1940'.
49 Vernon Kell's service spanned from 1909 to 1940, earning him the title of the longest serving head of any civil service department.
50 ISOS and ISK messages are now available at the PRO under HW 19.
51 Hinsley and Simkins, *British Intelligence, Vol.4*, p.315.
52 Hinsley and Simkins, *British Intelligence, Vol.4*, p.67.
53 *Camp 020*, p.41.
54 West, *MI5*, p.250.
55 *Camp 020*, p.41.
56 *Camp 020*, p.41 and KV 4/8, p.4; and Hinsley and Simkins, *British Intelligence, Vol.4*, p.71.
57 Other German espionage organizations included the SD, RSHA and SIPO.
58 Kindly supplied by Georges Van Acker and Roy C. Nesbit – see Ladislas Farago, *The Game of the Foxes*, pp.280 and 328.
59 KV 4/7, Ch.1, p.1.
60 KV 4/7, Ch.1, p.4.
61 Andrew, *The Security Service*, p.222.
62 KV 4/7, Ch.1, p.3; and Andrew, *The Security Service*, p.223.
63 KV 4/25, 'Monthly Summaries of the LRC 1943–1945'.

64 KV 4/7, Ch.1, p.8.
65 KV 4/7, Ch.4, p.6.
66 KV 4/7, Ch.1, p.6.
67 Ibid.
68 KV 4/8, p.2.
69 Ibid.
70 *Camp 020*, p.107.
71 FO 371/70830 paper CG 2290/G, p.7.
72 *Camp 020*, pp.57-8.
73 Letter from a collective group of Camp 020 secretarial staff to an unknown newspaper in response to the representation of Colonel Stephens in the BBC *Spy* series. This was also confirmed in an interview on 26 May 2000 between the author and two other members of the 020 secretarial staff, Mrs Ward-Thomas and Mrs Williams.
74 West, *MI5*, p.147.
75 Josef Jakobs, a parachute agent, was shot in the firing range at the Tower of London on 14 August 1941.
76 Nigel West, 'German Spies in Britain', *After the Battle*, No.11, p.13.
77 Interview on 26.5.2000 between the author and two members of the Camp 020 secretarial staff, Mrs Ward-Thomas and Mrs Williams.
78 *Camp 020*, p.127.
79 KV 4/7, Ch.4, p.5; and KV 4/8, p.56.
80 KV 4/8, p.61.
81 *Camp 020*, p71.
82 KV 4/8, p.69.
83 Andrew, *Secret Service*, p.275.
84 Masterman, J.C. *The Double Cross System 1939–1945* (London: Pimlico, 1995; first published 1972), p.3. The italics are Masterman's.
85 KV 2/114, Engelbertus Fukken Personal File.
86 Andrew, *The Security Service*, p.17.
87 *Camp 020*, p.237-9.
88 KV 4/210 ISOS intercepts of Fidrmuc 14 Jan 1942 to 3 May 1945.
89 KV 4/68, Minutes of the Twenty Committee for the period April to October 1944.
90 Oliver Hoare, PRO Press Release, 18 April 2000, and KV 2/197.
91 KV 2/200.
92 KV 4/63 Minutes of the First meeting of the Double Cross Committee, 2 January 1941.
93 *Camp 020*, p.259.
94 Nigel West, 'MI5's Secret Interrogation Centre', *After the Battle*, No.74, p.53.
95 KV 4/63, Early memorandum contained within the Minutes of the XX Committee, 2 January to 21 August 1941.
96 West and Masterman provide the best sources for Double Cross agents.
97 The most recent (May 2000) of these adaptations is the film *U-571*. This film credits the US Navy with the capture of an Enigma codebook, which was in reality found on a German U-boat by the Royal Navy.
98 ULTRA became the codeword given to intelligence obtained from the decryption of high-grade ciphers of whatever source – German, Italian or Japanese. In the US, it was also referred to as *Magic*. However, the term ULTRA was not in general use during the war except as a specification attached to MOST (later TOP) SECRET documents. Hinsley and Simkins, *British Intelligence in the Second World War, Abridged Edition* (London: HMSO, 1993), p.23; and M. Howard, *British Intelligence in the Second World War, Vol.5: Strategic Deception* (London: HMSO, 1990), p.13.
99 *Camp 020*, p.58. The italics are the author's.
100 Curry, *The Security Service*, p.206.
101 Hinsley and Simkins, *British Intelligence, Vol.4,* pp.11-12.
102 Andrew, *Secret Service*, p.654.
103 FO 371/70830 paper CG 2426, p.4. This document identifies one important aspect of HUMINT, namely technical information such as 'Beam' (used by the German bombers), acoustic mines, V-weapons and enemy atomic research.

A
DIGEST OF HAM

Volume One
A DIGEST OF HAM
ON THE INTERROGATION OF SPIES

HAM

HUNTERCOMBE

DIEST

BAD NENNDORF

1940—47

EDITOR'S NOTE

This history has been written at the instance of M.I.5. In all it
has been written three times. It suffered from a wealth of material.
Paradoxically the chronological Case-history lacked sequence because
of ramifications and the ever changing scene. Above all it did not
and cannot recapture the strain of those anxious years. The first
part then is a digest, which admits of allusions here and there to
trends of international espionage, to policy and to administration.
The second part touches upon the methods by which the answers were
obtained. The third part is pure intelligence and should be of value
to a student with leisure. The rule of anonymity has been respected
in relation to the regular officers of the Security Service. This is
particularly satisfactory in regard to the Editor who himself must
surely be interrogated one day. At once he can disclaim all
knowledge whatever of such a history. Pressed further, he may admit
to a correction of a sentence here or there; he was very busy at the
time. Cornered, he can plead he only wrote a part of it; and this is
true. The rule of anonymity has been violated in regard to certain
distinguished politicians, members of the Civil Service, and
temporary officers of the Security Service, because their part in
the disruption of the German Secret Service must be to them a
lasting satisfaction.

PART ONE

A DIGEST OF HAM

The story of Ham is stranger than fiction; indeed, as a work of
fiction it would violate the probabilities. It is a history which
has roots in M.I.5 in 1936, when the menace of German espionage was
recognised by few. It is the work which continues through Ham and
Huntercombe, through Diest and Bad Nenndorf, where at last the
failure of German espionage has been acknowledged by the Germans
themselves.

It is a history which cannot do justice to the ten years of
endeavour. It cannot be regarded in perspective because it is only a
part of the pattern of M.I.5. It cannot attain the impersonal
because the views, for better or for worse, are those of the man in
whom the command of those four establishments was vested in the
years. The interrogation of spies from all over the world in many
cases was personal, and the result is as fine a cross section of
rank evil as will be found in the annals of humanity. And for what
the final impression is worth, it is this - there is more racial
hatred, there is more evil, there is more determination to destroy
in this world today than ever there was before the war. The urgency
of those years, therefore must never be forgotten. And if bitterness
in this history here and there is apparent, it is not of malicious
intent, but rather a warning that the Munich mentality has been
resurrected. There is again the avoidance of issues which in
thinking people is tantamount to moral cowardice. It is apparent at
home, where a long suffering race is sick unto death of the German
issue and the resultant policy is to reduce the Occupation to the
bone. It is apparent in Germany, where the policy of KEITEL is
forgotten, that every male between 16 and 60 in Britain was to be
deported for slave labour and that each one of our women was to
breed for the German Reich. In the British Zone "Mil Gov mit uns" is
now a sneer of German contentment. That people, stained with
atrocity, are welded together in hardship regardless of creed, and
they have little respect for the token force which is to keep them
under control and is prepared to be friendly at one and the same
time. They remember they were bankrupt in 1925, and they do not
forget the extent of their staggering conquests within fifteen
years. In the American Zone there is a certain unevenness, and maybe
that is well, for at least it gives the Germans an uncomfortable
guess. In the Russian and the French Zones it is different.
Territorial expansion is a reality whatever they say in Conference.
And if they are baulked of their ambitions, two things will happen;

firstly they will lay waste the fair lands in dispute, and secondly they will see to it that Germany will not be against them in the third war.

But this is not the end of the trouble in Germany, for in this quixotic age an ally is an enemy at one and the same time. In the prophetic words of a great statesman, the Colossus astride Europe is Russia. And that ally is spying upon us in a large, a very large way.

Withal there is the mentality that still thinks in terms of soldiers, sailors and airmen; of tanks, ships and aircraft; every one of which in this atomic age is obsolete. The stark reality is that security lies in the atom bomb, and it is the responsibility of the Intelligence Service to know how best it can be used for us, and on the instant, when and where it is to be used against us. The responsibility is appalling and the anxiety is equal that the Service should have adequate resources.

The Disruption of the N.S.D.A.P. in the U.K.

Ten years ago, M.I.5 had the vision to penetrate the N.S.D.A.P. in Britain. There was infiltration of the Brown House in Bayswater, and the provincial organisations all over the Kingdom. Slowly, tirelessly and perhaps thanklessly, the investigation proceeded. BOHLE was the king pin, Kapitän KARLOWA was the executive in England, and RIBBENTROP was the ardent supporter. The implications were wide and their methods were ruthless. Pastors, seamen, merchants, actresses, prostitutes, domestics and crooks, Germans and Austrians all, were dragged into their net. If a Hun was antagonistic to the Nazi creed, he was hounded out of employment. That was all there was to it. Some were as zealous as they were pompous; others were blackmailed and became blackmailers in turn. But as always with the Teuton, with an increase in power there is a flood of arrogance and indiscretion, and long became our black list of the N.S.D.A.P. and D.A.F. devotees. In the result Plan SNUFFBOX was born. The objective was the liquidation of the Nazi Party on the outbreak of war. Unbelievable as it may seem, that final duty was allocated to one officer and one secretary, and she a minor in years. Strength lay, however, in the co-operation of the Chief Constables, secrecy was preserved, fervour was conspiratorial and good relations abounded.

Then in August 1939 Parteigenossen to the number of some six hundred prudently fled the country. That left eight hundred, and by the outbreak of war seven hundred or thereabouts were safely in gaol.

In effect the German Fifth Column had been brought to an abrupt halt. That was an incalculable gain, as England, alone in Europe, was to remain singularly free of this cancerous influence

for the rest of the war.
That was disruption with a vengeance.

The "Phoney War"

But smug satisfaction was shortlived, for that was the period of the
"phoney" war. Germans were still naturalised. Eminent Englishmen
advocated the release of eminent Germans, for how otherwise could
they avoid a charge of Fascism, a creed they themselves were notion-
ally fighting? Surely HANFSTAENGL (No 7 in the Partei) was a man of
culture, a man who would play the piano to soothe the Soothsayer in
a tantrum. And SCHIFFER (GOERING's predecessor in command of the
Prussian Police) was a refugee from Nazi oppression. Was it not a
discourtesy in these enlightened times to suggest that these
gentlemen were capable of telling a lie? Would it not be possible to
carry out interrogations with the customary decorum of the Courts?

To the duties vested in B.8 of detention and interrogation
were added the prevention of naturalisation and release. A
subsection was formed to join issue with official bodies such as the
Advisory Committee, with unofficial bodies such as the Society of
Friends. All bent upon equity to the Boche in the misunderstood days
of this perilous war. Other societies were more spurious; they
prospered because of the vested interests of the paid secretaries;
but under democracy in war they could not be ignored and their
nuisance value to the enemy was appreciable.

A second subsection of B.8 was established to deal with the
security of the internment camps. The possibility of the German
invasion of Britain was as real to the prisoners as to ourselves,
and they organised themselves into reinforcing centres. German
merchant seamen were concentrated around Portsmouth, which for them
was convenient as an answer to a prayer. In one camp discipline was
so lax that a wireless transmitter was found. In another, visits to
the dentist were a joy ride for the day, for the guards were corrupt
and made drunk. One day there was an inevitable miscount and a party
was returned as correct. Later, a prisoner returned unescorted and
alone, and was refused admission to the camp as the numbers were
officially correct. Stool pigeons were employed, but for lack of
supervision they played fast and loose. As always, the shortage of
trained staff was the critical problem.

Yet another subsection of B.8 was set up to deal with the
Tribunals, all ready to release so-called reliable internees when
general internment was ordered. Again the Police forces were zealous
to a degree; furthermore, they had tumbled to the fact that charges
of moral turpitude could carry much independent weight.

Certainly they were colourful days, if anxious to the verge

of desperation. Raiding took place by day and by night, and the
bubbling enthusiasm of Special Branch at the Yard was a solace
indeed. We went from the vestry of the German Church in Dalston to
shabby apartments in Notting Hill Gate. There was a luxury flat in
Addison Road and a pied-à-terre in the White House where two Irish
sisters kept a man we required. There was a rubbish dump in Victoria
where the records of the Partei had been jettisoned by an incautious
Hun. There was the spiritual adviser to RIBBENTROP had a
Parteigenosse to boot; Pastor WEHRAN was arrested but released
within the hour, presumably on the same score. That was too much,
and he was arrested again for sending a hacksaw in a cake to a
parishioner in internment. There were others of that ilk, German
agents in Seamen's Homes in ports such as Hull. One evaded arrest
because his ordination as a priest in the Church of England
intervened. The Registrar General was induced to prevent a marriage
whose aim was to gain British nationality. The Public Prosecutor was
persuaded to proceed against a gardener in bigamy because he had
spuriously married a women of great beauty from UFA for a fee. The
safe of the German Air Attache was traced to the Pall Mall Safe
Deposit. Notwithstanding the slogan of the business, "Safety,
Security and Secrecy", it was blown open by a crook who gave his
services to the Crown for nothing but a smile. The reaction of the
proprietor would have been reasonable in peace. Next time would we
be good enough to call after office hours, as this sort of thing had
a bearing on the confidential nature of his business? An R.A.F.
officer in "Ops" was arrested, for he had enemy connections and held
the King's Commission in a false name. There was also some little
unpleasantness in the States in the past. High larceny, they called
it, to the tune of some eighty thousand dollars. That arrest, in the
end, was upheld in the Lords. A woman from the Luftministerium in
Berlin had become a lady companion in the home of a naval officer of
high rank. There was a prostitute from Austria who tittered with
Army personnel to a dangerous degree. There was a French duchess
impoverished to the point of a coronet on a papier-maché suitcase
from a half-crown store. A borderline case was a card sharper on the
London-Brighton run, but the Yard took her under their wing. There
was the daughter of a senior French officer of Lorraine whose
personal integrity was undoubted. Wilfully she married a German. In
turn he fled to Eire and deserted his wife to her fate. That she
well knew, but proudly she defended him to the end. It was one of
the few cases wherein loyalty had meaning. There was a dentist in
Seaton with an anglicised name. In peacetime he made a strange
competence by selling ready-made teeth in standard sizes to replace
those lost by holiday-makers in the sea. In war he was bribed by
internees until he became an internee himself. There was the

Countess COSTENZA

Margarete OTTO (TITFORD)

grandson of the Iron Chancellor, a playboy monied by marriage, who
was sponsored by many. The discovery of his N.S.D.A.P. card in his
bureau rendered his "word of honour" denial somewhat thin. Then,
notwithstanding a warrant, a man in high favour fled the country with
a fortune in pearls when the currency restriction for the man in the
street remained at £10. There was a partial board residence place on
the uneven numbered side of a square, the porticos of which were
secured by cemetery chains. Hun was the proprietor, and
accommodating, for he supplied full board at weekends for a modest
supplementary fee. It was raided in a large way by ourselves and the
Yard, for it was peopled by Germans, black students and typists, and
lastly by persons of moral turpitude in whom the Home Office were
interested. "Thorough" was the official designation of the search,
and thorough it was, like a direct hit from a thousand pound bomb.
"Just one last look over my instructions, sir. Ah, the premises
should be left, insofar as possible, in the condition in which they
were found. That blotter was on the table - just so. Never mind about
replacing the mantelpiece and the floor boards. Fritz won't want this
outfit anymore."

A motley but a menacing population in war; a welcome
addition to the incarcerations that Plan SNUFFBOX had effected.

Interrogation of some four hundred took place at odd hours
in odd places; in Wandsworth and Holloway, at the Oratory Schools,
Olympia, Cannon Row and the Yard. The much publicised evidence
before the Nuremberg Tribunal in 1946 relating to the Reichstag fire
is not new. It has been in our possession since the interrogation of
KAHAN. Then again, Eva BRAUN was not the first of the amours of the
Führer. Before the war he had been financed by the daughter of
BECHSTEIN, the pianoforte man; but the trace of the Jew was
inconvenient; so, true gallant that he was, he forsook her; and the
interrogation of SCHIFFER is the authority therefor. KRAGOULSKI was
interesting, a leader of the Hitler Jugend, with the eyes of a
fanatic and the ambition to become one of the Gauleiters of England.
There was the son of a U-boat commander who found a remarkable
market for Eldorado ices at the entrance to a prohibited area. There
was a Boche in Siemens-Schuckerts, whose arrest was upheld not only
for Nazi activity but for the seduction of the wife of a British
medical man. At Holloway a raven-haired beauty laid bare her bosom
for sympathy, notwithstanding the presence of a secretary as staid
as she was severe. Bilingual in German was the secretary, but she
boggled at "hussy", so we called in a wardress to restore decency
and respect until the interview was done. At Holloway again there
was a scene when a short-lived recruit to MI 5 saw fit to liberate a
domestic of charm and order a dinner at the Berkeley to celebrate
the day of her freedom. At the Oratory Schools a classroom was used,

at one and the same time, by an officer who was changing for tennis, by an infatuated German couple who were disposed on his bed, and for the interrogation of Raymond WINGS, whose attention would stray to lascivious pictures on the walls. "With Wings to Success", that was the claim of a dynamic personality who cured stammering among socialites with pedigrees as long as their purses. Mesmerism, so he hoped, would be his weapon in interrogation; instead he was incontinently marched out as a fraud because he was made to stammer himself. It was the story again of the physician of old. At Olympia, an interrogation was the signal for the attendance of officers from the Brigade who had nothing better to do than to offer unhelpful suggestions. And when they were rebuked these men of infinite good fellowship would apologise and suggest a short adjournment for a thimbleful of gin. Then at the Yard there was the joint interrogation of an officer from Alsace by the French and ourselves. "Traitor, answer my questions before you die, as you certainly shall before the sun has set." That was the classic opening thundered by Commandant Dumas which led to a piercing shriek of despair and an unfounded suspicion of foul play.

Would there never be some place where there could be discipline and dignity, some ordered procedure which the professional spies in due course would fear and respect? No. War was still in its democracy. Finance and Habeas Corpus were involved, inter-departmental difficulties arose. Above all, Questions in Parliament. The horoscope for Ham was not reassuring. There would be some delay.

General Internment

In the Spring of 1940 two conferences were held in the office of the Privy Council, at which three members of the War Cabinet, Mr Attlee, Mr Greenwood and Sir John Anderson, were present. At each of these conferences two officers of M I 5 were in attendance.

Deportation of Category A enemy aliens was ordered. On 15 May 1940, five days after the invasion of Belgium, Holland and Luxembourg, the internment of Category B enemy aliens was carried out. Then came the troubled humiliations. On 28 May the Belgian Army surrendered. On 10 June, with that innate infamy for which she is so justly noted, Italy fell upon France and joined in a war of no danger to herself. On 22 June the French signed their armistice. On 30 June the incarceration of Category C enemy aliens was complete.

Again that was disruption with a vengeance.

But satisfaction on this occasion was not so short-lived. The Tribunals to consider the hard luck cases were busy, but the country at large was awakening at long last to more urgent things.

(II.)
HAM 1940 to D-DAY 1944

A historical fact now comes into focus. It weighed in the German decision to postpone the invasion of this country.

Germany at the time of the fall of France was without source of information from England.

Twice the German organisation had been incontinently disrupted. Plan SNUFFBOX was the first, general internment was the second. Conjointly M I. 5 and the Police had disposed of the remaining subversive elements.

In terms the German Fifth Column had been wiped out.

It therefore followed that the enemy would introduce professional spies and the presumption was sound that they would do it in Teutonic fashion on a big business scale. The hope was that preparation would be indifferent for lack of time, and if only the first spies could be caught and properly broken there would be a flow of information which would gain momentum in the manner of snow which is rolling into the valley below.

The establishment of a proper prison for spies was therefore of paramount importance. To this end contact was made with the Home Defence Security Executive. Lord Swinton and Sir Herbert Creedy took an immense personal interest in the problem and their influence was to be felt to the end of the war. Several country houses were offered, but the choice fell on Latchmere House at Ham, between Kingston and Richmond. In the first place it was near London, an official convenience; in the second place it had been a "home for neurasthenics" and had lunatic cells all ready made for a prison. The C.O. was given carte blanche and the impression was that he could be spared for this venture for two afternoons a week. In fact it was a whole time dual appointment for over six years.

Difficulties abounded, only to be overcome. Various Departments of State became aware of this high-handed requisition and sent priority claims with orders to take over at once. Possession being nine points of the law, the C.O., Stimson and Short established a squatters' title on 10 July 1940, and rival departmental deputations, each in turn, were rebuffed. The large premises were furnished, the camp was fortified, Intelligence officers and secretaries were engaged, Guard officers and troops marched in, all within seventeen days.

listening apparatus in the interrogation rooms and the cells. On 27 July 1940 the first batch of prisoners was incarcerated. They consisted of subversive British elements, certain enemy aliens whose cases were of operational importance, together with a number of suspects of German and other origins brought over from Dunkirk during the evacuation of France. Lord Swinton was able to report to the Cabinet that an interrogation centre for spies had been established and was in working order.

In retrospect the introduction of British elements was a political success but a tactical mistake. The British Fascists, notwithstanding their enemy leanings, claimed British privileges at one and the same time. They demanded legal representation; they claimed, as a Constitutional right, appeal to the Judges; they threatened proceedings for illegal detention, as Ham had not then been formally appointed "as a place of detention" under the Defence Regulations by the Home Secretary. All in all, they were certainly a treacherous bunch. Given power they would have abused it in the manner of the Hun; without power they were shabby nonentities, and gutless to boot. Lee Vaughan HENRY, DOMVILLE, McKECHNIE, SHELMERDINE and BATTERSBY are names that recur. CAIN of the Yard dealt with Vaughan HENRY, who resisted arrest, and it was well that the fiddler was no brother of the gallant inspector. The quick answer was to remove the British elements to Ascot, and by October 1940 Ham settled down to its proper role, namely the interrogation and detention of spies.

In the result, proper conditions could be imposed and these were approved by the Home Secretary. It was now possible to keep spies incommunicado for interrogation and later to retain them without fear of leakage of information and method. Spies as distinct from prisoners of war have no rights under the Geneva Convention, and an important result was that the Protecting Power, to say nothing of ambassadors, solicitors, religious advisers and voluntary organisations, were kept at bay.

At this time there were no precedents from the war of 1914 - 18 which could be followed. The camp was entirely a novel venture. There was no certain knowledge as to the methods which the enemy would employ or the magnitude of his effort. Thus both in Intelligence and in administration it was necessary to proceed by improvisation, by trial and error. The warning is that the tempo of modern war for such means is too fast.

One handicap was the fact that there was no pool of Intelligence officers trained in the handling and interrogation of spies. Most of the early officers were recruits from private life or by personal recommendation; many were commissioned ad hoc. An interrogator is born and not made. A breaker is one type, an investigator another. And the paradox is that the barrister is seldom the one or the other. The breakers were few and far between, and their total over the war can be counted on the fingers of one hand. The investigators in many cases made up for their lack of

personality by enthusiasm and drudgery. The officers who failed, and
it was no fault of theirs, were many indeed. Directionally a quick
appreciation is needed, and transfer; otherwise they lose faith in
themselves. The problem for ever is acute and the only solution is a
permanent cadre with conditions that attract. For the successful
officers have high qualifications; they have languages and drive and
they command high salaries in other fields of endeavour.

Another handicap was that the fighting soldier had little
sympathy for "Intelligence excreescences" and was apt to offload the
worst in his battalion when called upon for officers and men. In the
case of Ham this was at first particularly true, for there was a
literal procession of malcontents, unreliables and medically unfit.
A man reduced to the ranks, another under a suspension of sentence,
and a third who is "excused carrying a rifle", none of these, so to
say, carry confidence. Solution was reached, howsoever, with the
Adjutant General who ordained that the Commandant could handpick his
men and, for that matter, discharge them at will. A trouble-free
unit was in due course the result, and too high a tribute cannot be
paid to fine men who did a dull job well - so well that they never
lost a spy. A grand record. Indeed many of them volunteered for
Belgium and Germany and were sorry to leave in the end.

The third difficulty was the one of command, and it was only
a fortuitous circumstance that one man happened to hold the
qualifications of Chief Intelligence Officer and Camp Commandant at
one and the same time. There is no room for diarchy in war, and
M.I.19 with its various organisations came round to the same view.

The First Phase at Ham

The first distinct Intelligence phase at Ham began in September 1940
with the operational spies who landed in Kent, namely, WALDBERG, Van
den KIEBOOM, MAYER and PONS. What they lacked in preparation they
made up in Nazi faith. Indeed, WALDBERG was so certain the invasion
of England had begun that he demanded to be taken to the nearest
German Staff Officer. Three were hanged; PONS was acquitted,
promptly re-arrested and interned. Then came […]. He was broken in
straight interrogation, and Intelligence momentum began. […] had
struck up a great friendship with […], a fellow spy under training,
also intended for England. Privately they arranged to meet at the
"Black Boy" in Nottingham. […] in due course, was caught, and of him
alone a saga could be written. Unfortunately he was mishandled on
arrest, mishandled again by amateurs in interrogation, and finally
handed over to Ham as unbreakable. It was a crisis indeed, but he
was broken in due course by steady cross examination. Amongst other
elements, our knowledge of the private meeting at the "Black Boy"

had outstanding effect. Within the day [...] was "turned" and it is to the credit of MI 5 that he became the most remarkable double agent of the war. The record included the capture of RITTER and JOB, and the award of two decorations by Hitler for services rendered.

On the 30th September 1940 a signal was received that Vera ERICHSEN, De DEEKER and WAELTI had been captured in Scotland. [...] was asked about the woman and showed much agitation. He had last met her in Brussels with RITTER and a personal contretemps came to light. After dinner RITTER send Vera ERICHSEN home, unescorted in a tram, and the woman was angry indeed. That slight incident was twisted in interrogation. She had been followed by the British Secret Service, even on to a tram after a social scene with RITTER. Vera ERICHSEN was unnerved but, like most women in espionage, broke by instalments. Amongst other matters it transpired that her journey by seaplane to the Moray Firth was in fact the second; the first expedition by boat had been fouled by bad weather. One of her companions, she admitted, on that first journey was a most revolting man; a creature who chewed his wine glass and bled disgustingly in front of women. He was some uncouth journalist called EDVARDSEN. Inevitably EDVARDSEN followed after. He, in turn, was startled by our knowledge of his dubious parlour trick before the fair sex. The incident strengthened our claim to omniscience and EDVARDSEN confessed even to the hiding place of a sabotage tool which would have proved just that outside corroboration required in a trial. But fortunately for EDVARDSEN and his companions LUND and JOOST, some spies had already been hanged in England to deter others, and the policy was wisely changed to the establishment of the human reference library to incriminate others.

Next came the lone GOOSE, who was dropped by parachute in Northamptonshire on the 3rd October 1940. He belonged to the notorious 800 zur Besonderen Verfügung (the Lehr Regiment, Brandenburg). He was well equipped but his mission was so faulty that it was foredoomed to failure. He was to cover the territory of N.W. England, roughly between Bedford and Liverpool, including the towns of Leicester, Birmingham and Coventry. His mission covered meteorological data, reports on the morale of the British people and particulars of road barrages and obstructions. He was to remain in England until the proposed invasion took place, and then rejoin the invading army. He was given carte blanche with regard to his itinerary. He knew of no contacts in England. He was left to choose his accommodation as and where he thought fit. GOOSE, lacking initiative and for the matter courage proved a dismal failure.

Of the early sea cases JONASSON arrived with a mission in "La Part Bien" in Plymouth on 23rd September 1940 and EVERTSEN in

WALDBERG

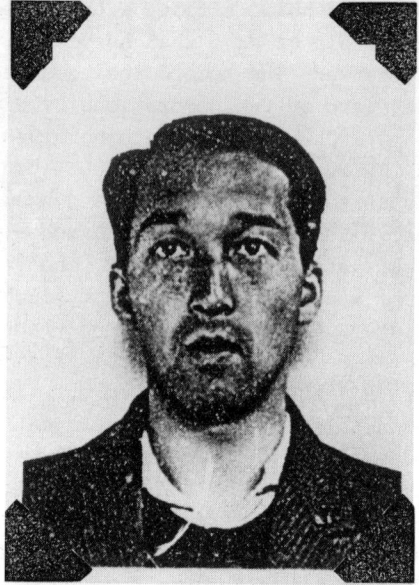

VAN DEN KIEBOOM

MENEZES

HELLMUTH

DRUCKE & DE DEEKER

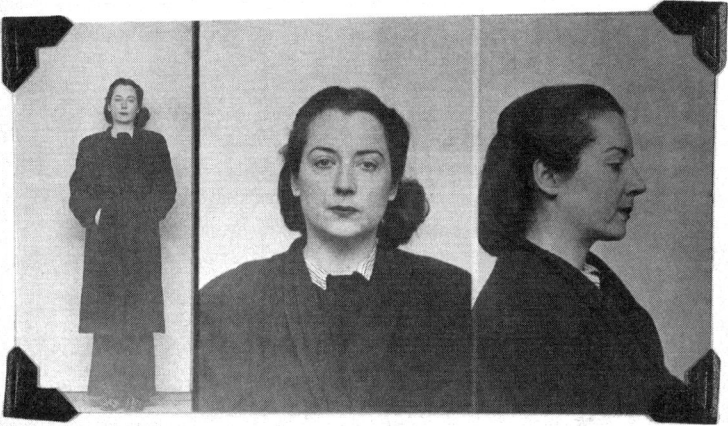

Vera ERICHSEN

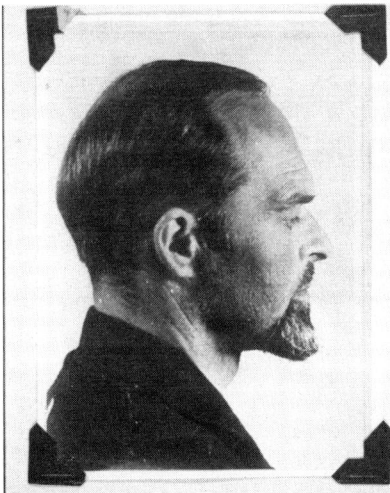

FINCKENSTEIN

the "Josephine" at Fishguard on the 12th November 1940. SKORZISKO
came alone in an open boat. Apart from being a spy he was a potential
nuisance because of his fantastic inventions. Each was discarded in
turn, and he died of a broken heart, firmly believing that we had
stolen the fruits of his genius. The last of the early batch of
spies was the FINCKENSTEIN/K.C. HANSEN party of meteorologists, who
were hauled off their fastness on Jan Mayen Island by the Royal Navy.

It is probably just to emphasise that these early cases,
which led to so many invasion ramifications, yielded to
straightforward interrogation. The times were against us, the
conditions were against us and Intelligence aids had not been fully
developed. Because of their outstanding importance, many of them are
dealt with in detail in the succeeding Case Histories.

The came trouble to Ham in no uncertain way. On 29th November
1940, Ham was hit by a land-mine which burst on the roof. Casualties
were few but material damage was enormous. In perspective it was a
taste of the tribulations the country was to suffer. The Officers'
Mess, living quarters and the offices were destroyed. The prison was
"open"; the men's lines were wrecked. The listening installation was
useless; there was no telephone, no heating, no water, no window, no
light. Evacuation was advised, but that momentum in Intelligence, on
which stress has already been laid, would have been lost. So we
lived with the prisoners instead and carried on just the same.
Interrogations took place in the mortuary and precedence in the bath
was granted only to prisoners due for trial at the Old Bailey.

The incident, none the less, was not without compensation,
as the dividing line between reconstruction and expansion became
blurred and a far better camp in due course was the result.

The Reserve Camp, Huntercombe, or Camp 020R

In January 1941 a lone German raider broke through the clouds by day
over Richmond Park and elected to drop a stick of four bombs over
Ham all over again. One bomb burst within two feet of a sentry box,
but the sentry within, by a miracle, was unhurt. Unconcernedly he
volunteered to continue his tour of duty. The only material damage
was the loss by blast of one regimental cap badge. The Regimental
Sergeant Major, of the Grenadier Guards, was by no means impressed.
Indeed such was his rigid sense of the fitness of things that he
duly laid a charge against the wretched sentry for being improperly
dressed. Official speculation then arose whether this second attack
on Ham was premeditated for a recurring accident ceases to be an
accident. Apparently Ham had already justified its existence and the
decision was reached that no further risk could be taken. In
consequence the Commandant was instructed to plan a duplicate camp

at Nuffield. Thus Huntercombe, or Camp 020R, came into being.
Primarily it was intended as a reserve camp. It was large enough to
absorb Ham in time of crisis and to provide for the future
commitments of a long term war. It included a hostel at Wallingford
where some 80 female staff could be accommodated. The decision was
wise, but the cost, about £250,000, was high, and it is for
consideration whether M.I.5 should not have a permanent lien on the
place. In the event, Huntercombe was never put to full use as the
Germans were good enough to leave Ham alone. The camp, howsoever,
did become the oubliette; the place where enemy spies, no longer of
interest, were allowed to vegetate until the end of the war. There
the prisoners learnt much about the British Constitution; they
whiled away their time by writing petitions to the King, to the Home
Secretary and to the Judges. Sometimes they gave good advice to Mr
Churchill and Mr Anthony Eden. Occasionally they tried to escape. In
the end it became a soulless camp, and much sympathy is due to the
officers and men who carried out their dreary task so
conscientiously and well for so long a time.

The Second Phase at Ham

The next distinct Intelligence phase may be conveniently considered
as beginning in 1941 and ending on D-Day or thereabouts. It was then
that the octopus was fully grown; tentacles stretched far and wide
and information was sucked in and thrown out in ink with remarkable
speed. From Iceland to Madagascar, South America to Egypt, Greenland
to the Azores, Ankara to the Belgian Congo, the Gold Coast to the
North West Frontier, Trinidad to Portuguese East Africa; of such
were the peoples, the languages and creeds, to say nothing of the
sweepings of belligerent Europe and of the states whose neutrality
was a glittering farce.

In particular, members of the German Secret Service do not
forget to this day the disruption caused by the confessions of two
of their spies. The repercussions were far and wide.

The first case is that of MENEZES, the clerk of the Portuguese
Embassy in London. He was a loose-mouthed youth, probably of
homosexual tendencies. He was recruited by the Germans in Lisbon.
His instructions were to send information by secret ink through the
diplomatic bag. Next he contacted the Italians who conceived the
same plan as the Germans. Thus in true opéra bouffe tradition the
Axis partners, unknown to each other, used the same spy and probably
exchanged the same information with much cordiality and Fascist
salute. The final revelations were so startling that the Portuguese
Government had the courage to incarcerate a score of agents in
Portugal, some German, some Italian and some Portuguese who were

officials in the Ministries. MENEZES was sentenced to death at the
Old Bailey, but was reprieved as a gesture to the good faith shown
by the Portuguese Government.

The second case is that of HELLMUTH, the Argentine Pleni-
potentiary to HIMMLER and HITLER. Under instructions, high-handed
action was taken by the British authorities at Trinidad. His
diplomatic cover was ignored. He was flown to Bermuda, and from there
was brought by H.M.S. "AJAX" to England. Tension was high, as without
a written confession of espionage there would have been trouble
indeed at a time when England could ill afford it. A confession, in
fact, was obtained and the Americans are of the opinion that the case
of HELLMUTH was the direct cause of the overthrow of the RAMIREZ
Government so hostile to the Allies at that time. But apart from
the war significance of the case, it was of great interest from an
Intelligence point of view. It was not an instance of isolated
endeavour, rather did it take its place in a long series of difficult
investigations. The interrogation of a score of South American spies
at Ham had proved conclusively that Germany aimed unequivocally at
world domination. The cases of BATICON, PEREZ GARCIA and RUIZ
embarrassed the Spanish Government as much as they stung Germany.
HOPPE and OLIVERA followed. Then came HELLMUTH. He had an SD
connection, which unmasked Amt VI, with SCHELLENBERG at the head of
an organisation controlled by HIMMLER himself. After the first few
interrogations HELLMUTH regained his nerve and bitterly blamed
himself as well as ourselves for his amazing defection. He became
recalcitrant and remained an ingrate to the end. He disapproved, in
terms as measured as they were futile, of the haven of rest provided
for him for the duration of the war.

The majority of the spies were as treacherous a gang as
could be found in the universe. It would be invidious to pick out
the most despicable, but the names of many recur who have all the
necessary qualifications. There was PACHECO, the Cuban dancer, who
communicated syphilis to his wife but did not warn her in case she
had given it to him in the first place. SCOTT FORD, while in the Navy,
gave away the position of H.M.S. "MALAYA", to say nothing of convoy
positions and secrets of Gibraltar. His motive was lust, greed and
self-aggrandisement. He figured himself Leiter of the Gau of
Hampshire, to include Portsmouth, after the end of the war. He was
well hanged. There was STEINER, the Belgian who posed as a refugee
of culture and erudition. Actually, for money, he married a German
woman, the mother of a Jewish bastard, and she was in trouble with
the Gestapo therefor. Then, for want of more money, STEINER peddled
"Kleenezi" brushes in Europe. Next he advertised with handbills a
brothel in the rue Van Iseghem in Ostende. Again for want of money
he betrayed his country and worked for the Germans as a spy. Finally

HOPPE

PACHECO & his wife dancing

PACHECO at Ham

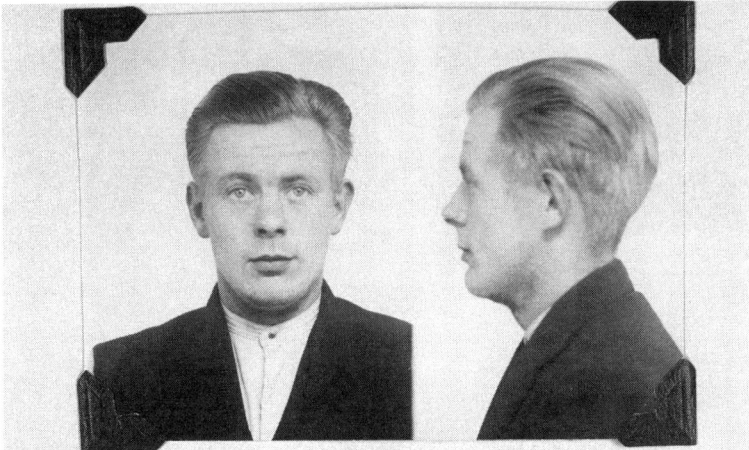

SCOTT FORD

Sobhy HANNA

NAUJOCKS

he was good enough to offer to work for the British Secret Service free of charge. There was ABEN, the Dutchman who betrayed his compatriots to their death. His motive was money and status, for his ambition was to be called "Captain" along the Dutch waterfront. JOB was a decayed English traitor from Fresnes, the internment camp near Paris. His was the mission to bring money in jewels to [...]. For that he was hanged. Sobhy HANNA was an "avocat" from Egypt, tall, swarthy and indecent, who impressed the Parisians. He bought thousands of acres of the Sahara and thereby duped a grasping Frenchwoman into marriage. He congratulated the Duke of Windsor on his marriage, and framed the formal acknowledgement as proof positive of powerful connections. In turn Sobhy HANNA worked for the Germans and then offered "on his honour as an Egyptian" to work solely for us.

NAUJOCKS "preserved" Polish bodies from prisons and sent them to the Polish border. These bodies, some still in suspended animation, were then riddled with bullets and so disposed to trump up a charge of Polish aggression on the sacred frontier of Germany. 'Real evidence' for the Führer, and thus, in part, came about the advance into Poland and the Second German War. NAUJOCKS was also a principal in the kidnapping of STEVENS and BEST, or "the Venlo affair". A thug? But in the hierarchy of evil, headed by HIMMLER, HEYDRICH, KALTENBRUNNER and POHL, NAUJOCKS stands in comparison a saint. Lastly in the galaxy of talent came PEEREBOOM, the Jew, coaxed into espionage as much by the disadvantages of blackmail as by the advantages of money. In England he became a stool pigeon of no distinction, and finally died of a fatty heart on the way to hospital.

A few men, very few, were brave. Joachim JAKOBS, the German, was one. He told the squad at the Tower to shoot straight. CHAPMAN was another. What a man! Discharged from the British Army in peace, he graduated through Hyde Park offences to be a master crook, "wanted" for safe blowing in many parts of the country. He drifted to Jersey, was interned by the Germans and witnessed the murder of his friend. He was trained by the German Secret Service as a saboteur. They considered him a safe bet as he would not dare, because of his past criminal record, to give himself up to the British. Actually that is exactly what he had the courage to do on arrival by parachute. Notional sabotage of the De Havilland works at Hatfield was carried out and communicated to the Germans. He then had the immense courage to return to Germany where he became something of a legendary figure. Again the Germans sent him here, but his time we kept him. What can be the future of such a man? Still anti-social, he has faced extreme danger and tasted easy money; above all he is allergic to work. LALLART, too, a Frenchman, was a brave man. He sought service with the German Secret Service in

order to betray them. He was taken by U-boat to Rio de Oro and made
a classic desert journey with the Germans to Port Etienne, where he
promptly betrayed his companions. His improbable story was thrown
out by the French but accepted by Ham, and it is satisfactory to
know that it was confirmed as correct by a prisoner named AHLRICHS
who was interrogated at Bad Nenndorf in 1945/46. An inconsequent
note is that the face of LALLART repays study. The like of it has
been seen in the past at Oberammergau.

Innocents abroad in war understandably come under grave
suspicion. Who but a man, stark staring mad, would choose a time of
invasion to cross the Channel in a canoe merely to start life
afresh? But such was De la FERE, under a false name, with false
papers, bogged in falsehood until he revealed the momentous secret
that his papa was one of the great Unknown. After weeks of inquiry
he was cross checked as innocent. Then followed the official Idea to
"release the man sweet", but the C.O. had more trouble than enough
on his hands. In terms De la FERE lied himself to the threshold of
the gallows. De la FERE answered faintly that he had come to realise
not only the time, but the craft also, were unsuitable and that such
conduct would never recur.

Van ACKERE, the weeping and romantic fat Belgian, was an oaf
of the same kidney. He escaped with his Beloved to the Unoccupied
vineyards of France, where they worked hand in hand for a pittance
in francs. But always the loss of liberty beckoned to them and they
finally sailed in a fishing boat from the spy ridden coast of Normandy
to England. The reality was incarceration in Ham and Holloway, where
they lied assiduously in a fanatical endeavour to help each other.
In the end there was no case. Again the official Idea; but this time
it was delegated with success. "Soldier Van ACKERE, put on your
uniform. You are a free man again." Uncontrollable weeping was the
reaction. "Oh Mister Officer, what a beautiful moment!". Van
ACKERE's Beloved turned the scale of adiposity at 280 pounds. Lastly
there was GROBBEN, the seaman. But the case of this man with a
straight eye was different. He had been enlisted by the German
Secret Service under duress. At Gibraltar he had the immense courage
to call for a Security Officer and to say he had no intention of
carrying out his mission. Instead, all information was at the
Allies' disposal. From the British point of view, infiltration was
the danger. At Ham, in due course, he was cleared. He was given
money which he declined to count. Rather was he intent on an old
silver ring, and when he had put that on his finger he felt a clean
man again. He left with a smile.

CALVO, the Spanish Press Attaché in London, was as
treacherous as he was entertaining. That dangerous ignoramus,
Alcazar de VELASCO, was his master. There was a link with Japan.

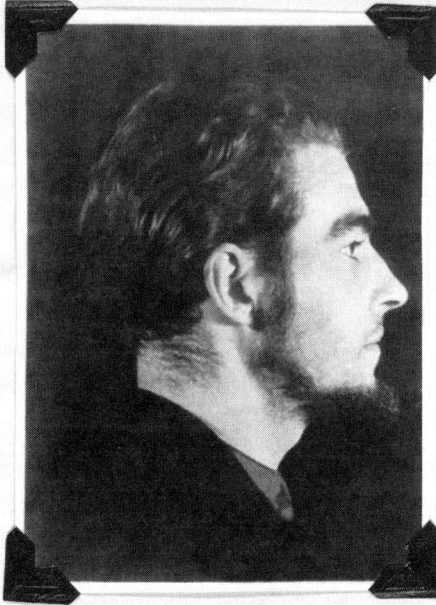

LALLART

CALVO

Serrano SUNER was involved and much diplomatic pressure was exerted. The Duke of ALBA was in a quandary, but his link with Berwick led him to a welcome impartiality. Evidence, in the end, was overwhelming, and it remains to be seen how CALVO, the journalist, can turn his misfortunes to advantage. MEISS-TEUFFEN was an Austrian/Swiss of good family recruited by I M for a mission in South Africa. He sailed single-handed in a 20-tonner to Bathurst. There he fooled the local Security officials, who gave him clearance. Thereupon he disclosed the fact that he was a German spy after all, but had no intention of carrying out his mission. For this bombast, he was inconvenienced by a sojourn in Ham which he plainly resented. MAYER from Jugoslavia was good value. His spy name was protected, but he was beguiled into a discussion on the great military commanders of the past. Talk drifted to Napoleon, and he was asked, as a matter of interest, to list his lieutenants in order of greatness. Glibly he gave NEY and quickly followed with MURAT. A stare….and from that instant a break had been achieved. The incident was not forced but later he admitted it was his spy name.

SERAFIMIDES was a Greek master mariner from Lourenco Marques. He sold convoy information from the Straits of Madagascar to the Germans and Italians, but so twisted was his reasoning that he convinced himself he was a friend of the British. De FREITAS, also a man from the sea, reported shipping movements by W/T to the Germans. His final mission was to tail the Armada for the invasion of North Africa; he was caught just in time.

STEVENS of the South American group of spies gained notoriety by an attempt to escape. At Huntercombe, with the connivance of fellow prisoners, he hid in a false marrow bed. The check on return of the working party led to a search and his discovery. LECUBE was a colourful character, a "futbolista" from Madrid. He kicked a mild looking warder in the stomach, only to wake up half an hour later to the fact that he had attacked a professional welter-weight by mistake. SALAMON and MOCSAN were picturesque figures, from Hungary, of great nuisance potential. SALAMON was a mariner who, by some process best known to himself, achieved diplomatic status. MOCSAN, his friend, had a wooden leg which he put to alternative use for the smuggling of cigarettes. Some of their time they spent in writing illiterate appeals to the Home Secretary. By way of a change they would write long screeds of advice to Mr Churchill on the Balkan situation.

KRAG was a Nazi fanatic from Schleswig-Holstein, and rebellious to the end. He organised a hunger-strike, but that was nipped in the bud. It is a fact that a man can do without food but he cannot do without liquid. Prisoners were therefore confined to their cells and provided with glucose and milk. Frustration set in within seventy-two hours. To SAETRANG, the spy from Panama, should go the credit for the only successful suicide at Ham. His was the ingenuity of a determined man who defies all administrative precaution. A window can be broken, or glasses smashed, or a femoral artery spent within a few moments. SAETRANG gagged himself, made a noose from stripped clothing and jumped from a bed which was upturned. Those unsuccessful in suicide include […] who cut veins in his wrist, and BATICON, who swallowed three-inch nails from his bunk. But of all the strange cases there was that of VIANA DOS SANTOS, who tore himself apart. He was sent to the Lunatic Asylum at Banstead, only to be returned, as such action is apparently quite a normal manifestation of the sane. Out of chronology was General PRUETZMANN at Diest, who hanged himself and was buried on the ramparts in the darkness of the night. HABENICHT at CSDIC also hanged himself and was finally buried in a local cemetery.

GILINSKY was a financial genius whose international operations in peace were as shady as they were successful. His story was that he bribed the Abwehr to pass him out of France to America under cover that he was an agent. In his own phrase, he merely used them as a 'guichet' for a ticket to freedom. To his everlasting indignation he was disbelieved and held as a contact of the German Secret Service. Nor could he understand the tortuous processes of the English legal mind. He had been forcibly removed from the ship in Trinidad. He had been taken against his will to England. He was then served with a formal "refusal of leave to land" under Defence Regulation 18B(A). And because there were no facilities for deportation in war he was imprisoned. Even that was not all, because we found 40,000 dollars which he had effectively smuggled through the controls of France, Spain and Portugal, to say nothing of the British controls in Trinidad and England. GILINSKY with his fortune could have been the natural successor of ZAHAROFF of the last war, and the only certain thing is that he would have been on the winning side.

BONZO, a Vatican lawyer of dual nationality, was the best of the Italians. He could have been dangerous in the Argentine, but the venture failed on account of Latin incompetence and jealousy. He maintained he worked for Italy rather than for Mussolini. Certainly he exposed without compunction the infamous frauds perpetrated by VOLPI and CIANO. One certainly is of the STAVISKY, KRUGER, HATRY variety. CIANO faulted a tender of five million lire for public works by the simple expedient of withdrawing the Fascist membership card for a technical indiscretion. VOLPI stepped in with a tender of eight million lire, only to find obstruction from CIANO again. In due course the CIANO group were awarded the contract for eighteen million lire. There was no bad blood between VOLPI and CIANO; they split the difference.

GILINSKY

BONZO

MANFREDI

MANFREDI, the baron, was a decadent Italian aristocrat. His reactions to an imperfect brief amounted to a frenzy. He was charged, inter alia, with sabotage of bridges on his estate in the Golfo di Manfredonia. "But there is no water, therefore no river, therefore no bridge. For that I am manacled and brought from my country to England." Later it transpired that his wife had been in touch with HIMMLER himself and MANFREDI's indignation at arrest turned into a fearful tirade against Fate. MOCHI, of the Italian Consular Service in Tangier, had a chequered war career. He was appointed to Jidda and crossed the Arabian Peninsula by truck from Baghdad. His experiences, if they are true, are reminiscent of the journeys of Philby. Later he was transferred to Tangier and was involved in a scene in the Consulate on the collapse of Italy. He adopted the attitude of the correct civil servant who obeyed the orders of his King. For that reason he advised the Consulate officials that they should surrender. The remainder, however, were Facists and they threw him through a glass door for his pains. Later he journeyed to Madrid and was there invited to proceed to England to clear himself. He was curiously unappreciative of the atmosphere of Ham and of his prison companions.

For the Intelligence officers it was a strange, urgent life. They lived in cells, above cells in the prison. Each sound could be heard, each move of a prisoner, of a warder, of a sentry without. Steps could be counted from an unseen cell to the closet. Even that could be turned to good account, for a recurrence of these visits meant a guilty conscience in a prisoner, and the time was perhaps ripe for asking questions all over again. It was a life among prisoners and stool pigeons, of heavy militarism and barbed wire; of the urgency of war and the determination to win that great battle of wits - to succeed against a professional spy who is fighting for his life. For interrogation there is not golden road to success. Again it is stressed that a "breaker" is born and not made. Personality, above all, is the quality that counts. Then comes experienced direction; there must be a definite but flexible plan; the right man must be chosen; the scene must be set for the first vital interview. Team work must count, when one man must stand down without pique in favour of another. Pressure must be maintained by day and even by night. The shrewder the spy, the less time must he have by himself in order to plan. He must be cajoled by a stool pigeon or irritated by a prisoner who is antipático. In some cases he can be wrong-footed by a Court of Assessors, composed of fellow prisoners, willing to ingratiate themselves with the authorities and round on the prisoner by the hour in his cell. Patience and perseverance are not without value, as success in one case was achieved after seventy-seven days. Violence is taboo, for not only does it produce

an answer to please, but it lowers the standard of information.
There is no room for a percentage assessment of reliability. If
information is correct, it is accepted and recorded; if it is
doubtful, it should be rejected in toto. All in all, it is a
business, this particular form of counter-intelligence, of ruthless
endeavour, of ninety-nine per cent frustration and sweat, of one per
cent satisfaction and reward. Time had no meaning, and it was no
uncommon occurrence to interrogate throughout the night. Physically
and mentally it will wear down the strongest constitution in the
end. Claustrophobia sets in, but what is worse is a disease akin to
a chronic dysentery of the East. A neurosis they called it, which
requires no medicine but "a change of occupation and rest". Strange
people, psychiatrists; even in war.

Yet withal there was room for satisfaction, for during the
phase 1940-44 Ham became recognised as one of the two most important
sources of information in war, comparable in accuracy indeed to the
other, which was ISOS itself. There was momentum. And I knowledge
can be measured by such things, there were hundreds of spies inside
the prison and well over a hundred thousand Intelligence cards in
the Registry at Ham. In addition there was a great accumulation of
information in codes and cyphers from many parts of the world, in
sabotage, W/T and kindred subjects. Such specialist matter required
great care and knowledge, for the technicalities are in foreign
languages and the reliability is nil unless the complete confidence
of the spy has been gained. All these ramifications of Ham led to
interest from other services and finally from other countries. The
DMI's in succession came to see us. There were visits from the DNI
and the RAF. A liaison of very lasting value was formed with M.I.19.
Indeed, that liaison culminated in the mergers at Diest and Bad
Nenndorf. There were visits from the FBI and the North West Mounted
Police, from the Director of Security in India to the Resistance
Movements of de Gaulle, the Belgians and the Dutch.

Administration presented little difficulty once a sound
system had evolved. The Home Secretary and his nominees took an
ever-decreasing interest, and visits from officials became rare with
the passing of time. In the world of the soldier, the Director of
Prisoners of War regarded the camps as star camps and in the last
year of war was too busy to inspect them at all.

(III.)

HAM - FROM DEFENCE TO ATTACK - D-DAY TO THE END

Operational as distinct from the normal C.I. phase of Ham is conveniently considered in relation to the period from D-Day, 6 June 44, to the Armistice, 8 May 45.

The contribution of Ham, and this includes the forward establishment at Diest in Belgium, to "Operational Intelligence" cannot, however, be evaluated. In the first place it is again merely a part of the M.I.5 pattern and it links up with the "Cover Plan", with "Diversionary Operations" and Security at large. In the second place the Germans relied in part on information from agents in England whom they trusted, but who in fact were operated by M.I.5; and with these activities this history does not deal. In the third place Hitler was by then living in the clouds of Berchtesgaden, in semi-celestial state, surrounded by sycophants, and it is quite impossible to gauge the effect of any Allied Intelligence activities upon the wandering mind of that erratic megalomaniac.

The German Secret Service, however, had definite plans in the event of invasion. They had agents in England in whose integrity they believed, and they sent others. They trained line runners for tactical information. They had a network of "stay-behind" W/T agents quite scientifically disposed over France, Belgium, Holland and Denmark. They engaged fanatics from autonomous movements such as that of Brittany who were prepared to work against their country for ideological motives. They tortured and blackmailed Resistance members into treachery. They finally relied on saboteurs in "bunkers" to operate in No Man's Land and on the sacred borders of their Vaterland. None of these dangers was overrated, for if the war was to be prolonged each would have developed by experience into a menace indeed.

In consequence the whole situation came under anxious review in order to provide the field with the best and most speedy assistance possible. Plans were laid for spies to be flown from the field to Ham and for reports in each case to be returned in the same manner within the week.

The Americans joined in the consultations. Major-General Bissel, Brigadier-General Sibert and others from the U.S. Army paid visits. The upshot of these visits was that Ham would cover the American requirements until they themselves could set up a similar organisation in France. In the meantime U.S. Army officers were detailed to Ham to gain whatever insight into the work time would permit. Good comrades and very intelligent they were, and it is hoped they liked us one half as much as we liked them.

German C.I. measures at that crucial period deserve reference and are dealt with in sequence.

(a) Agents operating before D-Day

First there were German agents in England who were working under British control. Their activities are not a part of this history, but they certainly contributed to the misconception of the German General Staff that the Pas de Calais was our main objective and that Normandy was a diversionary operation.

For the rest it is difficult to assess German interest in invasion. Clearly it was a stock question in the mission of any agent. In the early cases interest appeared remote, for the Germans believed in their ultimate victory and in the impregnability of the Atlantic Wall. The later cases indicate confused direction. A selection of the cases examined at Ham include Pierre Richard Charles NEUKERMANS, a Belgian Air Force Officer. His career of espionage on behalf of the Germans dates from November 1939 in Belgium until his arrest in England in February 1944. The most important part of his mission was to report invasion plans. For that he was hanged under the Treachery Act.

[…] was an Icelander who, blackmailed by the German Secret Service on account of his Black Market dealings in Germany, undertook an espionage mission to report on Allied troop movements in Iceland. He came under suspicion in Iceland and was sent to Ham by the Americans. He broke down under interrogation and it transpired he had been sent to Iceland in a U-boat. There was TIKHMENEV @ De MONTBRON @ FRESSAY, soi-disant Frenchman of rare cunning and aplomb. He maintained he had actively assisted the Allies in an underground movement in France and had allowed himself to be recruited as a German spy in order to assist the Allies' counter-espionage service. Sent to England for further investigation of his case, he became the victim of chance; perhaps a chance in a million. He was recognised by a casual acquaintance and the fat was in the fire. He had, in fact, been sent by the German Secret Service on a mission to report on service matters, particularly in relation to concentrations of landing barges and ships. Van HOVE, the waiter from Belgium, was willing to betray his country for a fee. His mission was directly connected with the invasion of the Continent. By his own admission, he had no loyalties. He was duly executed. A Lieutenant in the Norwegian Army, Knut BRODERSEN, accepted a mission in England on behalf of the German Secret Service to report by secret writing on invasion movements. WILMAN, a so-called Polish refugee, was recruited in Hamburg by the German I.S. and was given a mission in the U.K. or Canada, to obtain information on military installations and invasion plans. He was a high grade technician, for he was to purchase an ordinary wireless set and convert it for transmission purposes.

The case of CHAPMAN is dealt with elsewhere. The second part of his mission was definitely connected with troop movements.

A case of outstanding operational importance is that of FRESENIUS/BJORNSSON/JULIUSSON. The Germans sent this trained and well found party by submarine to Iceland, where they landed on 30 April 1944. Their mission was to report troop concentrations, as the Germans had been led to believe that a great concentration of American forces was taking place in Iceland for an invasion, possibly of Norway. Under interrogation at Ham the men proved extremely stubborn, but a break was finally obtained "through weakness into strength". In effect the story was pieced together from the underlings BJORNSSON and JULIUSSON, and FRESENIUS, the leader, was faced with a hopeless task of evasion. FRESENIUS, being an intelligent man, then gave the whole unvarnished story. Their subsequent handling is not a part of this history.

(b) Line Runners

"Frontlaufer" was the designation of the German spy detailed to penetrate the Allied lines and return with tactical information. Personnel selected were traitors. They were paid handsomely by results, but were subject to blackmail. They were trained to observe and to report back to field W/T stations. The German Army was briefed to pass to Headquarters any civilian who claimed to be a "Frontlaufer" and to belong to Eins C.

These spies appeared to be of poor quality, but it would have been a mistake to underrate them. Men of this kidney usually work for the winning side. In the early days is seemed they were working assiduously for the Germans. Once, however, the Allies were firmly established in Normandy the enthusiasm waned. Later still of course they would have us believe that they never intended to work for the Germans at all. One went so far as to advance the proposition that he accepted and spent money from the Germans in order to sabotage their treasury.

The sum total of the information obtained from these line runners was invaluable. They betrayed their fellow students at the spy schools and this led to further arrests. They gave information which, pieced together, yielded the design of the network of "stay-behind" agents.

COLLOMB, aged 21, was a member of the P.P.F. until he joined the new Fascist Party. Through a friend of his in this Party he was recruited for service in the S.D. His first mission was given to him

TIKHMENEFF

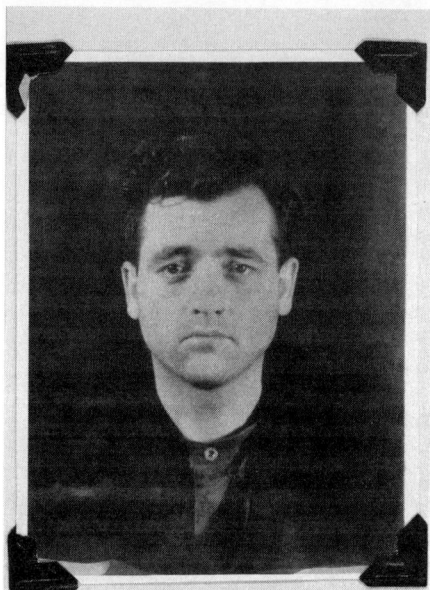

NEUKERMANS

BJORNSSON

FRESENIUS

in June 1943, when he was to penetrate an escape route into Spain. In due course he became a "Frontlaufer" in the area of Caen. He was ordered to report on civil administration, security controls, the food situation and Allied shelling from the sea. Later he got cold feet and, by some tortuous process of reasoning best known to himself, thought it would be well to surrender and make a partial confession. The whole truth was obtained only after considerable trouble.

BIANCHI, a Swiss, naturalised French, was a remarkable youth. Before the age of twenty-one his record included two criminal convictions and an arrest for espionage. Stealing, receiving, assault, battery, subversive activity and espionage all came to him with equal facility. He graduated to the German Secret Service through the P.P.F. His mission was to observe Allied traffic on roads and to locate artillery emplacements in the Escoville area. In due course he was arrested by the British and with much sincerity told his cover story. Passed to a Civil Affairs Camp, he survived further interrogation and was allowed to join the French Army. He was finally arrested after denunciation by his companion, GIRKA, a boy of eighteen, who had been with him at the outset.

PIAT was another young criminal. His qualifications for the German Secret Service included the perpetration of a bomb outrage in the Paris Synagogue, a sentence of imprisonment and membership of the P.P.F. His mission was to ascertain Allied concentrations and to identify units in the Calvados area. Arrested by a British sentry, he confessed to the F.S.P.

NOTERMAN saw no future in religion. He exchanged isolation in a monastery for eight months imprisonment for larceny. He was sent to Germany for forced labour. On his return he joined the Maquis for a brief period. Later he became a member of the Fascist Milice and through this organisation was put in touch with the Germans. By then he was trained in W/T and unit identification. He was given an operational mission in the Aunay-sur-Odon area. Arrested by two British soldiers, he first told a story which was an improvement on the cover story given him by the Germans. This, he explained, was because he had been told that the British shot suspected spies out of hand. Later, however, he was prevailed upon to tell the truth.

The vicious circle of personal treachery is well illustrated by the MANET group of cases. MANET himself was a failure in everything he touched. In 1929 or thereabouts he was a volunteer in the French Air Force. Later he became an inspector of mines, a dealer in antiques, a hospital superintendent, a sawyer in Morocco, a peddler in insurance and an agent for an Italian pastry firm. In 1940 he became a soldier, was taken prisoner and escaped. He then joined the TODT Organisation for a temporary living and drifted easily into espionage on behalf of the Germans. He failed generally

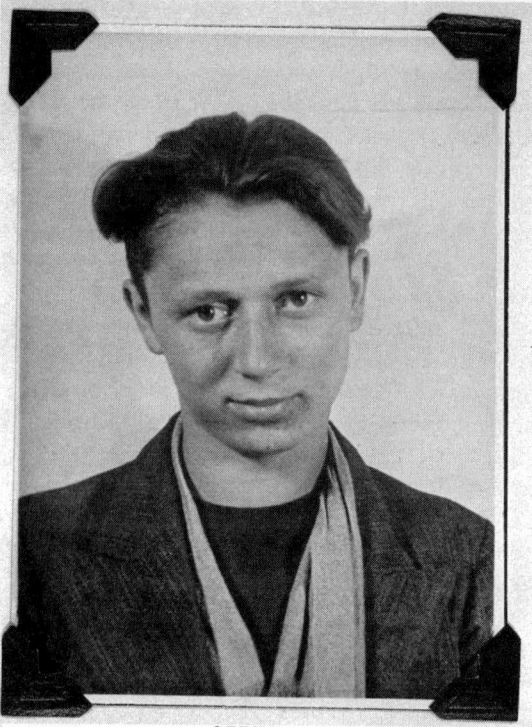

GIRKA

PIAT

in his training. On this record the Germans, with their flair for
the appropriate, made him a talent scout. MANET recruited PRIEUR, a
radio technician who won the Croix de Guerre in 1940 and found
nothing odd in joining the Germans in 1944. In turn PRIEUR failed in
his training, particularly in W/T. The wife of MANET was next on the
list, but she succeeded in W/T where her husband had failed. The
Germans, in desperation, linked the three together. MANET and PRIEUR
were to obtain information and pass it to Madame MANET for onward
transmission. The group was posted to St Malo. PRIEUR at last was of
assistance, as he had taken to himself a servant girl, Marie
RENAULT, as a mistress. Her premises were suitable for W/T
transmission. Heavy Allied bombing, however, interfered with their
plans and the group decided to leave. They placed the W/T
transmitter in the care of Marie RENAULT's mother, but she thought
better of it in due course and threw the set into the village pond.
PRIEUR then began the grand betrayal. He was arrested by the F.F.I.
at Lanhelin and was severely beaten. He betrayed his mistress, Marie
RENAULT, who had her hair clipped in the F.F.I. fashion of the day.
Then both PRIEUR and Marie RENAULT betrayed the MANETs, who were
rounded up by the F.F.I. All four members of this shabby outfit were
sent to Ham and gave much trouble under interrogation, as each
version was totally different and contradictory.

Another interesting case was that of ANDERSEN and his wife,
both examined at Ham. ANDERSEN was recruited as a W/T agent in 1940
for duty in the French Unoccupied Zone. He married in 1942 and
recruited his wife into the Service in 1943. They were established in
Marseilles under commercial cover as "stay-behind" agents in case of
the invasion of the South of France. The wife was infiltrated into
the U.S. Army as an interpreter. They sent much valuable information
to the enemy. But they laboured under a grievance, for the wife had
to sign for the pay of an agent which was pocketed by the Germans.
The investigation was difficult, but a break was effected by a cross
ruff. They were an unclean couple, dirty in body, mind and spirit.

An equally important affair was that of GOBIN and his wife.
GOBIN was recruited in 1940 and his wife was a principal. He worked
under cover of the Bureau de Ravitaillement in Brussels, but
operated a W/T set in a house in Antwerp. Madame GOBIN was
undoubtedly comely, but it may have been a coincidence after all
that the house was often inspected by Korv Kapt KOCHLING when the
husband was out. These two spies were of high grade and of great use
to the enemy. Because of the husband-and-wife element, the
investigation was difficult to a degree, but the wife was played off
against the husband and a break was effectively obtained within a
short but anxious space of time. An interesting side light in this
case was that the Field Security Section twice failed to find the

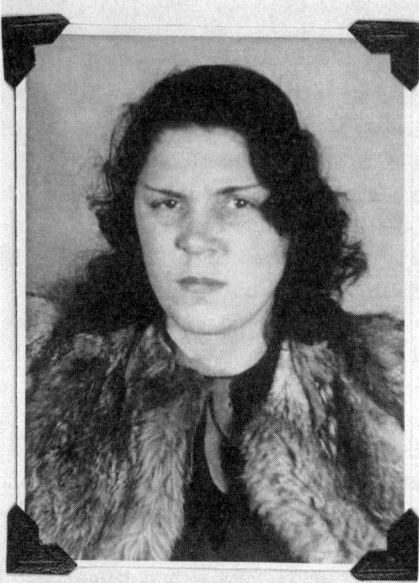
Helene ANDERSEN

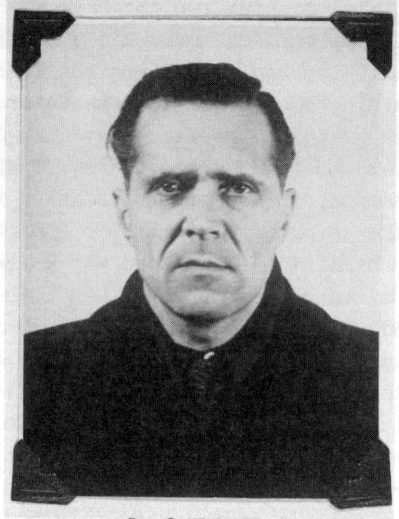
Svend ANDERSEN

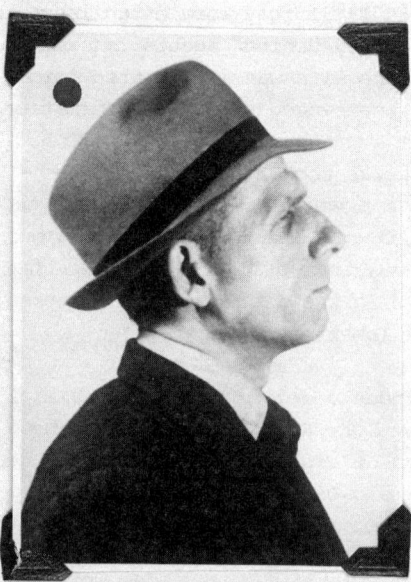
Joseph GOBIN

Mathilde GOBIN

W/T set in a bureau minutely described in the Interrogation Report. The GOBIN's, in consequence faced fearful wrath, but remained firm. A third search was demanded and the set was found. Cunning concealment or shoddy search; probably something of each.

(c) "Stay-Behind" Network

"Stay-behind" agents were generally spies, men and women, of sound training and long service. They were given cover businesses, they were well paid and they were soon absorbed into the normal life of their appointed town. Before invasion they were discreetly inspected from time to time. Generally speaking they were a formidable gang of traitors.

A typical example in this category is Fernand SCHMITT, a Frenchman born in Strasbourg. He was recruited by the German Secret Service in 1940. At Ham he was persuaded to give details of the staff and students at the schools at Chateau Lambeau in Brussels and at Chateau La Croix, Lille. He himself was trained in W/T, codes and cyphers and in secret writing. His mission was operational. He gave minute descriptions of 44 enemy agents, 16 espionage addresses and 19 suspected agents. He gave his W/T frequencies, call signs and spy name. Lastly, his network of "stay-behind" agents in the Pas de Calais area is worth examination.

More spurious than Fernand SCHMITT was EEMAN, the black marketeer of Knocke. He bled the country that bled for him. In addition, as a house agent he approached estate management from an entirely novel angle. He would requisition a house to pay off old scores and de-requisition it again for a fee. Yet such are the vagaries of human nature that he fought well enough for Belgium in the last war.

(d) Agents from Autonomous Movements

"Divide and rule" is a principle as old as the hills. In espionage the principle can be put into practice through Separatist movements. It requires political knowledge of a high order. It requires finesse, for the fanatic works for ideological motives and will reject anything base.

The Germans blundered into this field with their usual aplomb, but generally failed. They sent Otto MAYER to play off the Croats against the Slovenes. They paid court to Eire, but never understood that mentality. They deputed Sobhy HANNA to foment trouble among the students in Egypt. Through BRANDT they confused the politics of the Faqir of Ipi with the ethics of a jihad.

In France, however, they came within measurable distance of success through GUERIN and VISSAULT de COETLEGON. GUERIN had a

Otter
(peut-étre Ostende)

Frosch
(Dunkerque)

Dromedar
(Dunkerque)
Poste qui a été aboli

Fink (femme
s'appelant Lisette)
Poste situé en Belgique
n'ayant jamais répondue.

BERLIN
(Bürg)

- BRUSSELS (Vogelsang)

TOURCOING
15iéme AOK

COLOGNE
(Conrad)

Nashorn
(peut-étre
NAMUR)

LILLE
(Tournes)

WIESBADEN
(Wilja)

BENNETT
Lillebonne

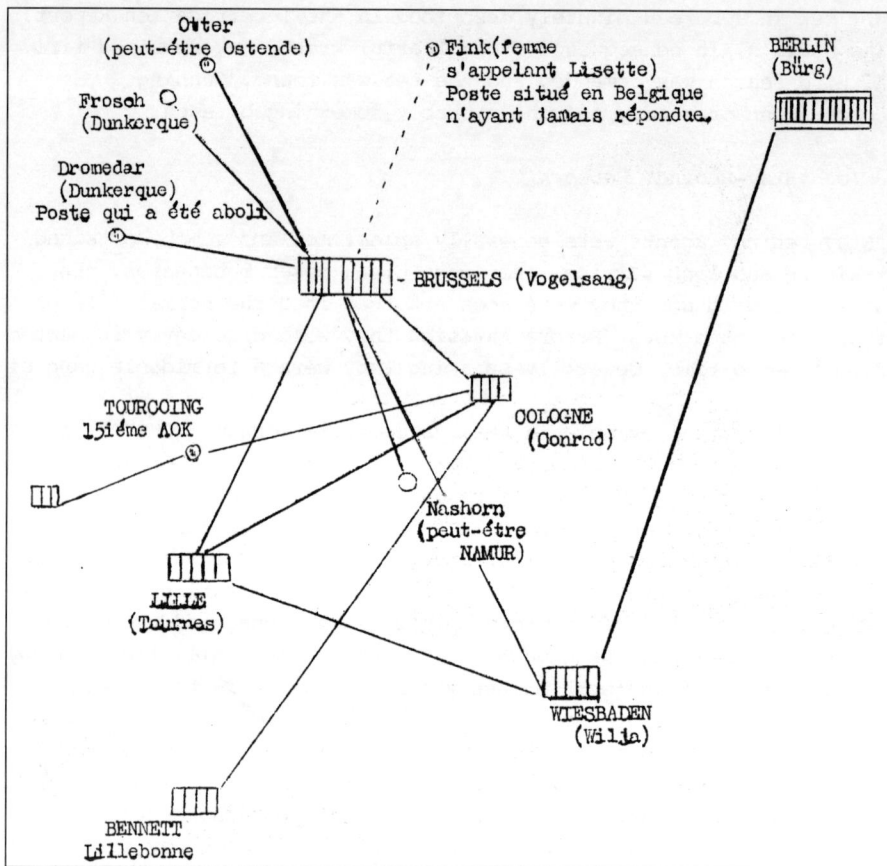

burning faith in the independent rights of Brittany. His reasoning
was tortuous. He was willing to betray France who would not
recognise his idealism in favour of Germany who promised autonomy.
To gain his ends he would be unscrupulous to a degree, yet it is
doubtful if he would do anything dishonourable outside his
obsession.

GUERIN was a dangerous enemy; COETLEGON conformed more to
the German espionage type. Both were trained as "stay-behind" agents
and had the battle of Normandy swayed back and forth, these two men
would have been a potent evil indeed.

(e) Traitors from the Resistance Movement

There can be little sympathy for a member of the Resistance Movement
who had been tortured and blackmailed by the Germans into treachery,
unless he can answer satisfactorily two questions. Firstly, when
under duress, did he do the least possible damage to his country?

VISSAULT DE COETLEGON

LINDEMANS

Secondly, did he reveal the entire truth at the first available
opportunity to the Allies when he came into their hands again?

The case of LINDEMANS, the enormous Dutch brute, well called
"KING KONG", comes under such consideration. Originally, for the
Dutch Resistance, he fought bravely. He was a good shot and a good
killer. Ultimately he was caught by the Germans and blackmailed into
working for them. On the arrival of the Allies in Belgium he was he
was caught by the Germans and blackmailed into working for them. On
the arrival of the Allies in Belgium he was attached to the staff of
Prince Bernhard. He was regarded as a hero, but the fact was that he
continued to work for the Germans in the fateful days of Arnhem. At
Ham LINDEMANS threw an epileptic fit and luminol was administered.
The "priority" was demanded from the field, and with the doctor's
agreement interrogation began. It was the first and the last
interrogation carried out under a drug. It was certainly the wrong
drug for intelligence purposes, as it had a steadying effect.
LINDEMANS, for hour after hour and day after day, was obdurate.
Success, none the less, was achieved through a series of partial
breaks, and these cumulatively were valuable. To wind up the case,
however, certain outside reactions were required, but they were
never forthcoming. Perhaps there were too many cross currents. Later
the body was transferred to Holland where again factions arose. Some
though LINDEMANS a hero; others know him to be a traitor. Finally a
decision was made to prosecute but LINDEMANS anticipated the result
by committing suicide.

If LINDEMANS of Holland was guilty of Arnhem, then in
treachery he must rival MIHAILOVITCH of Yugo-Slavia; and their names
will reek to the end of time.

(f) Saboteurs, "Bunker" and other Agents

There is evidence that the Germans had made considerable
preparations for espionage protection on the German border. In the
event, the speed of the attack and the general demoralisation of the
German Army rendered them ineffective.

There was the case of RAINER, an SS officer of the Götz von
Berlichingen Panzer Division, who had fought through the campaign in
Normandy. He transferred to the Höhere SS und Polizei Fuhrer in
November 1944 and was trained in an espionage school at Hülcrath
together with members of the SS Hitler Jugend and Ordungspolizei. The
indication was that they should remain in "bunkers" which were specially
prepared, transmit operational information and harass the L of C.
RAINER was a fair type of German and gave considerable trouble under
interrogation. In the ultimate, however, details were obtained of the
training schools, of fellow students and of a network of "bunkers".

Another case was that of SWEERTS. This man was a Belgian who chose to work for the Germans. He was well trained and finally became an SD officer of Amt VI. He was in constant touch with those notorious villains SCHELLENBERG and SKORZENY. He worked well for the Germans and visited Spain on their behalf as a guest of the Falange. In September 1944 he undertook to penetrate the Allied lines but was then good enough to desert to the winning side. He duly betrayed the German Secret Service and gave a mass of information on the RSHA. Indeed, he went so far as to assert that he interested himself in the RSHA with the deliberate intention of handing over this information to the Allies. Be all this as it may, it was found all very valuable in London. No doubt by so doing SWEERTS satisfied his own conscience that he was a good patriot.

The Forward Unit at Diest

After the battle of Normandy a decision was reached at SHAEF, Versailles, to set up forward investigating units in the American and the British sectors. Ham was to continue with the heavy and, so to say, long term C.I. cases.

The American Army selected Revin in the Ardennes. A British signal detachment […] was loaned to them and the C.O. of Ham was deputed to liaise. Investigations began in November. Work was carried out under difficult conditions, but the establishment was well forward and they gained in the time factor. The American Intelligence officers achieved remarkable results and their advance information on the Siegfried Line was vital. Later, during RUNDSTEDT's counter-attack in the Ardennes they were nearly overrun, but that was the luck of the toss.

21 Army Group considered Brussels, or thereabouts, a suitable location for their forward unit. M.I.5 and M.I.19 were asked to join forces, but for some obscure reason connected with Finance and War Establishment it was considered a U.K. instead of a 21 Army Group commitment. A reconnaissance by the C.O. and an officer of M.I.19 took place in November 1944. The citadel at Diest was on offer and was accepted. It was a mediaeval sort of place with dungeons and moats and excellently suited for the purpose. The R.A.F., however, were in part occupation and decided with some gaiety to extend. Breendonck, a Belgian fort with a dark record of Gestapo torture, was suggested by an officer with Hollywood ideas, but that proposition was summarily rejected. A second reconnaissance was carried out and Val Duchesse, on the outskirts of Brussels, was selected. The premises were duly evacuated in January and work was begun. Later 21 Army Group cancelled this arrangement in favour of Diest again, which was no longer required by the R.A.F. It was not

therefore until 12 March 1945 that the unit formed. It was called No 1 Det CSDIC(UK), BLA. It averaged some 12 Intelligence officers, 4 Administrative officers and 105 other ranks, contributed by Ham, CSDIC(UK) and PWIS(Home). It came under command of the C.O. at Ham, but was generally administered by a special staff section at 21 Army Group. The detachment functioned until 30 September 1945, when it was absorbed by CSDIC(WEA) at Bad Nenndorf in Germany.

Among the civilian elements there were some picturesque creatures. KRAMER, known of course as "the Beast of Belsen", was held at the request of the War Crimes Commission. Under orders he was not interrogated and little at first hand is known of him. It is, however, of some interest to note that he went to the scaffold like a craven, in marked contrast to Irma GREESE, who died with the serene courage of a fanatic.

Josef SCHREIEDER, a Gestapo official of The Hague, was a routine case. Originally he withheld information, but at Diest he gave satisfactory Intelligence on Gestapo methods in Holland and on treachery within the Dutch Resistance Movement.

PRAETORIUS of Ast Hamburg was of more interest. He had a long and possibly creditable record of service as a permanent official of the German Secret Service. His interests covered espionage in the UK, USA and South America. Korvetten Kapitän STIEGE was a man of much the same kind. He was involved in Spain, Portugal, South America and the Far East.

Then the case of GROTHMANN is of passing interest. GROTHMANN, Heinrich HIMMLER and MACHER were arrested near Meinstedt by three Russian soldiers. HIMMLER was wearing civilian clothes and had a black patch over one eye, whilst GROTHMANN and MACHER were dressed half in uniform and half in civilian clothes. In view of this disguise they were not recognised by the Russians, who handed them over to the occupants of a British Army car. The men were twice interrogated, but HIMMLER was not recognised. GROTHMANN says that this was not surprising, since HIMMLER, in civilian clothing and without his glasses, appeared as an ordinary type of middle class German. Later the three prisoners were taken to Westertimke and then to Luneberg. There HIMMLER finally admitted to his proper name. It is history that HIMMLER committed suicide by potassium cyanide.

(IV.)

HAM - NORMAL C.I. FROM D-DAY TO THE END

Apart from the operational intelligence which developed from D-Day at Ham there was the normal, and as it proved, heavy C.I. commitment. Many of the cases were of outstanding interest.

Carl EITEL, alias CARLOS, ship's steward on board the "BREMEN", joined the Abwehr in 1934 as a transatlantic courier for PHEIFFER. He was branded as an agent in the U.S. spy trials of 1938, but apart from that his career was such that any self-respecting Service would have discharged him with ignominy. Not so with the German Secret Service. On the outbreak of war they re-employed him variously in Genoa and Lisbon, and he roamed as far as Brest. In Lisbon he complicated his career by inducing the Americans to employ him as an agent double. In Brest he threw his family affairs into confusion by taking unto himself a French harpy. He began to fake Intelligence and dabbled in the Black Market. He was recalled to Berlin, but the Germans, with their inimitable flair for misplacing trust, gave him a mission to "redeem himself". He was charged with the delivery of money and W/T material to agents in danger of being cut off by the Allied advance through France. EITEL of course pocketed the proceeds. He was then lost in the German retreat. He failed to surrender and was finally arrested by the French. He was sent to Camp 020 as a "privileged daily visitor", but steps were pretty soon taken to have him incarcerated in a proper manner. It was then and not until then that his full activities and treachery came to light. Later he was joined by PHEIFFER, and he became so subservient that he asked for the privilege of doing odd jobs. He took a singular interest in washing his master's dirty linen, an arrangement which suited PHEIFFER well enough. Yet EITEL must be written down as a successful crook. For years he had received pay from two masters, robbed the Intelligence tills, and made a fortune in the Black Market. At the time of his arrest this shark was the proud possessor of an hotel and half a million ill gotten francs.

PHEIFFER himself was a good German but a bad Nazi. As such he was perhaps one of the better Abwehr officers. His knowledge of the Abwehr, its organisation, activities and personalities was certainly encyclopaedic. He was keen and worked hard, but became disgruntled because the results of his work were misapplied by his Nazi masters. In keeping with his character and as a member of the Naval officer corps, he had his loyalties, and it is doubtful whether he would have given us information had he not believed in the total collapse of his country.

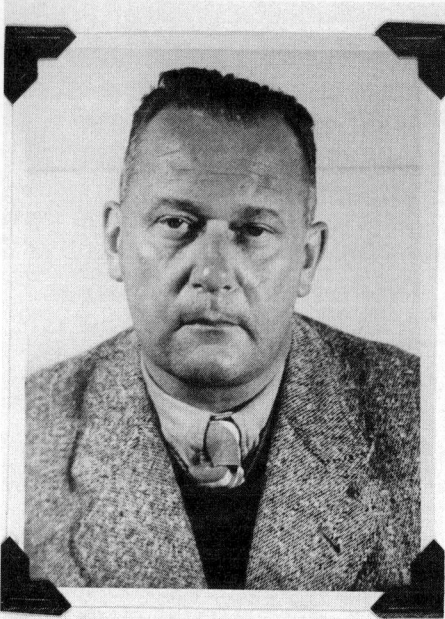

PHEIFFER

PHEIFFER & his secretary

EITEL

KRAEMER

Karl Heinz KRAEMER was an important German agent in Stockholm, and it is well that his organisation was penetrated in due course. He was a lawyer by profession, but reported to RITTER of Ast Hamburg in 1939. He went under cover as a German Legation Secretary and had the advantage of currency exchange and the diplomatic bag. His network of agents was respectable and his contacts included members of the Swedish and Japanese Secret Services. After the capitulation KRAEMER and his secretary, Nina SIEMSSEN, were sent to Ham. There was nothing in the woman, whose personality was that of a relation who types country house menus with no marked success. The capture of KRAEMER, on the other hand, was a very good investment. It warranted his transfer from Ham to Bad Nenndorf for further vegetation.

A vignette of a White Russian is not easy. Elie GOLENKO belonged to the officer class, once the pride and now the outcast of his race. Shiftless they must be, because they are bone idle; and espionage to them is as popular as an interest in a night club or a manicure shop. GOLENKO was decayed but he had lived on his wits. He had served in the Intelligence Services of the Greeks, the Finns, the French, the Germans and the Americans. He considered the British unintelligent because they would not round off his brilliant career by taking him into their Service. In the scheme of things he had no loyalties. At one time he maintained he was the White Russian concerned only with a feud against the Red Russians. Later he was trapped into the admission that he had given false information to the Germans against the Red Russians. The real fact is that he operated a W/T service in the office of the "PARIS-SOIR" on behalf of the Germans and swayed many an engagement before Stalingrad in this way. At Ham for a while he was urbane because he traded on the assumption that the German code was known only to himself.

Probably the most fantastic case which ever came to Ham was that of KRAUS. The Austrian was recruited by Theo SCHADE, and was posted to Paris under cover as an official of the SIEMENS combine. He kept a Frenchwoman in a 'third floor back' until he discovered she was a species of princess. He promptly promoted her by marriage and de-requisitioned her family home where he could live in greater ease at no expense to himself. He moved then in a higher stratum of French society and was able to betray to the Germans and to their death one or two of the new friends he had thus made. The Germans were pleased and gave him a decoration for his social treachery. For secrecy he kept it in a flower pot and watered it each day to keep his memory of the Vaterland fresh. Later he linked up with a misguided British officer who was enamoured of his wife's sister. He was smuggled as a batman in British uniform to England. On the voyage he was detailed to guard German prisoners and was rebuked for

GOLENKO

KRAUS

his slovenly drill and indifferent dress. On arrival in England
KRAUS and the British officer paid a visit to the sister-in-law who
was in hospital. There, another admirer with flowers was found, and
a first class brawl took place in the ward. After a month of
unseemly incidents of this kind KRAUS became anxious because he had
no British papers and he was then induced by his family to call at a
police station "to comply with the usual formalities". KRAUS was
arrested, the British officer was dismissed the Service, the wife of
the British officer resigned from a Government appointment, and
finally the princess petitioned for divorce. At Ham KRAUS seemed
little abashed. First he endeavoured to claim British nationality
through his half British wife. Later he magnanimously offered to
negotiate a loan in the City of London on behalf of "an Independent
Austria". It availed him nothing. Slowly, inexorably, the whole
sordid history came to light and the shabby career came to an end by
deportation to Germany.

Friedrich OLMES was an odious type of Hun. Bumptious to a
degree, this upstart looked younger than twenty-four years. He came
into prominence as the inventor of an anti-tank weapon which
intrigued the amateur soldier Hitler in the manner of a new toy. He
claimed further successes with his weapon at Cassino and thereby
contacted GOERING, HIMMLER and GOEBBELS. Then came the unsavoury
incident when his commanding officer, a homosexual, decried his
fighting at Cassino. OLMES seems to have lost favour for a time. He
was suspected of complicity in the affair of 20 July 44, but was
cleared. Inevitably he bounced up again and was employed by the
RSHA. Repugnant though he was, he had brain and talked with some
learning at Ham on war inventions and in particular on German
progress on the atom bomb.

Von LEDEBUR was a man of many contradictions. He was not a
Nazi but he dabbled in dirty business on behalf of the Abwehr. Then
he would have a pang of conscience and do something quite
respectable. At one time he fought on the Eastern Front; at another
he associated with Charles BEDAUX, that shady trader and spy. He was
party to a trans-Saharan expedition on behalf of the Germans, but
his proved abortive. Then he veered again, for there is evidence
that he saved some personal and business friends from the Nazis by
sheer force of personality. His method was interesting. He recruited
his friends into the Abwehr and sent them on notional missions to
Spain and to freedom. He would "control" them himself during
pleasant journeys to Spain, and would send back concocted
Intelligence to HANSEN, the gullible Amtschef in Berlin. In early
1944 he became somewhat bored and decided to change masters.

[…] them after the Putsch of 20 July 44. At Camp 020 his
strange story was subject to minute check and it must be granted in

his favour that he was seldom found wanting. Later he proved a willing prison agent and obtained valuable information from creatures such as SCHELLENDBERG and KALTENBRUNNER, whom he candidly despised.

It is a far cry from China to Ham, but WEIDEMANN answered the call. In him Hitler had great faith, and finally sent him to San Francisco as German Consul General. In due course he made his way to China and became responsible for much evil in that harried land. His property was fascinating. He had translated his money into 22 carat gold ingots and pearls, together worth the ransom of a king.

UNVERSAGT, the very correct official of the Abwehr, saw nothing incorrect in becoming a first class turncoat. For years he had recruited and trained agents for England such as WALDBERG, NEUKERMANS and FRAVAL. It was convenient that they came to Ham, and more convenient still that he was good enough to come himself, as he was able to check their stories. He certainly anticipated interrogation, and such was the efficiency of his paper work that he almost wrote his own report.

Korvetten Kapitän WICHMANN was another officer of the Abwehr, but possibly a better type than UNVERSAGT. He fought in the German Navy in 1914-19. He retired by rejoined in 1934. Very soon he joined the Abwehr and became Ast Leiter of Hamburg. That Ast was comparatively efficient in the years and WICHMANN can perhaps claim credit for it. Of much information which he gave possibly the most interesting related to the German plan for the invasion of Britain.

A late capture was General Friedrich WOLF, former German Military Attaché in Chile and subsequently German Naval, Military and Air Attaché to Argentina. His first contact with the Abwehr was in 1934; and he was thus in the hypocritical world of diplomacy an open spy. At Camp 020 this socialite arrogated to himself all the dignity of a fighting soldier, but it is doubtful whether he had ever heard a shot fired in anger. There was much posturing, bombast and nonsense about Conventions which availed him nothing in the face of the evidence of men such as HELLMUTH, BATICON, PEREZ, RUIZ, HOPPE and OLIVERA. The main value to Ham of this upstart general was firstly that he provided information relating to the German network in Argentina which led to its rapid disruption, and secondly that he confirmed in outline Intelligence already obtained. The main value of Ham to the General was that he learnt a few lessons in elementary manners and discipline. He graduated to CSDIC for further hospitality.

Another late capture was Luitpold WERZ, ex-German Consul and Legation Secretary in Lourenco Marques. His main object was to live in comfort with his mistress, so that G.I.S. funds did not come amiss. He linked up with the local Italian consul, CAMPINI, and

there is little doubt that these officials were responsible for
shipping losses around the Cape and in the Straits of Madagascar.
They traded also on ideological links with the OSSEWA BRANDWAG.
Names that recur in this group of cases are ELFERINK, about whom
much was known but from whom a confession was never obtained;
SERAFIMIDES, the Greek master mariner; MUELLNER, the piano tuner;
and Basil BATOS, as old and unprepossessing as his mistress was
young and attractive.

The C.O. saw KALTENBRUNNER, Von RUNDSTEDT and SKORZENY at
Wiesbaden in the American Zone. The Americans sent KALTENBRUNNER to
Ham and RUNDSTEDT to M.I.19. SKORZENY they retained. Von RUNDSTEDT
was one of the few Germans for whom there could be any respect. He
was a small man, of great dignity; a soldier every inch of him, and
shrewd. There is evidence that he fought for Germany rather than for
Hitler, that Hitler would lose patience but could not do without
him. In Normandy RUNDSTEDT was right and ROMMEL was wrong. In the
Ardennes RUNDSTEDT argued for a limited objective but Hitler
overstretched in a hallucination for the coast.

SKORZENY, to be fair, was a man of great courage and
enterprise for, after all, his paratroop expedition did snatch
MUSSOLINI from captivity. But to transform a commando into a Major
General in the twinkling of an eye is hardly smooth progress to
administrative success and it is only a Hun who would think of it.
In captivity SKORZENY was an ambling alp, amused by the paradox that
the smallest G.I. in the American Army appeared to be in charge of
him. Indeed, stock entertainment was to photograph the guard
standing under the outstretched arm of the prisoner. There is a
naive gaiety about the Americans. In the Ardennes they organised
S.S. prisoners of war into companies of a hundred to fill up the
shell holes in the roads. In charge of each hundred of the picked
men of Hitler was a coloured G.I. - "as black as we find them in the
chow lines."

Reverting to KALTENBRUNNER, Hitler reposed more trust in him
than in HIMMLER and GOERING. Perhaps it was because he was an
Austrian, a plebeian, a sycophant and a thug. He had tremendous
force of character and the suave manner of a trained lawyer. His
defence was sound because it was simple. He maintained it at Ham and
he did not deviate from it throughout his trial at Nuremberg. In
paraphrase, there were no excesses. But if there were excesses they
were carried out under the direct orders of the Head of the State or
through the indiscipline of lower subordinates of whom he had no
knowledge whatever.

He had a wife and family, but he seemed singularly detached.
He had a mistress and twins, but for them he was very much
concerned. Through notional blackmail on this account he was

KALTENBRUNNER

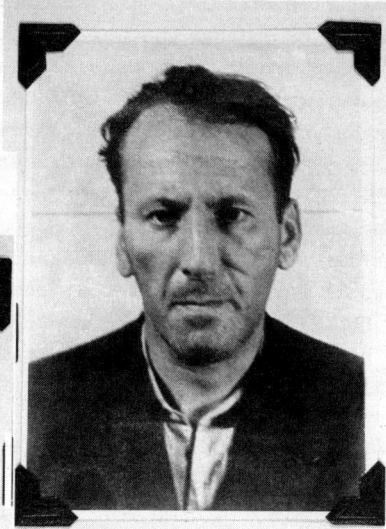

KALTENBRUNNER

SCHELLENBERG

SCHELLENBERG

occasionally constrained to give information, but he hardened soon
enough. He would quail when he was shouted at in the manner in which
he shouted at others, but he never lost his nerve. It seemed he knew
he must die, and would play his own game to the end. It was through
men such as this that the régime of the Nazis prevailed long after
the dictates of common sense spelt unconditional surrender.
KALTENBRUNNER was a giant in evil, ruthless to a degree, and bitter.
In every line of his vicious face restrained power is to be found.
It was a passing regret that the Intelligence investigation could
not be completed before his trial as a war criminal began.

For a history of SCHELLENBERG much vitriol is required. He
was the henchman of HIMMLER, who made him Chief of Amt VI. In terms
it was his duty, if the word can be coined, to Himmlerise the German
Secret Service. SCHELLENBERG accepted the job and it is true to his
character that he disliked the master who fed him. He was a traitor,
of course, in the end. He contacted BERNADOTTE while the Germans
were still fighting and aped the rôle of a friend of the Allies.
Actually, all he wanted was to save his skin. In office he would be
a vile enemy; in captivity he was a cringing cad. In office he would
ruthlessly cut down his opponents; in captivity he would as
ruthlessly betray his friends. In the property of SCHELLENBERG there
was a slim volume of Kipling's "If", given to him by BERNADOTTE's
daughter in return for some flowers. Have the first four lines ever
been in more bitter quotation?

(V.)

CSDIC(WEA) IN GERMANY

The last phase until the next war is CSDIC(WEA).+

Bad Nenndorf is a place of singular charm which has prospered for 150 years on first, second and third class mud. The curative value for the Kraut who suffers from obesity is an admixture of mud and sulphur. The assumption is reasonable that there would be a mountain of residue over the century. Nothing of the kind. They use it over and over again. But the bathrooms lent themselves to prison conversion and that saved many months of basic construction.

The site was selected by the C.O. in June 1945. On 30 June 45 an advance party took possession of the Schlammbads, the messuages and tenements, and the usual curtilege of wire was in place in due course. George Street, Elisabeth Street, Ham Avenue and Latimer Lane took the place of Adolf Hitler Strasse, Bahnhof Strasse, Wilhelm Strasse and Kramer Strasse. And in exchange for claustrophobia there is at least the satisfaction of an oasis in Germany where a Boche is imprisoned for trespass.

The original establishment was generous, but in practice was never filled. Later there was a reduction to the bone. That was inevitable owing to Treasury requirements. Then trouble began. Work was on the increase, demobilisation took heavy toll and replacements were inexperienced. Reconstruction became essential and there followed much understanding from those charged with retrenchment. Today there is a structure for a thoroughly competent organisation.

The functions include, in an ascending scale of importance, the clearance of historical cases, the examination of scientific and technical issues, the disruption of subversive organisations within, and Counter-Intelligence in the British Zone.

+ The corresponding establishment set up by the Americans is at Oberursel near Frankfurt. With a pretty sense of poetic justice they selected the premises of Dulag Luft, a notorious camp where the Germans subjected R.A.F. and American prisoners to heat and suffocation in the hope that they would give information. A windowless cell, no bigger than a cupboard so that a man could not lied down, took one back to the times of the Doges, but there was the modern refinement of an electric radiator with three adjustable elements.

(a) HISTORICAL CASES
  (i) The Last Days of Hitler

The last days of Hitler in the Führer-bunker in Berlin had all the drama of a penny-dreadful. Everything is there, the fall of the Reich, the marriage, insanity and suicide of Hitler, the disappearance of BORMANN, the murder of GOEBBELS' five children and the suicide of the parents, the execution of FEGELEIN, the daring flight of Hanna REITSCH, the escape of the emissaries with Hitler's Will and political testament, the message for the resurrection of the Nazi creed, and finally the usurpation of GOERING and HIMMLER in favour of Grand-Admiral DOENITZ.

And yet in fact it is living history and it must be written one day. CSDIC's interest was in relation to the missing Wills, how many there were, who had them and where the emissaries were to be found. That information was obtained by the interrogation of LORENZ, a Press official in the Bunker, and the subsequent confrontation of DIETRICH, Presse Chef. Later Von BELOW, personal A.D.C. to Hitler for so long, was broken in straight interrogation. The rest of the mournful tale was in part obtained at CSDIC and in part from outside sources.

LORENZ left the Bunker on 29 April 45, and evaded arrest until 25 May 45 in Hannover. There, in the name of George THIERS, a Luxembourger; he made administrative reference to the F.S.S. but was detained. In due course he revealed his true identity, and was sent to a camp in Fallingbostel. It was not until some months later that typed copies of Hitler's and GOERING's testaments were found sewn in his jacket. He was reticent and withheld much information. He was admitted to CSDIC on 17 Nov 45, and was broken by 29 Nov 45. The gist of the information is as follows:

Sender	Recipient	Documents	Destination
BORMANN	Standartenführer ZANDER	Hitler's political and personal testaments. Hitler/BRAUN marriage certificate.	To contact DOENITZ: failing him, the nearest German High Command, then Berchtesgaden; lastly, British or US lines.
General BURGDORF or KREBS	Major JOHANNMEYER	Hitler's political testament. Possibly Hitler's personal testament.	To contact DOENITZ or nearest German High Comannd. To contact Gen. SCHOERNER in the south; lastly to make for British or US lines.
BORMANN & GOEBBELS	Heinz LORENZ	Hitler's political & personal testaments.	To contact DOENITZ or nearest German High Command. Lastly to make for British or US lines. If all else failed, to publish at discretion for historical purposes.

The documents were held genuine by CSDIC on the grounds of comparison of signature, the trend of their content, the rational distribution and, lastly, check and countercheck on LORENZ. The report was subjected to check by the Americans and was released by them to the Press a month later.

Von BELOW had been the personal adjutant of Hitler since 1937. Comparatively young at 43 as an Oberst in the G.A.F., he was not only a fanatic but a ruthless self-seeker of the worst possible Nazi type. He was arrested on 7 Jan 46 in the guise of a student of Bonn University. The professorial staff were all very surprised that they had harboured such a man, but that fatuous attitude did them no good. It was then unfortunate that a number of zealous persons interrogated Von BELOW before he was sent to CSDIC on 8 Feb 46. One novice, indeed, came to the conclusion, since he could get no information out of Von BELOW, that there was none to be had, and wrote him off as a straightforward person. In the result the man became stubborn to a degree, and a strong Intelligence section at CSDIC, bereft of every interrogation advantage, failed. It was clear, however, that the man was lying and it was only after further considerable difficulty that he was finally broken on 15 Feb 46. The truth was that he had been given two letters in the Führerbunker on 29 Apr 45, one from Hitler to KEITEL and the other from General KREBS to JODL. Von BELOW, unable to deliver them, burned them so that they would not fall into Allied hands. Von BELOW was invited to reconstruct them and they rang true. The one from Hitler to KEITEL, since it is of historical importance and of psychological interest, is quoted:

"The fight for Berlin is drawing to a close. On the other fronts as well the end can be expected within a few days.

"I am going to commit suicide rather than surrender.

"I have appointed Grossadmiral DOENITZ my successor as Reichspraesident and Oberbefehlshaber der Wehrmacht.

"I expect you to remain at your posts and to give my successor the same zealous support you have granted me; and to do your utmost to fight gallantly to the end.

"Two of my oldest supporters, GOERING and HIMMLER, have broken faith with me at the last minute.

"The people and the Wehrmacht have given their all in this long and hard struggle. The sacrifice has been enormous,

"My trust has been misused by many people.

"Disloyalty and betrayal have undermined resistance throughout the war. It was therefore not granted to me to lead the people to victory.

"The Army General Staff cannot be compared with the General Staff in the World War. Its achievements were far behind those of the fighting front.

"The Luftwaffe fought bravely. Its Commander-in-Chief has been unable to maintain the superiority of the years 1939-40.

"The Navy has wiped out the disgrace of 1918 by its morale during this war. It cannot be blamed for its defeat.

VON BELOW

SCHWERDT

"The efforts and sacrifices of the German people in this war have been so great that I cannot believe they have been in vain. The aim must still be to win territory in the East for the German people."

From Von BELOW there is confirmation of the story of Hitler's Will:-

"I remember having seen in Berlin three copies of Hitler's private testament. I did not see the political testament. BORMANN showed me the private testament after the Führer had told me that I was to countersign it.

"A photostat copy of the original of Adolf Hitler's private testament has been shown to me, and I certify that it corresponds to the original."

Finally, more light was thrown on the last days of Hitler by Hanna REITSCH, a test pilot of supreme courage. The Americans held her, but allowed us to see her. She it was who accompanied GREIM, the successor of GOERING as Commander-in-Chief of the German Air Force. GREIM, on his flight to Berlin, was wounded, but Hanna REITSCH took control over the slumped body and landed in the inferno. Later she flew GREIM out again in a Fiesler Storch, oblivious of the Russian barrage. What a woman. She it was who was encased in a V.1 as a human check on the gyroscopic control. An improvised undercarriage would have introduced an artificial element, so the idea was to observe, and then ..... crash land. Seven intrepid volunteers broke their spines by impact on landing. Undismayed, REITSCH was the eighth. She landed safely in a field. In detention she was a wild bird in a small cage.

(ii) <u>The Liberation of Mussolini in September 1943</u>

Of less importance but of equal interest is the interrogation of Otto SWEERT, SKORZENY's lieutenant in the dramatic liberation of Mussolini from detention in Gran S'asso in September 1943. Otto SWEERT proceeds as follows:- +

"Early in August 1943 SKORZENY, then SS-Obersturm-führer and later head of all SS-Jagdverbande, ordered me to go to Italy (Rome) to join a "Kommando" consisting of about 30 men elected from the various SS-Sonderkommandoen.

+ The language is weird but because it is vivid it has not been edited.

"I joined the "Kommando" at Frascati. The men of the
"Kommando" wore ordinary German parachutist-uniforms. From
Frascati the unit was transferred to the Lake Albano. The
"Kommando" consisted of 6 or 7 officers and abt. 25 privates
who had no idea of what was to take place. The det. too knew
nothing in spite of the fact that we had asked SKORZENY for
the occasion of the journey. Some of the officers got
special tasks, but none of those around them was told about
the nature of these tasks.

"Now and then SKORZENY turned up to inspect and kept in
contact all the time with Generaloberst STUDENT, who was the
head of all German parachutists in Italy. The administration
of the "Kommando" was subject to a parachute-unit called
MOORS.

"The 4th and 5th of September the "Kommando" participated in
the disarmament of the Italian Army. The det. and 15 men
from the unit disarmed a regiment of artillery and a medical
unit.

"September 11th the det. learnt from SKORZENY that the
actual subject of the action in Italy was to liberate
Mussolini. In the morning of September 12th the det. was
ordered to make all military preparations demanded for the
liberation of Mussolini. I was to chose 15 of the fittest
men from the Sonderkommando and to get a car ready for
departure towards Pratica di Mare.

"At about 11-o'clock the same day the det. reported together
with 15 men who had volunteered for participation in the
liberation, to General STUDENT. The det. and the general now
had a short conversation whereupon the latter gave a summary
of the whole situation to all the pilots (from the Henschel
air-craft) and to the pilots of the 11 gliders
("Lastensegler") and the officers who were to participate.
SKORZENY who was the leader of the action explained the
present situation and gave the various officers their
respective tasks. It was planned to start at 1-o'clock p.m.
from Practica di Mare with the 11 gliders at their disposal.

According to the plan the 11 gliders were to be drawn up by
air-craft. The 11 gliders were manned as follows:

4 planes occupied by parachutists with the task to occupy
and secure the plateau, where the hotel in which MUSSOLINI
was staying, was situated.

The 5. and 6. planes (pilots: the det. and SKORZENY) had the
task to storm the hotel and to get hold of MUSSOLINI unhurt.

The remaining 5 planes had the task to occupy the funicular
railway-station (Drahtseilbahn-station) and to establish
contact with the valley station and to see that the 6 planes
already arrived performed their tasks.

"SKORZENY told the detachment how he had traced MUSSOLINI's
place of captivity.

"On an unknown date MUSSOLINI went to see the Italian King
and after that time no information about MUSSOLINI's
residence appeared.

"From various SS-officers (names unknown) they had learned
that the island of Sct. Magdalena was MUSSOLINI's first
place of residence. An SS-officer who had been sent to the
island disguised as a sailor, ascertained that MUSSOLINI was
staying in a castle in this island. Always acting like a
drunken sailor he made friends with the population of the
island and among his friends there was a gardener who
brought fresh fruit to the castle in question every day. The
sottish sailor asked the gardener to accompany him to the
castle. By this he ascertained that MUSSOLINI was staying
there and he reported this to SKORZENY, who at once
contacted the German Navy in Corsica, and made all
preparations for a landing in Sct. Magdalena in order to
liberate MUSSOLINI.

"On a flight necessary for this purpose SKORZENY crashed
into the sea near Corsica (probably owing to sabotage), but
he and the crew reached an Italian rock where he was found
by the Italian "See-notdienst".

"All preparation for the liberation of MUSSOLINI in the
island of Sct. Magdalena were in vain, as information
appeared to the effect that MUSSOLINI had been transferred
to another place.

"New results of the investigations concerning MUSSOLINI's

place of residence pointed towards the hotel at Gran S'asso. Photos of the hotel and its surroundings including the plateau in the Apennines were necessary. SKORZENY himself flew over the plateau in order to take the photos.

"On the basis of these photos a discussion took place about the liberation of MUSSOLINI.

"In order to have cleared up whether MUSSOLINI actually was staying at the hotel in question the O.C. of the Carabiniere, watching MUSSOLINI, General […], had to be sent for and interrogated.

"The general was in Rome and on September 12 about 1-o'clock he was fetched and taken to Practica di Mare by an SS-officer whose name the det. does not remember. Although the Italian general declined to give details he gave so much information about MUSSOLINI's place of residence and the guard that they were able to plan an action in detail.

"The Italian general refused to participate in a flight in order to point out where MUSSOLINI was staying.

"SKORZENY insisted that the general was to be persuaded to participate voluntarily in order to prevent unnecessary blood-shed. The general was to be placed in the det.'s plane and the det. succeeded in persuading the general to go with them giving the general his word of honour that nothing would happen to him.

"At 1.15 p.m. 11 planes started together with their gliders making for Gran S'asso.

"There was no wireless in the planes. In each glider there were 9 men. At 2 p.m., flying about 3,500 m. above the sea, they saw the hotel at Gran S'asso which was situated about 2,100 m. above the sea. In spite of the fact that the det. could not see any of the first 4 planes he and the pilot made up their minds to land. After having dived vertically the det.'s plane landed about 50 yards from the hotel. On landing the roof of the cabin flew open, so that the det. was able to get the Italian general out of the plane very quickly, and they went together up to the hotel. The det. and the general first entered the dinning-room, and at the same time SKORZENY's plane landed. As they did not find

MUSSOLINI they entered the telephone-and-telegraph room of the hotel, where they cut off all cables. Then SKORZENY turned up. Thereafter they climbed a wall, which was 3 yards high, in order to get into the yard of the hotel. In the yard there was gathered about one company of Italian soldiers. During the general confusion a window on the first floor was opened, and who turned up: MUSSOLINI!

"Now SKORZENY, Hauptsturmführer RADL, his A.D.C., GFOLLER, and the det. rushed into the crowd of soldiers who were so amazed that they quite forgot to use their arms, and proceeded to MUSSOLINI's room on the first floor. The det. adds that those 4 mentioned were the first to cross the yard.

"SKORZENY saluted MUSSOLINI with the words: "Duce, der Führer schickt mich, Sie zu befreien!". Thereafter a longish conversation between MUSSOLINI and SKORZENY followed, and in the meantime the det. carried out various orders given to me by SKORZENY. The det. was to take care that the other German soldiers, who had arrived now, disarmed the Italian unit and established contact with the funicular-railway-station and telephone contact with the air-field of Aveccano.

"The Italian general was likewise received by MUSSOLINI, but they were very cool to each other.

"When all orders had been carried out they awaited an aircraft from the aerodrome of Aveccano. After about half-an-hour the plane arrived and landed direct at the plateau, and after a very bad start SKORZENY and MUSSOLINI flew back to Aveccano. From there they proceeded by air-craft to Germany to "der Führer". SKORZENY ordered the det. to take the troops to the valley-station, besides he was to take care of the wounded soldiers and finally to return to Aveccano. On September 13 at 11-o'clock the det. arrived at Aveccano from the valley-station in a car. Thereafter he proceeded to Germany.

"The Italian general got a car at the valley-station and drove back to Rome.

"MUSSOLINI's wife and two children were likewise liberated from their captivity at Remini and taken to Germany."

Enemies though they are, it was a good piece of opportunism. SKORZENY's name forthwith became a by-word. Otto SWEERT, in turn, was decorated but could not remain clean. Later he indulged in war crimes in Denmark for which he will die. He knows he must die and has made half a dozen attempts to escape from CSDIC. On one occasion he broke his bars, climbed incredible defences and was at large for twelve hours. By then he had obtained a completely new set of clothing from a villager and looked a respectable member of society. That he was rounded up was a credit to CSDIC. Had he escaped it would have been a lasting disgrace. So little separates success from failure; so vast, howsoever, are repercussions.

(iii) Other Historical Cases

Oberst Leutnant Nikolaus RITTER was perhaps the most notorious of German spymasters in the early stages of the war. At that time he was based on Ast Hamburg. In 1941 he had left Hamburg to lead a Sonderkommando charged with the planting of spies in the Western Desert and the Near East. Later he commanded the anti-aircraft defences of Hannover with singular lack of success. A considerable force of Bomber Command passed over one night. RITTER, with a sigh of relief, gave the order to stand down, only to find Bomber Harris had ordered a feint. The destruction to this day defies imagination, and it is pleasant to recall that the R.A.F. casualties were singularly few. At CSDIC RITTER gave a full, if time-blurred, account of his several enterprises in the service of the Abwehr. In all frankness he admitted his failure as an Intelligence Officer, but adduced it in part to the superiority of the British Security Service. Latterly he usurped from a German general the command of the squad of prisoners employed in cleaning the Officer's Mess. In this way he can dream of the Guest Nights of the past and distribute the cigarette ends of today.

AHLRICHS, the Kapitän Leutnant, was for some five years a leading figure in the I Marine Section at Abwehr HQ. He was responsible for the despatch by sea of several agents, by U-boats or small craft. There was the "MERCATOR" enterprise; Roby LEIBRANDT's installation in South Africa, and the KOEPF and BAARN expedition to Brazil. He was able to provide considerable information which confirmed and supplemented Intelligence already in our possession. Among other points, he justified the view that the French agent LALLART, dealt with elsewhere, was loyal to his country.

A mine of information on the organisation, functions and activities of the Gestapo was Horst KOPKOW. For several years he was Leiter of Referat IV A 2 of the RSHA, working under that evil genius, Gruppenführer Heinrich MUELLER.

SIMMROSS FIEBIG was a German national, born in Madrid. He earned several dishonourable mentions in despatches from Ham and was good enough to accept an unavoidable invitation to CSDIC in Germany. At a distance in war he appeared a sinister influence; at close quarters in Germany he is a fraud from the gutter. His mentality is best illustrated by quotations from a statement of his life which he chose to write in the language of Balliol:-

"German Embassy (Military-Attaché) called me up 9 or 10 July to provide a post as Wehrmacht-Interpreter in France. I was astonished and refused sorringly, telling him that I was Spaniard and official State Employee. My mother becomes very angry and show me the document. She express her and father's wish. That was a terrible dilema! And then after 24 hours I made my worsest footstep, best minded to follow parents wish and bloody feelings".

"I don't mind to put me in your hands naked, because you have proved to be right and I felt it is my duty after my mistake".

Came POHL, the most unrepentant of them all. Genocide was his mission. That was the policy of his Government. He agreed with it. He carried it out. No regrets.

He agreed to a compromised total, between three and twenty million human beings.

What manner of man was this who could perpetrate such crimes without question? The only answer was fanaticism in a creed which came within measurable distance of conquering the world. POHL was a Naval officer in the Kaiser's war, but was later transferred to the SS and became a General-Leutnant in the Waffen SS. After eighteen years of marriage which resulted in three children, he divorced his wife in favour of Eleanora Von BRUENING, who was introduced to him by HIMMLER. She was not a high Party functionary but a practising member of the Lebensborn. This SS association glorified illegitimate children from pure Aryan stock. The women bore POHL her fourth and first legitimate child.

LAHOUSEN, a military carcerist of the Abwehr, fell with Admiral CANARIS. In anger he surrendered papers to the Americans. In revenge he deliberately betrayed the twenty-two thugs at Nuremberg. Now in a cell at CSDIC he had bitter regrets. Twist and turn as he will, he can never escape the stigma of Judas. By the German nation at large, he had committed the unforgivable. He has betrayed the German Army of which he was once a proud officer. By his fellow prisoners, always so ready to judge, he is shunned as a thing

somewhat unclean. In his captors he discerns a faint but inevitable
contempt. In affairs of the conscience caste notions and treachery
are ill wedded companions.

(b) <u>SCIENTIFIC AND TECHNICAL ISSUES</u>

The examination of such matters involves much routine work and is
not of outstanding interest excepting to the experts concerned.
Names which recur in this scientific and industrial connection are
STINNES, BOMKE, SIEDERSLEBEN and BROCHHAUS.

A swindle on a Nazi scale was revealed in the case of
Phillip REEMTSMA, who was Germany's leading tobacco magnate. In
April 1933 the firm was placed on the Nazi "Korruptionsliste" for
illegal remission of tax debts. REEMTSMA's quick riposte was to
corrupt Hermann GOERING himself. GOERING graciously accepted a
"donation" of four million marks and a promise of an annual
contribution of one million marks. In consequence of this little
arrangement the personal income of REEMTSMA soared from 525,455
marks in 1933 to 6,048,137 marks in 1934 and 59,794,912 marks in
1941. It is satisfactory now to note that his luxurious home in
Hamburg is a British officers' country club.

Information on such subjects as "Techno-Industrial
organisers of the Nazi era and their contribution to German economy"
and "the pursuit of the classic German policy of centralisation and
its results", was provided by LANDFRIED, an elderly Civil Servant.
He was possessed of remarkable mental powers and agility, but at
first claimed that his memory had suffered from the "great shock of
arrest". Later, however, he gave himself the lie by producing
information as valuable in its details as in its soundness. Like the
rest of his kidney, he now wishes to be a good European - for the
sake of Germany.

VAGELER was an interesting character who gave information at
CSDIC on technical and scientific subjects which aroused
considerable interest in the two Zones. A specialist in colour
photography for aerial geological surveys, forestry and oil-
cracking, he was a man of high intellect but of Nazi persuasion. His
personal ambition impelled him to take a deep interest in the
development of the "German Colonial Organisation". That organisation
was designed to govern British, French and Belgian colonies at the
end of the war.

The rest is the history of F.I.A.T. and S.T.I.B. and the
interest of CSDIC is incidental.

(c) <u>SUBVERSIVE MOVEMENTS</u>

A very satisfactory feature of the Occupation has been the close liaison between the American and the British Intelligence Services. It certainly proved valuable during the last months of 1945 when a subversive movement sponsored by old leaders of the Hitler Jugend gained momentum.

For investigation purposes the operation was called "NURSERY".

The Americans penetrated the organisation in their zone and the trail led north. The primary objective of the movement, of course, was the resuscitation of the Nazi creed. There was money in abundance, indeed ten million marks had actually been distributed for preliminary expenses. One of the schemes was to penetrate existing industries and to establish cells; another design was to penetrate the schools. An extensive organisation was set up for forging identity documents and plans were laid for removing SS tattoo marks. The true touch of the Nazi was discernible in the symbolism of a "blood-flag". This holy relic had been carried in the abortive Munich Putsch of 9 Nov 23. The venerable martyr, Heinrich HIMMLER, had been the standard bearer on that memorable occasion.

By Dec 45 matters had gone far enough and a decision was reached to pounce in both zones. First arrests were effected by the Americans in late Dec and by the British in early Jan 46.

BÜDAUS and LOHEL, ringleaders, were sent to CSDIC. They had some courage and were possessed of a certain fanaticism. At first, under interrogation, they were stubborn, but they ran true to Nazi type. Once broken, they broke completely and finally grovelled. Eleven of their kind were then examined and the deluge of confessions, denunciations and counter-denunciations became somewhat embarrassing. The mass of information, with difficulty, was reduced to a report of two hundred pages. Repercussions were satisfactory. Some six-hundred persons were deeply implicated and most of them found themselves in gaol.

It is always difficult to decide exactly when action should be taken in subversive movements of this kind. To strike too soon results in the escape of ring-leaders who may live to fight another day. To strike a little late is dangerous as the situation may get out of hand. Military and political issues also are involved. In the case of NURSERY there were some who felt action had been taken too soon, but subsequent evidence proved the decision was correct. That particular movement died out and something in the nature of an intelligence coup can be claimed in both zones.

But this is only a beginning, for no sooner is one subversive movement killed than another is born. Operations

"Lampshade" and "Deadlock" are of yesterday, "Globetrotter" and
"Brandy" are of today, and there is more trouble than enough brewing
for the future.

The evidence of the German resurrection, however, is not
only in the subversive movements themselves, but in the changing
outlook of the Germans. "Sweet are the uses of adversity", and
sometimes it seems as if the British and the American authorities
are blind to the eternal cunning of the Hun. The vicious circle 'No
food - no coal' - 'No coal - no production' 'No production - no
export' 'No export - no import' 'No import without CREDITS' and
'Without credits - no reparations', these are the old tunes which
can clearly be heard all over again. Indeed the plan of Dr. Müller,
more impertinent than naive, is worth examination. It has been
accepted by the authorities:-

(1) Basic ration of 2,000 calories in place of 1,550 today, with
    30 grammes (about an ounce) of fat in place of seven. German
    industrial exports to pay for food imports.
(2) Priority for German industry in exploitation of Germany's coal
    and iron resources. Production of coal and iron to be stepped
    up at full speed. Importation from abroad of raw materials and
    means of production needed for German industry. Revision of
    Level of Industries Plan and of present reparations schemes
    "which make any reconstruction of the German economy
    impossible".
(3) Credits to facilitate purchase of raw material and foodstuffs.
    Full participation by Germany in world export markets under
    normal business conditions.
(4) Reform of price and wage system.
(5) Reform of monetary system.
(6) Reform of the present "crippling" scale of taxation
    (prescribed by the Control Council) so that incentive towards
    intensive and rational efforts lacking today may be restored.
(7) Immediate cessation of the total or partial dismantling of
    plants with the exception of such as exclusively serve
    armament purposes.

In terms the Germans are in process of bringing off the same
coup today as they did with the assistance of the Dawes Plan of 1923.
This is no place for a political diatribe. But the fact
remains that only a label distinguishes the German democratic
parties from the normal subversive small organisations every Secret
Service must watch. Indeed these parties are already corrupt. There
is evidence of the suborning of the police; there is evidence of
black market activities on behalf of the trusty adherents. Little

fundamental divides them; they are tolerated merely because they perform lip service to the Western Powers. The Germans are not impressed by the democratic way of life and they will turn to their 'One Party' system just as soon as the occupation ends. Deep down in the German mind it is not the Nazi creed that has failed, but rather the leadership which did not produce world domination. One day the patient, inarticulate mass will again throw up a demagogue. He will be no leader, just a radical opportunist. He will mouth the obvious, the sufferings of the people; he will resurrect the shibboleths of the herrenvolk and rant for that lebensraum for which there is no need. And because the German 'Partei' system, which knows no healthy opposition, is inseparable from the State itself, the opportunist will interpret criticism as an attack upon the Vaterland and he will arrogate to himself any appreciation whatever as his due. If history is definable as a lesson never learnt, then war will come again; only the time factor is in issue, and that is dependent upon the circulation of the atomic bomb.

(d) COUNTER-ESPIONAGE IN THE BRITISH ZONE

There is unassailable evidence of Russian espionage within the British Zone in Germany.

At this stage it is impossible to write a history, but indications that trouble is brewing are undeniable, from cases such as those of SCHNUR, ALBRECHT and Van DAM. Of many extracts that can be made from information obtained, two possibly are outstanding.

Erika SANDER, a shrewd informer, states that nearly all Russian officers are convinced that war with the Western Allies is inevitable. They claim that only Russia did any serious fighting against the Germans and that now the Western Allies are trying to reap the benefits of Soviet victories. Moreover, the Allies are supporting Fascism with the intent of creating a bloc against the U.S.S.R.

Of far greater importance, however, is the testimony of METZGER. This man has been found reliable

A reconstruction of a conversation between Hella VUOLIJOKI, a Finnish writer indicted in 1943 on a charge of espionage on behalf of the U.S.S.R., and VISHINSKY himself deserves quotation in extenso:-

> "VUOLIJOKI expressed regret that the Comintern had been dissolved, because this would have been the most suitable organisation for furthering the aims of the desired "evolution" (towards world Communism and the sweeping away of Capitalism).

"VISHINSKY replied:-

'Even if we have dissolved the Comintern, that does NOT mean that its work is not continuing. Remember our work in Finland; we are working elsewhere in the same manner. The whole of the capital of the Comintern will be committed in this gigantic task. The sum involved is $86,000,000 (eighty-six million dollars) and is being used, amongst other purposes, for "Intelligence work" within the Armies of the Western Allies, who are war-weary to a degree, but the largest field of operations if of course amongst the working classes of all important States such as France, Britain, U.S.A., Brazil, China, Persia, Iraq and lately also Italy. Furthermore, we are supporting the exiled Republican Government of Spain in Mexico.

'It is not necessary to conquer by force of arms when other methods will do. The Capitalists know this very well and will contribute a lot of money towards our downfall; they are only a small clique, however, and represent an ideology which belongs to the past and is doomed to disaster.

'It is not, of course, improbable that our opponents, when they realise the hopelessness of this situation, may try to combat us by force of arms. But first, it is doubtful whether their men would be prepared to fight, and secondly we are the better soldiers; lastly we would have the greater part of the German population on our side and they already sympathise with Communism. The Germans would doubtless join us, because they have nothing to lose, and also because they are brooding on schemes of revenge.'

"VUOLIJOKI then asked whether VISHINSKY thought a use of force by the Western Powers would be likely in the immediate future. VISHINSKY replied:-

'Quite out of the question; they are too busy with their own problems and are, in addition, very war-weary. The British working class will never stand for a preventive war against Communism. The Capitalists in Britain would risk such a war only if they considered that war was the only means of keeping the capitalistic system on its feet.'

"VISHINSKY then went on to warn VUOLIJOKI:-

'Beware of the machinations of British agents in Finland;
keep a particularly watchful eye open.'

"VUOLIJOKI approached the subject of war once more and
VISHINSKY proceeded to boast about the performance of the
Red Army, saying:-

'If one day we are really forced into war, we shall reach
the Rhine in the shortest possible time. France is already
sympathetic to Communism. We and the Germans on the Rhine, a
Communist France...........Yes, the Channel will be damned
narrow then!'

The view of this pleasant ally is confirmed to some degree
by Van BERKER, who says that propaganda meetings are held regularly
in the armaments factory of DEPPER & Sons, Dresden. The speakers are
generally Russian officers. The theme of the speeches is the
inevitability of war between Russia and the Western democracies.
When the day of reckoning comes the British "will retreat across the
Channel with bare feet". Indeed, nothing in the world can now stop
the victorious Red Army and the German worker must realise that
their salvation lay with the Red Army, which alone was in a position
to reunite all Germany.

   ALBRECHT and Sonja BROSCHINSKI had definite missions to
penetrate CSDIC(WEA). When ALBRECHT failed, the Russians relied on
Sonja, aged seventeen, whom the British would never hold, owing to
her youth. At the present time she evinces much feminine resentment
that her plan has failed.

   The case of BACH/KURTH/HOFFMAN relates to plans hidden in
the former GAF Institute for Aerodymanics in the Harz Mountains. The
three men were instructed to filter over the border and obtain the
documents. When they had dug up the documents the opera bouffe came
to an end.

   The case of KALKOWSKI is as interesting as it is
disquieting. Unfortunately some of the revelations are too
sensational to set out until they have been checked. SILBERMAN,
perhaps, will prove of equal importance. At first sight it seems an
instance of direct operational espionage.

   The cases of GLEICH and WILHEIM have points in common. The
W/T set on which they were trained, and which they were to use
during operations, is an American type agent set which, according to
their descriptions, appears to be identical in both cases. One such
set is now in our possession. Although both men had been connected
with W/T in the German armed forces, they were each given 7 to 8
months' W/T course. Even political indoctrination was considered

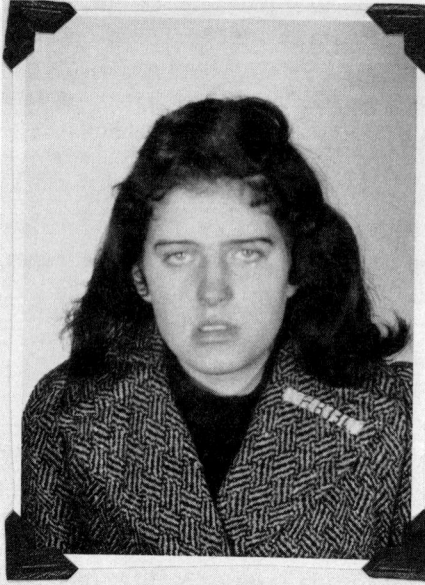

BROSCHINSKI

KALKOWSKI

HAU

important: "The Lt.-Col. gave Prisoner frequent talks on political subjects. Though the subjects may have varied, the theme was always the same - the blessings of Bolshevism, and the iniquity of Western democracy......".

GLEICH's mission related to military espionage. WILHEIM, on the other hand, had already worked as a Russian agent against the Germans during the war. He had a more important mission. Besides forming his own agent-network in CUXHAVEN and HAMBURG to obtain Naval Int, he was to recruit a German girl who was to marry a British soldier, and continue her espionage work for the RIS in England. WILHEIM himself was to obtain seaman's papers, so that eventually he could act as a courier between agents in the UK and the RIS.

These two agents surrendered themselves voluntarily to the British authorities. How many more of their kind have remained faithful to their Russian masters and are now operating in the British Zone, complete with WT transmitters, can only be surmised. That they exist cannot be doubted, for it is confirmed not only by KALKOWSKI, but also by a statement obtained from UHE: "Prisoner (UHE) was to pass all information obtained to Claus HALFKATH, who would transmit it on the W/T set which he operated in HAMBURG......".

The extent to which Polish and Russian official bodies abuse the privileges granted to them in the British Zone can best be demonstrated by the cases of HAU and DURBAYLLO.

HAU was told that the Russian or Pole who was to accompany her would be in possession of papers identifying him as a member of an important Russian or Polish delegation. These papers would be perfectly in order, and proof against scrutiny. HAU, who was supposed to be attached to this delegation, thought that she would be given a foreign passport before her departure for the British Zone.

DURBAYLLO @ KAMINSKI was recruited in the Atlantic Hotel, HAMBURG, by two Russian ships' Captains whose ships were lying in ports in the British Zone. He was also to be introduced to Col GOLENIKOV, member of the Russian mission in Hamburg.

The Russians have always been fond of mass Intelligence, even in peace time. However, their present effort, as revealed in recent CSDIC reports, shows an intensity of Intelligence work which justifies only one conclusion, namely that the Kremlin have decided on the conquest of Europe, if necessary by armed conflict. As a first step they require all the relevant information and their Intelligence Services seem to concentrate on the following main tasks:-

(a) Penetration of the armed forces of the Western Powers.
(b) Economic espionage (which includes the inducement of German

scientists and technicians in the Western Zones to cross over
to the Russian Zone and work for the Russians).

(c) Intelligence and propaganda among the German population in the
Western Zones (which includes the information of Russian
inspired subversive movements).

To assist Russian agents in their work, W/T communication
has been established between agents in the Western Zone and their
directing bodies in the Russian Zone.

In view of this massive Intelligence effort, coupled with
the feverish Russian efforts to develop long-range rockets and atom
bombs, it seems fair to say that the Intelligence forces of the East
and West have already joined issue, as a preliminary to open
conflict between Russia and the Western powers.

(VI.)

E N V O I

The cross section is complete. In itself it is an appalling indictment on the civilisation of today. It is stark and there is no embellishment. In half-an-hour notwithstanding a certain judicious levity, it is said to induce in the reader a profound depression. In the years certainly it has induced in those who lived cheek by jowl with these vicious elements a lasting realism.

In London, Ham, Huntercombe, Diest and Bad Nenndorf 400, 480, 73, 205 and 350+ cases respectively were examined. In the chapters which follow more details are given. To forty-six countries must attach the distinction of providing spies for Germany. Thirty agents came in clandestine fashion by submarine, parachute, seaplane or small craft. The rest posed as refugees from Nazi oppression. Less than three dozen were women. Thirteen men were hanged, one shot. That number at first sight is depressingly small, but the policy was deliberate to keep spies alive that they might betray their friends, and the dividends were handsome indeed. Another consolation is that many of them were deported to their country of origin, where they were either executed in addition to the incarceration they had suffered, or were imprisoned all over again.

The value of the history is difficult to assess. Insofar as the past is concerned, there was solid achievement. Over a long term war the measures were adequate. The German Secret Service acknowledged it was beaten by the British Secret Service. Thus the complacent will be satisfied. But in total war there is no time for improvisation, argument, conference and speculation. Twice in this generation we have run the appalling risks of unpreparedness, and it is salutary to remember the dangers when Britain stood alone against Germany at her zenith.

If there were to be another long term war, much could be learned from this history. Recommendations would be many and they would be sound. It could be pleaded that there should be an adequacy of trained Intelligence personnel. It would be reasonable to have an interrogation centre ready at the beginning of the war rather than an improvisation ten months later in the face of invasion. It would be well to have a war establishment sanctioned in advance to save the time of trained Intelligence officers from haggling over the necessity for a warder or a sanitary man. Women are as dangerous as men, but they cannot be housed in a place such as Ham because of democratic inhibitions. The provision of adequate office equipment

---

+ Up to and including 31 December 46.

would make it unnecessary for trained and bilingual secretaries to have to turn the handle of a duplicator, in the manner of a mangle, for five years. And so it could go on until the formidable list were complete.

But there will not be another long term war. It is the age of the atomic bomb and talk of international control is as smooth as it is empty.

The overt act must be stillborn.

The British Secret Service must be so powerful that it can unerringly predict the use of the atom bomb. It must be so trusted that its advice to drop an atom bomb on the enemy will be acceptable. In terms there must be a complete reorientation of war policy, and from that derives a reorientation of Secret Service policy. In provocative language the Service must be maintained on a war footing even in time of peace.

The elements of war are present. There is a fundamental variance between the "Big Four". Two powers require integration; two powers demand disintegration. And notwithstanding fleeting agreements the ideological incompatibilities remain. The social hostility of the Russian in Berlin is scarcely veiled; the friendship of the French, as often as not, is a veneer. In Germany itself there is a national resurrection, unnoticed from day to day, but crystal clear if a comparison is made with the situation six months' ago. Eighty million Germans who have tasted world domination are not lightly held in subjection.

Germany now, not Belgium, is the cockpit of Europe; and war will start from the East again. The incident which will provoke it, whether in Poland, or Germany or Russia, is of no consequence. The force of evil is there. VISHINSKY is credited with a boast, but there is nothing original about it, for it is the way the international mind is working today.

Let the boast be a warning and a fitting envoi:-

'We (the Russians) and the Germans on the Rhine ...... a Communist France .... Yes, the Channel will be damned narrow then!'

PART TWO
ON THE INTERROGATION OF SPIES

The stake is high. It is the life of the spy against the security of
a country. In roulette the odds are on the Bank; in contre-espionage
the odds disappear. The long term policy gives way to the vital
present; in the atomic years to come the time factor will be more
vital still.

Yes, the fascination of gambling is present, and with it the
strange urgency of war. And if ever a cliché could be justified, it
would be in relation to this subject. It is a war of nerves. Neither
side can be sure of success. No spy, however astute, is proof
against relentless interrogation. Some unforeseen circumstance, some
trivial lapse, is pounced upon, exploited by the interrogator, until
a break is complete. Yet no interrogator, however talented, however
experienced, can guarantee such a break. A failure in timing, a
mistaken appreciation of a Balkan character, a bad trace, a delayed
document, how many times have such things spelt ruin?

Seemingly, a logical approach would be an examination of the
characteristics of a spy, of the consequent characteristics of an
interrogator. But in fact this is not possible. Character is
complex, the variables are infinite. Moreover, there is no time here
to sail the seven seas, to wander in the highways and byways of the
continents, to rummage in the gutters or stir the political middens
of the capitals of the world. Nazi espionage ranged from Iceland to
the Cape, from Buenos Aires to Hong Kong, from the Armada at Madeira
to the U-boats at Madagascar, from Egypt to Shiraz, to the frontier
and beyond, to Newfoundland, Lagos, Greenland, Gibraltar - where you
will - to the belligerent countries of Europe, to the jackal lands
whose neutrality was a glittering farce.

Forty-four countries threw up spies on behalf of Nazi
Germany. Of consequence there were some five hundred spies all told.

The Nature of the Spy

Yet, broadly, what manner of man is the spy? Is he a patriot, brave?
Is he of the underworld, a subject of blackmail? Is he just a
mercenary, who will sell a ship for the dollar, the piastre, the
escudo, the franc? Is it possible to approach the problem in another
way, are there national as distinct from individual characteristics?

The patriots are few, and these brave fewer still. They can
be counted on the left hand. One, JAKOBS, a German, told the firing
squad at the Tower to shoot straight. A second was LALLART, the
Frenchman who joined the Germans in order to betray them. Landed at

Rio de Oro, he trekked the desert sands to Port Etienne, where he handed over his U-boat companions. The volatile French believed him and fêted him; then they disbelieved him and well nigh executed him. It was left to the English to prove that he spoke the truth. The third was rather the master of spies, KALTENBRUNNER, the Chief of the RSHA. Never once under interrogation did he show fear. The genius of evil had run his course. His day was done. He knew he must die. A lover of the macabre will find satisfaction in the fearful photographs of the hanged men of Nuremburg, but one, at least, died serene in his faith in the Nazi dominion over the world to come.

The spies of the underworld are legion. Craven crooks, for the most part, they are prey to blackmail. And herein lie truths so fundamental, so often forgotten, and certainly so seldom understood by the German Secret Service. Firstly, a man blackmailed into espionage is an unwilling spy. Secondly, a man blackmailed into espionage can equally well be blackmailed into confession. Thirdly, a man blackmailed into espionage and caught by the enemy may well turn upon his original oppressor. The dull-witted German calls that treachery, while the man himself calls it revenge. Generally, these men of the underworld have opted for evil; certainly they have done little to fight against it. Then somewhere down the fast running stream they have dallied with the bait of easy money in espionage. Often it is just a question of following a career of crime, of tracing the associates; somewhere, somehow, the trace of espionage will come to light. At other times the interrogator proceeds by paradox. He expects the unexpected. It is human nature in reverse. No single streak of decency is discernible. Only one thing is certain, self preservation. To avoid the hangman's rope, that is all important. Wives, children of wives, mistresses, children of mistresses; a few snivelling tears and they are forgotten.

Spies who work for money alone are few but they are dangerous. They have no home anchor, as often as not they have no collateral. They cannot be blackmailed. They prosper by results. Without conscience they collect information and impart it to the highest bidder. Often they will sell it over again to another Secret Service foolish enough to buy. The holocaust which may result from their act is of no consequence to them. GOLENKO, the White Russian, was an outstanding example. In succession he had served the Greeks, the Finns, the French the Germans and the Americans. The British, he dismissed them with a shrug of the shoulder; they were too stupid to take advantage of his services. EITEL, of the Hamburg-Amerika Line was of the same kidney. He worked for the Abwehr until he was placed on the retired list through notoriety; it was of no fault of his own. At the beginning of the war he was re-employed, he double crossed the Germans and the Americans, fell into the arms of a

French harlot and slid easily enough into the Black Market. His confession to the British Secret Service was complete, so was his surprise when he received no monetary reward. His cup was full when his goods were estreated.

National characteristics in spies are equally inconclusive. There are some who say the Hun is the bully who, once figuratively beaten, will cringe. The Scandinavian is a bore, he will hold out long after the stage of intelligent surrender. The man of the East will bargain. The man of the West will bluster. The Latin, however, will cause trouble; he is quick, he is proud, he is astute, he is stubborn; he is temperamental, he changes from day to day. Such, however, are possibilities rather than probabilities, and it is merely the courting of danger for an interrogator to depend upon any such fleeting phenomena.

The growing conviction is that the broader the survey the more certain it is that generalisation is without profit. The truth is that the interrogator must treat each spy as a very individual case and for that matter, as a very personal enemy.

Characteristics of an Interrogator

The difficulty of setting out the requirements for a first class interrogator is more apparent than real. In theory, remarkable attainments are essential. In practice an average officer is posted and the best use is made of his limited qualification, enthusiasm and experience. If and when any headway is made he is usually required for service elsewhere or the war comes to an end. Certainly no machinery exists for the retention of his services; he is lost for any future emergency and the lessons must be learnt, in the hard way, by trial and by error in time of peril, all over again. In the next war there will be no time for this parlous procedure.

Interrogators are of two kinds. Firstly there is the "breaker", the man whose duty it is to reduce the spy to the stage of speaking, and of speaking at least some truth. He is a paragon, so to say, who is expected to overwhelm and disintegrate all opposition. Secondly there is the investigator who, given the advantage of the "break", must deal with the minutiae, check and counter-check, analyse, collate and report.

It is customary to say a breaker is born and not made. Perhaps the first class breaker has yet to be born. Perhaps he has yet to be recruited from the concentration camps, where he has suffered for years, where, above all he has watched and learnt in bitterness every move in the game. First and foremost there must be certain inherent qualities. There must be an implacable hatred of the enemy. From that is derived a certain aggressive approach, a disinclination to believe without independent corroboration, and above all a relentless determination to break down the spy, however hopeless the odds, however many the difficulties, however long the process may take. Indeed, in the classic case of Ernesto HOPPE, seventy-seven days of attack, frustration, sweat and disappointment at last brought their reward.

Some smugness not unnaturally attaches to linguistic qualifications. Rich is the advantage of a man who can claim to be bilingual. But where does he stand in global war which throws up spies from scores of foreign lands? Again, a linguist is not, per se, an Intelligence officer. So often linguistic ability goes with the qualities which fail to impress a particular spy. A sailor does not react to the scholarly approach. The peasant suspects the urbane man about town. The regular officer of the Wehrmacht does not respond to a man accustomed to the negotiations of trade. Proportion, perhaps, is reached in the contention that the breaker should confine his undivided attention to the spy, the relentless pursuit of his plan, and indeed leave interpretation, the taking of notes, and the custody of property to others.

A formidable consideration may well be religion, if it exists, in a spy. Like to like is the rule.

Not infrequently the barrister will fail. Maybe something personal is wanting in his attack. Not unexpectedly he regards the case as an intellectual foray. He feels bound by the ethics of his profession. He depends upon his brief. But great is his discomfiture when there is no brief worth a tinker's benediction, just an intuition that a man is a spy - no more. Too soon then will this man of law break into a dissertation on the possibilities. On the one hand something is possible; on the other hand, howsoever, the contrary is reasonable. And what manner of use is this in war? Once it is accepted that dealing with the average spy is dealing with human nature in reverse, then professional ethics must be put in reverse. Every spy is presumed to be guilty until he is proved to be innocent. That at once was a challenge accepted by one or two members of Lincolns Inn in war, and there seems very little reason why more lowly brethren from other places should not also proceed, in war, upon similar and salutary lines.

What else can be said? Obviously a man of experience is required, essentially a man of common sense. If he has travelled, so much the better. If too he has seen war, lost much, that is an advantage. The wider the range of his interests the better. A spy will talk ships to a man who knows little ships; he will talk desert war with a man who understands the meaning of thirst; he will talk Latin logic with a man who had the patience of Job. Maybe he will not say much to a young man, however enthusiastic; perhaps he will be reticent with a socialite or a man about town. So much depends upon personality, upon mood, upon the man who can impress or cajole, blow hot blow cold, stand down at the psychological moment, without jealousy, in favour of another officer.

The Objective

Truth in the shortest possible time.

Some information in time is worth more than an encyclopedia out of date.

The length of a sound C.I. Report is often in inverse ratio to the labour expended upon it.

The ideal for a preliminary report is a signed confession. In itself it is a short report; it is a holding document; it is a stage in the investigation from which a spy cannot recede.

A fair example is found in the case of COPIER. The outline appears in a covering report; detail, damning to a degree, is set out in the confession.

The "Yellow Peril" reads as follows:-

"1. COPIER is pro-German, to this day a fanatic, and certainly proud of his conduct. His glory, in his esteem, is his faith. His undoing is the obstinacy of a weak man, for he is unable to see he is a traitor to Holland. His tragedy is myopia; indeed, for practical purposes, in a fast moving world, he is blind. He must peer for enlightenment, but even this has become a heel-clicking drill. Because of his disability, he was rejected for the Waffen S.S. Service then became a gnawing obsession even to the point of envy when a soldier came back without an arm from the front. His principles are unattainable, for he talks of "Honest National Socialism," which is a contradiction in terms. There have been brushes with the louts of the Party because he would not follow his tenets to the logical conclusion of barbarity. After years of frustration, howsoever, the Nazis made use of this man of ideals, but it was done with a sneer. "QUAX" is the buffoon of a pilot in the propaganda film, "QUAX, der Brockenpilot." So "QUAX" he was called, but it left him bemused, and it remains for us to place it together:-

"Auf einmal hörte ich in der Frauenschule lautes Lachen, und hörte aagen:

'LEONIDAS and MAX der BROCKENPILOT.
QUAX das sind Sie, C : sagte AUGNER gegen mich.'

"Vielleicht hat dieses eine Bedeutung?"

They chose him for a parachute mission but even in his preparations
his conduct was odd. They offered him extra money for his wife; but
this he rejected. They promised him employment after the war, but he
was in no way impressed. "Pflicht" was the torch of this thwarted
evangelist, but the character is such that he could never succeed,
and the facts as they emerge are enough for an opera bouffe. The
parachute release tapes of himself, of BECK, his companion, and of
their respective equipments were crossed. He made a signal, probably
the wrong one, but in any event it was misunderstood. COPIER was
pushed out, without further ado, and lost his equipment; his
companion fell to his death like a stone. COPIER was hurt when he
landed, but his intention was firm to carry out his mission. That he
feebly admits. Then came a peasant on the scene, and COPIER had a
pistol. But the "Pflicht" of today gave way to the chivalry of yore,
for the peasant was old, so COPIER did not shoot. Instead the old
man led him to captivity, in the ultimate perhaps to his death as a
traitor. So much for the character of COPIER. Himself, he ran true
to the form of "QUAX, der Brockenpilot." GOEBBELS, in his turn, made
a hash of his trade.

"2. Under interrogation, COPIER put up a good fight. In the
field he denied his companion, until he knew he was dead. He refused
to give the names of his masters in the German S.S. At Camp 020, he
pursued the same course. He withheld information, but mainly to
protect others rather than himself. But little by little he found it
was of no use. Day after day evidence bore upon him that the Nazis,
through their incompetence, had betrayed him. He listened to the
counsel of a Dutchman who had also been betrayed. To-day, the man is
disillusioned, and his confession is almost complete. To his credit,
howsoever, it must be recorded he is still unafraid."

The Confession is as under:-

I, the undersigned William COPIER, this twenty-fourth day of
February, nineteen hundred and forty-five, admit to the following
facts concerning my activities on behalf of the German Secret
Service.

1. First Contact

My first contact with the German Secret Service was on the
twelfth of October, 1944, with a certain BOES in Groningen.

2. Members of the G.S.S. known to me.		BOES	Groningen	October 1944
		ROEPKE	Groningen	Oct. '44
	Kpt.Lt. alias	SCHUCHMANN⎫ SCHROEDER⎬	Groningen, Rotter dam.Goor, Weilbach,	Oct. '44 Jan. '45
		AUGNER	Weilbach	Jan. '45
	Leutnant	WEISHEIT	Gronigen, Rotterdam	Nov. '44
	Leutnant	SCHURMANN	Weilbach	Jan. '45
	Hptm.	BURCHARD	Goor	Dec. '44
	Leutnant	GASTEL	Weilbach	Jan. '44
	O.Funkmr.	STRAKKE	Goor	Dec. '44
		WODNIK	Goor, Weilbach	Dec. '44- Jan. '45
		WURST	Rotterdam	Nov-Dec. '44
		CARO	Goor	Dec. '44
		MOLOCH	Goor	Dec. '44
		ERICH	Weilbach	Jan. '45
		FORTGEN	Goor	Dec. '44
	Frl.	BAETEN	Goor	Dec. '44

3. **G.S.S. Agents:** BECK, deceased

POSTEMA, suspected agent — Goor — Dec. '44

VENEMA, suspected agent — Goor — Dec. '45

4. **G.S.S. addresses visited by me:**

Scholtenshuis. Groote Markt. Groningen S.D. office
Rijksstraantweg, Groningen — G.S.S.Dienst- stelle.
(Erasmushuis), Hooghuis, Coolsingel 102, W/T training. — Rotterdam.
Villa in Diepenheimscheweg, Goor. — Dienststelle
Frauenschule, Weilbach. — Dienststelle
⎧Jahnstrasse 1, Weilbach — ⎫ — Billets.
⎩Bach(hof) strasse 13, Weilbach ⎭
Airfield near Zellhausen, near Frankfurt a/Main.

5. **Training.**

In: Rotterdam	By: WURST	W/T ⎫ codes ⎭	Nov.- Dec.'44
Goor	WODNIK	W/T	Dec.'44.
Goor	Hptm. BURCHARD	Military ⎫ matters ⎭	Dec.'44

6. **Spy names**

(Lt.) JUCHTER — given by Lt. WEISHEIT in Rotterdam, also used in Weilbach.

Herr C. — used in Weilbach by almost everyone I met there, and perhaps in Rotterdam.

COP — name given me with which to sign my W/T messages.

	COR	– Emergency call-sign. Probably used while practising in Goor.
7. Money received from the G.S.S.	10,000 florins	Groningen, from Lt. WEISHEIT
	2,000 dollars	Weilbach
	£300	Weilbach
	2 diamond rings value 1800 RM	Weilbach
	1 gold box value 450 RM	Weilbach

For receipt of the above I always signed in my own name.

8. **Mission** Descent by parachute from an aeroplane in the neighbourhood of Breda; set up a W/T set; and report back military information by means of W/T to a reception station somewhere in Germany. Specific missions would later be conveyed to me by W/T messages.

9. **Activities con- nected with my mission:** I jumped on January 23rd, 1945, from a German plane, in which was also luggage for my task, containing a set, money and a spade. I landed in Belgium, without finding my luggage, but I carried on me a Personalausweis (Identity card) with 2 false entries and money which I had received from the G.S.S.

10. **Intentions on landing:** If I had found my luggage, I would have carried out my mission described in para. 8 above. If questioned, I would have concealed my mission.

11. **Subsequent conduct after arrest by the Allies:**
a) I told a false story and held back information when I was interrogated in Belgium.
b) I did the same in England up to February 16th, 1945. Since that date I have given full information.
c) I confirm that I have now given true and complete information.

Written and signed by me freely and without duress.

24th February 1945, England. (Signed) W. COPIER.

With nine erasures, (on original) (signed) W.COPIER. "This confession was written and signed in my presence. XXXXXX."

The Network of Investigation

Interrogation is only a part of a pattern. It may be the foreground, it may hold the highlight of a jigsaw picture, but all said and done it is only a part of the whole.

It is the inexperienced interrogator who arrogates to himself credit for a break or credit for a completed report. It is the Intelligence Officer of sense and experience who insists upon assistance from every conceivable source before he starts his battle.

A spy is picked up through a trace, an intercept, a mistake on the part of the spy himself, through the work of an agent-double, the treachery of a fellow-spy; through these and many other means well known to M.I.5. Early information is in a Special Registry. There are documents on the spy himself; there is the possibility of real evidence such as secret ink concealed in his clothes. There is the man who can fit one piece of information into another and give it meaning. Early information is passed to the Central Registry, and the bells start ringing all over again.

Only a novice will plunge into an interrogation unarmed. His action is as fantastic as a man who would play bridge with the dummy face down. He finesses for a card which is already in his possession.

The machine, the system, the network, call it what you will is complex indeed. During the war the following establishments existed:-

M.I.5 for espionage	- Camp 020	- Ham
	Camp 020R	- Huntercombe
	Diest	- Belgium
	CSDIC(WEA)	- Bad Nenndorf, Germany *
M.I.19 for P.O.W.	- CSDIC(UK)	- Beaconsfield
		Wilton Park
		Latimer
	CSDIC(MEF)	-
	CSDIC(INDIA)	-
	and others.	
Field for Ops	- Interrogation Teams under O.I. organisations of Army Group and lesser formations.	
Screening Establish-ments	London Reception Centre for M.I.5, P.W.I.S. for M.I.19.	

+ Later under Intelligence Division, C.C.G. (B.E.) and known as D.I.C. 74 H.Q. C.C.G.

On the Conduct of a C.I. Investigation

(a) Preliminaries

The penalty for espionage is death. If the spy tells the truth he
may live. There is no guarantee; it is a hope, not more.

The quicker the spy realises that fundamental position the
better.

Psychology and discipline should produce that result.

Arrest must be efficient. The less said the better. The
quicker the handcuffs are slipped on the more pronounced is the
effect of stark reality. The quicker ill fitting and shabby prison
garb take the place of sartorial elegance the more profound and
depressing is the effect.

No exceptions. No chivalry. No gossip. No cigarettes.

Incommunicado is the watchword.

The remaining preliminaries are all calculated to maintain
discipline and to reduce the morale of the spy. Rules must be framed and
rigidly observed. Otherwise, in the urgency, in the excitement of the
moment, some vital clue, some obvious precaution will be overlooked.

Take property as an example

Property must be removed, sorted, listed. A meticulous search of the
body and of clothing must follow. Nikolai HANSEN had secret ink in
the cavity of a tooth. HIMMLER had cyanide in his mouth; GOERING
kept his poison in his navel for over a year. Cotton, impregnated
with secret ink, has been threaded into the collar stuffing of a
coat. A full-stop in a love letter may mean much. GILINSKY slipped
Security at Trinidad and Customs in England with 40,000 dollars by
the means, old-age, of a false bottom to the drawer of a trunk. BLAY
Pigrau had a password in the fly-buttons of his trousers.

Take documents as another example

Passports and identity papers must be checked for forgery before
interrogation, even if there is no time for immediate examination by
violet ray. All names and addresses whatever in letters, papers or
notebooks should be seen by the local registry before interrogation
and there should be no delay in forwarding them to the Central
Registry for conclusive check.

Odd notes, even hieroglyphs, demand intelligent study. A
trivial entry in one page of a notebook coupled with another in a
distant page may well be the key to a code; and if it is discovered,
it is at once a trump card for a break.

An outstanding example arises in the case of Osmar HELLMUTH. An extract from the "Yellow Peril" is as follows:-

"Before the arrival of HELLMUTH at Camp 020, the extent of HIMMLER's indirect influence in the Argentine was unknown. I was told that any information on his organisation would be welcome, and in particular, the identity of the chief. During the first interrogation it was ascertained from HELLMUTH that on leaving the "CABO DE HORNOS" at Bilbao he was to repair to the Hotel Carlton, where he would be approached by a certain individual with the password: "SALUDOS DE PARTE DEL SR. SIGMUND BECKER", ("Greetings from Herr Sigmund BECKER"). HELLMUTH was to reply: "AH, SI, EL HAUPTSTURMFUEHRER", ("Ah, yes, the Hauptsturmführer"). HELLMUTH not unexpectedly was reticent on this subject, but I was able to obtain from him that the Hauptsturmführer was in fact a certain Sigmund BECKER and I got a description from him.

"Confirmation was found shortly afterwards without reference to HELLMUTH. On the outside cover of a cardboard folder carried by HELLMUTH were five pencilled words. An officer had the bright idea of translating the Spanish into German, with the following results:-

Seguismundo	=	Sigmund
Panadero	=	BECKER
Principal	=	Haupt
Temporal	=	Sturm
Conductor	=	Führer

"Later still, the property of Diego BELTRAN underwent the usual laborious check. Industry was rewarded and two of many dozen photographs were identified by HELLMUTH as those of Juan HARNISCH and Sigmund BECKER."

"Yet another link in this chain is that HELLMUTH admitted he was to contact SCHELLENBERG in Berlin. Now SCHELLENBERG is the head of Amt VI, which comes under HIMMLER."

"The last interesting sidelight on this particular part of the case was that HELLMUTH was at pains to make drafts of his statements in pencil in his cell before proceeding on a typewriter with a fair copy. He was accordingly given a book rather than odd scraps of paper, and while HELLMUTH was seen by an officer and myself one night, I arranged for the book to be intercepted. Among the facts which came to light on comparing the draft with the final statement was a note which dealt with the friendship which exists between HARNISCH and SCHELLENBERG. HELLMUTH apparently thought this dangerous for he carefully crossed this out in pencil and did not allow it to appear in the final form."

Another interesting example is set out in a description of the investigation of MESQUITA DOS SANTOS.

"Between the time of his detention in Africa and his arrival at Ham, MESQUITA had made no admission of contact with the enemy. The case gave cause for considerable anxiety. In the first place, the investigation began at a time when the Foreign Office were experiencing difficulty with the Portuguese nationals on charges of espionage, so that a written confession was necessary. In the second place, MESQUITA was an intelligent man and the original evidence against him was decidedly slender.

"But it was noticed at Camp 020 that he had travelled out to Lourenco Marques in the same ship as Sobhy HANNA, and this led to a re-examination of the whole of Sobhy HANNA's property in the hope of finding evidence which would incriminate MESQUITA. Now in that mass of property had been listed a certificate issued by the shipping company to passengers on the occasion of "Crossing the Line". As is the custom at equatorial dinners on shipboard, such certificates are passed round for signature. Various signatures, some affected by stimulants, were compared with the passport signature of MESQUITA. The searchers were rewarded with the chance in a million. In fact, on German agent had unwittingly given his signature to another German agent; and such was the inscrutable decree of Providence that both the agents and the document were vouchsafed unto the examining officers at Ham.

"It now remained for the coincidence to be put to good use. The Commandant decided to convey to MESQUITA that he had been covered by a British agent, and covered so successfully that the British agent had even induced MESQUITA to provide him with his signature. In addition it was possible also to put to good use the name "TOME", for MESQUITA had used that name in his telegram to Lisbon and a cross-check was available from ISOS that "TOME" was, in fact, his spy-name.

"The Commandant interrogated MESQUITA at the earliest opportunity after the marshalling of all the facts. He addressed MESQUITA as "TOME". He asked him for a signature, and was promptly rewarded with a false one. But this eventuality had been anticipated. His passport was produced, and he was asked to explain away the difference.

"MESQUITA was now off balance, and he certainly did not regain it when he was told that he had not only been covered by a British agent as far as Lourenço Marques, but that he had also been good enough to present that agent with his signature. The certificate was produced and compared. Then MESQUITA was sent to his cell with a direct order to write out a full confession against time. This order was obeyed, and thus it came about that a good

basis was established for further investigation and the Foreign
Office had their evidence for the Portuguese Ambassador.

(b) <u>The Plan</u>

Since it is team work that counts, there must be a plan, clear and
definite, understood by everyone concerned. Admittedly it must be
flexible, admittedly it may have to be changed; but the
responsibility is from first to last in the Commandant. A precious
interrogator, a secretive soul, or a poseur is an outstanding
menace. The ideal arrangement is for a Commandant to interrogate
with the whole weight of his establishment in support. Various
factors militate against this system, but in a crucial case it is
well worth while to call a halt to all other activities until the
case is broken. It is the attack in maximum force at the critical
moment that is decisive.

(c) <u>The first vital interview</u>

A board of officers is appointed. The atmosphere is that of a
General Court Martial.

One officer interrogates. In no circumstances whatsoever
may he be interrupted. Unless he issues an invitation, no other
officer may put any question whatever.

In urgent cases two officers alternately take summaries.
The summary progresses by shifts in an adjoining office. A quick
report should be available for a D.R. within an hour of completion
of the interrogation.

The interpreter sits next to the interrogator. Unless
other facilities exist a stenographer is present and is relieved
unobtrusively every half hour.

An officer may be required as property master. Instant
production of any item of evidence is his duty.

The prisoner is marched in and remains standing to
attention throughout the proceedings. No liberties, no
interruptions, no gesticulations. He speaks when he is spoken
to. He answers the questions; no more, no less.

Studious politeness, the courtesy of a chair, the friendliness
of a cigarette, these things breed familiarity and confidence in a
spy. Figuratively, a spy in war should be at the point of a bayonet.

It is prudent to fix identity at an early stage in the
proceedings. If it is difficult to get specific information as to the
real identity of persons such as STALIN, MOLOTOV and TITO, because of
their political aliases, how much more necessary is it to obtain it
in relation to a spy because of his underground activities?

Early in the war one young officer thought he knew much. Somewhat myopic in vision, he relied upon academic training. He disapproved of a break. He marshalled his facts. He set out some three hundred questions. He gave the spy the benefit of the case against him. Courteously he invited him to react. With equal courtesy came back the answer:-

"Sir, I regret I am not Mr X."
"Ah - so none of my questions apply."
"Sir, that is so."

The officer reported back it was a case of mistaken identity. He was wrong again. But the spy knew the case against him; he knew also the gaps. It took a month of Sundays to break the man; few of the gaps were ever filled.

What is the secret of success in interrogation? Firstly, perhaps, the knowledge, it may be as slender as an intuition, then the man is a spy. Secondly, the motive which drove the man into espionage. Given a shred of evidence, the rest is a matter for personality and experience; and an interrogator should be ashamed of himself if he fails.

What should be the attitude of the interrogator? The bitter, uncompromising approach is as effective as any. And as with a man, so with a women - no quarter. And often how profitable, the instant there is a glimmering of an admission, to make the man write it down. Still standing, he can write down the second admission, and the third, until the cumulative effect undermines his morale. How easy to wriggle out of a verbal lapse; how difficult to erase a written admission? Such admissions, one after another, are the milestones on the road to surrender. Pressure must be maintained.

Pressure is attained by personality, tone, and rapidity of question; insistence upon an immediate answer, recapitulation. The requirement is a driving attack in the nature of blast which will scare a man out of his wits.

Again, as with a man, so with a woman. There is no room for chivalry in modern espionage.

Never promise, never bargain. The man's neck is in your grasp. Never forget it; never let him forget it.

Never strike a man. For one thing it is the act of a coward. For another, it is unintelligent, for the spy will give an answer to please, an answer to escape punishment. And having given a false answer, all else depends upon the false premise.

Break off when a confession in writing had been obtained. Set the prisoner further questions, against time, in his cell. Send for him again, whatever the hour of the night, and continue until the goal is achieved. Blow hot, blow cold. No respite, no time to recover, no time to plan.

Mental hell. Worn out, dispirited, dejected, a time will come when there is absolute surrender. The man can stand the strain no longer.

The strain upon the interrogator is equal if not greater. The difference? Why, the interrogator is free, and the spy is condemned. The interrogator can celebrate; they spy can console himself in solitary confinement with his failure.

But this is the bright side of the picture. If the interrogator fails during the first vital hours, trouble untold is in store. And each interrogator of experience has tasted the bitter dregs of disappointment. Probably he is a better man for it.

On Special Devices

(a) The use of "M" and Indirect Interrogation

The value of "M" is extremely difficult to assess. The professional spy is warned of the danger of "M" during the early stages of his training. Furthermore the problem of protecting "M" in some cases is almost insuperable, and once a spy becomes suspicious of the existence of "M", the warning goes out to his companions and a complete reallocation to prison blocks must result. There can be no doubt, howsoever, that the installation is essential. There is the chance of the odd remark, the link in the chain; there is the advantage of covering a stool pigeon at work; there is the indication that a man is ripe for interrogation.

M.I.19, on the other hand found "M" of inestimable advantage in regard to prisoners of war. Their general experience was that the direct interrogation of prisoners of war often failed, even when the toughest methods were used. This was due mainly to the different mentality of P.W. as opposed to that of C.I. suspects. The notes of an officer of great experience in this class of case are as follows:-

1. "PW had nothing on their consciences; they considered themselves soldiers who had done their duty until by the misfortune of war they had fallen into enemy hands, and even after capture they felt that it was still their duty to assist their country by withholding information which might be of value to the enemy. Tough methods in face of such an attitude were sometimes successful during forward interrogation in the field, when PW were still aware that if they failed to reach a

PW camp, no one would be any the wiser, but once they had
passed through cages, filled in forms and been allowed to send
postcards to their relatives, they were fully aware of their
rights and of the fact that they were under the protection of
the International Red Cross. Moreover, many of them were
familiar with the relevant clauses of the Geneva Convention,
and threats on the part of the IO would be received with a
contemptuous smile or would even evoke the retort that if
anything of that sort happened, the IO might get himself into
serious trouble. This attitude was particularly prevalent in
the first years of the war, when all PW, with very rare
exceptions, were arrogantly confident of victory; in the later
stages, when the possibility of defeat became more and more
apparent, many PW became "co-operative", but even so a
considerable number remained obstinate to the end.

"In view of this, various devices and tricks were used at
Interrogation Centres in the rear areas overseas and in the UK,
and were often developed to such an extent that the chief aim
of direct interrogation became the creation of a frame of mind
suitable to the use of such devices. Some of the devices used
are dealt with in the following paragraphs.

2. "M" Cover

"In the early stages of the war, "M" was used in a very
unscientific manner, being operated almost entirely by
interrogators who, immediately after interrogation, would
listen in and endeavour to assess whether their PW had told the
truth or not. Notable successes achieved during the "Blitz"
period, however, made it clear that "M" offered vast
possibilities and it soon became a highly organised department
with a permanent staff engaged exclusively on this work. Rooms
were covered from early morning to midnight and in special
cases even throughout the night. IOs, who had at first resented
"M", especially when it produced flat contradictions of their
reports, soon realised that, properly used, it would save them
a great deal of time and work, and that close liaison with "M"
was in their own interests. It soon became a rule that no IO
ever interrogated without first consulting the "M" operator
covering his particular PW, thus avoiding the interruption of
an interesting conversation by the removal of a PW from the
cell for interrogation and ensuring that the "M" operator would
know exactly what the IO was after and would be able to watch
for the essential points when the PW returned to his cell. "M"
was also used as a check on the ability of new IOs, and

although, when informed of this, they were at first extremely indignant, they soon learned that even the best IO can sometimes misunderstand a PW's statements and that the existence of a permanent and verbatim record of an interrogation could be useful when doubts as to the accuracy of a statement were raised at higher levels. Eventually IOs became so anxious to have their interrogations covered that this imposed too great a burden of the "M" staff, and it became necessary to lay down that only really important interrogations could be covered.

"M" also had many other advantages, among which were the following:

(a) It sometimes revealed that PW possessed knowledge about subjects on which the IO would never have dreamt of interrogating them. An outstanding example was the case of a PW sent to the UK as an expert on Diesel engines (which he undoubtedly was); he was kept in solitary confinement for five weeks while under interrogation by technical experts; when at last he was "associated". "M" cover revealed within a few hours that he also knew a great deal about V-weapons and the resulting "M" report contained valuable information on the V-1 and V-2, a year before these weapons were first used. Another instance was one of the SCHARNHORST survivors; once sunk, the SCHARNHORST was of no particular intelligence interest, but "M" revealed that this survivor had been on board the TIRPITZ when she was attacked by midget submarines and produced the first eye-witness account of what had happened on that occasion.

(b) "M" also served as the only possible check on the veracity of German or Italian SPs.

(c) It revealed the existence of escape plots.

(d) It revealed that the Germans were using new inventions of which nothing was known and about which PW would otherwise never have been interrogated.

(e) It served as a check on the attitude of the warder staff towards PW.

(f) If outside (eg Allied) officers obtained permission to see PW alone, it was the only means of ascertaining what was said.

The disadvantages of "M" may be summarised as follows:-

(a) Good "M" operators are even rarer than good interrogators. It is an error to suppose that knowledge of the language is the only qualification; background knowledge and a flair for what is important are essential, and the transcribing of records demands infinite patience. Of some 200 officers, WOs and Sjts who worked in the "M" room at CSDIC/UK during the war, not more than a dozen can be said to have been really first-class, and even they sometimes slipped up badly.

(b) To provide effective cover, even for a dozen rooms, a very large "M" staff is required.

(c) The use of microphones is nowadays common knowledge and some PW proved to be so "mike-conscious" that nothing could be obtained from them via "M". It is interesting note, however, that this was comparatively rare; most "mike-conscious" PW were under the impression that the danger period was the first hour or so after interrogation; hardly any of them realised the extent to which they were being covered and there are few men who can resist the temptation to talk about themselves and their experiences when confined in a cell with one or two other men for days on end. Hence the necessity of a large staff to provide constant cover.

(d) The existence of an efficient "M" room encourages IOs to rely too much upon it and to neglect direct interrogation which, however good the "M" cover, is nevertheless the only means of extracting information from certain types of Prisoners."

(b) The Stool Pigeon

Vitriol is an indifferent medium in which to portray a stool pigeon in any land whatever.

Essentially he is a despicable character, treacherous to a degree, mistrusted by both sides, and a lasting anxiety to any administration. To call a man a spitzel, a cimbel, lokduif or a mouchoir, is worse than the casting of doubt upon the parentage of a man down Silvertown way.

Risks abound. The introduction of a stool pigeon is a crude device against which a spy is warned during his elementary training. It follows that the stool pigeon, ab initio, is suspect. Equally does it follow on the other side that everything said by this man of treachery must be subject to cover or independent corroboration, preferably both. Then when the stool pigeon fails, as almost invariably he does fail, the interrogator earns the contempt of the spy, the investigation is irretrievably lost, the man himself is blown to the rest of the prison, and an overall reticence may well affect other cases under inquiry. Next, equity is such that the gallant gentleman cannot be punished for his original espionage crime for the very good reason that the prosecution themselves do not come to court with clean hands. The consequence is that the man becomes body nuisance number one in an espionage prison for months, maybe for years. In the ultimate, when the war is over, the stool pigeon blackmails the Secret Service concerned into the grant of his freedom, a pension, and ever increasing increments thereto.

In circumstances such as these, it is perhaps not overstressing the case to suggest that creatures of this kidney should only be used as a last resort.

Two cases fall outside this melancholy conclusion. First there is the man who is not, properly speaking, a stool pigeon at all; rather is he the trained agent introduced to act that part. Great must be his histrionic and linguistic ability; infinite must be the patience in priming him for his part. Clearly, he must be a first class secret service agent, an individual found, perhaps, once in a generation. The second type, equally rare and no less gifted, is the stool pigeon freak who responds to training, subtle handling, who proceeds without brief, and gives no information at all. He is an instrument of psychology. The Belgian, HUYSMANS, was an outstanding example during the War. He was promised nothing, nothing at all. His only glimmer of hope was to save his life, to save the life of his wife. Himself arrested in Lisbon and sent to England, capital was made of the fortunate circumstance that his wife followed in another plane. HUYSMANS was told the British could snatch her from the clutches of the Germans. In due course, she was prevailed upon to write to him from Holloway Gaol. The omniscience and power of the Secret Service were thus proved. HUYSMANS was permitted occasionally to meet prisoners. He did not know what their cases were about. Quite simply he gave advice. Because of his worldly experience he carried conviction; because of his genuine ignorance of the cases he carried sincerity. First he would tell his own story, rich in detail, essentially true. Then he would dilate upon the strange power of the British Secret Service; he could quote the incident of his wife. He would talk of the fairness of British methods. Sorrowfully he would depart and remain away until the spy himself asked to see him again. That too, had to be finessed and sometimes adroitly refused by the Authorities themselves who hoped against hope the request would be repeated.

Then followed HUYSMANS second approach:- "I do not wish to listen to your story; I have too much trouble of my own. All I can say for myself is that I am alive."

Further urged by a desperate spy to help he would refuse again:- "The responsibility is too great. All I can say is that I spoke the truth, they checked every word of it - and I am alive."

Later, perhaps, the odd message would be delivered:- "Number X is, I think, ready to talk. Perhaps he will react to sympathy,

this one, rather than to heavy interrogation. It is for you,
honoured Sir, to decide. I do no know his case."

In retrospect, HUYSMANS is one of the most fascinating
espionage studies of the war. But desperate was the anxiety. Every
move was planned, words weighed, cover kept; we were never
suspected. Essentially he had one master only; obviously he was
sparingly used.

In the ultimate, freedom was HUYSMANS' reward. Maybe he will
carry an uneasy feeling to his grave, that he is still being
watched.

(c) The Cross-Ruff

The Cross-ruff is a process which can be effectively used in the
case of joint spies. Since their cover story is common they tend to
work in concert. There is a pact to keep silence. If one breaks,
however, in interrogation the other usually follows suit.
Segregation is the first essential and extremely heavy interrogation
of the weaker character then follows. If successful the results are
reduced to writing and the principal is then faced with the
defection of his comrade. Usually he is intelligent enough to
appreciate the hopelessness of the position and surrender.

One case is that of Joseph and Mathilde GOBIN. The covering
report of 19 January 1945 set out in the second part of this paper
sufficiently sets out the facts.

A second case is that of the Icelanders FRESENIUS, BJORNSSON
and JULIUSSON. FRESENIUS was the master while the other two were no
more than his servants. They were kept separate, and to reverse a
phrase, the lead was taken through weakness into strength. First a
partial break was obtained from BJORNSSON. This resulted in a
limited admission from JULIUSSON. JULIUSSON was played against
BJORNSSON and vice versa. The result was an accurate background of
the whole mission, and FRESENIUS, the master, was then attacked with
much success.

The outstanding feature of this very important operational
case at the time of "D" Day is that the bulk of the information was
obtained within 48 hours.

(d) Confrontation

Confrontation, in theory, seems such an obvious and effective
weapon. In practice, it is a most dangerous expedient which may well
ruin the whole course of an investigation.

One case in point is that of VERLINDEN and LAUREYSSENS.
VERLINDEN was the informer; he was trustworthy, his evidence against

LAUREYSSENS was damning to a degree. VERLINDEN, […] had actually introduced LAUREYSSENS to the German spy master, HOFFMAN. He had provided accommodation for LAUREYSSENS. He exposed the details of the mission. He described how LAUREYSSENS had earned his keep in LISBON by pin pointing targets and AA defences in SWANSEA. LAUREYSSENS admitted the contacts, but swore they were purely social. Nothing would move him. Confrontation was the only solution. VERLINDEN told his story with obvious sincerity. LAUREYSSENS with impressive calm, looked VERLINDEN straight in the face and denied all knowledge of him whatever.

Another case was that of EDVARDSEN, DE DEEKER, Vera ERICHSEN and WAELTI. Here EDVARDSEN told his story with obvious conviction. Against DE DEEKER and WAELTI complete failure must be recorded:

WAELTI denied ever having set eyes on him before and DE DEEKER (though he admitted having understood EDVARDSEN's story which was told throughout in English) contented himself with the ironical comment that the gentleman's memory was too good and he appeared to have got the story off by heart.

This failure was redeemed in part by success against Vera ERICHSEN. She did in fact retract some previous information and substitute new detail which certainly discomfited DE DEEKER and WAELTI in turn.

If resort is had to confrontation obvious precautions must be taken. The interrogator must be certain the informer will give his evidence at the critical time; he must ensure that only relevant information is given.

When confrontation is complete, argument and questions must be prohibited. Finally there must be a definite plan to meet either success or failure.

Failure in such cases is complete and utter, and an interrogator who has not anticipated the contingency is a novice indeed.

(e) Assessors

Ever on the search for the unexpected approach in interrogation the use of "assessors" came to mind. It smacks of the opéra bouffe, but then it was calculated to deal with an opéra bouffe type. In a word the volatile Latins were involved. The ideal was to hark back to pavement café days, when half a dozen men gathered together, all spoke at once, all argued with the illogical logic of the Mediterranean and ended up with stilettos drawn or complete exhaustion.

The "assessors" are fellow spies whose cases are long since dead. Some have spoken the truth and are ready to live; some have lied and are ready to die. That is the theme of the opening address. Courteously they are asked to be seated, to consider the case of a fellow countryman who is in trouble, to assist him if he is wayward, to encourage him if he is in doubt.

Sometimes it works like a charm. The unbroken spy is marched in. Alone he stands. When he makes a ridiculous reply, reference is made to his countrymen. They are invited to give an opinion. When the spy loses his temper, they are invited to calm him. When they side with their countryman they are reminded they are doing themselves no good. When they side against him they are told there may be hope at least for their families to work again in peace in the vineyards, to sing again under a moonlit sky.

Yes, it can work like a charm. In the case of LECUBE, it failed, but at least an assessor broke down completely and volunteered to confess. LIPKAU was the name.

But when the interrogator himself is exhausted, why, all he has to do is to dismiss them all to a cell where they can discus the events of the day in peace. Then it is the turn of those who must cover six people who shout at once, of those who cry or laugh, curse or plead, fight or keep silent.

Who is the man under inquiry? Which of the six?

In the early hours of the morning, when the morale is low, it is well to send the orderly officer to demand written replies to a questionnaire, otherwise there will be trouble for all.

To stage all this with success? Many weeks.

A contrast is the case of GISKES. Ah, that was a grim business. One Teuton, the superior officer of the other, preceded this man to his cell. He ordered him to sit on the other side of an improvised interrogation table. Relentlessly the examination proceeded. The questionnaire was answered, each page was numbered, each page was signed, each erasure initialled.

But with all their confounded tantrums the Latins are less detestable than the Huns.

(f) The Legend of Cell Fourteen

"You will now be sent to Cell Fourteen.

"In time of peace it was a padded cell, so protected that raving maniacs could not bash out their brains against the wall. Some recovered. Some committed suicide. Some died from natural causes.

"The mortuary is conveniently opposite.

"In time of war accommodation is short. Cell Fourteen is no longer a padded cell. Now there is little difference between that cell and any other cell. Perhaps it is remote, and cold and a little dark. That is all. But for some reason the sinister reputation persists.

"Some spies believe in the supernatural. They say certain psychic elements are present. Some spies suffer from claustrophobia. Some spies have a guilty conscience and know no peace.

"Results are interesting. Some spies have told the truth and have been transferred. Some have committed suicide. Some have passed out for the last time to their judicial hanging - their rich desert.

"I shall not see you again. I do not know how long you will be there. Petitions will be ignored. Only if you decide to tell the truth will you be allowed to write.

"But just remember this, that we are winning the war in spite of you - one man only - in captivity. Maybe you are holding back information which is already in our possession. Maybe you are more of a fool than a hero.

"For the rest, you will be interested perhaps in the movements of the sentry who will cover you each quarter of the hour. Perhaps he comes to check. Perhaps he comes with food. Perhaps he comes - to take you away - for the last time."

At first sight that address is sheer unadulterated melodrama. But the fact remains that it proved successful on many occasions during the war. Much depended upon delivery, atmosphere, timing - last but not least upon the personality of the interrogator.

To use a phrase hackneyed in melodrama - it's not so much what you say but the way that you say it.

Effects varied. A German lost his arrogance. A Spaniard lost the glint of his dark and fiery eye. An Egyptian visibly wasted. An Italian gesticulated wildly for writing materials within the hour. A Frenchman lost his nerve and talked of the "cellule des condamnés." An Icelander remained unmoved; between Cell Fourteen and the land of desolation there was no contrast.

Danger lay in the finality of Cell Fourteen. If it failed, then little hope remained of a break.

The lesson of Cell Fourteen lay in the exploitation of a trivial circumstance, the existence of an old padded cell. The Intelligence officer responsible asked himself this question: "If I were a captured spy, what would I hate most in my predicament?" Thereafter it became a matter of psychology - to say what would hurt the mind most.

(g) The Technique of "Blow Hot-Blow Cold"

Some spies have diplomatic cover, they have grandiose delusions, they are always on their dignity. Fortunately, in war, liberties can

be taken. The diplomat is reduced to the state of a common
prisoner. He wears ill fitting prison clothes and there is
nothing more disconcerting to a poseur than to relieve him of his
pince-nez, his false teeth and his bootlaces. The grounds are
humanitarian - in case the prisoner feels impelled to commit
suicide.

Then the stage is set. The diplomat is brought before the
interrogation board. He is subjected to a withering fire of
invective. One of the officers attempts to intervene and is sourly
rebuked. One or two unimportant mistakes of fact are made. The man
is then summarily removed without an opportunity of saying a word
for himself.

His indignation is intense, but so also is his fear.

Then, by chance, the officer who intervened on his behalf,
is the orderly officer of the day. He treats the diplomat with
courtesy; a link is established. The Commandant is an unreasonable
man. The process of investigation, however, is inexorable. Much is
known of the diplomat; the Commandant intends to get the rest from
him. He does not appreciate sensitive people, he treats all spies
alike. He is a hard man. He know no mercy.

Perhaps the officer could smoothe the way to a dignified
statement of fact? Perhaps further painful scenes, such as that of
the morning, can be avoided?

Perhaps the diplomat and his family can be saved from the
terrors of blackmail?

"Sleep well, and if you would like writing materials, or if
you want my assistance, I will come. I will try to help you."

The scheme and variations of it succeeded in a number of
cases. The officer who had acted like a snake in the grass was
usually regarded an an "English Gentleman" while the Commandant had
the invidious distinction of being likened to HEYDRICH.

(h) The Cover Story

The cover story is the protective armour of the spy; that
manufactured by the Germans had many chinks.

To be effective a spy must live his cover story. If he
professes to a knowledge of Liverpool he must know the way to the
Adelphi; if he claims familiarity with Brighton he must know
something of grotesque in the Regency quarter. In London he must
know something of the rivers, the Underground, the sparkling and the
shabby hotels.

And so in reverse, the interrogator must live the cover
story with the spy. If he has not been there, he must toil through
the maps, the tourist guide books and the photographs available.

Endless, driving questioning on detail may result in that very
pleasant moment "You lie - you have never been there."

Sometimes an astute spy will make a partial confession and
set out the rest of his activities in a plausible tale. HANSEN
landed in England by parachute. He immediately admitted to a W/T
set. What more could a novice interrogator require? Here was an
honest man, a man who hated the Germans. But somehow it all sounded
too plausible. Perseverance resulted in a remarkable cover story.
HANSEN was to be very candid, if caught. No doubt he would get his
release. Then he could return to the scene of the drop, for it was
there that he had concealed a second W/T set which he could operate
at leisure under little suspicion.

+(i) "Sympathy Men"

"Sympathy Men" were used to a considerable extent by the Germans
during the war and to a limited extent by ourselves. Their role was
to gain the confidence of PW by expressing sympathy with their lot
(a good opening was to pretend to have been a PW oneself in the
1914-18 war) and, in the guise of welfare officers, to provide PW
with cigarettes and other comforts, this being done allegedly
against camp regulations. The "Sympathy Man" thus gained the
reputation of being a man who could be trusted and could then try to
obtain information, sometimes by using the "BF approach", eg by
asking a U-boat rating infantile questions about submarines and
gradually leading up to some technical point which it had not been
possible to elucidate by direct interrogation or via "M". In other
cases the "Sympathy Man", without actually asking questions, would
try to get the PWs' minds on to a certain topic and then leave the
cell, hoping that the "M" reaction would obtain the desired
information.

"Akin to the use of "Sympathy Men" was the practice of
sending Army officers out with GAF or German Navy PW as escorts,
on walks etc, in the hope that they would talk more freely to an
Army officer on technical subjects than they would to an officer
of their own branch of the service. Here, too, the "BF approach"
could be used with advantage, or else the officer, having previously
made sure that the party included one English speaker, would
converse with the latter while listening to the conversation of
the others."

+ An officer of M.I.19 writes on items (i) to (m) as they are
applicable more to Prisoners of War than Spies.

(j) <u>Interrogation of the Wrong Prisoner</u>

"A warder would be instructed to enter a cell late at night, wake a
PW and bring him to the interrogation room, where he would find an
IO, apparently slightly intoxicated. The IO would adopt the tough
attitude and ask the PW technical questions which he could not
possibly answer, but which his cell-mate could. After half an hour's
grilling the PW would be returned to his cell the "think it over".
He would, not unnaturally, be rather exasperated, and would relate
the incident to his cell-mate, repeating the questions he had been
asked, whereupon the cell-mate would laugh heartily at the IO's
stupid mistake, congratulate himself on not having been asked those
questions and in many cases supply the answers, which would be duly
recorded by "M".

(k) <u>Faking of Newspapers</u>

"By arrangement with one of the newspapers, a few copies of a daily
newspaper would be printed containing a spoof article in place of
one of the same length which had appeared in the normal edition.
These copies would then be given to selected PW and "M" would keep
watch. A successful instance of this occurred in late 1941, when two
U-boar officers were given a paper containing an alleged Admiralty
communiqué giving the numbers and commandant's names of U-boats sunk
to date, some of the numbers and names being intentionally wrong. In
due course the officers came across the paragraph, discussed it
eagerly and laughed at the mistakes; this put them on the right path
and the eventual "M" report gave an almost complete picture of what
U-boats and commanders were still operating at that time."

(l) <u>Exploitation of Rank-consciousness</u>

"The German respect for rank is such that it was found advisable for
all IOs to hold the rank at least of a captain, whatever their
status in the eyes of the paymaster. With senior officer PW,
interrogation by a full colonel frequently made a favourable
impression, while with the more snobbish of the German generals, the
temporary elevation of the IO to the peerage was found effective."

(m) <u>Drink</u>

"The practice of giving PW a bottle of whisky to drink in their
cells, in the hope of loosening their tongues for the benefit of
"M", was tried, but was NOT a success. It was found that the PW
generally became either sentimental or bawdy, and information of

value was rarely obtained. The practice died a natural death when the shortage of whisky became acute.

There can be no standard form as every espionage case has its individual characteristics. There are, however, certain underlying principles. Furthermore a standard framework is worth consideration so long as it is not used for slavish interpretation.

Underlying principles are as follows:-

(i) A short report in time is worth an encyclopaedia out of date.

(ii) Fact, and fact only, must appear in the report.
"On the one hand the spy may mean......
On the other hand the real fact is probably......"
How many times has this gibberish been seen?
A report containing that sort of thing must be thrown out at once. In terms the interrogator has not done his job.

(iii) The proper place for opinion, interpretation and a call for action is in a covering memorandum.

(iv) There is no room in any report for a percentage assessment of reliability.

(v) Sentences must be short and to the point - Gibbon is dead.

A
DIGEST OF HAM

Volume Two
CASE HISTORIES

HAM

HUNTERCOMBE

DIEST

BAD NENNDORF

WALDBERG/MEIER/PONS/Van den KIEBOOM (+)

If complete justification were needed for the creation of Camp 020,
it came at a very early stage in its history. Britain faced imminent
invasion. The enemy could be expected to introduce his agents
immediately before the event, since his potential in the sphere of
Intelligence through spies in situ had been completely destroyed by
timely and energetic action in the years before the war and the
months of its course.

The first attempt, rather falsely alarming in its local
magnitude, was made in the neighbourhood of Dungeness in September
1940. Four pre-invasion agents, acting in pairs, made an almost
simultaneous landing within a few miles of each other. They were Josef
Rudolf WALDBERG, a German, and three Dutchmen: Karl Heinrich Cornelis
Ernst MEIER, Stoerd PONS and Charles Albert Van den KIEBOOM. They
arrived in the early hours of 3 September 1940. MEIER and WALDBERG had
left Le Touquet via Boulogne in one fishing boat, PONS and Van den
KIEBOOM in another: both boats had been towed by German minesweepers,
under cover of night and mist, to within a mile of the British coast
near Dungeness, and the agents made for the shore in dinghies.

Before making land MEIER and WALDBERG, alarmed by the
proximity of a British patrol vessel, jettisoned a weighted packet
containing a circular code and maps (these were subsequently
recovered). Leaving their boat to be washed away by the receding
tide, the two men carried ashore their radio transmitter, a parcel
of food, and personal belongings. The transmitter they buried
temporarily in sand; the food was deposited in an empty boat drawn
up on the beach; and the two men snatched a 'few hours' sleep
against the wall of a house.

Towards dawn they crept across an open stretch of ground
with their retrieved equipment until they found suitable refuge in a
ditch covered by shrub. Some hours later MEIER, who spoke reasonably
good English, set off in the direction of Lydd in quest of drink. He
found an inn and got into conversation with an Air-Raid warden, with
whom he had some drinks. Somewhat ingenuously over-zealous, he soon
began to make enquiries as to the disposition and number of British
troops in the area. The warden was equally zealous, and more alert.
He asked to see MEIER's identity card. MEIER became flustered. He
admitted that he had no such document; he was a refugee, he
explained. Unconsciously he betrayed his companions as well: "We
arrived last night". He was promptly detained.

+ Admissions to Ham prior to the WALDBERG group included 20 British
Fascists and 27 subversive or espionage characters. Case histories are
not given as they are of insufficient importance.

After some three hours of prevarication under police questioning, MEIER confessed to his mission and disclosed WALBERG's whereabouts. The latter had waited patiently through the day on MEIER's return. At 20.30 hours he decided to send out his first wireless message in an emergency code, reporting the position of their landing and the jettisoning of their papers. In the early hours of the next morning he sent a second, more urgent message reporting the probability of MEIER's arrest and his own alarming position: he demanded that an aeroplane be sent to pick him up. He had just prepared a third communication for transmission - like the others, painstakingly recorded in his notebook - when he was arrested.

PONS and Van den KIEBOOM, in the meantime, had been given even shorter shrift. Immediately on landing they unpacked their transmitter and other equipment and began to transfer it across the coastal road while looking for a safe hiding place. Van den KIEBOOM was about to cross the road with one of his packages when a car containing two British officers pulled up. They challenged him and promptly took him in charge. While waiting to be handed over to the police, he asked urgently to be allowed to visit a lavatory and succeeded in ridding himself of such incriminating evidence as a code, map and reagent for secret ink.

PONS, who had been busily engaged in unloading, somewhat innocently approached a group of people standing nearby, claimed to be a Dutch refugee, and enquired when he might be. He, too, was handed over to the police.

All four men were questioned at Seabrook Police Station and eventually made damning admissions. By 6 September they had been admitted to Camp 020.

The agents were already partially broken; but it was vitally important and urgent to extract from them the full details of their recruitment, training and mission, and to learn whether any further agents might be expected from the same source. The Commandant called a conference and discussed the matter with the respective case officers. Policy and tactics were agreed upon. In such a group investigation it was essential to concentrate at the outset on the weakest link. The indication, assisted by the Orderly Officer's report on the men's demeanour in the course of his last inspection, was that WALDBERG was the weak link.

Thus the initial onslaught was against WALDBERG. His disclosures under persistent, detailed interrogation served to provide material for use against the other three. MEIER and PONS spoke readily enough in their spleen against the shabby preparation of their adventure by the German Secret Service, a fact of which they were constantly and shrewdly reminded by their interrogators.

Van den KIEBOOM, who lived alternately in hope and fear of
an imminent German liberation, required less gentle persuasion to
part with his version of the story. In the result it was found that
WALDBERG, who was described by his companions as the enthusiast of
the party, was a pre-war agent of Ast Wiesbaden, who had been
detailed on this mission after attachment to Ast Belgien, Brussels.
The other three were more hastily recruited a few weeks before they
set out. MEIER had been recruited at The Hague, PONS and Van den
KIEBOOM in Amsterdam; all had been trained in Brussels.

They had been given a short-term operational mission: to
report on troops, airfields and planes, AA defences, ships under
repair and civilian morale. WALDBERG received further instructions
which he was to withhold from his companions. He was to seize a
motor-boat and made for Boulogne. Immediately on arrival there he
was to report his return; and on the following day he would return
to the Dungeness area with one of his former Brussels instructors,
"Werner UHL" @ "WERNER" (+)

All four recruits had been assured before leaving France
that their precarious life in England would be short. The German
armies would soon rescue them on British soil. It had been gently
put to them that in the most improbable event of their prior capture
by the enemy, they should name Brest as their port of embarkation.

On 7 September 1940 Van den KIEBOOM was instructed by
interrogating officers to transmit a message to his German masters
reporting that PONS had been shot and the rest of the party had gone
into hiding for three days. On 24 October all four spies left Camp
020 for trial at the Old Bailey. Rather contrarily, in view of the
controlled message sent to Germany, PONS alone escaped the death
sentence and execution. His plea that he had been suborned into the
German service was accepted. He remained at Camps 020 and 020R until
after the cessation of hostilities and was then deported to Holland.

All four men had served their purpose from the counter-
espionage point of view as spectacularly as they had failed in their
espionage mission. The information wrested from them at Camp 020 was
to prove invaluable to the British Security Service. Results of
interrogation were instantly and progressively communicated to MI 5:
names and descriptions of potential agents, names of English contacts,
details of German Secret Service organisation, personnel and methods.

+ "WERNER" was later identified with Werner UNVERSAGT, who was to be
responsible for the despatch of many agents admitted to Camp 020 in the
years to come, some of them in transit to the gallows. He was a
familiar character, indeed, when his own career ended, appositely
enough, with his capture at home and his transfer to cells at Ham which
had housed his luckless recruits.

Thus, at a crucial stage in the war, there became available to the British authorities a pointer to future enemy espionage plans. Nor was the usefulness of the fourfold case limited to immediate events. When, in 1941, Theo DRÜKE @ François de DEEKER (later to be convicted and hanged as a spy) was admitted to Camp 020, one of his admissions was that he recognised a photograph of Van den KIEBOOM as that of a former employee at the Hotel Victoria in Amsterdam, a centre of German espionage activities. Later still, a seaman agent, Johan Johansen STRANDMOEN, was shown the photographs of the four spies and confessed that he had been a member of the crew which had brought over PONS and Van den KIEBOOM.

In the meantime, there was to be little respite for the interrogating officers at Camp 020. A new case, with novel features, had presented itself on 7 September, only one day after the admission of the four Brussels agents. It was a foretaste of things to come under a determined and co-ordinated plan formulated by the OKW: the Operation "LENA". This called for the urgent recruitment and training of invasion agents to be dropped by parachute in different areas of England to report by radio all information calculated to be of value to an invading army. An order was issued to all Abwehrstellen to this effect, but the Eins Luft Section of Ast Hamburg, under the then Major Nikolaus Fritz Adolf RITTER(+) was made responsible for the special training and conveyance by air of the agents.

The first of the "LENA" men to arrive in the UK was [SUMMER] a Swedish journalist. An abortive attempt had been made to land him on the night of 1 September, but the plane in which he was carried from Rennes had been picked up by searchlights and the pilot, Oblt GARTENFELD, who was to feature in the same rôle in several later cases at Camp 020, decided to make for Brussels. The second attempt, on the night of 5/6 September, was successful. [SUMMER] had rejected GARTENFELD's suggestion that he carry several auxiliary parachutes for his heavy equipment; he had elected to have his radio transmitter strapped to his chest and chose to be dropped from a height of 5,000 feet. His descent on farmland near Denton, Northants, was precipitous: the weight of the set caused him to fall forward heavily on landing, and he was knocked unconscious. Some five hours later, at 0630 hours, he came to his senses, cut himself free of the parachute and dragged it, with himself and the transmitter, into a nearby ditch, where he fell asleep. His detection was ignominious rather than dramatic: a farmer's boy found him asleep and told his employer; the farmer 'phoned the military

---

+ Later prisoner at CSDIC(WEA)

authorities; and not long afterwards [SUMMER] found himself in Northampton Police Station.

No protestations of innocence could be expected of him at Camp 020 on the following day. It would have been difficult for him to explain away a parachute, radio transmitter, £200 in notes, […] tablets, a false identity card, several maps and a loaded pistol. But [SUMMER] for all his Swedish nationality, was a fanatical Nazi; he could be expected to put up a fight when required to disclose his contacts and mission.

He was given little chance to entrench himself. The first interrogation elicited the names of several of the Abwehr officers with whom he had been in contact in Hamburg, seat of his controlling Stelle, and elsewhere. He claimed to have been recruited for his mission only some two months earlier, but admitted that he had been in England, "working as a journalist for a Swedish press agency", in 1938 and 1939. Pressure on him reached its most acute stage when he was asked to disclose the names and other details of agents who might be expected to follow on his footsteps.

[SUMMER] prevaricated, then gave slightly. There was another agent, due to arrive by the same means, in a matter of days. He was loth to give the name and other details; the man concerned was a personal friend. For the first and last time in the history of Camp 020 a promise was made to a prisoner: [SUMMER] was assured that the life of his friend would be spared. It was a momentous decision, and it was to prove felicitous, for upon that promise devolved many of the most spectacular wartime successes of the British counter-espionage service.

The agent in question was [TATE], another Hamburg trainee. He would be arriving very shortly and was to be dropped somewhere in the region of the Fens. […] and he had pledged themselves to meet on a certain day outside the "Black Boy" inn at Nottingham. A description of [TATE] was obtained, communicated to M I 5, and immediately issued to Police authorities throughout the country.

[SUMMER's] own case was quickly disposed of, since he had agreed to work as a double agent. Details of his mission, training, contacts and all means of communication given him had already been obtained when he was put at the disposal of B.1.a and left Camp 020 on 9 September, two days after his arrival there.

The estimate of [SUMMER's] character and outlook made at Camp 020 allowed for subsequent developments, which were spectacular. The agent had been working for some time under control when, in an access of ideological conscience, he decided to attempt to regain Germany. His effort at the outset was determined. He overpowered his guardian at his place of controlled residence, stole £5, commandeered a motor-cycle and canoe and made off in the direction of the Wash. The effort was wasted; he could not carry his scheme through; and he gave himself up to the Police.

Inevitably he found his way back to Ham. His loyalty was still to his German masters and himself. He made an attempt at suicide by cutting the arteries in his wrists with a razor-blade. He was found in his cell in a pool of blood, but prompt action saved his life. He reacted unexpectedly after recovery by disclosing that he had, in fact, been in contact with the German Secret Service since October 1938, and that his subsequent stay in the UK had obeyed espionage motives. He had reported regularly on public utilities, harbours, aeroplane factories and other matters of interest to his masters.

Despite these new admissions, [SUMMER] remained at heart a Nazi, an attitude from which he never departed throughout his long internment at Camps 020 and 020R. Although now disciplined and not otherwise troublesome, his escape mania was a constant menace. He was the only prisoner at either camp who ever attempted to cut his was through the formidable apron of wire surrounding the buildings and compounds.

In the meantime [SUMMER's] friend, had arrived in England according to schedule. He had been parachuted by GARTENFELD near Willingham, Cambs, on the night of 19/20 September 1940 with a W/T set and full equipment. He landed heavily and sprained an ankle, a fact that speeded his detection and detention, which in itself was inevitable in view of the information obtained from [SUMMER] at Camp 020 and disseminated from there via M I 5.

Shortly after landing [TATE] concealed his equipment and hobbled into the village of Willingham in his neat blue suit to make some purchases. His English, acquired during a long sojourn on the Gold Coast, was good; but it was foreign and this, with his appearance and movements in a rural place, aroused immediate suspicion. He was questioned and arrested on the evening of his landing. On his person were found £132, $160, a genuine Danish passport in his own name and a forged British identity card in the name of "WILLIAMS".

[TATE] made no admission under police interrogation. He arrived at Camp 020 on 21 September. The case had aroused such interest that three outside officers were permitted, at the request of M I 5, to undertake the initial interrogation. It proved abortive. [TATE] stoutly maintained that he had come to England some weeks ago by boat from Denmark, where he had run into trouble with the Germans. The last three months, he said, he had spent in tramping the English countryside from West Hartlepool.

The external intervention in the interrogation had not been happy. Now one of the visitors followed [TATE] to his cell at the close of that first interrogation and, in flagrant violation of the Commandant's rigid rule that no physical violence should ever be used at Ham, struck the agent on the head. The incident led, on immediate representations by the Commandant, to the instant recall of the visitors from the camp.(+)

With the departure of the outside officers, intensive interrogation of [TATE] began that same day. He stuck to his story at first, although it did not stand up to straight insistent interrogation. He could not reply with any conviction or certainty to points raised about his alleged wanderings over England. They were simple questions: What about his itinerary? Where had he stayed and how had he managed to keep his clothes clean and pressed? Where had he last had his hair cut?

[TATE's] defence was determined, despite his consciousness of its weakness; but he was fighting a losing battle. He was floundering amid inconsistencies and incongruities when it was decided to give him the coup de grace by recourse to the material provided by [SUMMER] The evidence was twisted so that [TATE] would believe that he had been betrayed by his "best friend". There was disclosed to him the information and description of himself given by including the proposed meeting of the two agents at the "Black Boy" in Nottingham.

His reaction was immediate and dramatic. [TATE] lost all his previous composure, cursed "the swine [SUMMER] and blurted out that he would tell the whole truth. He held back little. He told of his recruitment by I/Wi in Hamburg; of his training under different officers, including Major RITTER; of his meeting in Brussels with other agents, including Kurt Goose (see below); and he disclosed his mission, which was similar to [SUMMER].

In his new standpoint [TATE] seemed to be a sound double-cross prospect. He was persuaded that his betrayal had not begun with the capture of [SUMMER] it had been implicit in the cynical carelessness of his preparation and despatch by his masters in Hamburg.

[TATE] agreed to work as a double agent. Under his direction his W/T set and other equipment were recovered. His first transmission was made from a second-floor room of Latchmere House: he signalled the fact of his landing and gave advice of his injury. He continued for some time to transmit from an equitation school close by the camp. For fear that German D/F-int might pinpoint his transmitting position and discover the ruse, it was recommended by the investigating officers that [TATE] be placed forthwith at the free disposal of his controlling B.1.a officer and transferred to his more proper operational area.

+ Henceforth interrogations at Ham, in all but the most exceptional cases of a technical or highly privileged nature, were conducted exclusively by the camp staff.

[TATE], who was later to be appointed paymaster and contact for further agents despatched by his misled German masters, who twice awarded him the Iron Cross for services rendered, was to prove a most successful and profitable controlled agent throughout the war. Skilful direction of his activities and reports provided not only opportunity for deception of the enemy, but gained advance information leading to the detection of other agents and their neutralisation.

Vera ERICHSEN/Karl DRUEKE/Werner WAELTI/Gunnnar EDVARDSEN/Legwald LUND/Otto JOOST

It was fortuitous that […] was still at Camp 020 when a trio of new agents arrived in the UK out of the blue. Information which was extracted from him was instrumental in securing the only "break" in a difficult and long-drawn investigation.

At 0310 hours on 30 September 1940 a man and a woman of foreign appearance presented themselves at the Scottish railway station of Portgordon, observed that the station name had been obliterated, and enquired where they might be. After some deliberation they bought tickets to Forres. The station-master was suspicious. He didn't like their manner or their appearance; their clothes showed signs of exposure. He reported their presence to Portgordon Police Station, which received them shortly afterwards.

At the railway station the woman had told the village policeman that she was Danish and her companion, who spoke no English at all, was Belgian. She claimed that they had recently arrived in Scotland from London, on a visit. At the police station she retracted. She now said that she had sailed with her companion from Bergen some twelve days previously in a fishing boat; they were refugees from Nazi oppression. She gave as a reference Sonia, Duchesse de CHATEAU-THIERRY of Dorset House, London.

History does not record whether the local police were impressed by the invocation of exotic nobility. They were busily engaged in examining the papers and the luggage of the couple, which were intriguing. The woman had a British identity card in the name of Vera ERICHSEN and £69 in Treasury notes. The man had a Belgian passport in the name of Franziskus DE DEEKER; a British identity card and traveller's ration book with a Sussex Place, London, address; and £327.10.0 in notes. Most embarrassing of all was the man's suitcase. It contained a wireless transmitter, a fully loaded revolver, a cardboard disc code, a list of British localities corresponding with the more important RAF aerodromes, and some food.

Shortly afterwards an inflated rubber dinghy capable of carrying four persons was discovered drifting towards Cluny Harbour,

Buckie. Enquiries were instituted at once to establish whether any other persons might have landed from the same dinghy. At 1800 hours it was reported that a suitcase which was damp and had particles of sand adhering to it had been deposited at the Left Luggage Office at Waverley Station, Edinburgh. A porter stated that it had been left there of behalf of a man who spoke with a foreign accent. He had arrived on the Aberdeen train and had stated that he would reclaim the suitcase later in the evening.

Watch was kept at the Edinburgh Station. In the late evening a man, instantly recognised by the porter as the owner of the suitcase, arrived there and took up a position some distance from the Left Luggage Office. The porter went up to him and asked whether he wished to take out the case. The man produced the ticket and was promptly surrounded by waiting police officers. He attempted to resist, but was overpowered as he tried to reach for a Mauser pistol in his pocket.

On his person were found: A Swiss passport in the name of Werner Heinrich WAELTI: British identity card and traveller's ration book; £195 in notes; a railway ticket, Edinburgh to King's Cross; a book of graph paper. In a brief case he was carrying at the time of his arrest were ten maps of English and Scottish counties on the East Coast, a compass and a book containing extracts from the international "Q" code. The suitcase was opened. It held, among other things, a wireless transmitter, a disc code and a book of graph paper. WAELTI, like DE DEEKER a few hours before him, professed to be hugely surprised at the revelation.

On the following day, 1 October, DE DEEKER and Vera ERICHSEN, who was to be accommodated for holding purposes at Holloway Gaol, were received at Camp 020, WAELTI arrived on the next day.

The woman, who had wavered already under police interrogation, was obviously the weak link in the combination, and the first attack was concentrated on her. Before opening the interrogation the Commandant decided to consult who might have some information on her. There was no positive evidence to link […] with ERICHSEN beyond a certain similarity in the equipment of the three with that of […] and […]

[…] was asked what he knew about a woman called VERA. He denied knowledge of any VERA. He was taxed, at a venture, with lying. The result was gratifying. […] admitted somewhat shamefacedly that he was "frightened about VERA", and then confessed to a meeting in Brussels with a certain Vera ERICHSEN when in the company of Major RITTER. It had happened as recently as August 27th. He had been standing with RITTER in the lobby of the Hotel Metropole when a woman came up to the Major, who was apparently expecting her. All

three had a drink at the hotel, then went on to the Restaurant
L'Ardennaise for a meal. […] gathered at the time that ERICHSEN was
a Hamburg agent who was to be despatched shortly to Spain. She
appeared to be in high favour with the Hamburg officers which, he
explained, had accounted for his "fear of betraying her". But she
had left them in a huff that day in Brussels, because RITTER had
packed her off home in a tram. Some days later Vera had lost her
husband, Hauptmann DIERKS of Ast Hamburg, in a car accident.

The stage was set for the interrogation of ERICHSEN. The
opening address, in no squeamish terms, clearly shook her. When it
was put to her that prevarication would be fatuous since she had
been under the close and constant surveillance of the British
Intelligence Service in Brussels - an assertion backed by details of
her drinks and meal with RITTER and her tantrums over the tram - she
decided to make a partial confession.

She admitted recruitment several years earlier by the
Germans Secret Service, and previous service for the Russians. She
had formed a liaison with DIERKS, the I M specialist of Ast Hamburg,
under whose direction she had latterly worked. DIERKS, whom she
claimed to have married, had recently been killed in a car accident;
the driver, DE DEEKER, a close friend of her husband, had been
seriously injured.

The rest of her story, it soon became apparent, was
purposely confused to cover DIERKS and her more recent paramour, DE
DEEKER. She blamed her intended contact in London with the Duchesse
De CHATEAU-THIERRY, with whom she had lived in London in 1939, on
RITTER; and although her other admissions deeply implicated both DE
DEEKER and WAELTI, she disclaimed any knowledge of their recruitment
or mission. She did no know DE DEEKER, whom she had first met in
Brussels some months earlier, to be a GIS agent, despite his close
association with DIERKS; WAELTI she knew not at all.

Later Vera ERICHSEN became very angry, particularly about the
omniscience, ubiquity and sleeplessness of the British Intelligence
Service. Perhaps it riled her that she had been followed and did not
know it. Femininity asserted itself to make a far-reaching
correction. RITTER, […] and herself did not have drinks at the Hotel
Metropole and dinner at L'Ardennaise. It was the other way about.

She seemed less worried that the other facts should be got
right. Little by little in the weeks which followed, and with
infinite patience, the interrogators sought to piece together the
story. For no help was forthcoming from WAELTI or DE DEEKER. Their
stories, separately heard, were that they had no knowledge of the
contents of their respective suitcases, which they were to hand over
to contacts who would approach them at certain rendezvous in London.
DE DEEKER claimed to know nothing about wireless or about WAELTI.

WAELTI admitted that the Germans had tried to train him as a radio operator but they had given it up as a bad job and compelled him to bring the suitcase to England for delivery to an unknown man. For the rest, DE DEEKER and WAELTI had 'rien à dire'.

Confrontation with ERICHSEN was a failure. She urged them to tell the truth. They stuck to their story, thin as it had worn. The interrogators pressed them with undeniable evidence in the presence of the woman. They remained unmoved. One of them ironically commented: "Gentlemen, you waste your time on such unimportant people....."

Controlled association was tried. In innocent confidence ERICHSEN told DE DEEKER: "Ils savent à peu près tout". There was no reaction from her accomplice. Association of WAELTI and DE DEEKER produced no more than furtive whispering which could only heighten the incipient despair of the investigating officers.

Progress with the cases had practically reached a standstill. A tactical switch was made to an older officer who had been advocating a new approach. He was inclined to think that there might be some small element of truth in the men's stories. It was put to the test: two fruitless journeys were made with the agents to the ABC restaurant in Baker Street and to Victoria Station where, they claimed, they were to be approached by the persons who would claim the suitcases.

The processes of attrition were resumed. DE DEEKER still insisted that he had left Norway in a fishing-boat, and that he had not previously know ERICHSEN. WAELTI, with careless inconsistency, admitted having been flown to the Scottish coast in a seaplane. He denied any prior knowledge of DE DEEKER and the woman; he had never had anything to do with them before the flight. He doubted whether he would have recognised them again, for when they had been in the dinghy together it was too dark to appreciate their features......

ERICHSEN, in the meantime, had very nearly succeeded in telling the full truth about the journey. The party was originally to have crossed from Norway in a fishing boat. A fourth person was to have accompanied them: Gunnar EDVARDSEN, a young Norwegian journalist with a sabotage mission in the UK. He had a large trunkload of equipment, and it had ultimately been decided that he should leave Norway on another opportunity.

EDVARDSEN had apparently made a pass at ERICHSEN during the Norwegian interlude. She was coldly contemptuous of the advance and spoke derisively of his naive effort to impress her by chewing a glass at a party held in Bergen on the night of 17 September.

ERICHSEN was ready enough to betray the outsider EDVARDSEN, but her intimate associates, DE DEEKER and WAELTI, continued to enjoy for a time the protection of her dissimulation in their respect. She maintained that DE DEEKER's appearance in Norway had caused her intense surprise; she had not seen him for some time and had no idea that he would be travelling with her to the UK. WAELTI was, of course, still the complete stranger ....

After their landing in Scotland from the seaplane and dinghy, she said, WAELTI had gone off on his own. She had intended to go to London, call on her friend the Duchesse and then give herself up to the authorities.

And DE DEEKER ? ERICHSEN slipped into a damning admission. She didn't know the <u>exact</u> purpose of his mission; at the same time she was to help him. They were to find an address in Soho which had been provided by RITTER's assistant, Dr KRAEMER(+) as a hideout. Later they were to go out into the country and obtain information about aerodromes and troop dispositions. The relevant reports were to be transmitted to Germany by wireless by DE DEEKER.

As impasse had been reached in the investigation when, on 25 October, a second group of German agents from Norway reached Scotland. A police constable saw three men of foreign appearance in the road outside Nairn Police Station and took them into custody. They were the Norwegians Gunnar EDVARDSEN and Legwald LUND and the Saarlander Otto JOOST. They claimed to be refugees who had landed in a rubber dinghy after escaping from Norway in a fishing cutter, the "BOREAS". Each man had exactly £100 in his possession. Later in the day a slashed rubber dinghy and an aluminium oar of the type in use by the Luftwaffe were found on the coast.

The three men were transferred to Camp 020 on 28 October. EDVARDSEN's photograph was at once identified by Vera ERICHSEN as the intended saboteur met in Bergen. The commandant decided to use the "omniscience, ubiquity and sleeplessness of the British Intelligence Service" trick again. He substantiated it with the detail of the glass-chewing act at Bergen on the night of 17 September, when EDVARDSEN was collected at a party with other German agents. EDVARDSEN was suitably impressed and broke(++). He admitted recruitment in Norway for a sabotage mission in the UK in which he was to be assisted by JOOST. Theirs was a quaint mission. They were to race up and down the British highways on bicycles and cut

(+) KRAEMER himself passed through Camp 020 in 1945, and was held at Bad Nenndorf in 1946.
(++) EDVARDSEN broke completely at that first interrogation. So completely that he admitted having buried his insulated clippers in a sand dune shortly after landing, and gave the location with such accuracy that they were recovered soon afterwards in the place indicated. The extraordinary case thus presented itself of an enemy agent blithely providing the real evidence which could be used for his own prosecution to death. He was fortunate indeed that such proceedings were not instituted against him.

telephone wires with specially insulated clippers. LUND, he said had separate orders to establish contact with some anonymous person at the Scandinavian Seamen's Home in Glasgow.

LUND, who followed EDVARDSEN into the interrogation room, tried to rest on his refugee story. He was soon shaken out of his pretension. With reluctant alacrity he confirmed the story told by EDVARDSEN.

JOOST proved the least tractable of the three. He admitted nothing until confronted with the other two. Even after his investigation had been shelved, to cut losses on the lesser cases, it was felt that he had not made a full admission.

The "BOREAS" agents were not, in themselves, of any great importance, although valuable information was obtained about the activities and methods of Abt II of Ast Norway. EDVARDSEN, however, was valuable as a potential new aid to the solution of the greater problem.

He learned in Bergen that DE DEEKER and ERICHSEN were experienced agents employed by Ast Hamburg. WAELTI had been described to him as a skilful agent who had operated in Paris during the Battle of France. He had seen the two men enciphering a message in a Bergen hotel with a disc code. WAELTI had later rigged an aerial on the "BOREAS" and locked himself in the cabin, obviously to transmit the message. EDVARDSEN could dispose of ERICHSEN's story that the arrival of DE DEEKER and WAELTI had cause her great surprise. He had been to Bergen station to meet all three when they arrived together under the guidance of Dr MÜLLER, an Abwehr officer. They had come from Oslo, where they had spent only one day en route from Hamburg.

It seemed reasonable to suppose that confrontation with EDVARDSEN might break both DE DEEKER and WAELTI. The attempts failed. WAELTI glibly denied ever having seen EDVARDSEN. DE DEEKER contented himself with the ironical observation that the gentleman's memory was too good to be true; he had the whole story just pat.

But the new information from EDVARDSEN was not without its value. It served to goad ERICHSEN into yielding fresh details of the Hamburg venture, though she still refrained from further exposing DE DEEKER and WAELTI.

There was no notable progress in the month of November, which was spent in part in the interrogation outside Ham, by Camp officers, of two of ERICHSEN's London contacts, the Duchesse de CHATEAU-THIERRY and a Miss COSTENZA. The Duchesse, who was no intellectual giantess, told of her pre-war relations with ERICHSEN and "Dr RANTZAU" (RITTER). She was herself quite evidently a low grade agent on the threadbare fringe of High Society, which she was to have exploited for espionage purposes. COSTENZA, another international hanger-on to London Society, had been in the pay of the Germans for some time and had earned arrest some months earlier. She appeared to have a certain personal attraction, but, judged by results, she was no Mata Hari.

On the night of 29 November Latchmere House was hit and badly damaged by a bomb, causing considerable physical inconvenience both to the staff and the establishment. The bomb, followed a few days later by news of the execution of WALDBERG, MEIER and Van den KIEBOOM, who had enjoyed a wide circle of acquaintances among the inmates of the Camp, appears to have had its repercussions. Associations between prisoners could no longer be covered owing to the disruption of the special devices. DE DEEKER and WAELTI were not allowed to see each other. […], a Belgian seaman agent, was enlisted as a stool-pigeon and given access to DE DEEKER, to whom he was to confide that he was expecting repatriation to Belgium very shortly.

DE DEEKER, whose nerves were probably on edge, took the bait. On 5 December he prepared a letter in shorthand addressed to a certain "SPITZENBERG" at 5 rue Faider, Brussels, and asked […] to deliver it on his return to that city. […] delivered the letter to the Orderly Officer. The name and address was immediately communicated to SIS for reactions; the shorthand letter was despatched post-haste to the School of Codes and Ciphers.

No results were to hand on 13 December when DE DEEKER, whose confidence had been systematically gained by the camp Medical Officer, who was acting as the "sympathetic and understanding link" between prisoner and Vera ERICHSEN, somewhat unexpectedly confessed to the MO that his real name was Karl Theo DRÜKE, of 5 rue Faider, Brussels, and that he was a German national.

On the following day came the SIS trace on the name and address which had been submitted: a German agent named DRÜKE had lived with a certain STUTZENBERG at 5, rue Faider; the date of his birth was 20 March 1906 (the birthdate, too, coincided with that in "DE DEEKER'S" spurious passport!).

There followed, from the School of Codes and Ciphers, a transcription of DRÜKE's note to "SPITZENBERG". It was couched in extraordinary language: the writer was either showing the first signs of mental derangement or was employing phraseology that had been convened for emergency use. But these eccentricities affected only details and niceties of the text, which clearly revealed: DRÜKE's activities in Norway; the names of several of his GSS contacts in that country; his close friendship with "SPITZENBERG", a known German agent; an attempt to communicate the fact that EDVARDSEN "is very suspect" (a clear case of meiosis); and a staunch determination to remain faithful to his masters.

All this was rich material that could not yet be used, but on 23 December, in a further paroxysm of nerves, DRÜKE "officially" disclosed his true identity to the Orderly Officer and acknowledged that he had always been aware of the contents of the suitcase which had been carrying when arrested. But he refused to give any information about the German Secret Service, his own mission to England or details of any contacts that he was to have made there.

About a week earlier, however, DRÜKE had sent a letter to Vera ERICHSEN through the Medical Officer urging her to do everything to save herself; he expected to spend the rest of his life in prison. She wrote back through the same channel urging him to tell everything for the sake of their unborn child. She wasn't pregnant at all, but she confided to the MO that the little personal touch might sway her lover.

It didn't. DRÜKE refused to respond. The new emotional situation, it was decided, could be capitalised. The MO was instructed to sound ERICHSEN as to her willingness now to tell the whole truth herself. The woman agreed to do so. On three separate occasions during December and January the MO visited her and interrogated her on the basis of an agreed questionnaire. As a result a tolerably clear story of the whole case could be prepared and valuable details were obtained of characters involved in it who were continuing operations on the other side of the Channel and the North Sea.

ERICHSEN confirmed DRÜKE's true identity before he had made his "official" admission in that respect; she revealed that he had been a member of the GSS for some years past and stated that she had first met him at an Abwehr address at The Hague which had been given to her by her friend the Duchesse. But she maintained to the end her plea of ignorance of the real nature of DE DEEKER's mission in the UK.

On 16 January WAELTI, who had been transferred to Brixton Prison following threats of suicide which might yet allow him to cheat the gallows, was returned to Camp 020. He was told, in all truth, that EDVARDSEN's story had now received full confirmation from Vera ERICHSEN and that DRÜKE had revealed his true identity. He was advised that this would be the last opportunity to help himself by making a confession. He was adamant to the end: he had nothing to add to his previous statements.

The time had come to close the case. There was ample material for the successful prosecution of DRÜKE and WAELTI.(+) They

---

(+) The story of WAELTI has, apparently, never been known in detail. RITTER has stated at Bad Nenndorf that he believes his true name to have been KELLER. LIKE DRÜKE @ "DE DEEKER", he was a V-mann of I M Hamburg; both received the general "LENA" training and mission under RITTER's subordinates, although they remained, primarily I M agents.

were found guilty after trial at the Old Bailey, sentenced to death, and hanged. ERICHSEN, whose real name was SCHALBURG, remained in detention.

The "Case of the German Agents Sent to the United Kingdom by Seaplane from Norway" has been told at length, not because it had any great intrinsic importance, but because the development of its investigation presents a classical example of the difficulties faced by the interrogators of spies and the resource and resources brought to bear against them. The officers concerned were not rewarded with the personal satisfaction of "breaks" in the cases of DRÜKE and WAELTI. It is unlikely that overmuch Intelligence was lost as a result. And, after all, DRÜKE and WAELTI could be, and were, hanged on the evidence available.

Kurt Karl GOOSE

On the night of 3/4 October a new spy had been dropped to earth by parachute near Wellingborough, Northants. He was not unexpected. [TATE] had described how he had been asked in Brussels to hand GOOSE a pistol, and how GOOSE had confided to him that, as a member of the Wehrmacht, he would be taking his Soldbuch and uniform in order to claim the status of a Prisoner of War if captured by the British.

The circumstances of his actual capture allowed of neither vainglory nor artifice. The first hours after landing GOOSE spent in hiding behind some bushes. When day came he cut up his parachute and disposed of the pieces by introducing them into rabbit-holes. The rest of the equipment and himself he deposited in a small barn about a mile from the spot at which he had landed. He was found there at 1920 hours by an outraged farmer who promptly handed him over to the police. He was wearing civilian clothes at the time; a Luftwaffe uniform and his Soldbuch were found later, with the rest of the now familiar impedimenta of an invasion agent, in the barn.

GOOSE arrived at Camp 020 on the following day. He offered no resistance to interrogation. His story was unremarkable save for one feature: he was the first member of the Brandenburg Lehr-Regiment zbV 300, an Intelligence and sabotage unit, to fall into British hands. He had been a geological student in the US between 1936 and 1939 and had returned to Germany via Japan in early 1940 to volunteer his services. His knowledge of English led to his prompt drafting into the Brandenburg unit. After a refresher course in infantry training - he had been called up in 1935 for two eight-week periods - he was attached to an Abwehr bureau in Brussels for three weeks' intensive specialised training, including radio transmission.

GOOSE agreed readily to work as a double agent, but he was unsuccessful in his attempts to establish W/T contact and therefore remained at Camp 020. Although he had been claiming that he never had any intention of operating in the UK as an agent, but was anxious to escape detention in order to make his way back to America and away from Nazism, he blotted his untidy copybook by attempting to bribe a warder soldier into smuggling out of the camp a letter addressed to the German Embassy in Dublin. A case for his prosecution under the Treachery Act was drawn up but not pursued.

The only open channel of communication left to Britain after the German overflow into the narrow seas was the line to and from the Iberian Peninsula. The Germans could be expected to exploit it to their own ends by the employment of seamen agents. The turn of the year 1940/41 brought confirmation of this suspicion.

The first case to be brought to Camp 020 was that of the Belgian seaman [...] who has already been mentioned in connection with DRÜKE. [...] had fled Belgium in the pilot boat in which he was serving at the time of the Allied debacle in the Low Countries. The ship reached Bayonne on 22 June 1940, day of the French surrender to Germany. She was boarded by a man wearing British battledress and the name of HOFFMAN, who begged to be allowed to work his passage on the ship's flight to Lisbon, and was allowed to do so.

Shortly after arrival in Portugal HOFFMAN approached [...] and invited him to work for the Germans, claiming that he himself had lost all his papers to an unhelpful British consular officer and was intending to collaborate with the Germans in order to secure a full pardon.

[...] agreed, received cursory instructions in observation and reporting for espionage purposes, and was shown how to prepare communications in secret writing. Some weeks later he signed on as a member of the crew of a Dutch merchant ship and received a written questionnaire calling for information on Britain.

The fact that he and other seamen had been consorting with Germans in Lisbon had been denounced to the British authorities there by one of his friends and compatriots, Jack VERLINDEN, and he was promptly arrested on the ship's arrival at Newport, Mon.

[...] caused no difficulty from the Intelligence or disciplinary points of view at Camp 020. On the contrary, he proved an enthusiastic and effective stool-pigeon, and it is his activity in this respect rather than any special interest offered by his own case that has won him more than passing mention in these pages.

SKORZISKO

An interesting and perplexing arrival at Ham in November 1940 was one SKORZISKO, a German national who claimed to be a Communist, to have fled his native land after the rise of Hitler, and to have

lived precariously in several European countries since then.
Latterly he had been living in France, and the arrival of the
Germans had made his position untenable. He had decided to flee to
England.

It was the manner of his flight rather than his antecedents,
of which nothing was known from other sources, that caused suspicion
to fasten on him when he arrived off Chesil Bank in a 9-foot dinghy
in July 1940. He may have been telling the truth, but he did not
help to clear himself when he claimed to have spent four days alone
in his dinghy since leaving the north French coast.

The case, which was in all conscience complex enough, had
been further complicated by the time that SKORZISKO was transferred
to Ham some four months after his arrival in England. The elementary
step of checking his story by examination of his physical condition
at the first opportunity after his landing had not been taken by the
authorities who had dealt with him.

SKORZISKO's story at Camp 020 was unshakeable. He had either
hardened by this time or was still telling the truth. But the story
had to be subjected to every possible check. Camp officers with
experience of the sea were inclined to doubt the account of the
crossing. With the scrupulous fairness that characterised
investigation of all cases, independent expert opinion was sought; a
request was made to the Admiralty for a report on the weather
conditions during the material time and for a considered view on the
likelihood of such a journey in such a craft. The report was
economical in argument and lamentably inconclusive: the journey was
"possible but not probable" in the conditions given.

Pressure on SKORZISKO was maintained over a long period, but
brought no new light on the case. He was transferred to Camp WX
(Stafford) and eventually died in hospital.

Axel COLL

A series of cases investigated at Camp 020 in November 1940
underlined the anxiety of the Germans to establish regular
meteorological stations in Greenland and on Jan Mayen Island, in the
Arctic Circle, and marked the frustration of their efforts. The
cases were interesting, too, because, ab initio, so far as their
examination at Camp 020 was concerned, ISOS had become available as
a brief and a check.

Independent physical detection of the first German venture
fell to a patrolling Norwegian gunboat, the "FRIDTJOF NANSEN"
(Captain ULLRING), which intercepted the SS "VESLE KARI" in King
Oscar's Fjord, Greenland, and took her under escort. Captain ULLRING
was regrettably innocent of the greater prize which had fallen into

his hands: a number of relief and relieved wireless operators in the German meteorological service were abroad the seized vessel.

ULLRING told the men that it was most likely that the "VESLE KARI", a Norwegian ship, and her crew and passengers, Norwegian also, would be released and permitted to return to Norway! One of them, Axel COLL, voiced a preference for England: he was a master mariner and would like to join the Free Norwegian Navy. ULLRING was willing and bought from COLL an excellent Leica camera at an agreeable price.

The "FRIDTJOF NANSEN" mad a round trip of the area and picked up a few men, wireless operators and at least one scientist, who had been dropped by the "VESLE KARI" in what later transpired to have been an agent-planting expedition. The gunboat landed most of the men in Iceland; the majority eventually regained Norway and one contrived to make Copenhagen via Portugal and Spain.

Only three of the men opted for England: COLL and two wireless operators. They were lodged in Pentonville Prison on 12 September for examination. By the time that the intercept material had roused real interest in their case, the two operators had left the UK for Canada on representations from the Norwegian Government that their capture had been due solely to the Norwegian Navy.

Thus COLL made a lone visit to Camp 020, where he was received in November 1940, to explain himself and his colleagues. He offered no resistance to interrogation and gave valuable information on the preparation of the "VESLE KARI's" Arctic Odyssey and the personalities concerned. An interesting link with the Vera ERICHSEN/EDVARDSEN cases was provided when he named a certain Carl ANDERSEN as one of the German officials concerned in the project; for ANDERSEN it was who made the plans for the sailing of the "BOREAS" at the time when it was proposed to sail all four agents to Scotland together.

COLL's own part in the Greenland venture was curious and perplexing even to himself. Originally the Germans had intended to give him command of a ship servicing the meteorological stations with personnel and stores. This scheme had been dropped and COLL, who was no expert at handling a camera, had been given a Leica and told to provide a pictorial record of the "VESLE KARI's" trip. It was his impression that this was merely an excuse for his presence in the ship and that on her return to Aalesund, the port of departure, he would also be asked to report on navigational and other aspects of the journey.

Coll was very much the simple sailor, with the engaging quality of being a stickler for accuracy: his verbal statements were often corrected or amplified by unsolicited written notes. He had a code of morals all his own. He had visited a dentist shortly after his arrival in England; and instead of paying the fees out of the money obtained from ULLRING for the Leica camera, he wrote to his brother for financial aid. His explanation was that he could never use "German money" - originally he had described it as the proceeds of "legal booty obtained from the Germans" - for fillings which would remain permanently in his mouth! But he could, and did, use it to buy supplementary food and tobacco.

When the information in his possession had been exhausted by detailed interrogation, COLL, who was in bad health, was transferred to internment in the Isle of Man.

M/V "LA PART BIEN"

The arrival at Plymouth on 23 September of the M/V "LA PART BIEN", with a crew of three and no passengers, despite the provision at short notice of reasonably comfortable accommodation for such, represented the complete failure ab initio of a new espionage venture from across the Channel. The crew, a Swedish skipper and two men, had been recruited by the Abwehr Nebenstelle at Brest and provided with the motor-vessel. They were to make for Le Touquet and there pick up "passengers" for England, to be clandestinely landed.

A faulty compass and the presence on board of a cask of heady wine, which was not left long unbroached, influenced Skipper JONASSON's navigation: instead of making Le Touquet he hit England.

The first story told by the men at Plymouth was decidedly simple and would have been true if it had been complete. They merely stated that they had received orders from unspecified Germans to proceed to Le Touquet; instead, they had come to England. They were landed as refugees and directed to London for routine examination.

It was not until the month of November, when new information had been obtained from them and from other sources, that it was decided to transfer them to Camp 020 for more detailed interrogation. Their examination here presented little difficulty and provided information of considerable value on the personnel and activities of Nest Brest.

M/V "JOSEPHINE"

A new attempt by Nest Brest to land agents in the UK was registered in the month of November, when the M/V "JOSEPHINE" put into Fishguard with a crew of five and three Cuban passengers. The captain, Cornelius EVERTSEN, a Dutchman, informed the naval control that they were all refugees from France bound for Ireland; but one of the passengers (the Cuban PAZOS-DIAZ, who died in a UK hospital in 1942) had developed an abscess and was in urgent need of medical attention, so that they had made the nearest port.

The men were landed and sent to London for routine interrogation. They adhered as first to a common cover story: that they were refugees from Nazi-occupied France escaping to Ireland. EVERTSEN, the leader, told a long and circumstantial story so complex that it could not stand up to cross-examination. He broke at Cannon-Row Police Station: he admitted that the party had sailed from France under German sponsorship. Examination of the eight-fold case at the police station ceased abruptly; the men were transferred at once to Camp 020.

EVERTSEN, now a very scared man, tried to confuse investigation of the case by seeking to minimise his own rôle in it. Another member of the crew, KRAG, was decidedly truculent; but the rest, and especially the Cubans, were willing enough to talk. From the counter-intelligence point of view, their transfer to Ham proved, in the result, to be extremely profitable.

The story itself was simple and sorry. The "JOSEPHINE" was under Abwehr orders and her crew were conscious of their tainted employment. The three Cubans, all of them refugees from Spain, where they had fought on the Republican side in the recent war, had been picked up in Paris by a Hungarian talent scout of the Abwehr. They had received training in sabotage in Brest; their mission in England was to pose as refugees and obtain employment in some factory in the West Country which they would then proceed to incapacitate.

With sabotage material packed in tins labelled "Green Peas", the three agents were placed as passengers in a boat, the "JACQUELINE", and set off for England during September. Extremely bad weather caused EVERTSEN to return to Brest.

The "JOSEPHINE", a new boat with the old crew, had been favoured with rather better weather in November, but it was still not good enough for the passengers. The seedy Cubans wanted to die, but not on terra firma. They consigned all German souls to hell and their spurious tins of peas to the ocean deep.

When they were in sight of England, EVERTSEN tried to persuade the Cubans to land at the point which had been indicated on a chart by the Nest Brest officers. Only one of them (ROBLES) was in any condition to reply to the invitation, and he palely but categorically declined to go ashore without his prostrate copains. When PAZOS-DIAZ' condition was seen to be serious indeed, EVERTSEN agreed to make Fishguard after urgently instructing crew and passengers to adhere at all costs to their cover story. He was the first to depart from it, and one of the last inmates to depart from Camp 020R on its dissolution; with the exception of the unlamented PAZOS-DIAZ, his crew and passengers bore him company during those years of reflexion.

Josef JAKOBS

The lull in airborne espionage traffic ended at 2100 hours on the night of 31 January 1941 with the arrival near Romsey, Huntingdonshire, of a 43-year old German, Josef JAKOBS. He lay in a field with a broken ankle, draped by his parachute and surrounded by his equipment, until 0930 hours on the following morning, unable to move. He had been boldly shy hitherto of betraying his presence, but by this time the physical hurt had become unendurable. He drew a revolver and fired it into the air to attract attention and succour.

He was quite unsympathetically taken into custody, for the police are zealous and such visitors are rare in Huntingdonshire. An inventory was taken of his property. It made interesting reading: two identity cards, one in blank, the other in the name of "James RYMER"; a ration book in blank; a portable radio transmitter; a partially destroyed circular code (No. 9); a Shell touring map of England; £497 in notes, and a Mauser revolver.

A routine statement was taken from JAKOBS. He admitted that he had been despatched to England to send back weather reports to Germany. Of course he had never, never intended to carry out his mission; he had accepted it in order to escape from Germany. He would really like to make his way to America, where he had an aunt living in Illinois ....

He found himself at Camp 020 on the following day. The first interrogation, to which he was brought on a wheeled stretcher, was a painful affair. But it would have been improper, in view of the man's distraught condition, to go into the full details of his case at this stage. Instead, admissions were obtained from him on the salient features of his contacts, training and mission for immediate transmission to M I 5.

The man's agony could not be prolonged, if only in the interests of coherence and concentration; he was despatched to hospital after that preliminary step. He did not return until 15 April. The respite had obviously fortified his spirit. It soon became apparent that he was now determined to fight back. He was a doughty opponent across the interrogation table, shrewd and courageous. He sought to retract some of his earlier admissions; he volunteered no information of any great value; he agreed to work under control only with manifest reluctance. Such facts as were dragged out of him were the fruits of perseverance and perspicacity.

JAKOBS' moral strength probably stemmed from his patriotism. He had few other moral qualities. He had started life as a respectable dentist, but he had gone into decay: he had served a sentence of imprisonment in Switzerland following deals in counterfeit gold; he had drawn handsome if unsavoury payment out of

Jewish migrations, though himself an Aryan; he had disgusted even
the Gestapo by such activities and had been briefly confined by
them. He would still have his interrogators believe that he had
accepted his espionage mission only after consultation with his
Jewish friends and in order to canvass funds for their organisation.

The actual circumstances of his recruitment were never made
clear. He spoke vaguely of "Nachrichtendienst" officers in Berlin,
Hamburg, The Hauge. He gave few details of his training in weather
reporting and radio transmission and little information about his
contacts; he professed to know nothing about Abwehrstellen as such.
When he named "BRUHNS" at Hamburg and "ZEBRA", the radio instructor
at The Hague, it was clear that he knew of and was known to at least
two Asten; but the identity and station of his controlling officer
and Stelle could not be established with any certainty.(+)

For JAKOBS remained stolidly true to his masters and
fellows. He acknowledged acquaintance with another agent, Karel
RICHTER, a later arrival by parachute, only when it was evident that
his colleague was already known to us. At a subsequent confrontation
with RICHTER he bore himself with apologetic resignation.

JAKOBS was manifestly unemployable as a double agent; as a
tome of reference in the living counter-espionage library that was
being created at Camp 020 he would have been drawn blank. There was
no good reason why he should continue to live. He was prosecuted
under the Treachery Act and sentenced to death. He died at the Tower
of London on 15 Aug 1941, a brave man. His last words directed the
"Tommies" of the firing squad to shoot straight.

<u>Joseph Auguste LAUREYSSENS/Jack VERLINDEN/Karl Hendrik VAN GILS</u>

On 4 February 1941 an examiner of the Postal Censorship in London
opened an airmail letter addressed to:

"M Maria Jose DOS SANTOS,
Rua 20 Abril 48 II,
LISBON."

It had been posted at Erith before midday on 30 January. The writer,
one "AUGUST", professed ardent love for Maria; he spread himself
over several pages of blue notepaper to convey the tender message.

(+) RITTER has stated at CSDIC(WEA) that JAKOBS was probably a recruit
of Sonderführer FRISCHMUTH, of the independent "Stelle Bremen" (later
"Referat Roland"); "BRUHNS" (Hauptmann BOECKEL of Ast Hamburg, another
inmate at Bad Nenndorf), has confirmed his training in Hamburg; "ZEBRA"
(Uffz ZEBRALLA, now also at Bad Nenndorf) was to win mention in many
cases at Camp 020 throughout the war).

With the detachment from emotionalism in third-party affairs bred by familiarity with such communications, the conscientious examiner read on unmoved until one of the middle pages was reached. Then the practised eye detected something between the lines. It looked closer. The surface of the paper had been methodically disturbed. The orderly scratches ran on to the next page, then everything was smooth again.

These must be the "traces consistent with writing in secret inks" with which few censorship examiners are rewarded in an otherwise thankless and dreary task. The examiner submitted the letter for laboratory tests.

The reaction on the traces was immediate and positive. A secret message in Flemish had been sandwiched between the lines of the open text. Photographic copies of the developed writing were taken and the text submitted for translation. It proved to be a report on the attack made by a German plane on "our ship....near Buoy 4".

The alarm was sounded and search for the agent began. Inside a fortnight he had been identified, traced and arrested. He was Joseph Auguste LAUREYSSENS, a member of the crew of the Belgian coastal steamer "VAE VICTIS", which was lying at Erith on 17 February.

Close to the man's bunk were found a bottle containing invisible ink, a pen with a white substance coagulated on the nib, blue paper identical with that used in the intercepted letter, an airmail label and two visiting cards of Maria DOS SANTOS. To one of these he had added his name in pencil: LAUREYSSENS, Auguste". He was changing his clothes in the ship's pantry before being taken ashore and tried to rid himself of another piece of incriminating evidence: a photograph of himself with Maria. But the picture was found, and with it a second airmail label.

The ship's log of the "VAE VICTIS" was also revealing. The entry for 26 January read in part:-

"1602 hrs: Not far from Nore Light, vessel attacked by low-flying bomber..... Attack occurred at B 4 buoy Barrow deep."

Ashore, under police interrogation, LAUREYSSENS assumed an air of injured innocence and intellectual insufficiency: nobody understood his Flemish and he was misunderstood, he whined. He knew nothing about the intercepted letter; the liquid in the bottle, the pen, the paper . . . these things didn't belong to him. . .

Three days later, on 20 February, he arrived at Camp 020, bringing with him all the negative phrases and histrionic tricks that he had mastered since he was detained. His was a bad case indeed, but he succeeded in making it inordinately trying to resolve. He defended himself with all the low cunning that he could summon, and he must have been a master of deceit, even among his fellow Flemings.

Under interrogation at Camp 020, LAUREYSSENS played dumb in the intellectual sense: he was "only a poor, illiterate seaman". To reinforce this plea and to disown his letter to Maria, he consistently wrote all his statements with a pencil held between thumb and first finger, dispensing altogether with such literary refinements as capital letters and punctuation. He blamed the embarrassment of the secret inks, the paper and the unfortunate letter on two mythical land-bound characters, "JEF" and "TOON", who almost came to life in his agile imaginings. To suit his evasive purposes he endowed them at different times with syphilis, platonic affection for Maria, authorship of the intercepted letter, ownership of its instruments, and extreme mobility. They were even more ubiquitous than the British Secret Service. For "JEF" and "TOON" were not only bad types, but bad pennies: they turned up at every British port and on every occasion that their creator was in trouble.

But it was his perverse obstinacy in refusing to admit demonstrable facts, rather than his equivocations, that saved his life. LAUREYSSENS was never broken; but his interrogators at Camp 020 and their willing collaborators, inside and outside the establishment, not only established his guilt beyond all doubt, but succeeded in piecing together practically the whole story of his venture in espionage.

As in the ERICHSEN/WAELTI/DRÜKE case, all resources of Camp 020 were mobilised against him. The most effective proved to be three other prisoners.

The first chapters of LAUREYSSENS' story of espionage were produced in remarkable detail by Jack VERLINDEN.

[…] VERLINDEN had recently been admitted to Camp 020 on suspicion of having withheld knowledge of other German agents recruited in Lisbon. The charge was disproved. It was established that VERLINDEN had played true throughout: he had reported many facts to a British consular official in Lisbon who, with tranquil negligence, had omitted to forward the information.

Among the agents whom he had so fruitlessly denounced some weeks before was LAUREYSSENS himself. VERLINDEN had actually introduced LAUREYSSENS to the enterprising Herr HOFFMANN. He had found the flat in Lisbon that the agent was temporarily to share with Maria Jose DOS SANTOS, who was to provide cover for the communications in secret ink in which LAUREYSSENS was trained. He outlined the questionnaire which had been handed to LAUREYSSENS on his espionage mission in England, and described how LAUREYSSENS had earned his keep even before leaving Lisbon by pin-pointing important targets in Swansea and giving the disposition of AA defences in the area, which he had recently visited as a seaman(+).

LAUREYSSENS admitted the contacts, but insisted that they were purely social. On that point he was immovable. The impasse called for a confrontation. It failed dismally. LAUREYSSENS, with impressive outward calm, flatly denied ever having seen or met VERLINDEN . . .

VERLINDEN has lost sight of LAUREYSSENS after the agent sailed for England via Seville in a Swedish steamer in October 1940. The confection of the next chapters in the story called for new sources of information. The framework was supplied directly to the interrogators by LAUREYSSENS, who contributed a fair account of his movements but was obdurately reticent or equivocal about the less innocent activities that attended them.

It was decided to bring into play […], the enthusiastic stool-pigeon who had a similar Lisbon espionage background. His success was gradual, but complete. Soon he had won LAUREYSSENS' confidence. LAUREYSSENS began to talk vauntingly of his ascendancy over his examiners and to disclose facts which he felt he had so successfully withheld from them.

Full confirmation was obtained by […] of VERLINDEN's detailed account of the Lisbon story, even though he had not been fully briefed on the points or permitted to associate with VERLINDEN.

The rest of the story was well developed by […] under the expert direction of the camp officers. LAUREYSSENS boasted to him that he had sent at least seventeen reports in secret writing from ports which included Seville, Workington, Liverpool, Middlesborough, Sunderland and London. He gave all the details, with contacts and dates.

He spoke of his determined but unsuccessful attempt to recruit in England another Belgian seaman, Karel Hendrik VAN GILS. VAN GILS was promptly arrested and brought to Camp 020, where he confirmed the fact in the teeth of LAUREYSSENS' manifest displeasure and vehement dissidence.

[…] continued the good work. LAUREYSSENS admitted to him authorship of the intercepted letter posted at Erith, while still maintaining "upstairs" that the fanciful and wicked "JEF" and "TOON" were to blame. He went further, to provide fresh evidence against himself: he boasted that the British had failed to detect the ingenious course which he had adopted to record for his subsequent report, details of the bombing incident. He had made an immediate note of it in indelible ink on the lining of his coat sleeve.

(+) There is reason to believe that the severe blow subsequently struck at the town by the Luftwaffe was largely assisted by briefing based on the information supplied by LAUREYSSENS.

On […] urgent report, the coat was at once examined. The aide memoire was certainly there. It read: "26 J 4 ur B.4". Ingenuity was not taxed to decipher it: "26 January 4 o'clock Buoy 4".

Although from the Intelligence point of view the LAUREYSSENS case was satisfactorily resolved, it must rank as one of the failures of Camp 020. The ultimate objective had been his prosecution to death. This called for the extraction from the man of a full confession, and the production of fresh real evidence, for by some lamentable mischance the secret writing on the intercepted letter had been wiped off the paper after development and copying.

But LAUREYSSENS remained unbroken, and the new evidence obtained, conclusive as it might appear, could not guarantee conviction under fastidious British justice. A model but unloved prisoner, he remained at Camp 020 until 1945, when he was repatriated with a strong recommendation that the ready justice of liberated Belgium be meted out to him.

DE JONGE

Concurrently with the undoubted agent types there passed through Camp 020 during this period a cosmopolitan cavalcade of refugee suspects who had come under notice as a result of information obtained from Camp 020 prisoners and double agents or the dissatisfaction of their interrogators at preliminary examinations. Several of them were found to have had relatively trifling traffic with the enemy and were rapidly disposed of by transfer to less formidable places of detention.

There were also the guiltless, who had to be proved innocent. Now an admission of guilt from a known agent was difficult enough to obtain in many cases: to prove a suspect innocent was even more arduous. He could often prove his own unsuspected worst enemy by producing a circumstantial story or detail that was quite unacceptable under distrustful if logical examination. Investigation was always scrupulously fair; but where the slightest element of doubt existed, the man was held. The stakes in counter-espionage are too high to allow of squeamishness. If a suspect did eventually leave Camp 020 a free and wiser man, he might almost be said to have qualified for canonisation.

There was nothing saintly, however, about Jan Roelof DE JONGE, a Dutchman whose case may be taken as typifying those unfortunates who, in the ultimate, were found guiltless of espionage, if not otherwise innocent. DE JONGE was arrested in Gibraltar in February 1941 after making a tactless public enquiry as to the sailings of convoys. There were adverse reports against him

from other sources, and it was natural that he should gravitate to
Camp 020.

DE JONGE's story was sordid indeed. He had been expelled
from Germany in 1934 as "an enemy of the State". It could have been
a redeeming feature in his career, but it wasn't. On investigation
of the claim it was found that he had proffered a German prostitute
a mean fee; that she had protested obscenely; and that a group of
Storm-troopers had upheld her demands. DE JONGE had somewhat archly
retorted that he was unaware that Nazis were also pimps. The insult
to German womanhood and Nazi honour cost him four months'
imprisonment and expulsion.

A couple of years later DE JONGE and his wife conspired to
defraud the brothers Littlewood, of football pool fame, by forging
coupons. He anticipated the Dutch court's verdict by fleeing to
Casablanca before returning to Antwerp indirectly to conduct a local
agency for Mr Murphy's football pools. Anti-pool legislation caused
him to flit further and further south until the outbreak of war
found him in Tangier, couponless and without prospects.

He ventured into the food trade with Spanish Morocco and
failed to make a success of it. He dabbled in other low level
business and lived on an allowance from his father.

A chance meeting with a German in Tetuan, who asked him to
deliver a letter to another German in Tangier, brougt him, in an
unprecedented flush of righteousness and honesty, to the office of
the French Consul in Tangier. He was enlisted as an agent of the
Deuxième Bureau and embarked on a directed flirtation with the
Germans.

After fair and profitable dalliance with the French, DE
JONGE's blood and conscience finally asserted themselves: he
determined to rehabilitate himself as a Dutchman. There was some
official delay before he succeeded in winning acceptance for service
in the Free Dutch forces. It was his impatience to be enlisted that
caused him at Gibraltar to make the fateful enquiry about convoy
sailings.

Having lightly admitted at Camp 020 to his contact with
German agents, thus substantiating much of the evidence which had
accumulated against him, DE JONGE could not prove that his
connection with them had obeyed the directions of an Allied
Intelligence Service. His French controlling officer had disappeared
from Tangier into French North Africa and could not be traced. His
own vehement protestations of good faith were, not unnaturally,
unacceptable, and it was not until December 1944 that evidence was
obtained to confirm his story and justify his release.

DEL CAMPO

A new low in agent grading was struck by a more adventitious seaman, a remarkable young Cuban national, José Antonio DEL CAMPO y Palaez, who laid questionable claims to the doubtful Spanish title of Marqués de San Carolo. He had lived more wildly than wisely in Madrid for several years. His dissolution had emptied his purse and broken his health. But in his rake's progress he had met probably everyone in Madrid, not excluding the lowest level representatives of the German Secret Service. They had impressed him into their employment. He had signed on a ship bound for America as a coal trimmer with the sinister clandestine espionage mission of buying popular technical magazines in that country. He never got there. His ship put in at a British port and he was arrested. Shortly afterwards he arrived at Camp 020.

He proved proudly haïf under interrogation. His confession was immediate and full; the incidental information which he provided, especially on the Falange and its connections with the Germans, almost too full. There was no arresting him when he began his verbose and scandalous survey of the Spanish scene. He was as prolix as he was prolific, and three glutted weeks went by before he was firmly silenced. He remained proud and willing throughout his four-year stay at Camps 020 and 020R, where his nostalgic memories of Spain were turned to good account in many subsequent cases.

On the night of 7/8 April two young Norwegians, [MUTT and JEFF], were transferred in Scottish waters from a German seaplane to a rubber dinghy. They landed on the coast of Banffshire and surrendered at once to the local police.

Their arrival had not been unexpected and preparations had been made for their reception. They were rushed to Camp 020, rapidly interrogated, turned round and handed to B.1.a as double agents; their detention in the camp had lasted no more than 24 hours, and in that time their story, which was checked against ISOS material, was broadly established. They had been recruited and trained in Norway by characters who were already familiar and had been equipped with a radio transmitter, sabotage equipment, English and American money, two bicycles and other material.

TER BRAAK

J. Willem Ter BRAKK has no rightful place in this history of Camp 020, which knew of him only by report. His name is recorded here merely as that of one of the few candidates fully qualified for admission who never entered its gates.

Ter BRAAK, a parachute agent, had landed in England as long ago as November 1940. A suspicious Cambridge landlady had denounced him outright as "a spy". The information was not followed up. A local Food Office official might have detected him when he called there for a ration card with false documentation, but didn't. In some access of conscience or fear, Ter BRAAK finally decided during the month of April spectacularly to announce his presence and end his espionage venture by shooting himself in a Cambridge air-raid shelter.

M/V "TAANEVIK"

A new Norwegian spying expedition organised by the Germans fetched up at Wick, in Scotland, in the M/V "TAANEVIK" during the month of April. The skipper, Henry TORGERSEN, naïvely explained to the local authorities that he had brought a cargo of sardines which it was intended to convert by sale into whisky, coffee, tea and other beverages needed in Norway, wither they proposed to return. The story was too simple and good to be wholly true. TORGERSEN, with his companions, Bjarne HANSEN, Hans HANSEN, and Johan STRANDMOEN were promptly consigned to Camp 020.

There it was soon established that all four men had been in the pay of the Germans for some time. They had been sent out to Scotland on the present trip by the indefatigable but ineffectual "Karl ANDERSEN", whose shadow had already made its debut in the cases of Vera ERICHSEN and EDVARDSEN, among others.

TORGERSEN and Hans HANSEN were found to be sinners only to a minor and shabby degree: they had received employment simply as sailors. Bjarne HANSEN, on the other hand, had an unsavoury history. He had known "ANDERSEN" since 1920: together they had been engaged for years in smuggling spirits in Norwegian waters. In July 1940 "ANDERSEN", now a spymaster, had engaged him to sail the famous "BOREAS" to the Shetlands to obtain intelligence about Allied shipping and convoys. The unprincipled HANSEN coasted round for a few days, falsely reported that he had been to the Shetlands, and with dishonour to his fellow thief, pocketed the equivalent of £60 for the service.

STRANDMOEN, too, had come into "ANDERSEN'S" sphere and had been sent by him in 1940 to Brest as a member of the crew of a small vessel destined to run agents to the British coast. He had, in fact, been in the fishing smack which landed PONS and Van den KIEBOOM off Deal. He was much impressed and very frightened when his interrogators produced photographs of the two men and pointed ominously to a cutting in the "Obituary File" reporting the execution of Van den KIEBOOM.

STRANDMOEN and Bjarne HANSEN had been instructed, certainly, to sell the cargo of sardines and buy whisky and tea, with which they were to return to Norway. But they had an espionage mission, too: they were to report fully on their return anything of interest which they might have observed or learned during their British sojourn.

In outline the case would appear to have been easily disposed of; the relative report, when issued, ran only to four and a half pages. But as was to occur in many future cases, this gave no clue to the laborious processes by which the facts were finally established: the length of the report, the Commandant commented in submitting it to M I 5, "is in inverse ratio to the work involved on a troublesome case of no little complexity." And the "TAANEVIK" case, at that, was relatively unimportant.

Karel RICHTER

In the course of an interrogation of Josef JAKOBS on 29 April 1941, a description had been obtained of another agent who might be expected to arrive in England in the immediate future. Within the fortnight the man had made landfall in a field near London Colney. He was Karel RICHTER, a 29-year old Sudeten German. He had been dropped by parachute from a plane captained by GARTENFELD at 0315 hours on 12 May, after flying from Schipol, in Holland.

RICHTER buried his espionage baggage in such frenzied haste that he included with it his emergency ration of salami and brown bread. He went into immediate hiding; but three days of fearful cogitation on a empty stomach persuaded him that even if discretion were the better part of valour, food was the best part of well-being. He walked into London Colney and up to Police Constable Scott, who was parading the High Street on his lawful occasions. RICHTER complained feelingly but gutturally of sickness due to lack of food and drink; he begged urgently to be sent to hospital. PC Scott was not impressed into precipitate sympathy. He knew his drill. He told RICHTER that he had better come along with him, young man, and the agent found himself under arrest.

As soon as his identity had been clearly established and the news conveyed to M I 5, arrangements were made to receive him at Camp 020. He arrived there in reasonable good health and unreasonable frame of mind. He showed no anxiety to make a confession. He was quite convinced that the Germans would soon launch a successful invasion of Britain. He felt, and said, that soon he would be sitting on the right side of the interrogation table.

His obstinacy and disputaciousness were soon overcome, though not without trouble. The facts about himself revealed by JAKOBS were produced for his discomfort; and when JAKOBS, carefully groomed for his reluctant rôle, was brought into the room for confrontation, RICHTER slipped and began gradually to break.

But seventeen hours of interrogation were necessary before he would reveal the place where he had hidden his equipment. The Commandant himself took RICHTER, with a number of Camp officers and troops, to the point finally indicated by the agent. RICHTER led them to a hedge bordering the field in which he had landed: piece by piece the physical instruments of espionage, radio adaptor and all, were unearthed.

Only a few yards away from this scene of activity was a small picnic party. It included a very small girl who, in piping voice, enquired of Mummy what those soldiers might be doing over there. Mummy scarcely looked up: "Never you mind, dearie; you never know what the military are up to next." And the little girl never knew ....

RICHTER's story developed slowly. He was reluctant still fully to betray his masters, whose early vengeance he feared. But gradually the details were extracted from him.

He was a merchant seaman who had deserted a German ship at Hamburg in August 1939; he had no wish to face the wartime perils of the deep. He visited his home in the Sudetenland, took farewell of his family, and fled to Sweden, en route to the US, where he hoped to settle. But his papers were not in order; the Swedes deported him to Germany; the Gestapo seized him as a deserter, and he was thrown into a concentration camp.

His liberation followed a talent-spotting visit by Hauptmann BOECKEL, of Ast Hamburg, who sold him his freedom against an undertaking to work dangerously on behalf of Germany. BOECKEL had him trained in air intelligence and radio transmission, then dropped him as inept for his own particular purposes. He was taken over by Hauptmann PRAETORIUS, the I/Wi (Economics) expert, and received further training both in Hamburg and at The Hague. He was to have been despatched to England in January 1941, by sea, but the conditions in the Channel at this time of year were thought to be adverse. On 9 May a second attempt was made to land him in the UK: RICHTER was placed in a motor-launch at Delfzijl and taken to within a few miles of the English coast before the crew decided that the ground-swell would not allow of a safe landing. Three days later he was successfully introduced into England by GARTENFELD's plane.

Perhaps the most interesting feature in the case of RICHTER was his mission. At first he insisted that he was merely to deliver £400 - out of the £550 and $1400 in his possession - and a quartz crystal for the control of radio frequency to another German agent whom he was to meet at the Regent Palace Hotel in London. When he had carried out these instructions, he was to concentrate on meteorological reports, details of the electrical grid system in England, and general Intelligence, including controls on roads and at railway stations.(+)

Later RICHTER confessed that the most important point in his mission was to check the reliability of the agent whom he was to contact at the Regent Palace Hotel. This man proved to be none other than […] PRAETORIUS had told him that recent messages from [TATE] had given rise to the suspicion that the agent was either under control or had been substituted by another man. […], said PRAETORIUS during his briefing of RICHTER, "is our master pearl; if he is false, then the whole string is false."

RICHTER was apparently to use the quartz crystal himself on [TATE's] transmitter, if the reliability of the latter were undoubted. If necessary, he could also use the adaptor which would enable him to transform any popular type of radio receiver into a transmitter, or even build his own set from components that might easily be purchased. But it had been impressed on him by his masters in Hamburg that he must make every effort to return to Germany to report in person at the first opportunity. To this end he was to obtain a boat or launch at some South Coast port, possibly with the assistance of other agents.

By the time that he had decided to reveal his complete mission, RICHTER was convinced that he would hang. He was not disappointed. He was executed in London in December 1941.

On 19 July 1941 a 35-year old Irishman, dropped out of the night sky over Eire under a parachute which had been specially selected for him by the diligent Hauptmann GARTENFELD. [BASKET] concealed his parachute and a suitcase containing a radio transmitter in a hedge and hitch-hiked into Dublin with a second suitcase containing his more personal belongings. He took a train from Dublin to Athlone and visited his brother Patrick to enquire into the division of their later father's estate. He returned to Dublin and took train for Belfast; on route he asked to be put in touch with the British military authorities in Northern Ireland; and on arrival in Belfast he repaired at once to the headquarters of the Royal Ulster Constabulary to report that he was a German agent with urgent and valuable information to impart to the competent British authorities.

By 22 July he had been well received at Camp 020. [BASKET] owned no loyalty to the British. He had been involved in an I.R.A. gun-running enterprise as the producer of forged frontier passes, and had served a nine-month sentence on discovery of his enterprise.

(+) BOECKEL has stated at CSDIC(WEA) that […] was suspect in Hamburg after he had reported that he had been stopped at a London railway station and asked to produce his identity documents. His claim to have satisfied the authorities concerned was not wholly convincing.

The Eireann Government had offered him a free pardon, a large sum of money, and free passage to the USA if he would disclose the exact nature of the contraband and other details of the gun-running scheme. [BASKET] the rebel, was true to his ideals: he refused to betray his associates and suffered his prison sentence without complaint.

He made it quite plain at the outset of his interrogations at Camp 020 that he had no love for the British Government; he made it equally plain that he had much less love for the Germans. He told his story frankly and fully without prompting and without fretting over the delay in his release and return to Ireland.

[BASKET] had worked in England for some time after completion of his Irish sentence. In May 1940 he had moved to Jersey for the potato-lifting season. He was caught the by the German invasion. In about November he made a determined bid to sail alone to England in a 22-ft motorboat, but the heavy south-westerly gale which was raging swamped the boat, flooded it engine and carried it ashore on a beach of the Contentin peninsula.

[BASKET] was found by a group of German soldiers and sent on for interrogation at Carteret. Four days later he was seen by two German officers from Paris who proposed that he go back to Eire, with their assistance, to act as a German agent, working against the hated British in the North. [BASKET] agreed with alacrity: there was nothing that he wanted more than to return to his native land.

He was driven to Paris and lodged in an apartment to which came a stream of German I.S. instructors in radio, meteorology, secret writing. He was a popular recruit and pupil; he met many Abwehr officers and NCOs from the notorious Hotel Lutetia and enjoyed the confidence of them all. He studied the men, their methods and their haunts with close attention; he had decided already that he would betray them all, with their bags of tricks, to the British.

His Irish contrariness got him into trouble only once in Paris. He was at Freddy's Bar at the Normandy Hotel one night and was overheard by the German soldiery speaking English. Some inspired officer decided he must be an English spy, and cried "Engländer". Another pointed a gun at him. The insult and the menace were too much for [BASKET]. He slapped them down, and himself into gaol. His friends of the Lutetia secured his release on the following day.

[BASKET] received further training at The Hague and also made a two-day visit to Brussels with one of his would-be masters. He learned more about the German Secret Service and its personnel and improved his radio transmission.

In January 1941 he was ready to be planted in Eire. GARTENFELD allowed him to chose his own preferred place of landing, and he opted for the Curragh. The plane left Schipol airport in the direction of Athlone, but after two and a half hours' flight, when they should have been nearing the Irish coast, the heating system broke down. They were flying at an altitude of some 30,000 feet at the time, and GARTENFELD decided that weather conditions militated against a safe landing; he ordered the pilot to turn back. By the time they had landed again at Schipol everyone save the pilot, who was wearing an electrically heated suit, had suffered severe frostbite.

The Luftwaffe personnel was despatched to military hospitals at The Hague and to a hospital at Suresnes, where he remained for three months. "WERNER", one of his most assiduous sponsors, called on him daily with expressions of German sympathy and fond hopes for the future.

[BASKET] left hospital in May and received fresh training and instruction both in Paris and at The Hague; in both places he learned much that would be of value to the British, for he was an exceptionally observant and intelligent type. By July he had been voted fit and ready to land in Eire. His despatch on this occasion suffered no hitch. It might have been more profitable to the Germans if it had, for [BASKET] as a source of accurate information on the G.S.S., was indeed heaven-sent to the British. The volume of Intelligence which he yielded to them in defiance of his narrower nationalism was surpassed only by its quality. And having spoken, he left Ham Common with a clear conscience, probably to continue in his home land the legitimate struggle against the English oppressor.

Edward EJSYMONT

A complex and unsavoury case presented itself at Camp 020 in July 1941 with the arrival of a Polish Air Force cadet, Edward EJSYMONT, who had made a voluntary statement to OC Troops in HMT "SCYTHIA", when bound from Gibraltar to the UK, to the effect that he had been recruited in Spain as a German agent. EJSYMONT, on the face of things, appeared to have given a full account of his dealings with the Germans. Complications arose when Polish Intelligence links operating in Lisbon, where EJSYMONT had spent some time en route to Gibraltar, reported that their "special sources" had obtained information about him which suggested that he was withholding information.

The sources, on enquiry, turned out to be special indeed: three shifty Polish Jews who had befriended and shadowed EJSYMONT at the behest of the chief of the Evacuation Department of the Polish Legation in Lisbon. These three extraordinary agents, Jan MUHLSTEIN, Edward BALSAM and Jakob SUKIENNIK, had compiled a formidable list of charges against EJSYMONT, some of them allegedly drawn out of his own mouth.

EJYSMONT himself, under detailed interrogation, expanded his earlier statements and made new admissions, few of which might have been omitted previously with any studied sinister design. But on most of the accusations made by the unholy trio, he stood his ground with the determination born of innocence. MUHLSTEIN, BALSAM and SUKIENNIK, summoned to the UK for closer investigation of their wild charges, stood their ground with equal determination, but in their case it appeared quite clearly to have been born of greed and malice.

In his analysis of the case the Commandant stated his views in the following terms:-

"EJYSMONT had admitted that he is a disreputable fellow...... Particular accusations against EJSYMONT have been discredited (by the officers in charge of the investigation)..... I am driven to the conclusion that monetary gain is the true motive, not only of the Polish informants, but also of the Polish authorities who, after all, have sponsored these rogues. And if anything is required to fortify my view, I might add that the Polish authorities were extremely anxious to handle EJSYMONT as a double-cross agent against the Germans. In this way BALSAM and his confederates would establish for themselves a remunerative employment at rates which would be enhanced by time; and the Polish authorities, in turn, would have the benefit of grants from the British Government and establish themselves as an appendage to the British Secret Service....."

It was not the first or the last time that the investigation of a case at Camp 020 revealed the deficiencies of Allied Intelligence Services. A note of warning was struck; the advance which the Polish authorities might make in the future should be met with grave misgivings. For if they had been taken in by those patent rogues, BALSAM & Co, their Intelligence Service was worth just nothing at all; and if they were aware of the nefarious activities of their informants, then their conduct was contemptible in the extreme.

EJYSMONT was adjudged a potential source of danger to the security of the country in time of war; he remained in detention. He had an importunate father, a Colonel in the Polish Army in Britain, whose protestations and parcels of sweetmeats to his feckless son did not unduly embarrass the Home Secretary and his keepers respectively.

The Commandant's recommendation that BALSAM and SUKIENNIK share the fate of their victim was agreed; both were incarcerated at

Camps 020 and 020R, where the name BALSAM itself became a term of reproach applicable to any especially repulsive type.

Helmik WALLEM

On 8 July 1941 there arrived at Lerwick three Norwegians who had sailed from Bergen some days before in a small motor-vessel, the "HERNIE", from which they had been transferred that same morning to a loyal Norwegian patrol boat based on a Scottish port. They were Helmik WALLEM, Ingard Westerlid NILSEN and George LUNDE; they claimed to be refugees from Nazi oppression who wished to serve with the Norwegian Forces in the UK.

They were subjected to the routine examination at the London Reception Centre and satisfied their interrogators as to their bona fides. NILSEN and LUNDE were allowed to join the Norwegian forces; WALLEM was signed on a coastal steamer as mate and wireless operator.

Some weeks later it was discovered, with considerable alarm, that the "HERNIE" and the name "NILSEN" appeared in an ISOS message referring to a German espionage mission. The three men were swiftly rounded up and despatched to Camp 020 for proper investigation.

All three were left to stew overnight in their cells, a practice developed out of experience of the working of guilty men's consciences. Morning brought its reward. WALLEM had written a statement during the night indicating that he wished to make a confession. He was at once summoned for interrogation, and broke completely.

He was a seaman who had begun a radio course at Bergen Radio School in 1939; it had been interrupted by the German invasion of Norway and he had been unable to resume it until February 1941. Shortly afterwards he had come into contact with one "LUND", a member of the German Secret Service, after enquiring of a Norwegian friend if there might be any prospects of employment by the Germans on completion of his radio course.

"LUND", without ado, invited WALLEM to undertake a journey to England. It was not, he explained, a question of spying in that country. From past experience the Germans had learned that almost any supposed loyal Norwegian with radio experience who arrived in the UK at this time would be invited by the Allied Intelligence Services to return to Norway as an agent under Allied control. All that was required of WALLEM was that he accept any such proposition, return to Norway and hand over his transmitter and code to the Germans. The reward for such a service would be generous: Kr 10,000 in cash and the assurance of a promising future.

WALLEM accepted the proposition and an advance of Kr 100, for which he signed a receipt in his spy name, "Olaf NILSEN".

It was at once curious and confusing that the cover-name
chosen should have coincided with the real surname of one of the
genuine refugees subsequently persuaded to join in the flight from
Norway as cover for the sinister design. Ingard NILSEN was, in fact,
found completely innocent of any complicity in the plot; LUNDE, too,
was cleared; and both men were released when investigation of the
case was complete.

WALLEM, on the other had, remained in detention, despite
protestation that he had never intended to carry out his mission.
The claim appeared to have some support in fact. The Germans had
been right about the tendency of the Allied IS section concerned
gaily to recruit, train and despatch to Norway practically every
Norwegian with radio qualifications arriving in England. WALLEM, on
release from the London Reception Centre, had visited Norway House
in London. He had been asked whether he would be willing to return
to Norway, to work there as an agent. He had replied non-comittally,
and did not again broach the subject. His passivity in that respect
was the only creditable feature in a sordid story.

Alphonse Louis Eugène TIMMERMAN

In June 1940 a Belgian seaman, Alphonse Louis Eugène TIMMERMAN, was
rescued by a Spanish fishing boat when his ship, the "VILLE DE
NAMUR", was torpedoed by a German U-boat some 120 miles from the
coast of France. It would have saved time and trouble if he had been
allowed to stay in the water: two years later he was to die as a
German spy on the gallows erected for his special benefit in an
English prison yard

The espionage history of TIMMERMAN began only some months
after his return to Belgium following his rescue. It had no
highlights: his recruitment and training in Antwerp and his
mission - against Great Britain - were remarkably unimaginative.
The only new feature was evidence, obtained from him at Camp 020, of
Spanish officials' conscious complicity in German espionage
activities.

His training completed, TIMMERMAN was driven to the Spanish
frontier via France and escorted across by a Spaniard who also made
arrangements for him to be detained at the Nanclares Concentration
Camp for three days. Time being very relative in Spain, TIMMERMAN's
guide had little difficulty in obtaining from official sources a
certificate to the effect that TIMMERMAN had been held at Nanclares
for three months. This document was calculated to deceive the
sympathetic British into welcoming TIMMERMAN to their country with
open arms.

TIMMERMAN himself convinced a British Consul in Southern

Spain of his perfervid belief in the Allied cause: on the same day
he was signed on a British ship in Seville as a steward. One of his
fellow stewards, a knowledgeable man, didn't like his story of
facile escape from Belgium and monstrous sufferings in Spain: in his
experience, no prisoner of the France régime had ever left a
concentration camp in possession of anything, let alone two
excellent suitcases, tolerable Continental clothing and £100 in
brand new English notes. But he held his uneasy peace of mind and
his suspicions until later enquires showed them to have been
justified. On the ship's arrival in Glasgow, TIMMERMAN was subjected
to routine examination by FSP and sent to London for further
investigation.

The English steward's views on TIMMERMAN had only an
academic interest by the time that he was called upon to air them.
TIMMERMAN had graduated to Ham after failing to satisfy
interrogators at another establishment; and at Camp 020 he had
broken fully after uneven conflict.

Because he had failed to make any admission at his first
opportunity on landing in the UK, and because he was of no earthly
use as a source of counter-intelligence, TIMMERMAN was prosecuted on
the completion of his case and hanged in July 1942.

Eigil Dag ROBR

Eigil Dag ROBR, a despicable Norwegian traitor who had operated in
Sweden as well as in his own country, was spirited into England in
November 1941 by the subtle machinations of the British Military
Attache in Stockholm, who had some evidence of the man's black
record from a variety of sources.

His known and suspected background brought him automatically
to Camp 020. He broke completely only after three months of
unrelenting pressure. In its entirety his history proved to be even
more noisome than had been imagined.

The sordid story is best summed up in a contemporary
commentary by the Commandant:-

"Over a period of two years many evil personalities, both
traitors and spies, have been admitted to this
establishment, but I doubt whether there has been a
character more vile than that of Eigil Dag ROBR. His record
is almost beyond belief, for he has confessed to us the
names of nineteen fellow Norwegians whom he has betrayed to
the Germans for Kr 700 or 35/- per head. The total number of
betrayals may be even greater; but having regard to pressure
of time, the fact that we have put the halter nineteen times
round the neck of this Quisling, and the fact that the

Gestapo background of this case has been cleared to our Intelligence satisfaction, we deem it wise to call a halt to this remarkable enquiry.

"ROBR, during investigation, relied upon every art and device we have learned to expect from those who have truck with the Gestapo over a period of time. In the ultimate, after an enquiry which might well be described as a war of attrition, ROBR broke. For a time he was in terror of consequence; but with the resilience of the true guttersnipe, he regained his poise and as quickly turned to duress as an alternative defence.

"Soon the idea became attractive; his attitude changed from the aggressive to that of the martyr. He would have us believe that he is the unfortunate product of Nazi blackmail, that foundry of the modern Judas; in pursuance thereof he has asked even for those privileges accorded to the more venial offenders of this prison. The point is of importance, as he is play-acting and may well be word perfect at his trial.

"Viewed dispassionately and with the utmost charity, the betrayal under duress of one man or even two men may with bitterness be understood. But can there ever be extenuation for half a dozen, a dozen, or even nineteen betrayals over a period of two months, when pressure has lessened and blood had time to cool? Escape, imprisonment or even suicide were possible alternatives; but if ROBR thought otherwise, as in fact was the case, surely the full penalty should be exacted for treachery to follow nationals, strangers, acquaintances and school friends alike? And lastly, for what my observation over a period of four months is worth to the Norwegian authorities, I have to report that, while terror of consequence has occasionally been present, remorse has always been absent."

But Norwegian justice could not be meted out to ROBR in the UK. He remained in Britain safekeeping at Camps 020 and 020R until their dissolution in 1945, when his live body was delivered to the Norwegians for proper disposal.

Leopold HIRSCH/Oscar GILINSKY

There followed the HIRSCH/GILINSKY combination, as unpretty a brace of rogues as ever disported themselves in the darker chambers of high finance and commercial swindle. Leopold HIRSCH was a Parisian banker of Austrian origin who had engaged in politico-financial intrigues on a high if not disinterested international level: from arms running into Republican Spain to the economic bleeding of independent Austria; from the loan of silver to CHIANG-KAI-SHEK to abetment of Serge RUBENSTEIN's Chosen swindle. He had been imprisoned by the French for corrupting French newspapers, probably his most effortless accomplishment. He was freed by the invading Germans and made much profit out of his undeniable gratitude to them, which found expression in monstrous commission on his noisome services.

Oscar GILINSKY was HIRSCH's natural partner: a Jew, he came of a Russian family that had founded its considerable fortunes on the monopoly of oil sales for the ikon-lamps of the Greek-Orthodox peoples; he sold arms with which Spaniards on two political sides, and the futile Italian interventionists, might kill each other without discrimination or repercussion on the GILINSKY business charts. He sold telegraph poles to England and derived a steady annual income of £20,000 out of the single enterprise of persuading other acute business men to discount Soviet bills backed by loot. In the last stages of his interrupted career he had found a new source of material credit in diverting the sweated earnings of French prisoners of war in Germany into his own pockets by the sale to them of French Red Cross property. His own conscience had not worried him on this score, but he had been compelled to soothe a German official's with a sizeable bribe.

The sphere of activity of these two enemies of society was limited by the turn of the war. They decided to move to America, the land of the free. They found that they had to pay a high price. The Germans extorted from them a large sum of money, which hurt, and a promise to engage in espionage against the United States, which didn't.

They were arrested on the way out, in Trinidad. Under interrogation there they proved verbose but secretive. They were transferred to England and Camp 020, where their verbosity continued but their reticences ceased.

After they had made their respective reluctant admissions they lived in constant expectation of release to continue their nefarious activities. More than anything they rued the loss of time. which in terms of money, in their most modest estimate, spelt a Croesian era. For Camps 020 and 020R saved society of their depredations for almost four years.

Lest it be thought that no one could have loved HIRSCH, it should be recorded that he brought with him to England on his enforced visit a wife named Olly who continued to dote upon him in writing over the years. GILINSKY, in his unsurprising loneliness, was probably the happier of the two.

Thorleif SOLEM & Sigurd Edvard ALSETH

A new "Karl ANDERSEN" mission from Norway to the British Isles to get whisky and Intelligence came to light only nine months after two of the agents concerned, Thorleif SOLEM and Sigurd Edvard ALSETH, had been given the freedom of the country by one of the screening establishments. There had been a third agent with them, but he had preferred to return to Norway after a short visit.

SOLEM and ALSETH had arrived in the Shetland Islands in March 1941 in a small motor-vessel skippered by a certain Ingvald JOHANSEN, who was himself in the pay of the Germans. SOLEM and ALSETH admitted to their whisky mission, but shyly omitted to mention that it had any connection with any Germans in Norway. JOHANSEN, who was a Norwegian seaman, claimed, with pretty conceit, to be an honest and simple Norwegian seaman.

SOLEM and ALSETH were examined at the London Reception Centre and released for service with the Norwegian Forces. They opted for the Army and joined it together. After only a fortnight's service, SOLEM was discharged on medical grounds; ALSETH helped him celebrate the event by going Absent without Leave with him to London, where they bought much whisky and drank it.

In early May SOLEM was despatched by a Norwegian Intelligence Officer on some unimportant mission to Norway in the company of five others; he was good enough to return to the UK. In June he was arrested in Dover for entering a protected area without permission and was sentenced to two days' imprisonment. On release he was referred to the Norwegian Consulate General in London, which allowed him to join a Norwegian ship.

In the same month a Norwegian refugee, Sverre GISVOLD, arrived in the UK and reported that he had recently been imprisoned by the Germans as a result of denunciation by Thorleif SOLEM, who had claimed to be his best friend. A few days later SOLEM was arrested in Bristol - for refusing to work on his ship! He was handed to the Norwegian authorities. The Norwegians took the opportunity to interrogate SOLEM and GISVOLD together. They took no action against SOLEM on GISVOLD's charge of betrayal to the enemy; they released both men for service with the forces, and SOLEM joined the Norwegian Navy.

In December there was excitement when an ISOS intercept betrayed SOLEM, ALSETH and JOHANSEN for what they were: recruits of the German Secret Service. The first two were soon rounded up and taken to Camp 020. JOHANSEN had gone home.

The investigation of the case was long and difficult; it was carried out concurrently with other Norwegian cases. Pains were not spared, and in addition to numerous stormy interrogations of SOLEM and ALSETH, GISVOLD was seen and confirmed his accusation against SOLEM. The latter broke later and admitted also to having betrayed arms caches to the Germans even before the capitulation of Norway. He was an evil character with a dangerous subversive record. SOLEM and ALSETH, it was found, stood in relation as principal to accessory; the former active, the latter ineffective. But no distinction was made in their disposal: both remained at Camps 020 and 020R until the end.

Fernando CASABAYO

In January 1942 a Lance Corporal of the Pioneer Corps walked into the Spanish Embassy in London and very nearly succeeded in precipitating a first-class political crisis. He was a Spaniard, Fernando CASABAYO, who had fought against Franco in Spain and against the Germans at Narvik as a French Foreign Legionary before joining a special Spanish section of the Pioneer Corps in England.

CASABAYO had lost yet another battle for freedom in August 1941. His English girl-friend, a Plymouth bus conductress with a delicate sense of timing, persuaded him to marry her on the day before the birth of their daughter. This early acquisition of a complete family was to drive him into rashness and land him in trouble.

He felt that an Army allowance of 36/- a week was inadequate provision for a wife and child. Moreover, his recent Army courses had persuaded him that the special Spanish section to which he was attached was being trained for possible future operations against Spain. Much as he disliked Franco, he felt that this antipathy was exclusively an affair between Spaniards.

He decided to desert, seek a false identity and find work as a civilian: he would be getting better money and would not be called to fight against his compatriots. He tried to persuade the French authorities in London that he was a survivor of the Narvik expedition by name of Basilio BELTRAN. BELTRAN had died at Narvik, and CASABAYO had obtained his personal documents from a colleague. The French were not inclined to accept CASABAYO's suggestion that they provide him with an official identity document or discharge papers in the name of BELTRAN; nor was he moved to accept their invitation to join the Free French Forces.

In a fit of pique, CASABAYO ran off to the Spanish Embassy and told an official there that he was Basilio BELTRAN and that he was anxious to go home to Spain. He was told to come back later. On his second visit he revealed his true identity and invited sympathy by offering to disclose information about the Special Pioneer Company and its preparation for operations against Spain. Official interest was instantly aroused: a member of the Embassy staff, BRUGADA, obtained the details from CASABAYO. They included a description of a highly secret British explosive, "808", of which CASABAYO offered to obtain samples.

For his treachery CASABAYO received altogether £19, a forged identity document in the name of BELTRAN and promise of early repatriation. Only the money profited him. A source in the Spanish Embassy itself betrayed his actions to M I 5, but identified him merely as a Catalan serving in the Pioneer Corps.

CASABAYO, in the meantime, had re-established contact with his wife. He discussed his position with her; they decided that he must surrender to the police.

His identity with the wanted Catalan was soon established; a few days later he arrived at Camp 020. He proved more stubborn than repentant, and it was only after long hours of intensive interrogation that he made full admission of his sins, the gravity of which he never appeared fully to appreciate.

The fragile political situation between Britain and Spain did not allow of prosecution. The affair, moreover, had to be dissembled. CASABAYO remained at Camp 020 until the late summer of 1945; his wife received her weekly Army allowance and was led fondly to imagine that her husband was engaged in highly secret operations. She was allowed occasionally to correspond with him via a military address. In one such letter she communicated the news of the birth of a second child. It caused some alarm and despondency in her husband. Her sense of timing had become indelicate. More than the accepted number of months had passed since she and CASABAYO had been in propinquity.

Florent Sylvestre STEINER

Following information given at Camp 020 by Jack VERLINDEN (qv), enquiries began as to the whereabouts in England of another Belgian seaman, Florent Sylvestre STEINER, whom he had denounced as yet another HOFFMAN agent from Lisbon with a mission in the UK. STEINER had arrived in England in June 1941, and it was not until February 1942 that he was found in Liverpool, working at a garage owned by his brother. He was promptly directed to Camp 020 under escort.

STEINER had been in contact in Lisbon not only with VERLINDEN, but with at least two other Camp 020 colleagues, […] and LAUREYSSENS. His espionage background was very similar, but he appeared to have been in innocent contact with the Germans there, as a ready money-lender, for some considerable time. His preparation for espionage and his mission were cursory and inconsiderable, respectively.

But the investigation of his case was attended by much
trouble to himself and to his interrogating officers. He denied
knowledge of two cover addresses that had been found in his
possession close by some secret writing materials; he refuted any
suggestion that he had been given a mission in the UK.

After a long period of stubborn defiance, he finally broke.
He made a full confession which included directions as to his
disposal, in the property which remained at Liverpool, of further
secret writing materials.

There was no admission, nor indeed evidence, that he had
sent any report or communication to his masters in Lisbon. But his
possession of the requisite materials and his failure to disclose
his contact with and despatch by the Germans necessarily overrode
all his protestations that he had never intended to work on their
behalf. He was held at Camps 020 and 020R to the end, and was,
indeed, fortunate to escape prosecution under the Treachery Act.

Luis CALVO Andaluz

The pattern of espionage disclosed so far at Ham suggested that
Franco's Spain was more sinned against than sinning. That complacent
view was soon to be rudely shaken. The chosen instrument of
revelation was one Luis CALVO Andaluz, a leading Spanish journalist
who had represented important Spanish and Argentine newspapers in
London since 1932 and had acted for a time as Spanish Press Attaché.

M I 5 had been aware for some time past that insolent use
was being made by the Spanish Government of its Embassy in London to
provide cover for official spies working on behalf of Germany. In
September 1940 an ostentatious young man rejoicing in the name of
PIERNAVIEJA Del Pozo had arrived in England, ostensibly as a Press
correspondent in the employ of the Institute of Political Studies of
Madrid, an official organisation. Shortly after his arrival, he
contacted a Welsh Nationalist named [G.W.] who, under the direction
of M I 5, had allowed himself to be recruited as an agent by the
Germans in Belgium in 1939. PIERNAVIEJA gave [G.W.] a password
agreed with the Germans, handed him a sum of money to finance his
"subversive activities" and instructed him to obtain certain
information of use to "their common masters".

In January 1941 another Spaniard, a sottish parvenu of an
ex-bullfighter who had risen to dizzy political eminence under
Franco, arrived in London as "Press Attaché" at the Spanish Embassy.
He was ALCAZAR DE VELASCO, a servant of the Japanese as well as of
the German Secret Service acting under the orders of the Spanish
Foreign Minister himself, SERRANO SUÑER.

[G.W.] an adroit double agent, soon established that

PIERNAVIEJA's espionage activities were supervised and directed by ALCAZAR, with ultimate control vested in the Germans. PIERNAVIEJA was allowed to return to Spain in February 1941, since his detention would have compromised [G.W.] at this stage in their relations. ALCAZAR, whose boorishness had been remarked even by London Society, returned in the same month to Madrid. Both were expected to return to England in due course.

PIERNAVIEJA, who had given [G.W.] instructions to gather additional Intelligence in his absence, was to have returned to England in a matter of weeks. When it became evident that he would not do so, [G.W.] was instructed by M I 5 to seek a fresh contact at the Spanish Embassy who would serve as a link with PIERNAVIEJA in Spain, at least pending the return of ALCAZAR. The Embassy porter casually sealed the wartime fate of CALVO, hitherto unsuspected - and quite possibly innocent - of any subversive activity, by naming him as "the man to see"; CALVO, through his relations with the Press Section, was fully acquainted with PIERNAVIEJA, if not with his more sinister business.

[G.W.] was now acting not only as a double agent, but as an agent provocateur. He cultivated CALVO's curiosity in PIERNAVIEJA by retailing a few intriguing features of his true activities; and he promoted CALVO's intervention, as interpreter and later as go-between, in the relations which he now opened with ALCAZAR.

CALVO had taken the bait. Microphone cover of his London flat was at once instituted. It yielded a few of the man's contacts and the many obscenities which CALVO and his Russian mistress indulged; it lost M I 5 the services of one or two virtuous girl operators of the special devices.

ALCAZAR had returned to Spain in September 1941, and CALVO continued to act as a cut-out between the Spaniard and [G.W.]. From ALCAZAR he passed Intelligence and sabotage instructions and money to [...], from [...] he passed Intelligence and documents, fed to the double agent by M I 5, to ALCAZAR via the Spanish diplomatic bag.

CALVO had been pitchforked deeply into espionage. His arrest was contemplated in October 1941. The manner of his induction into the enemy service may suggest a certain injustice in such a course. But CALVO, as has been pointed out, was the chosen instrument of revelation and disruption of Spanish-German subversive activities against England. His arrest would bring to book a potential source of rich information on the organisation and means of communication of the Spanish group in England engaged in espionage on behalf of Germany; it would serve as a salutary warning to other Spaniards engaged in or contemplating such activities; and it would shake the distinctly unneutral Spanish Government.

CALVO was not arrested in October 1941. He was allowed to

continue his clandestine relations with [...] and ALCAZAR until, in January 1942, he left for Madrid.

He never admitted it, but the visit obeyed a summons from ALCAZAR. To the last he maintained that the Spanish censor's consistent slashing of his copy from London called for personal representations; moreover, he was required to give evidence in Madrid in the case of one LOJENDIO, a former member of the Embassy staff in London who had been ordered by the Spanish General Staff to collect Intelligence in England on general matters and on the conduct of Spanish Republicans in exile. (LOJENDIO had reacted against his employment as an informant when he began to suspect that the material he provided was being passed to the Germans. His chiefs thereupon recalled him to Spain and charged him with improper relations with the British Secret Service and the Basque Nationalist Movement, participation in a conspiracy to kill PIERNAVIEJA, and of undiplomatic contraction of debts).

The true reason for CALVO's recall was the intention to recruit him as a German spy in his own right for return to England. At the instance of ALCAZAR, he had an interview with SERRANO SUÑER, who put the proposition to him and spoke of England as a real enemy.

CALVO offered no resistance. He was put by ALCAZAR into direct touch with two German spymasters in Madrid. They gave him a mission in England, provided him with secret writing formulae and spoke of a radio transmitter already at the Spanish Embassy in London which awaited only the recruitment of a suitable operator. An espionage questionnaire, instructions for operation of the radio set, a coding system, cover addresses, secret writing material for his own use, together with money and fresh instructions for [...] whom he would continue to service, would be forwarded to CALVO, on his return to England, through the Spanish diplomatic bag. The radio would be put at his disposal, or at [...], by another member of the Embassy staff, VILLAVERDE, in whose safe keeping it was. A subsequent note from ALCAZAR, who was now engaged in furious flirtation with the Japanese, advised CALVO to do nothing about the radio transmitter, but gave tacit encouragement to his other plans.

The Germans were good enough during this time to provide M I 5, however unconsciously, with confirmation of CALVO's recruitment and return en mission the England. ISOS intercepts betrayed their high hopes of his imminent activity on their behalf.

M I 5 disposed that the illusory nature of their confidence in CALVO should be heavily underlined. Arrangements were made to arrest him immediately on landing in the UK on his return. CALVO was detained as he left the Lisbon plane at Bristol airport on the evening of 12 February 1942; the night had not passed before he found himself in Camp 020.

The political implications of the case called for an immediate confession which would meet the inevitable cynical protest of the Spanish Foreign Office. The onus laid on the Commandant was not light. Much was already known about CALVO; but the sources were all too highly privileged to be imperilled in the slightest degree. CALVO was a man of more than ordinary intelligence.

The circumstances demanded a shattering broadside on a wide arc at the first encounter. CALVO got it. Its weight overwhelmed him; whatever ideas he may have nurtured of meeting the challenge went by the board. He surrendered. He hastened to write and sign a confession that damned him irretrievably. It served to dry up the simulated spleen of the Spanish authorities; and it served as a sound basis for the fuller investigation which followed.

The case was pursued in detail over weeks and months. CALVO told considerably more than was known already, but rather less than had been expected. His personal story, though it was at variance in a few points of detail with [...] account of their relations, was satisfactorily established; but the additional intelligence in his knowledge proved both limited and vague.

CALVO, an extremely sensitive man, had not taken well to prison life. Spiritually he was a broken man within a matter of days of his admission. He had tried to send out an appeal for help to the Spanish Embassy. The message was readily accepted for transmission by a soldier warder of gypsy origin who was not easily to be seduced from his wartime allegiance to the State. He delivered the message, not to the Spanish Embassy, but to the Orderly Officer. The opportunity was exploited: the warder was given a sight of the Embassy building and was otherwise primed to pass back a notional verbal reply. The stratagem was successful, but its dividends negligible until it was turned and capitalised by impressing on CALVO the suspicion that, at the Embassy, he was a forgotten man. CALVO talked more readily then.

A temporary relapse into hopeful thought won him a somewhat empty success over the security defences. In the wisdom of an outside State Department, a member of the Spanish Embassy was allowed access to CALVO at a convenient cover establishment. By some inexplicable lapse of discretion, CALVO had been given foreknowledge of the meeting. He had prepared a short note, successfully concealed it during search before leaving the camp, and deftly delivered it to his visitor during the handclasp which he was allowed to give him. The fact and the text of the communication were dutifully reported by a double agent within the Embassy itself. Subtle handling of the situation again allowed of its application, in CALVO's lasting disfavour.

A little grey ghost of a man by this time, CALVO was accorded the privilege of appointment as prison librarian. Over a period of time he qualified also to act as an assessor in the Courts of Logic which were instituted as a final recourse against the most stubborn Spanish prisoners who passed through Ham. His reaction to flattery was pathetic; but his proneness to compassion ultimately disqualified him as a logician. He was returned to his dog-eared books and his confused conscience.

Onofré GARCIA Tirador

The third Spaniard to qualify for interrogation and detention at Ham was a former Asturian gunman, Onofré GARCIA Tirador, who had fought bravely for the Republic in Spain, passively in France, and contrarily in England.

GARCIA had lived up to his matronymic. "Tirador" in Spanish is one who shoots; and in the Asturian miner's tradition of bloody finality in political argument, GARCIA had shot his bag of non-conformists with CNT ideology.

His faith appeared to have burned itself out shortly after his retreat in 1938 into uneasy exile in France, where he had combined membership of the Communist "MARSHALL Group" of refugee compatriots with treacherous flirtation with a Franco consul. The "MARSHALL Group", in all innocence, had nominated him as a valuable collaborator deserving evacuation to the UK on the fall of France. They did not know what M I 5 learned later from a secret source: that the Franco consul had reported to the Spanish Minister SERRANO SUÑER that "the pistolero Onofré GARCIA was now willing to work for the Franco Government by returning to Spain to organise anti-Franco elements and then betray them to the Government."

The "MARSHALL Group", […] was transferred to the UK, where it took up residence and activity pending further transfer to Mexico. On its disbandment, GARCIA opted to stay in England. He became, first a boilerman, the porter at the Cuban Legation in London.

He became homesick for Spain. He was no longer the impassioned partisan: his moral fibre was in decay; GARCIA was ready to bargain the lives of his friends for leave to return to Spain and a guarantee to live there unpunished and unmolested.

The promise of traitor service in the future, he realised, might not impress Franco's Government and its official representatives in London. GARCIA thought out a plan. He would report to a Free French officer that he was prepared to organise, from Portugal, an escape organisation operating to France through Spain. He would betray the scheme to the Spanish Embassy in London. Further to win their sympathy, he would betray also the plans recently prepared by members of the "MARSHALL Group" and Spaniards serving in the Free French and other Allied forces, for an eventual attack by the Free French on Spanish Guinea and Rio Benito. He persuaded himself that, as a patriot,it was his duty to report the scheme, with all its known and suspected authors and potential executors, to the Government which he now wished to call his.

GARCIA's compromise with his awful conscience directed him with some confidence to approach BRUGADA of the Spanish Embassy. BRUGADA was not only accessible, but ready to meet GARCIA on the latter's own ground. The Attaché called at the Cuban Legation to see the porter. GARCIA told him that he was worried by the current political unrest in Spain: he wished to offer his services for the elimination of anti-Franco elements. He wanted only a passport and a guarantee that retribution would not be visited upon himself for his misguided political past .... To this plea he added, "as of possible value", betrayal of his planned escape route for the French, the identity and number of Spanish Republicans serving in the Allied forces, and the existence of a plan to attack a Spanish colony.

BRUGADA was interested. He made copious notes. He promised to forward the information to Spain and the enquire at the same time whether GARCIA would be well received there.

GARCIA, the precursor of CASABAYO as a facile patriotic traitor, had no more traffic with BRUGADA before his reception at Camp 020. He was himself betrayed to M I 5.

He brought with him to the camp a lacerated mind and an ulcerated stomach. The evidence against him was complete. His story was known in detail. He was merely required to confirm it, and no great difficulty was experienced in obtaining the admission.

GARCIA's body was mended by the time that he was released from Ham on deportation to Spain in the summer of 1945; but the spirit of the pistolero had long since died within him.

Pieter Jan SCHIPPER

A case of some interest both from the counter-espionage and the operational points of view was that presented by Pieter Jan SCHIPPER, a Dutch seaman. He fetched up at a British port in March 1942 in the company of a Jew and a West Indian. The three men claimed to have boarded a steel launch at Ijmuiden and fled by sea from Nazi oppression.

It was quickly established at a primary screening centre that the Jew and the West Indian had indeed been oppressed and that they were genuine refugees. SCHIPPER, on the other hand, admitted to long service as a GIS agent; but he claimed to have had enough of the Germans and to be done with them, and to be a genuine refugee too, please.

It was a story that demanded immediate investigation. The main issue was whether SCHIPPER's final voyage from Holland to the UK obeyed a German Secret Service mission or represented a genuine escape. No less important was the extraction from the man of whatever Intelligence was in his possession. He was transferred to Camp 020 in early April. Within a fortnight an interim report had been issued that was rich indeed in information, for the man was not unintelligent, his powers of observation good, and his memory retentive and clear.

SCHIPPER's relations with the Germans, dating since December 1939, had been close; he had collaborated freely and willingly. His first task, set him by Kapitän-Leutnant Fritz STRAUCH - who was to acquire a certain disdainful notoriety at Ham, the journey's end of many of his recruits - was to plan the creation of a fishing fleet based on Holland which could be developed into a North Sea espionage network. STRAUCH's idea was bright: every trawler a mobile radio reporting centre; every boat paying for itself and its V-mann; and the whole Abwehr-blessed thing a source of much income for STRAUCH.

SCHIPPER'S espionage career was chequered. His fleet planning won him a certain respect from STRAUCH. He lost it, after much training in secret writing and radio, by botching at the outset a mission to Lisbon to seduce loyal Dutch merchant captains into German collaboration. He re-established confidence by negotiating the purchase by STRAUCH of Dutch trawlers at treasonable prices. He finally fell out of favour when he failed to produce valuable Intelligence for his masters. With Teutonic naïveté, STRAUCH told him that he had failed to prove himself a good Dutchman!

The Germans made a last effort to stimulate in the Dutchman some goodness to themselves. They had him arrested on a trumped up charge of betrayal of Abwehr secrets. They arranged his release, then hinted darkly that unless he collaborated more effectively in the future he might find himself in worse trouble.

SCHIPPER took the hint and the launch to England. There he remained until 1945, when he was returned to Holland. There were no longer any Germans in the homeland to face. There were only loyal Dutchmen, and their quarrel with SCHIPPER was more than just the Germans!

PELLETIER: Van ACKERE

Jean Charles PELLETIER, a young Frenchman trained in England and parachuted into France as an Allied agent, was a man of tremendous guilt. He had been captured by the Gestapo; under duress he had betrayed to them the names and locations of a score of other agents operating in France. The Germans acted upon that information, and looked for more. They impressed PELLETIER into their service: as an uneasy double agent and wandering Judas he played other Allied agents into German hands. They were still not satisfied: PELLETIER must get back to England, infiltrate Allied Intelligence radio services and report the names of new agents, new technical developments, new codes, new methods.

PELLETIER, still under duress, accepted. He reported the facts on arrival in England. At Ham the realisation of his enormities weighed gravely upon him. He sought alleviation by full confession and promise of good faith in any future employment which might be accorded him by the service he had so weakly betrayed. There are no second chances in espionage. PELLETIER was held in detention until he could be returned to liberated France.

Eugène Jean Constant Van ACKERE, a Belgian representative of the Frigidaire concern, was one of the bewildered innocents of Ham. He had arrived in England as a member of a small escape party which left Normandy in a fishing boat. Immediately on arrival he reported that he was the bearer of a message from two Allied agents to a named person at M I 6. M I 6 reacted with strong suspicion of attempted penetration by Van ACKERE, whom they guessed to be a German agent. In proper perspective, this mistrust of the Belgian had the flimsiest foundation: the name of the contact which he had been given was indeed that of an M I 6 official; but he worked in quite a different department from that with which the two Allied agents must be concerned. The flakes of suspicion developed into a snowball as unsuccessful effort was made to identify the Allied agents in question.

Van ACKERE paid a heavy price for the heresies of his chance acquaintances across the Channel and the not unnatural doubts of their London principals. For five whole months he was subjected to the most unrelenting pressure of investigation at Ham. His case officer, after prodigious effort, became convinced of Van ACKERE's innocence and reported to that effect. There was some conflict of opinion before the man was released. Many months later the accuracy of his story was established beyond any lingering doubt: the defaulting agents had been traced and admitted the innocent error of their commission .... It is improbable that Van ACKERE would have accepted their puzzled apology.

Sigurjon JONSSON/Jens PALSSON

Something outlandish suggests itself in the vision of a three-masted Icelandic schooner arriving at Vigo in wartime with a cargo of cod roe and leaving again with a full load of oranges. Strange things had happened in the between times. The skipper, Sigurjon JONSSON,

and the radio operator, Jens PALSSON, had been suborned by local
German Intelligence representatives into acceptance of a regular
weather-reporting mission. Icelanders are not notoriously
disputatious people, and when the Germans threatened to sink the
schooner in Spanish waters unless the skipper undertook service on
their behalf, there was no argument. JONSSON shipped the
responsibility and PALSSON the radio transmitter furnished by their
new friends of convenience.

During the long journey home to Reykjavik, JONSSON read the
weather and PALSSON communicated his findings on at least eight
occasions. As their next trip was to England, both men thought it
politic to leave the German radio behind; British contraband control
officers might take a jaundiced view of it. JONSSON decided to leave
it in the care of his brother-in-law, Marel MAGNUSSON, a truck
driver. It was dismantled, placed in two kitbags and left under the
stairs of MAGNUSSON's house. PALSSON, in the meantime, deposited his
espionage code with an old school friend, Hallgrimur DALBERG,
through his own fiancée. Neither MAGNUSSON nor DALBERG, had any clue
as to the nature of the property they were to hold for the two men.

JONSSON and PALSSON left Reykjavik for England in the good
ship "ARCTIC". They made a call en route at the Westmann Islands.
They were awaited there, for their masters had unwittingly betrayed
them in a radio intercept.

So JONSSON, PALSSON, MAGNUSSON and DALBERG came to exotic
Ham Common in the Spring of 1942. JONSSON, a dissolute old salt,
admitted his crime with little hesitation; PALSSON hesitated only
because he was afflicted with a stupendous stammer, so that he had
ultimately to write down his answers to verbal questions. MAGNUSSON
and DALBERG, the imbecile dupes and simple accessories after the
fact of espionage conspiracy, were packed off home and were glad to
see Iceland again after their strange interlude in England.

JONSSON's excuse for preserving the transmitter at all may
or may not typify Icelandic reasoning: he wanted to leave the set in
Iceland in case of trouble with The Authorities, to whom he could
then prove that although the set was indeed in his possession, it
was not being used! He also said that he regarded his acceptance of
the German mission merely as a "life insurance". It didn't work off
the water. JONSSON died in a British hospital in 1943.

Hilaire Anton WESTERLINCK

The success of the counter-espionage services in Britain and the
degree of reliability won by internal security measures were now
reflected in a more marked counter-Intelligence trend. Camp 020 had
proved itself as an Intelligence centre; M.I.5 could afford to

divert to the UK for examination enemy agents not intended to operate on British soil or in the immediacy of these islands.

An important case in point was that of a Belgian doctor, Hilaire Anton WESTERLINCK, who had been recruited by the Germans for agent service in the Belgian Congo. WESTERLINCK, once a "medecin à la mode" and then a practician in the Belgian Congo, had later become a ship's doctor. At the time of the Belgian capitulation his ship, the "THYSVILLE", had sought refuge first at La Pallice, then in Lisbon. The doctor, a craven defeatist, had played an active subversive rôle in engineering the repatriation of passengers and crew to Belgium. The fact was duly reported at Camp 020 by two Lisbon agents of the Germans, […] and Jack VERLINDEN.

It was not until some months after the Lisbon incidents that WESTERLINCK was actually recruited by the Germans in Antwerp. He had made enquiries into the possibility of resettlement in the Belgian Congo. His uneasiness to be off came to the notice of the Germans. They checked his record. The spirit which he had betrayed in Lisbon appealed to them. He fell easily for their suggestion that the good turn of exit facilities deserved the other of active collaboration at his destination. The contract was sealed over a glass of brandy.

WESTERLINCK paid three visits of instruction to Bremen, where he as trained in radio transmission and secret writing and coached in espionage duties. His GIS contacts were numerous and reasonably intimate, to the subsequent profit of British counter-intelligence records.

The agent left Belgium for Lisbon via Paris, where he made a few fresh contacts. He was accompanied by a wife who ignored the duality of their African venture and by two children unwisely entrusted to him for delivery to parents in Loanda.

In Lisbon WESTERLINCK maintained close touch with Abwehr representatives over some period of time, for there were difficulties in securing a visa for the onward journey. While his wife attended Mass to pray for his soul, WESTERLINCK received a refresher course in secret writing behind the locked door of his hotel room.

Not the least important reason for the delay in his sailing was the fact that WESTERLINCK was already under the close surveillance of the British Secret Service. When WESTERLINCK settled down to the mere business of waiting, it was decided to entice him to Britain to extract from him all the Intelligence by which he had come in recent months. The Belgian consular authorities collaborated. It was suggested to him that his arrangements could be more easily completed in London.....

WESTERLINCK passed the news to his masters, who were jubilant and immediately drew up an English transit mission.

WESTERLINCK and his wife were flown to England on 5 May 1942. That same evening she was housed at Holloway Gaol, he at Camp 020.

It was only a matter of hours, too, before a full confession was extracted from him. He had brought no radio transmitter with him, but other property in his baggage damned him irretrievably: [...] both important elements in secret ink formulae, were found at Ham during examination of his luggage.

On the strength of this discovery a statement was obtained from him under caution. It might have been used for prosecution purposes, but wasn't. WESTERLINCK had come to England only under advice. And besides, he had a greater value as a tome in the human reference library than as a closed book.

Tadeusz SZUMLICZ

A recurrence of the sordid Polish intrigues disclosed in the case of EJSYMONT occurred with the arrival at Ham of another young pole, Tadeusz SZUMLICZ. He had fled to France on the collapse of Polish resistance, and in Paris he had learned, even before France was overrun, of a Polish officers' conspiracy to seek a seperate peace. He took the secret with him to the Parisian gaol out of which he was subsequently recruited by the Germans as an agent-informant.

After much difficulty SZUMLICZ fled France and reached Madrid. There he told his story in part to Polish interrogating officers, pointing to his evidence of treason in high Polish quarters. The information was not well received by his compatriots, who apparently tried to silence him. They soon found a pretext: SZUMLICZ had run into a German in Madrid who claimed to be aware of his contact with and services for the Germans in Paris; and this German had begged him to continue the good work by penetrating Polish escape routes into Spain. SZUMLICZ made pretence of accepting the mission, but took no active steps to fulfil it. The Poles in Madrid, who were anxious to be rid of him, decided to indict him on a charge of high treason, alleging, among other things, that he had not disclosed to them his full knowledge of the "Peace Group Conspiracy".

SZUMLICZ was sent to England and directed to Camp 020. There he was frank about his reticences. He explained that he could not tell his compatriots everything because he knew too much and felt that his very life would be imperilled. The attitude adopted by members of the Polish Government in London served only to confirm SZUMLICZ' suspicion of victimisation. An appeal sent out from Camp 020 for checks on information given by the prisoner fell on deaf ears.

Once again in a Polish case, the interrogating officers at

Camp 020 found themselves called upon to unravel not only enemy implications, but also official Polish intrigue. The position was reached where SZUMLICZ, in fear of Polish official vengeance as distinguished from justice, became reluctant to give important information.

The Commandant, in a report to M I 5, set out in no uncertain terms his views on the case. He pointed out that if the information withheld by SZUMLICZ were germane to the investigation of the man's own story, he would not have the slightest truck with an attitude which might be described as one of barter. But the fact was that the information was important from a general Intelligence point of view, and it was intolerable that it was not reasonably available just because the Polish authorities could not be trusted to act in good faith.

The protest availed nothing. The Poles remained silent. So, in part, did SZUMLICZ, who nursed his secret and his fears for the future for three long years at Camps 020 and 020R. He was probably glad to be out of reach of his cynical compatriots over that period of time.

Hans Johann Franz Oskar von MEISS-TEUFFEN

In early March 1942 there arrived off Bathurst, Gambia, a seventeen-ton yacht flying, of all things, the Swiss flag. The sole occupant, a thirty-year old Swiss journalist, Hans Johann Franz Oskar von MEISS-TEUFFEN, finding himself becalmed, requested and obtained a tow into harbour.

Ashore he was subjected to something more than the local routine check. His call offered a break in the monotonous drill of the Security station. His story, a simple one of yachting pleasure combined with an African mission on behalf of an official Swiss trade department, was accepted by the Bathurst authorities after a fortnight's protracted examination. He was told that he was free to proceed on his way.

MEISS-TEUFFEN's conceit and pride were hurt by such light dismissal. The journalist in him asserted himself to break the first and last big story in an indifferent career. He flabbergasted the Defence Security Officer and his staff by announcing, at the dramatic moment of his own choosing, that he was, in fact, a German agent with a mission in the Belgian Congo. Frantic signals passed between Bathurst and London: it was finally agreed that MEISS-TEUFFEN be brought to England for examination at Camp 020.

His claim to be a fully trained German agent was no idle boast. That much was established at Ham, with a full assessment of his worth as such, within a few days. A recommendation from Bathurst that MEISS-TEUFFEN might be profitably exploited as a double agent was quashed by the findings at Camp 020.

MEISS-TEUFFEN's was a complex character. His background was Austrian and Swiss, with the Austrian influence dominant; but he lacked stability. He wasted a life of promise. Four interrupted years as a bank clerk, including one year as such in London, induced boredom. He reacted by conceiving the pretentious idea of covering the Italo-Abyssinian war as a journalist, but failed to take the elementary step of accrediting himself to a newspaper and obtaining adequate funds. He worked his way down to the Mediterranean by taking employment as a chauffeur. With careless disregard for both prudence and convention, he set sail for Alexandria en route to the front without a visa. The warlike Italians removed him from the ship at Naples. Undaunted, he bought a boat at Brindisi and set sail for Haifa. He lived there by his wits until April 1936, when he obtained employment on a Rhodesian estate. He failed to get any nearer to Abyssinia.

MEISS-TEUFFEN liked novelty. He was willing to try anything once. In Rhodesia he decided to become the fourth husband of a young Austrian woman, and decided within the year to make way for a fifth. In early 1939 he was hawking round London an idea of producing educational films on native African themes. The summer he spent in pleasant but unprofitable dalliance in Switzerland. The outbreak of war impressed him into a year's featureless and futureless bearing of Swiss arms.

That was not enough for MEISS-TEUFFEN. He must needs seek further complication to give zest to the enterprise. He had recently written and published "a comic article on espionage", and at this late stage in its composition he felt that he might get some real background for it. He deliberately provoked German interest in himself when applying for a transit permit by stating in writing that he hoped to visit British colonies on his African tour.

The ruse had the desired effect. Within a matter of hours the Germans were at the other end of a telephone call, inviting him to a rendezvous. He kept the appointment, accepted the inevitable offer of an espionage mission, and agreed to undergo training courses in Germany. His contact, a worldly fellow, advised him that he would need neither a Swiss exit nor a German entry permit for the purpose; he need only walk across a certain graveyard and hop into or out of Germany at his pleasure.

In due course the German Secret Service trained him in Cologne as a spy, provided him with a radio transmitter, micro-photographs, secret writing materials, cover addresses, money, false papers, a good boat, a reasonable cover story and a mission in the Congo. In October 1941 he was towed out of Bayonne harbour as far as

Cape Finisterre, where he cast off to sail single-handed to Bathurst by easy stages.

MEISS-TEUFFEN found the voyage most amusing. It certainly had its moments. The following are excerpts from his log-book:-

12 Oct 41	:	Solo voyage began; jettisoned W/T set which would not fit locker and might prove an embarrassment.
14 Oct 41	:	Stopped by British vessel; British lieutenant signed log-book.
16 Oct 41	:	Hailed by German submarine; tried to photograph it, but threatened with bombardment.
18 Oct 41	:	Arrived Lisbon, contacted by German in street who provided a password in case of future need.
2 Nov 41	:	Stopped by second British vessel.
3 Nov 41	:	Tempted to report to British Consul at Tangier, but felt under some obligation to the Swiss Officer for expansion.
30 Nov 41	:	Arrived in Casablanca, greeted in restaurant by German who gave the Lisbon password and asked whether he could help.
5 Jan 42	:	Again hailed by German submarine.
8 Jan 42	:	Arrived a Las Palmas, where a German gave password and asked whether he could do anything.
8 Feb 42	:	Arrived at Dakar, given the Lisbon password by a Frenchman in a white straw hat.
7 Mar 42	:	Arrived at Barthurst after about 2,500 sea miles covered in 39 days' sailing time.

Despite his initial reticence at Bathurst - explained away as a polite gesture to the British, who would find him out anyway - MEISS-TEUFFEN, who was subsequently released, spoke volubly and wrote lengthily about himself and the Germans. His information about Germans was interesting and valuable.

Johannes Marinus DRONKERS

In May 1942 HMS "CORENA" escorted into Harwich the Dutch yacht "JOPPE" with its crew of three: Johannes Marinus DRONKERS, a 46-year old ex-Post Office clerk from The Hague; John Alphonsus MULDER, a Javanese half-breed; and Jan Bruno De LANGEN, another postal employee.

All three men claimed, under investigation a the London
Reception Centre, to be hasty refugees from Holland. De LANGEN, who
spoke frankly, was soon cleared; MULDER attracted some interest by
contradicting himself at every opportunity; but it was DRONKERS
whose story rang least true. He was pressed on the many
improbabilities in his narrative of the escape, and after much
inconsistency of argument he broke. He confessed to having been in
the German service as long ago as 1938 and admitted that his present
visit to England was to have obeyed an espionage mission. He was to
have reported in secret writing on military and general subjects; he
called for his pocket dictionary and showed how he had lightly
underlined certain letters which together went to make up his two
cover addresses.

DRONKERS was a feckless individual. Although recruited by the
Germans for espionage in the UK in 1938, he had stayed at home and
written his "despatches from England" from there. He admitted that his
recent re-employment had awaited "sufficient financial inducement."

At Camp 020 his sordid tale was fully elaborated and
statements were taken from him for purposes of prosecution. Before
he left Ham for the Old Bailey and the gallows, DRONKERS was
unwittingly instrumental in clearing some of the suspicion into
which MULDER, at that time a fellow prisoner, had fallen. A covered
association between the two men was arranged. After a few banal
exchanges, DRONKERS confided to MULDER that he was a German agent
and that he had already made a confession. MULDER reacted violently
and with venom: for a full half hour he poured scorn and execration
upon DRONKERS for his shameless treachery. DRONKERS was hanged in
January 1943, but MULDER did not leave Camp 020 until April of the
same year, a free man.

John Henry Watkin PRICE

An Englishman gone native Portuguese was John Henry Watkin PRICE,
son of the doorkeeper at the British Embassy in Lisbon. He spoke
better Portuguese than English' and he had not resisted conscription
into the Portuguese Army. He worked for the Lisbon Tramways and
served with the Portuguese Air Force; he fought for a year in the
Spanish War as a private in the Spanish Foreign Legion; he became an
electrician, a mechanic, a chauffeur, and a minter in Spain. On the
outbreak of war he volunteered for service with the British forces.
The advance was rejected; the British Consul told him he was a
Portuguese. He joined the crew of a "mystery tug" manned by
Englishmen, the "COMMANDANTE AFFONSO DE CARVALHO", which failed to
live up to its local reputation during his stay aboard. He quit the
ship after a very commonplace row with the ship's cook.

The tug was to have been fitted clandestinely with a machine gun, and PRICE was aware of the fact. So were the Germans; and later PRICE was accused, somewhat capriciously, of having betrayed the secret to them.

Towards the end of April 1942 PRICE was still without work. He tried to get employment with the Portuguese merchant navy, and in the process was brought by a friend into contact with the Germans. They were interested in his ambition to become a seaman; they suggested to him that he might prefer to remain in England if once his ship touched there. He could earn good money by sending reports on military subjects; if England won the war, he would be safe and find a good job there; if Germany were victorious, he would be given splendid employment in Portugal. Kuno WELTZIEN, his Abwehr tempter, gave him some money to redeem his clothes and watch out of pawn and then instructed him in secret writing. The German produced some brandy and a few Havana cigars, because "these things were necessary if good work were to be done".

PRICE's blood was stronger than the brandy. He went home and told his father about Kuno WELTZIEN and his friends, but not about the money which he had received. Father PRICE was wild; he ordered his son to report at once to the British Embassy. The son did so and was encouraged to maintain contact with the enemy.

In June 1942 he arrived in Cardiff as second cook of the Panamanian vessel "INAKI"; he was promptly removed from the ship and sent to Camp 020 for investigation. His was not the straightforward case of the willing informant, because it had been complicated by unsubstantiated charges of betrayal of Embassy documents to the Germans in Lisbon. Further difficulty attended the enquiry because the man was scatterbrained and constitutionally incapable of telling the plain truth. For all that, he was unshakeable on the main outline of his story, and in September 1942 he was released.

Leon Ernest JUDE

Failure to disclose at the first opportunity any traffic with the enemy Secret Service, either for good or ill, could lead into trouble not only the traitor, but also the patriot. Such a one was Leon Ernest JUDE, a Belgian SABENA airline pilot, who, after many desperate attempts to escape to England, allowed himself to be recruited by the Germans for an espionage mission in the United States. It was his intention, on arrival there, to make his way to England as soon as possible, to volunteer his services for the Belgian Air Force.

JUDE's training was purely nominal: he was more adept as a

radio operator than his would-be instructors. His masters, who coveted an apartment and furniture he had already sold over their heads when they fancied it would be adequate collateral for his loyalty to them, treated him with some deference. They had imagined at first that his name had a Jewish ring, and they gave him the cover name of SALO (for SALOME) before they discovered that he was perhaps more Aryan than they. They got him to write that down on official paper and then showed him off proudly to all their Abwehr friends, so that later JUDE could produce a formidable list of espionage contacts.

JUDE eventually left for the United States via France, Spain, Cuba and Venezeula. On arrival he enquired urgently whether he might not be allowed to join the Belgian forces in the UK, and within a matter of weeks he was landed in Scotland. Neither in the United States nor England did he offer the information that the Germans had sent him out of Belgium as a spy, perhaps because, in his view, the preliminaries of escape from Occupied Europe were unimportant.

He only discovered that the end did not justify the undisclosed means when a friend denounced him to the Allied authorities. He was sent to Camp 020 to explain himself. The investigation there proceeded without difficulty, for JUDE was now painfully conscious of his omission and anxious to make amends. But his co-operation availed him little at this late date: he was adjudged unfit to be allowed liberty in the UK, and since no one else was interested in him, he remained at Camps 020 and 020R until his deportation to Belgium in 1945.

Johannes Franciscus WINTER

The only thing of any real merit that Johannes Franciscus WINTER attained in thirty-nine years of life was death by hanging. He was a Belgian seaman and ship's steward with an undistinguished record of service in British and German vessels up to the outbreak of war. He became a waterfront loafer for some weeks in late 1939 and was at one time tempted by a former colleague to accept employment with the Germans as a low-level informer on dockside activity. Probably the reward offered was insufficient to attract him, for shortly afterwards he found employment as storekeeper for an Antwerp packing and rubber company.

He was thus occupied when the Germans entered Belgium. They allowed him to keep the job and even promoted him to the status of a buyer. The opportunity to exact illicit commissions and to dabble in the Black Market was not missed. WINTER, whose salary with the firm was five marks weekly, could afford to buy, at the end of one year, a house costing some 100,000 francs.

These halcyon days were short-lived. WINTER was
again approached by his former steward colleague, Karl ULRICH,
and accepted an invitation to contact representatives
of the GIS. Blackmail played a part in his subsequent
recruitment, for the Germans were aware of WINTER'S nefarious
activities, but no great exertion of pressure was needed to
obtain his agreement to act as an agent either in Spain or on board
ship.

WINTER received instruction in secret writing and was
escorted into Spain with orders to report to a British Consul and
volunteer for service as a seaman in any ship sailing for Britain.
He was to resume his sea-going career after reporting to the Belgian
authorities in England and was required to report on convoys in
particular and marine subjects in general.

The Spaniards co-operated once again with the GIS to cover
an agent's approach to his task. They issued him with a five weeks'
detention certificate to counterfeit a three-day visit to the
Nanclares concentration camp.

WINTER visited the British Consul at Huelva and was directed
to Gibraltar. There he was twice interrogated by the Security
authorities, who cleared him and allowed him to sail for the UK in
the "LLANSTEPHAN CASTLE".

M I 5 had forewarning of his advent. WINTER was allowed to
pass through the routine channels to the London Reception Centre.
Two interrogations there failed to satisfy the examining officers;
at the third WINTER broke.

He was transferred at once to Camp 020, where he made a full
confession. He made no attempt to justify his acceptance of the
German mission or his failure to report it at the first opportunity
in Huelva, at the second, Gibraltar, and at the third in London. He
could only repeat whiningly, "I was a fool; I was afraid; I was
ashamed." His sole defence was that throughout the "LLANSTEPHAN
CASTLE's" voyage to the UK, he had remained below decks in order not
to observe any shipping movements which he might have had to report
to his masters!

There was only one future for WINTER, and that was its
negation. He was successfully prosecuted, sentenced to death, and
hanged in November 1942.

Duncan Alexander Croall SCOTT-FORD

One of the most important, and certainly the most obnoxious, of the
cases handled at Camp 020 in 1942 involved that happy rarity, a
British traitor. The man in the case was a former naval rating,
Duncan Alexander Croall SCOTT-FORD. On a lower scale than the

infamous BAILLIE-STEWART, SCOTT-FORD belonged in every other particular to the same stamp of renegade. There was a service background to each; lust, financial greed, ideas of personal aggrandisement were common.

SCOTT-FORD showed signs of criminal heedlessness at an early stage in his naval career. He was only eighteen years old when, in June 1939, while serving in HMS "GLOUCESTER", he became infatuated with a German girl a year younger than himself who was living at Dar-es-Salaam. To her he lightly imparted details of naval codes and other information calculated to be of value to her doting father, who was already living in the seventh Teutonic heaven of a promised Gauleitership of East Africa after the forthcoming march against England.

A year later, in Alexandria, he became embroiled with an Egyptian houri operating at a local nightclub. She was exacting and expensive. SCOTT-FORD cooked the official account books and there was suspicion that certain leakages of information from the cypher-room at this time might also be traceable to him. SCOTT-FORD was suitably court-martialled, dismissed the service with ignominy and sentenced to two years' imprisonment.

His mother, whom he hated, lodged an appeal on the grounds of his extreme youth. It was successful: his sentence was quashed after he had served six months. My Lords of the Admiralty endorsed his papers with a note to the effect that his discharge had really been honourable.

For all that, SCOTT-FORD found it difficult to get employment in England. He decided to go to sea again, in the merchant service. In May 1942 he was serving in a ship which called at Lisbon. He went ashore to a cafe, where he had a drink and picked up a girl with whom he spent the night. He spent most of the next day with her too. He left her late in the evening:

> "I went to the Lethis Bar. I went in and sat at the bar
> drinking alone for about twenty minutes, or possibly thirty
> minutes, but not longer. Then a man came in and sat on the
> next stool. I'd had two or three beers and was a bit muzzy.
> I afterwards learned that this man's name was RITHMAN."

RITHMAN led SCOTT-FORD down the familiar slippery slope with some ease. Before they parted he had promised the sailor that he would send a letter from him to the girl from Dar-es-Salaam, who was now back in Germany. He had also promised SCOTT-FORD 1,000 escudos if the latter could find out why all British ships had orders to be in port on 28 June. They arranged to meet on the following day.

RITHMAN brought a German friend with him to that rendezvous. Together they pumped SCOTT-FORD for information on shipping subjects, bomb damage and morale in Britain. He gave it. They gave him 1,000 escudos. At a second meeting in the offices of the local KRUPPS agency, he was more intensively questioned on a wide range of subjects. The game of question and answer lasted four hours. Another hour was spent in briefing on information and material required on his next visit to Lisbon from England. Among other printed matter, SCOTT-FORD was to obtain specimen identity, ration and clothing cards.

SCOTT-FORD's ship arrived in Liverpool on 20 June. On the following day, during routine Security examination, he was asked whether he had been approached by any German agents in Lisbon. He declared that he had; he gave details of the men concerned; but he claimed to have been recoiled from their approach as an honest British seaman. To a woman with whom he stayed for several nights he proposed a few hours later that she, too, become a German agent. She toyed with the idea because of the money, but later "she expressed some doubts about accepting work on behalf of the Germans which might result in the bombing of women and children". The prostitute's morals were better than SCOTT-FORD's.

He was back in Lisbon in late July. There he re-established contact with his German masters and gave them a full account of the route taken by the convoys in which he had sailed since their last meeting, with names of ships and casualties suffered. Some of the information was known to them already, for in several instances he was rudely corrected on his information. Altogether it was a stormy interview, and the Germans lost no time in chiding him on that score. Moreover, he had failed to produce the identity and other documents which he had promised. He was ordered to call back a few days later.

He never did go back. Shore leave was cancelled and the convoy sailed shortly afterwards. His ship reached Manchester on 18 August. MI 5, who had learned form ISOS of a certain "RUTHERFORD's" treachery in Lisbon, arranged an immediate interrogation in order positively to identify the agent with SCOTT-FORD. He stuck to his original half-truth: he gave fresh details of his contacts, but denied that he had given away any information.

On the following day he broke under pressure and was arrested at once. After the legal formalities of detention had been complied with, SCOTT-FORD was directed to Camp 020.

He was well roused by his first interrogation. At first he blustered and revelled in his crimes: he pointed without blushing to entries in his notebook showing that he had taken down full notes, complete with sketch-map, of the composition and disposition of his last convoy; he admitted quite blithely that he had intended to pass this information to the Germans in Lisbon on his return. He told of the glittering prizes which they had hinted at: he might become the German master of a German ship or even Gauleiter of the Plymouth area. The Gauleiter vision had so entranced him that he had written the word in his notebook too. He was going to suggest to the Germans that if for some reason the post was given to another, he would be satisfied with £5,000 in lieu!

As investigation of the case proceeded, SCOTT-FORD's attitude underwent a change. At last he had seen the shadow of the gallows. He cringed and whined and revealed himself to be a true coward. In the ultimate, when cornered, he had not even the courage of a rat to fight back.

But if the case was unsavoury, its Intelligence product was rich. Kuno WELTZIEN, of the PRICE case, again came into prominence; details of eleven other German agents, to say nothing of a legion of prostitute sub-agents, were obtained.

SCOTT-FORD was tried at the Old Bailey under the Treachery Act on 16 October 1942 and sentenced to death. A report on his case was issued from Camp 020 while he awaited execution. Its prompt publication had two objects: M I 5 might require elucidation on points which SCOTT-FORD alone might be able to answer: and someone in authority might be disposed to examine the case for a reprieve. The Commandant, in his covering comments, underlined the fact that not a single extenuating circumstance was to be found. "Indeed", he wrote, "there may well be many who will agree that death by hanging is almost too good for a sailor who will encompass the death of thousands of his shipmates without qualm."

There was no reprieve. SCOTT-FORD was hanged in November 1942.

Robert Charles Roger PETIN

On 26 August 1942, at the request of the Deuxième Bureau of the Free French in London, Robert Charles Roger PETIN, who had served in the French Air Force until the capitulation, was admitted to Camp 020 as "a self-confessed German agent, having written and signed a statement to this effect."

At the first opportunity at Ham, PETIN retracted the confession. It had been made under duress. He claimed to have been subjected to third-degree pressure by his French interrogators in London. He was medically examined: there were weals below his knee-caps not inconsistent with his story that he had been made to kneel on the sharp edge of a piece of wood.

At Ham PETIN was given every chance to tell his true story. In outline it was simple enough. He had escaped from France and come the England in September 1941. […] trained and parachuted back into France. A certain disregard for caution in himself and other French agents led to his capture by the Gestapo. He claimed to have survived interrogation without breaking on his espionage mission or blowing his colleagues. He had managed to escape the Gestapo and after some difficulty with the Spanish authorities in Madrid, had regained England.

Here he ran foul of the Free French authorities. He had given them reason enough to doubt him. He had lied to them as he had lied to every other authority, to give himself importance and to cover a little charge of desertion from the French Forces. He admitted at Ham that he suffered from "mythomane"; and this, with a natural anxiety to conceal the less commendable details of his earlier life, had led him into trouble.

There seemed little doubt that PETIN was not a German agent. An ISOS intercept in the possession of M I 5 supported this view. The German Embassy in Madrid had communicated to Germany a report from the Spanish police that they were holding PETIN, whom they knew to be a British agent newly escaped from France, for possible exchange against "a Spanish journalist arrested in London (CALVO)". The message added that the Spaniards might be willing to hold PETIN at the disposal of the Germans for a certain time.

PETIN's arrival in Lisbon en route to England followed so soon after interception of the message that the time factor alone cleared him of any possible contact with the Germans in the interval.

PETIN's maddening mendacity and contradictions did not endear him to his interrogators at Ham, but he was given a patient and fair hearing. In the result neither he nor the Free French authorities emerged from the affair with credit. Materially, however, the real loss was PETIN's: he remained under detention at Camps 020 and 020R until September 1945.

Janos SALAMON/Sandor MOCSAN

Connivance by Hungarian official departments in a German espionage mission to Brazil employing two Hungarians invested with official status came to light during 1941, when radio messages from Rio de Janeiro to Germany were intercepted by British monitoring stations.

The two men concerned, Janos SALAMON and Sandor MOCSAN, were forced by their own departing Legation to return to Europe in the early months on 1942, for all their efforts to remain in Brazil as "private citizens". It seemed that the Hungarian authorities had miscalculated both the duration and outcome of the war and the overweening loyalty to themselves, as apart from their Axis co-religionaries, of the two agents.

SALAMON and MOCSAN travelled separately out of Brazil. Each was picked off his Spanish ship by British control authorities at Trinidad, who had received warning of their passage. Thereafter their fates were conjoint, as had been their recent activity. Both were placed in a local detention camp, both interrogated at Halifax, Nova Scotia, en route to Britain; both examined and held at Camp 020 until October 1945.

At Halifax, as in Trinidad, both men talked much excited nonsense about diplomatic status, but in due course it transpired that these spurious legates were willing to admit that they had been working for the German and Hungarian Secret Services and that their activities included messages to the Germans not only by radio transmission but also in secret writing. The admission was wrested from them only after heated argument, despite the fact that both men had been apprehended in possession of notebooks containing real evidence relating to radio transmission, meteorological reports, indications that they had established communication with German agents in Mexico and Chile, and references to US shipping movements off Brazil. Moreover, in their desperation of ever getting sense out of the voluble Hungarians, the interrogating authorities in Halifax had seen fit to blow to the agents the fact that their radio messages had been intercepted and decoded, so that their final denials had a decidedly hollow ring. Notwithstanding the damning nature of the eventual confessions, it was decided that the two men be sent to Camp 020 for further enquiry.

The move was profitable from the Intelligence point of view. It was found that the background to the espionage activities of the two men was almost untouched. Details were obtained of their original recruitment in Budapest; training, despatch and operation under the direction of a certain Herr SEBOLD in Germany, who monopolised the attention and services of the Hungarians at the expense of the hopeful but helpless Magyar authorities. A mass of new material relating to espionage activities in South America and against the United States was also obtained, while the list of active agents and sub-agents in Brazil grew impressively.

SALAMON proved a difficult subject. He was a disingenuous character who required extreme patience in handling. Although the main features of his story were known already out of his own admissions in Canada, SALAMON now sought refuge again in his threadbare claim to diplomatic status. He _was_ a diplomat, he said; he had been tricked into captivity by the issue of a worthless British navicert; he had been unjustly accused of being a spy and been "questioned about the confidential aspect of his diplomatic activity in an independent, neutral State." He compared himself with Sir Stafford Cripps, who, as Ambassador to Russia, doubtless visited

Russian factories and would, on this precedent, be liable to
treatment in Hungary, not as a gentleman, but as a spy! When
required to divulge his spy-name, be boggled fastidiously at the
term and announced that his pseudo-name was Jose COSTA.

His attempts at equivocation went even beyond that. The
lapse at Halifax had made it possible, for the first and last time
at Camp 020, to make use of the actual text of radio intercepts.
They were produced to SALAMON. Most of the messages were addressed
to his German spymasters; their content was blatant espionage
material; they were signed by himself. SALAMON blithely announced
that they were perfectly innocent communications sent by him to
report his activities on behalf of the Hungarian Foreign Office.

He had a second passport, additional to his spurious
diplomatic document. It was in the name of SAROS. He insisted ad
nauseam that it was merely the Magyarised form of his own name,
until it was pointed out that MOCSAN, whose name was entirely
Magyar, possessed a second passport in the name of MAGU. Then
SALAMON retracted.

His egotism bordered on insanity. During his internment in
Trinidad, he applied to the Colonial Secretary for the post of
Social and Welfare Officer in the local Leper Colony. The acting
Colonial Secretary disillusioned and deflated him by reminding him
that he was an enemy national, and would he please make any further
communications as brief and concise as possible. He confessed to
being outraged by the discovery, in Recife, that he and MOSCAN were
not the only two German agents in Brazil.

The Commandant had portentous, unilateral words with this
gross prevaricator, and the way was opened for proper investigation
of his case, but even then he was no simple subject, and thirsty
long interrogations were necessary before a comprehensive report
could be produced.

While SALAMON had blustered and flustered, MOSCAN, who had
only one leg to stand on, had faced issues more squarely. As a mere
radio operator jealously limited to that function by SALAMON, he had
less to tell than his colleague, but was more ready to tell it. He
proved a useful, if dull-witted, foil against SALAMON, who never
ceased to reproach him for it in the purest Magyar.

Sobhy HANNA

Sobhy HANNA was born an Egyptian. He was a Copt. He was educated at
the Schools of the Order of St Mark, of the Holy Family, and St.
Joseph in Cairo. He became a dealer in electric equipment, a shady
lawyer, a salesman of Saharan wastes, a Member of the Order of the
Nile of King Fuad I (Fifth Class), a parasite on French military

disaster, and a German agent. Women of a certain age liked him. He also looked knowledgeable, because in Paris a middle-aged German, a complete stranger, approached him to seek advice in connection with an affiliation order which had been served on him.

HANNA, who practised law and deceit in France, decided to go home to Egypt when various decrees of the Vichy Government threatened seriously to interfere with his earning capacity in the half-world of the lawless. Difficulties in obtaining visas and permits, and the awful expense of it, all directed his springy footsteps on to German doorsteps. He accepted an ill-defined mission to engage in subversive political activity in Egypt, and a radio transmitter for the employment of which his orders were even less precise.

Allowances for his wife and children in France, for his equipment, living and travel expenditure were lavish. The Germans, bedazzled by his generous estimate of himself, took infinite pain in preparing his way back to Egypt. He decided to travel via Lisbon, Lourenço Marques and Dar-es-Salaam.

In Lisbon he vacillated over disclosing his German contacts to the British; at Lourenço Marques he effected a cautionary compromise by telling the British Consul that he would have information to impart at Nairobi or Mombasa; at Dar-es-Salaam he was arrested on orders of M I 5, who had independent and irrefutable knowledge from ISOS itself of his dalliance with the Germans and the importance which they attached to his mission.

HANNA had nothing to say at Dar-es-Salaam. He was brought to Camp 020, where he was not allowed to exploit his racial gift for mendacity under direct interrogation. But he remained economical of the truth in many particulars and its extraction from him was painful at either side of the table.

Even when fully developed his case presented many puzzling features, especially the exact purpose and scope of his mission. The Germans had not been explicit and Sobhy HANNA, with the worst will in the world, could not amplify his own final version of that point. Confusion became worse confounded when it was established at Camp 020 that his German contacts in Paris included several individuals already known from the LENIHAN case. HANNA, according to ISOS indications, was to be an Abwehr I agent; his own confession showed him to have been groomed for an Abwehr II mission of political subversion.

In the result, however, it became apparent that the Germans were themselves unsure of his exact future employment at the time of his departure en mission, and it seemed likely that new instructions and local contacts would have been communicated to him when once he was safely established in Egypt. HANNA was not allowed to arrive there until August 1945.

Pierre Henri MOREL

The confused loyalties of prostrate France were epitomised in Pierre Henri MOREL, a demobilised pilot of the French Air Force who lent his services as an informant with equal zeal to non-conformist Vichyites working against Germany and orthodox Germans working against Vichyites. He drew good pay and much applause from either side.

Towards the spring of 1942 MOREL allowed himself to drift into exclusive employment by the Germans. His principal in Paris, one SCHMIDT, had him well trained in the preparation of sabotage material and general Intelligence work, and then announced that MOREL's mission was against England. MOREL, in his confusion, was never quite sure whether he wished to work against England or not, but he accepted the invitation with alacrity. Not did he demur when SCHMIDT dangled before him a reward of one million francs if he succeeded in stealing a British 'plane from an RAF airfield and landing it undamaged in France. Should he not have the opportunity to perform that feat, MOREL was to seek employment in some Allied Intelligence unit and engineer his despatch to France.

MOREL left for England via Spain and actually reported his German contacts and mission to a British consular official in San Sebastian and later to other British authorities in Madrid. He was smuggled out of Spain into Gibraltar, where he composed a lengthy unsolicited critique of the bastion's Security defences, and was then shipped to England.

His anxiety to be "turned" and sent back to France created an unfavourable impression at the London Reception Centre, and he was earmarked for more detailed examination at Ham. Here it was soon established that MOREL had been reticent and equivocal on many details of his story. This attitude was not inconsistent with an overriding loyalty to the Germans, who held his wife as collateral against his defection. MOREL was held at Camps 020 and 020R until some time after the war was ended.

Luís MORALES Serrano

The case of Luís MORALES Serrano, Spanish soldier and German agent, was one of continuous difficulty at Camp 020. The original trace dated back to the beginning of 1942, when it became known to M I 5 from ISOS that a certain "Luís MARTINEZ Suarez", a Spaniard, was proceeding to Buenos Aires under instructions from the Brussels Stelle of the Abwehr. Inter-departmental issues of no little magnitude preceded the apprehension of the agent; policy forbade his immediate detention when his ship called at Trinidad, but he was finally arrested at Curaçao, in Dutch territorial waters, in March 1942.

At Trinidad, whither he was now transferred, it transpired that the man was travelling on false papers, and that the pregnant woman with whom he was travelling was not, in fact, his wife. "SUAREZ" proved, in truth, to be MORALES; and "Mme SUAREZ-MORALES", who aborted over the shock of detention and subsequently blamed the fact on individual officers at several British establishments, was actually Mercedes INIESTA Pozos, a woman of peasant origin who may at one time have been personable but always remained illiterate. MORALES, one of several Spanish agents collected by the Trinidad control over a period of some months, was sent to England for investigation at Camp 020.

His arrival coincided with intolerable pressure from the Spanish Government, and thus it came about that an urgent demand from the Foreign Office for "proof of guilt" lay on the Commandant's desk beside the papers just removed from MORALES' luggage. "Proof of guilt" at such short notice rendered an orderly and logical investigation impossible. However, the Commandant, with the case officers, proceeded by day and took advantage of the long nights.

MORALES, under unrelenting pressure, signed a written confession on the third day after his arrival. He admitted to a secret mission in Argentina, Chile and Mexico on behalf of Spanish official sponsors; he was to obtain Intelligence on US air defences and aircraft types and production; and he was to report in code via the Spanish Embassies in different countries to a cover address in Portugal.

The most curious feature of the case was that, while the evidence was almost overwhelming that MORALES was to have worked for the Germans through the Spanish authorities, he would never admit this to be true. After a time, faced with hints of the evidence, he admitted the soundness of the argument and offered to sign a declaration to the effect that he was working for the Germans, adding the rider that he did no know it at the time.

This attitude was of no use at Camp 020, and the Commandant refused to accept any such declaration. The effect of it, actually, was to make him re-examine every statement which MORALES had signed: he found that ISOS confirmed the accuracy of earlier statements and confessions, so that in those matters the investigation remained on a firm basis.

MORALES had declared that the Spanish Embassy in London were aware of his secret mission and relied upon his silence in view of the fact that, as a former officer in the Spanish Republican Army, he had been condemned to death by the Franco Government. The "protest" made by the Embassy on behalf of their "innocent" natural could only be regarded as a gross breach of diplomatic privilege.

The implication no doubt explained why MORALES became extremely anxious to communicate secretly with the Spanish authorities in London. He feigned illness by scratching his mouth to induce blood vomiting; he chewed soap to simulate symptomatic foams. In this way he hoped to secure a transfer to a hospital wherefrom he could more easily establish communication.

Frustrated, he then tried to smuggle a message out of the camp, but in this also he met with no success. Later he tried to stand on borrowed dignity by representing himself to be a Lieutenant-Colonel in the Spanish Army. He demanded preferential treatment as such; but it then transpired that, although he had the record of an Army officer, had had conveniently promoted himself to impress. To add to his troubles, there was information, confirmed in part by himself, that the end of his Army career coincided with a shortage of funds in the officers' Mess involving some 60,000 pesetas. Then, as a last expedient, Major MORALES had recourse to the grand gesture of suicide. Apparently the slitting of an artery appeared to him, but it all came to nought through pain engendered by the insertion of a domestic nib an very short distance into a vein.

Although MORALES' intransigently stupid attitude did not allow of a complete solution of the case, much was gained by it. Not only did it provide further evidence of unneutral conduct by Spanish officials, but also names - among them those of DUQUE and GOMEZ PIÑAN - which were to recur in cases investigated at Camp 020.

MORALES, an unmitigated and nauseating nuisance at Camps 020 and 020R, was held there in detention until December 1944, when he was transferred to a special wing at Dartmoor until some months after the war was ended.

Juan GÓMEZ de LECUBE

Of all the obstinate, stubborn, immovable and immutable Spaniards who ever came to Ham, Juan GÓMEZ de LECUBE, ex-professional "futbolist", greyhound owner, civil servant, devout Catholic and fully-trained German agent, was incontestably the most mulish. A testimonial to that effect, in terms, came to Camp 020 from a knowledgeable source: his own brother.

LECUBE's espionage history had been voluminously covered by ISOS intercepts. There was little about it that was not known. After identification with the known agent had been established beyond doubt, LECUBE was removed from a Spanish ship in Trinidad in the early months of 1942 while on his way to Venezuela and Panama, in the hope that he might amplify certain aspects of the known story.

Examination of his property revealed that his notebook

contained, seriatim, three entries which corresponded to known German cover addresses; the telephone number of a certain "Don LUIS", a notorious Mexican recruiting agent of the Germans operating in Barcelona; and a cryptic reference to the officer of a Spanish ship, also a known German agent. Among other strange items in his possession were phials of [...] the raw material of his known secret writing medium, and a toothpick ready wrapped in cotton-wool, its customary instrument.

The Trinidad Control authorities had instructions not to pursue the questioning of LECUBE beyond the establishment of his personal background. LECUBE was not loth to disclose this within the bounds of his discretion, although he did lapse unconsciously into further confirmation of the fragmentary but irrefragable ISOS story.

His removal to England awaited only the provision of transport. His innate rebellious spirit was probably promoted further by the company, en route to the UK and Ham, of Luis MORALES Serrano and the crazing INIESTA woman. LECUBE arrived at Camp 020 in October 1942, openly defiant of authority and truth. His interrogations, though intensive, were non-productive. He gave the softest answer or the most plausible explanation to every point of read evidence with which he could be challenged. He was willing to admit that he had been in touch with "Don LUIS" and other bad characters in Spain, but he "just did not know" that they were German agents. He used every negative in the rich Spanish language to deny all charges and accusations against him. The "nunca's", "nada's", "nadie's", "ningun's" and "no's" dropped as incontinently and as easily from his lips as the waters over Niagara.

By implication and by inference his guilt was well proven. But there was no persuading him to condemn himself out of his own mouth or to divulge the Intelligence known to be in his possession. The immovable mass had met the irresistible force. LECUBE's case officer went on leave; LECUBE spent that leave in the so-called "condemned cell", the horrors of which were largely psychological, although it lacked certain material comforts as compared with the ordinary cells.

By the time that active prosecution of the case could be resumed, LECUBE, who had found comfort in his religion in the absence of any company or provocation, had hardened. He had always been difficult, now he was impossible, to budge out of his intransigence. To cut losses, the case was temporarily shelved, the first complete failure in the history of Camp 020.

Many months later, in June 1943, a microphone check on LECUBE's cell revealed that he was in extremely low spirits and was invoking the name of God to protect him. The Commandant decided at once to exploit his moral weakness and to reopen the case. For weeks every new approach, every new device was tried against LECUBE. He was goaded into the most monstrous fits of temper; he was spoken to smoothly and sympathetically; he saw through it all. Fresh evidence was found in his property of sinister intent, including the camouflaged formulae for his secret inks, but LECUBE refused to speak.

A "Court of Assessors" was set up, consisting of Spaniards and South Americans who had been well and truly broken and who could be trusted to listen gravely and disgustedly to the evidence against him and then pester the temper and conscience out of him in controlled associations. With time some of them became as keen to break LECUBE as the investigating officers, but in sum they achieved nothing. Their impressment into the case, however, was not without profit, for after a particularly heated session with LECUBE over which the Commandant presided, one of the assessors (LIPKAU) was so much impressed that he elected to break on the last detail of his own story!

On and off, the case of LECUBE was pursued until the pressure of more urgent espionage traffic relegated him to the limbo of the forgotten at the Huntercombe cubliette. From there he bombarded the Home Secretary with glib but verbose demands for release and redress; his sole success was to win a transfer to Dartmoor in December 1944. But by August 1945 he could walk the streets of Madrid and Barcelona and proudly proclaim himself a Spaniard with the Spanish equivalent of guts.

Ernesto SIMOES

If character can be expressed in colour, yellow is probably the most fitting shade for the average spy. But the renowned Yellow Peril of Ham was not developed out of any such fancy. It is the practice in official files to record points of outstanding importance or summaries of earlier minutes on paper of a colour which will stand out against the white bulk of routine correspondence and records. Quick reference is facilitated: time is saved.

Yellow was the colour chosen by the Commandant for this purpose. In the course of time the "YPs" sent out from Camp 020 became something more than mere official documents. Personalities were their subject as much as stark facts; and personality became their keynote. It became the wont for the Commandant to preface each report on despatch from Ham with a concise and trenchant summary of and commentary on the case. Soon the Yellow Peril had won fame as well as attention.

Typical of its kind was that which accompanied the report in the case of Ernesto SIMOES, Portuguese spy in England. It is here

quoted verbatim not only as an example, but as the complete case
history:-

"To succeed through ineptitude is a paradox indeed, but that
in effect is the lot of Ernesto SIMOES.

"The first ten years of his manhood, if the term can be
applied to SIMOES, is a saga of drift. As an apprentice he
is loved by a wife and a daughter whom he fails to support.
With equal facility he applies himself to the manufacture of
munitions, geysers and soda-water bottles, with occasional
diversions in salesmanship and the driving of cars.
Dismissal and resignation from a long list of employments
alternate with monotonous regularity. Yet SIMOES is in no
wise deterred by this record behind him, for next he sets up
as "a specialist in new factories to be opened in Tampico".
Spurred on by this novel ambition, he travels to Paris,
Casablanca, Luanda and Johannesburg, and it is
characteristic of the man that he never reaches Tampico at
all. Yet the man never starves, nor for that matter does he
lack feminine company, for women in great numbers have in
fact found him endowed with great charm.

"Money for nothing is the creed of this ilk, and it is not
surprising therefore that SIMOES was watched with acute
interest by the German Secret Service in Lisbon and finally
employed by them. Yet it is curious that this man who lives
by his wits could not see through this fraud, for the truth,
rejecting training expenses, passage money and promises held
out, is that he risked his neck for a sum total of four
hundred escudos.

"His espionage training is superficial, for in three months
he was taught to communicate by secret ink only, but the
story is not to be rejected out of hand as improbable, for
those who have knowledge of this man incline to the view
that the Germans felt further instruction would hardly repay
the trouble involved. They admitted the outgoing secret ink
process was simple, but added with heavy sarcasm that it was
sufficient to pass the British censorship tests. More
interest, however, attaches to the developer provided for
incoming correspondence, which was handed to SIMOES in the
form of impregnated cotton-wool. Specimens were found at Ham
in the lining of his coat and were passed on for analysis to
the authorities concerned.

"His espionage mission also is simple, consisting as it does
of the following items of war interest in England:-

Construction and movement of ships;
Movement of troops;
"Anything of interest" regarding aircraft;
Arrival of American troops;
Economic conditions in England.

"Our contre-espionage service had followed the activities of SIMOES
long before his departure from Lisbon, but determined as an
experiment to watch him actively at work in this country. In due
course he was landed at Poole Airport on 29 July 1942, and
insinuated into the employment of Percival Aircraft, Limited, at
Luton.

    "In espionage his overt act consisted of contacting en clair
the German Secret Service from England to a cover address in Lisbon
- Mlle Lucia GONZALEZ, Rua Jardim do Regedor 29, $4°D$ - and receiving
in secret ink instructions from the German SS in reply. Real
evidence consists of materials found in the property of SIMOES,
which he admitted were handed to him by the enemy for secret writing
purposes.

    "Unfortunately SIMOES indulged in little other espionage
activity, notwithstanding the attentions of an active agent
provocateur. In fact he ran true to form. He pottered in espionage,
tired of it, and then drifted inevitably to women. In due course it
was decided to bring the contre-espionage plan to an end. SIMOES was
arrested and made a short confession at Luton Police Station.... The
rest of the story was obtained at Camp 020.

    "In retrospect, the case of SIMOES is not of importance. His
training was elementary. His contacts were few. He adds nothing to
our knowledge of the somewhat shabby WELTZIEN organisation in
Lisbon. His hostile potential was nil, as he was under contre-
espionage supervision. As a German spy he was a failure. As an
agent-double he would have been of no value whatever. The irritating
feature of the case is that he escapes trial under the Treachery Act
for the good reason that the agent provocateur is of more value to
us. In the result SIMOES, through sheer ineptitude, must live,
whereas a man of normal competence in like circumstances would have
met his death as a spy."

    He was returned to Portugal in good physical heath in
September 1945.

Gabriel Jules Emanuel PRY

The case of Gabriel Jules Emanuel PRY, young Belgian mathematician turned German agent, offered several novelties. PRY, who was only 25 years old, actually offered his services to the Germans before any approach had been made to him; he was at this time a frustrated insurance clerk and an avid reader of spy stories, and "he wanted to do secret work for Germany."

The opportunity to do so was soon vouchsafed him, for the Germans do not look gift horses in the mouth. PRY was put in contact with "the right people". They included a man called KARSTEN, of the Brussels Abwehrstelle, whose name was to feature frequently in other true spy stories written at Ham, and a woman named "CARMEN", who was a dowdy but adroit double agent provocatrice loyal to the Germans.

PRY's instructions were received usually through "CARMEN", who showed more enterprise and ingenuity than KARSTEN. She gave him his mission, which was to be in the Congo; he was to deliver a letter from a loyal official in Belgium to the Governor-General of the Belgian Congo, and hand to him further letters for delivery in London. The Germans hoped that PRY would then be entrusted with regular courier work between England, Portugal and the Congo. Naturally, he would allow his German masters to examine all the correspondence entrusted to him.

Should PRY fail to win preferment as a courier and remain in the Congo, he could report all manner of local Intelligence by a simple en clair code in letters written to cover addresses in Madrid and Lisbon. And if, by chance, he should be routed by the Belgians in Lisbon to the Congo via the UK, he could deliver his letters in London and there procure his employment as the bearer of the acknowledgements and replies.

"CARMEN", with inside knowledge of British escape routes into and through Spain, set PRY on the right track for Lisbon. He had an excellent cover story, for the author of the letters was dangerously innocent of the ill-use to which it was intended to put them, and the escape route contacts given to PRY by "CARMEN" were almost all proven supporters of the Allied cause.

And yet Pry failed dismally in his mission. The Belgian authorities in Lisbon sensed duplicity in his story; the kept the letters and routed PRY to the UK. There he was directed through the routine check at the London Reception Centre. He adhered at first to his cover story, but failed to convince his examiner. Under more detailed examination, he finally revealed his contact with the Germans, but still withheld important details of the true story. He was a poor dissimulator, and the examiner at the London Reception Centre recommended that he be subjected to more intensive questioning.

PRY arrived at Camp 020 at the end of October 1942, and a whole week went by before he could be persuaded to part with his jealous reticences, perhaps because he still aspired to the professorship in Mathematics at a German University which had been glibly promised to him by KARSTEN "on the morrow of German victory".

PRY practised mathematics at Ham and Huntercombe until February 1945, when he was delivered to the care of the Belgian authorities.

Manoel MESQUITA Dos Santos

Recruitment by the Germans of a Portuguese journalist living in Brazil to carry out a mission in south Africa after final training and briefing in Lisbon: here was an interesting departure from the normal enemy espionage practice as observed at Ham. The man in question was Manoel MESQUITA Dos Santos, a not unsuccessful journalist in Rio de Janeiro whose finances had long been in a desperate state. He had a wife and child to support; he had been despised by his more unctuous relatives; and he fell an easy prey to Germans who were aware of his talents and could offer attractive payment for their exploitation in the German cause.

MESQUITA, who was to be sent to Lourenço Marques with a view to his ultimate introduction as a German agent in to the Union of South Africa, received courses in secret writing and other instruction in Rio de Janeiro itself. Later he was despatched to Lisbon for vetting, training in wireless transmission, and to receive detailed orders from more adept members of the German Secret Service than those resident in Brazil. It was apparent from their suave and generous treatment of the agent at all times that the Germans expected much of him.

MESQUITA sailed from Lisbon for Lourenço Marques in April 1942. On arrival there he found that a permit to travel into and around the Union of South Africa was less easy to obtain than either he or the Germans had imagined. After some weeks he lost enthusiasm for espionage. Successively he offered to the authorities in Lourenço Marques ideas to dry meat and to develop the Portuguese colony, and in the second he succeeded in promoting a certain official interest. He was, however, handicapped by lack of funds, and it occurred to him that the Germans, of whose demands on himself he had been conveniently oblivious for some time, might finance him further. He sent a telegram to Lisbon, signed with his spy name of "TOME", and requested funds. The Germans still apparently had faith in him, although he had not heard from them nor they from him since his departure from Lisbon; eventually he received the equivalent of £200.

On completing a tour of the Portuguese colony in his personal interest and at German expense, MESQUITA decided to return to Portugal. M I 5 were determined that he should not reach Lisbon without being afforded the opportunity of explaining his brief career under German sponsorship, for ISOS had given warning of his employment as a spy. MESQUITA was arrested when his ship called at Freetown in October 1942, and a month later he was admitted to Camp 020.

Between the time of his detention in Africa and his arrival at Ham, MESQUITA had made no admission of contact with the enemy. The case gave cause for considerable anxiety. In the first place, the investigation began at a time when the Foreign Office were experiencing difficulty with the Portuguese nationals on charges of espionage, so that a written confession was necessary. In the second place, MESQUITA was an intelligent man and the original evidence against him was decidedly slender.

But it was noticed at Camp 020 that he had travelled out to Lourenço Marques in the same ship as Sobhy HANNA, and this led to a re-examination of the whole of Sobhy HANNA's property in the hope of finding evidence which would incriminate MESQUITA. Now in that mass of property had been listed a certificate issued by the shipping company to passengers on the occasion of "crossing the Line". As is the custom at equatorial dinners on shipboard, such certificates were passed round for signature. Various signatures, some affected by stimulants, were compared with the passport signature of MESQUITA. The searchers were rewarded with the chance in a million. In fact, one German agent had unwittingly given his signature to another German agent; and such was the inscrutable decree of Providence that both the agents and the document were vouchsafed unto the examining officers at Ham.

It now remained for the coincidence to be put to good use. The Commandant decided to convey to MESQUITA that he had been covered by a British agent, and covered so successfully that the British agent had even induced MESQUITA to provide him with his signature. In addition it was possible also to put to good use the name "TOME", for MESQUITA had used that name in his telegram to Lisbon and a cross-check was available from ISOS that "TOME" was, in fact, his spy name.

The Commandant interrogated MESQUITA at the earliest opportunity after the marshalling of all the facts. He addressed MESQUITA as "TOME". He asked him for a signature, and was promptly rewarded with a false one. But this eventuality had been anticipated. His passport was produced and he was asked to explain away the difference.

MESQUITA was now off balance, and he certainly did not regain it when he was told that he had not only been covered by a

British agent as far as Lourenço Marques, but that he had also been good enough to present that agent with his signature. The certificate was produced and compared. Then MESQUITA was sent to his cell with a direct order to write out a full confession against time. This order was obeyed, and thus it came about that a good basis was established for further investigation and the Foreign Office had their evidence for the Portuguese Ambassador.

In the fulness of time the case was further developed, for MESQUITA reacted by making a clean breast of his sins in the hope of averting a death penalty which it would have been impossible to impose upon him

Gastão Crawford DE FREITAS Ferraz

A German spy who might easily have jeopardised the success of the Allied landing in North Africa was Gastão Crawford DE FREITAS Ferraz, radio operator on the SS "GIL EANNES", depot ship of the Portuguese Cod Fishing Fleet operating in the Atlantic. The alertness of the Security Services and prompt action on their information by the Royal Navy led to his arrest on the high seas a matter of hours before his ship came upon the mammoth convoy of Allied transports carrying the invasion forces to French North Africa in November 1942.

It was towards the end of that month that De FREITAS, whose activities has been betrayed by ISOS, arrived at Camp 020. The investigation of the case was as outstanding in importance as it was exceptional in difficulty. Its importance derived from the fact that his position had enabled him to enjoy perfect cover to carry out his infamous work. The fishing fleet in which he worked had strong diplomatic backing, for not only did in involve reciprocal advantages held by the British fishing fleets off the Azores, but there was also the personal guarantee of two senior Portuguese naval officers that no vessel of the fleet which they administered would be guilty of unneutral conduct.

The difficulties of the investigation were various. The evidence against the known agent on the "GIL EANNES", which carried two radio operators, rested solely on ISOS, which yielded only a cover name. Even when there was good reason to believe that De FREITAS was clearly identified with the actual spy, use of ISOS was impossible. Moreover, there was no corroborative evidence in De FREITAS' property; he had jettisoned his code when his ship was stopped on the high seas. Lastly, the Foreign Office were anxious for an early written confession to justify the Portuguese Government.

Initial handling of the case needed to be judicious. De

FREITAS was called for interrogation. Play began with the classical opening: "What is your name?" De FREITAS gave it. The next move can hardly have been anticipated by the agent. He was handed a photograph of Kuno WELTZIEN, who was known to have been one of his many Lisbon contacts, and asked whether he recognised the man. After a horrendous Portuguese shriek of shock and anguish, De FREITAS melted into hysterics. No useful purpose could be served by further interrogation so long as the man remained en crise. He was returned to his cell and two stool-pigeons were introduced to him that night. There was no profit in the morning. In fact there was a loss: a sensitive secretary who had overheard the awful wail of recognition resigned.

In the afternoon of this second day, De FREITAS was given a smooth, sympathetic hearing on the blow hot, blow cold principle. Hysteria and fright were briefly dispelled. He yielded to artful cajolery: he admitted to his espionage employment and to the transmission of two messages to the Germans, one of them detailing shipping at St. John's, Newfoundland. He was persuaded to write a brief confession on the spot; and when he had signed it he was ordered to amplify it in a complete statement of his contacts and activities.

De FREITAS was broken, the requirements of the Foreign Office met. The relief of the investigating officer soon gave way to regret that justice could not be done to De FREITAS, for if ever a man deserved to die for espionage, it was he. Through the monstrous inadequacy of legislation at that time, there was no chance of trial under the Treachery Act. De FREITAS was to remain in detention at Ham and Huntercombe until September 1945. But if the authorities acted on the recommendation of the Commandant, he was preceded on his return to Lisbon by an invitation to the Portuguese Government that in due course they institute proceedings which would result in a resounding sentence for a spy who had brought that Government into official disrepute.

Charles Olivier BOYD

On 1 July 1940, while en route to Africa from New York in a British steamer, Charles Olivier BOYD, a South African student, was captured by a German raider and interned for a short time at a civilian camp in France. Soon afterwards ISOS revealed that he had volunteered to work for the Germans and was trained to spy for them in South Africa.

His sudden arrival at Gourock in November 1942 was therefore not expected by M I 5. Unadvised of his coming, the immigration authorities cleared him to proceed to visit a relative in Bo'ness.

BOYD's name, with that of all other civilians landing in Britain, was passed through M I 5 Registry check. The ISOS trace against him was on record. Two M I 5 officers travelled to Scotland immediately, effected arrest and were pleasantly rewarded with a partial confession on the train going South.

One of the officers concerned discussed the case with the Commandant shortly after BOYD had been received at Camp 020. He suggested that, if the man were carefully handled in interrogation, he might develop on his own volition into an agent-double: recent German espionage activity in South Africa indicated the desirability of such a step.

The Commandant interrogated BOYD in accordance with this agreed policy. At an early stage he became thoroughly disgusted with BOYD, who made no secret of his anti-British, pro-German outlook; but he held his peace in order to achieve the main objective, leaving information as a secondary consideration.

BOYD, a precious creature of half-baked ideals, showed no inclination to volunteer for double-cross employment. He ranted against the British. He claimed not to be impressed by the "cross-section of the race" with whom he had been in contact at his internment camp in France. He did not begin to appreciate that at Ham he was consorting with a more true cross-section of the Herrenvolk and their parasites.

Patience with him was exhausted. All traces of idealism dropped from him when he was brought face to face with the grim reality of his position. The wide yellow streak in him was brought to the surface when it was bluntly put to him that he might be hanged, for then he had no scruple in accepting with alacrity the possibility of becoming a double agent. But it was too late then, and the recommendation went out that BOYD, an unreliable character, receive the deserts of a spy and not the favours of a potential collaborator.

The further investigation of the case, untrammelled by considerations of finesse, yielded considerable Intelligence profit. His contacts included, among many Germans, two Spaniards who had featured at Ham in the MORALES case; a wealth of information was obtained on the personnel and technique at different GIS training establishments; and there was confirmation and amplification of much other knowledge of GIS personalities.

The South African authorities had been fully informed at all stages in the progress of the case. They accepted the Commandant's opinion of BOYD, and declined the have anything to do with him. In early 1943 BOYD was given the opportunity to consort with that cross-section of the British race with which he would have most in common. He was sent to Dartmoor.

Lucien Jules François LECOQ

The dismal failure of the MOREL mission led the Germans in Paris to recruit a new agent who might succeed in flying back to them a model of the newest aircraft in service with the RAF. The instrument they chose was no paragon of virtue or model of competence; but he could fly.

He was Lucien Jules François LECOQ, a young Frenchman who had been expelled from the French Naval Air Arm many years ago as a wilfilly stormy petrel with no more than a chronic nuisance value to the service. He followed no particular occupation over the next years, but spent his divorced mother's meagre income on learning to fly. He stole motor-cars and was twice sentenced in French courts. For two years up to the outbreak of war, he enjoyed unnatural relations with a wealthy man who made him a present of an airplane. On mobilisation in 1939 his record qualified him for service with "Les Joyeux", the notorious penal regiment of the French Foreign Legion.

In 1940 he was demobilised and hastened to marry into a prosperous family which put him into a fruit-juice bar business at Cannes. He bought an invention of doubtful value and had to sell the fruit-juice bar business to meet his commitments. He took work with his wife's step-father, but soon quarrelled with him. He returned to his homosexual friend, and quarrelled with him. Then he quarrelled with his wife.

As a change he decided to volunteer for the "Corps of French Pilots to Aid Germany in her Struggle against Russia". The decayed Frenchman who received him with open arms decided that he might best be used in the service of Germany in her struggle against Russia by flying to England and reporting back information about French pilots fighting with the Allies. But even that errand was too big for them to handle for themselves; they put him in touch with the GIS. The Germans, of whom he met several at this early stage in his treachery, were not particularly impressed by him and his idea of flying to England in his own plane. It was not for want of pertinacity on LECOQ's part that his first offers to the enemy came to nothing.

It was only in October 1942, after MOREL had come to grief with their earlier commission, that LECOQ was received by the Germans with any sympathy. He was given new contacts in the GIS: the same men who had recruited and briefed his luckless precursor. They gave him the same mission, their full support and their German blessing.

LECOQ took off from a French aerodrome in his Comper-Swift plane in the early days of December 1942 and alighted an hour and twenty minutes later at Marchwood, Southampton. To the local Security Officer he told a circumstantial story of hazardous escape from the other side of the Channel. Then he demanded urgently to be put in touch with the American authorities, with whom he had matters of importance to discuss. (His explanation later was that he wanted to interest them in the invention which had cost his fruit-juice bar business, and not in his more recent activities.)

The Security Officer was not impressed. LECOQ was directed to the London Reception Centre, where he maintained his demands and truculence. An indiscretion to a fellow detainee there led to his denunciation as a contact of the Germans. The LRC examiners could not persuade LECOQ to change his circumstantial story of escape, but they did lure him into new inconsistencies. A few days later he was transferred to Camp 020.

Here he proved extremely difficult to handle at the outset of investigation. He adopted the astonishing attitude that it was an impertinence for the British authorities to enquire into his activities. He made it plain that he was not concerned with the outcome of the war. Politically, this Frenchman insisted that he was a neutral; he bore no animosity against the Germans, he had no reason to love the British. He was a café conversationalist of the worst type. He was enamoured of the sound of his own voice, but considered it quite unnecessary to answer difficult questions. He was impertinent to his interrogating officer. He gave trouble to the prison administration. Finally, he gave extreme offence to a number of other prisoners with whom he was associated, resulting in a petition from them pleading for a discontinuation of any contact with them. He was a pariah among outcasts.

LECOQ, even after he was broken by process of attrition and his story extracted in its sordid entirety, gloried in outbursts of indiscipline. He posed as a man of courage who could endure much punishment. It angered him, and finally defeated him, that he was both pitied and ignored. Perhaps the last straw came when he smashed his cell chair to smithereens in a fit of pique, repented it, and asked for another. A prison NCO, on instructions from the Commandant, handed to LECOQ the wooden splinters recently collected from his cell, and suggested that he might care to put them together again.

From that moment LECOQ developed into a tame prisoner. He gave no more trouble before his shipment to France in the Spring of 1945.

Edward Arnold CHAPMAN

Fiction has not, and probably never will, produce an espionage story to rival in fascination and improbability the true story of an

English crook, Edward Arnold CHAPMAN, whom only war could invest
with any virtue, and that only for its duration.

CHAPMAN's pre-war career was not pretty. He was an Army
deserter before he was bound over, as a first offender, on a charge
of "being on enclosed premises for an unlawful purpose". A month
later he was sentenced to a total of nine months' imprisonment on a
new "enclosed premises" charge, for stealing a cheque and for
obtaining credit by fraud and money by false pretences. Not very
long after his release he behaved in Hyde Park in a manner likely to
offend the virtuous public and was caught in flagrante delictu. A
fortnight later he was sentenced to nine months' hard labour for
obtaining credit, food and lodgings by fraud. In 1938 he was wanted
in Edinburgh on a safebusting charge(+), but it was some time before
he was arrested, and in March 1939 he jumped his bail. Four days
later he was re-arrested in Jersey and received a sentence of two
years' hard labour for burglary and house-breaking. He endured this
enforced inactivity for four months and then escaped from prison. On
the day following the outbreak of war he stood unabashed in the dock
at the Jersey Royal Court and heard the judge pronounce on him a
further sentence of twelve months' hard labour for theft.

It would not be fair to CHAPMAN, a vain crook, to omit other
transgressions for which he was not required to do penance, but
which he admitted later with a certain diffidence. He attracted
women on the fringe of London Society, indulged in violent affairs
with them, and then proceeded to blackmail them by producing
compromising photographs taken by an accomplice. He confessed to an
experiment in sodomy. He did not blush when he related how, having
infected a girl of eighteen with VD, he blackmailed her by
threatening to tell her parents that she had given it to him!

That was the background of Edward Arnold CHAPMAN, aged
twenty-seven, when the invading Germans found him in Jersey sitting
disconsolately in his solitary confinement. They moved him to a
French prison. There he contrived to manufacture master keys which
allowed him to move freely at night between the men's and women's
blocks. These restricted adventures palled after a time, and CHAPMAN
decided that he might bargain for his liberty. He offered his
services to the Germans. Enquiries were made on his behalf, and
finally he was released to an Abwehrstelle in France, for the GIS
had noted with approval his excellent qualifications as a potential
agent.

The Germans, led by a Hauptmann GROENING and Hauptmann
PRAETORIUS (who now has something in common with his protégé, for he
spent some months in 1945 and 1946 in prison at Bad Nenndorf), set

---

(+) To the admiring Germans later he became known as "Safebuster".

about training him as a high-grade saboteur and spy. For once in a
way it had to be conceded that they did their work well: his courses
of instruction in sabotage, espionage and radio transmission were
thorough, and he was an apt pupil. In Nantes they had the wisdom to
accept this crook as an equal in an Officers' Mess. They pandered to
his vanity, granted him liberty and treated him with respect.

In the end he became something of a hero, for he won a wager
for the Mess by worming his way into a well-guarded arsenal and
placing there a dummy package of explosive, wholly unobserved.

The Germans came to love CHAPMAN, but although he went
cynically through all the forms, he did not reciprocate that
felling. CHAPMAN loved himself, loved adventure, and loved his
country, probably in that order. He saw in the Germans the source of
satisfaction of two personal and one patriotic emotion […] The
mission with which they entrusted him met all his wishes: he was to
be dropped in England by parachute to carry out sabotage and
espionage tasks and later he might be sent to the United States with
similar instructions.

Already before October 1942 ISOS had begun to record
CHAPMAN's practice transmissions from Nantes, Paris and Berlin and
there were pointed references to him in other intercepts. M I 5
expected "FRITZ" or "FRITZCHIEN" CHAPMAN to arrive that very month.
Arrangements were made to receive him under the code-name "Operation
NIGHTCAP". Warning was broadcast secretly to police and military
authorities throughout Britain; and M I 5 representative was posted
to Operations Room of Fighter Command to observe on radar
instruments the tracks of incoming enemy planes in order to identify
by its special behaviour the plane carrying CHAPMAN.

There was considerable delay in his despatch, and he did not
leave France until the early hours of 16 December. He was seen off
by members of the Nantes Mess, and the Chief of the Stelle promised
champagne all round on receipt of a message from CHAPMAN which would
herald the success of his mission.

CHAPMAN made landfall at 0225 hours on 16 December near
Littleport in the Isle of Ely. He rid himself of his parachute,
neatly stacked his radio transmitter and other equipment, and then
proceeded to haul a protesting Mr Convince out of a warm bed at Apes
Hall. From there he telephoned into police and invited them to
interview him and then put him in touch with the British
Intelligence Service, for which he had important information.

The policeman who came down to fetch CHAPMAN to his station
did not realise that he was the bull who had been taken by the
horns. Dutifully and phlegmatically he took down a short statement
which CHAPMAN signed. He telephoned the news to his superiors. Then
he sat down to make out his own report on the official stationery of

the Isle of Ely Constabulary. He headed it:- "Unauthorised Arrival from Enemy Territory".

The telephone call, in the meantime, had set in motion all the machinery prepared to receive CHAPMAN. He was collected from Littleport and rushed to Camp 020.

Interrogation began in the early hours of 17 December, and from the outset it was apparent that CHAPMAN, for once in his life, wished to be honest, possibly because the effort did not rob him of vainglory. By 1430 hours draft summaries of a series of interrogations by the Commandant were in the hands of M I 5 together with full verbatim transcriptions. In the YP which covered these papers the Commandant stated:-

> "Under interrogation CHAPMAN has been candid. There are remarkably few discrepancies in the material (ISOS) that can be checked, and the concensus of opinion among officers who have seen him is that they are natural inexactitudes. His motive (in reporting at once to the authorities) is a streak of hatred for the Hun coupled with sense of adventure. There is no woman in the case, and no bargain for rehabilitation. He is possessed of courage and nerve. My opinion is that CHAPMAN should be used for double-cross purposes, that Camp 020 is no place from which he can be used, but that he should be kept under active supervision".

Interrogation continued through the day. CHAPMAN revealed that his arrival and mission in England had been intended to be incidental to his ultimate impact on the United States in the German service.

CHAPMAN had been instructed to establish radio contact with his controlling Stelle at the earliest possible opportunity. As soon as M I 5 had approved his tentative employment as a double agent, he was driven out of Camp 020 with his transmitter and after a long diversionary tour was set down at the doors of an equestrian club a few yards from the camp gate. Here his transmitter was installed and an aerial rigged.

There was much speculation when CHAPMAN began confidently to send out his call-sign. It turned to excitement when acknowledgement and invitation to start transmitting came from the other side. The reply was faint and CHAPMAN, with little prompting, signalled his control to come nearer the coast, to move east, to move west, so that there was much breathless hithering and thithering that night on the other side of the Channel.

But there were also celebrations. CHAPMAN's success was toasted no less in the Officers' Mess at Ham than in Nantes.

CHAPMAN, in the familiar loneliness of a cell, was unable to respond to either.

    The investigation at Camp 020 continued. The Commandant despatched a new YP to M I 5:-

> "I put it to CHAPMAN that the German Secret Services were taking an abnormal risk in sending him, with his criminal record, to England at all, particularly if his present mission was of a secondary nature and the American sabotage adventure was the primary issue. CHAPMAN's reaction was curious. He said he had put this point himself to GROENING and PRAETORIUS. Apparently they laughed off this objection, and one said to the other that it was in the interest of the German Secret Service to send over such a man to England as he would not dare to betray them. I told CHAPMAN this was plain, unvarnished blackmail, and CHAPMAN, with some bitterness, said that he had felt it all along.

> "CHAPMAN told me that he was the first to realise that if he were liberated, he would have to be under control in a quiet country place. He said that the last thing in the world he would do would be to break surveillance. He had no desire at all to fall into the hands of the police. He added: 'As I figure it out, with my brilliant past, I am due for a stretch of something like fourteen years.'

There was a wistful quality in CHAPMAN's smile when the Commandant pointed out that the Germans themselves had come as near to betraying him as was possible. The evidence was produced: around the bundle of banknotes totalling £1,000 which they had given him as he stepped into the plane, the Germans had left a band clearly stamped with the imprint of the Deutsche Bank, Hamburg.

    CHAPMAN was released to B.1.a for active service as an agent-double on 22 December. With him went the Commandant's final assessment of his character:-

> "The story of many a spy is commonplace and drab. It would not pass muster in fiction. The subject is a failure in life, and those who train him do not appreciate he must fail in espionage as he fails in everything else. The motive is sordid. Fear is present. Patriotism is absent. Silence is not the equipment of a brave man, rather is it a reaction to dread of consequence. High adventure means just nothing at all.

"The story of CHAPMAN, the spy of the German Secret Service who landed by parachute, is different. In fiction it would be rejected as improbable. The subject is a crook, but as a crook he is by no means a failure. His career in crime has been progressive.... Latterly his rewards have been large, and no doubt he despises himself for his petty beginnings...... The man, essentially vain, has grown in stature and, in his own estimation, is something of a prince of the underworld. He has no scruples and will stop at nothing. He plays for high stakes and would have the world know it. He makes no bargain with society, and money is a means to an end! Of fear he knows nothing, and while patriotism is not a positive virtue, he certainly has a deep-rooted hatred of the Hun. In a word, adventure to CHAPMAN is the breath of life. Given adventure he has the courage to achieve the unbelievable. Discretion is not his strong suit, yet paradoxically his very recklessness is his standby. Today he is a German parachute spy: tomorrow perhaps he will undertake a desperate hazard as an active agent-double, the stake for which is his life. Without adventure he would be a rebel; in the ultimate he will have recourse again to crime in search of the unusual......"

CHAPMAN took up quiet country residence under the tactful surveillance of two FSP and surprised everyone by his meek conduct. He had time enough to think. He produced considerable additional information about his German contacts. An unprecedented quirk of conscience reminded him that a girl in Scotland had a child by him. He was allowed to communicate with her in writing, and M I 5 assumed guardianship over the stray and waif by opening a banking account in the woman's name and helping her to furnish a flat.

This was no act of charity. CHAPMAN was to earn his keep. B.1.a devised a brilliant programme for him. The Germans expected spectacular results of their agent, and they were not to be disappointed. It was decided to stage a damaging explosion at an important war factory. De Havilland's at Hatfield had been named by the Germans. Chapman, who inspected the site, agreed with his B 1 a controlling officer that the obvious and most damaging sabotage target was the power plant. A small, well-placed explosive would cripple the entire works over a considerable period.

The target was remote enough from the main buildings to justify restriction of advice of the forthcoming operation to a few key-men at De Havilland's. Rubble, carefully daubed canvas and odd pieces of machinery were judiciously strewn over and around the power plant; and in the night there was a loud but empty explosion.

By special arrangement a very limited edition of the "Daily Express" carried in its back page next day a small discreet paragraph headed: "Explosion at North London Factory". Copies of that edition were included in the batch of British newspapers despatched daily by air to Lisbon, in the sure knowledge that the Germans there would acquire a copy. CHAPMAN, in the meantime, was to transmit an exultant message reporting his triumph. The Germans might be inclined to check his claim: the dressing of camouflage over the "damaged" plant would deceive the eye of any camera in a reconnaissance plane; the excision of the news item from subsequent editions of the "Daily Express" would be explained by natural censorial objections.......

The Germans did not seriously doubt CHAPMAN's claim, but some time later it was agreed among them that he should return to Paris to report and for reassignment. It was left to the agent to find his own way back. The prospect did not dismay CHAPMAN: it offered high adventure, and he was confident that he could face the most searching enquiry into his recent activities in England.

In early March 1943 CHAPMAN signed on the SS "CITY OF LANCASTER" as an assistant steward in the name of "Hugh ANSON". A few days later he arrived in Lisbon and effected contact with the local Stelle, which sent news of his arrival to Paris. While he awaited instructions, the local Abwehr representatives decided that they might capitalise the services of this fabulous agent for their own greater glory. He was invited to place a coal bomb in his ship's bunkers and he accepted the commission. He returned to the "CITY OF LANCASTER" and handed the explosive to the ship's captain, who had been given a vague outline of the general picture, with instructions to hand it to the Security authorities at the first British port of arrival.

CHAPMAN was summoned to Paris. He travelled via Madrid, where he was received with deference by members of the local Stelle, and then helped on to Paris. There he was welcomed with much junketing, and the same was true of a transit call he made in Berlin en route to Oslo, the new station of his proud and grateful controller GROENING, who was holding down his position in the Abwehr solely as a result of the resounding triumph of the agent.

But the Germans did not accept CHAPMAN's story without question: he was subjected to searching enquiry which ignored no detail, even if the approach was fundamentally hopeful and friendly. CHAPMAN met the situation with infinite resource. His glib but assured version of events since his departure for England was finally accepted as complete and true. There were more junketings. CHAPMAN was granted a special bonus of 110,000 marks, the freedom of Oslo and a trim yacht in which to disport himself.

They were halcyon days for CHAPMAN and he enjoyed them for over a year. But it was not all play in Norway, and occasionally CHAPMAN had to act as instructor in radio and sabotage at the Oslo agents' school. This employment provided M I 5 with a useful check on his new activities, for in May 1944 two Icelanders who were broken at Ham, Sverri MATTHIASSON and Magnus GUDBJORNSSON, gave descriptions of one of their instructors, "FRITZ", which tallied in every particular with the prodigal Edward Arnold CHAPMAN.

CHAPMAN himself was not long in following them. The Normandy landings had taken place and the Germans could no longer afford to fritter away the services of one of their most successful agents. He was groomed for a straight espionage mission: to report on damage caused by the V.1 attacks, then at their height; activity at USAAF airfields; technical details of latest British submarine detectors, radar equipment on aircraft, and any information on the new type of square valve which permitted the exploitation of unused frequencies.

CHAPMAN repeated his parachute landing in England on the night of 27/28 June 1944 and again contacted the police. Soon he was in touch with his B.1.a controllers and shortly afterwards he made the first of three daily visits to Camp 020 for further investigation of his story.

Those days were well employed, for CHAPMAN was expansive in his conceit, both in the interrogation rooms and over lunch at the Griffin Hotel in Kingston, as the "doodle-bugs" puttered overhead or exploded in the near distance. There was an excellent check on his good faith in this return visit, but any qualms which might have been felt about a possible change of heart were dispelled when CHAPMAN, without prompting, named MATTHIASSON and GUDBJORNSSON among agents known to him during training in Oslo.

It became evident during interrogation that CHAPMAN had become endeared to his controller, GROENING. Later he admitted that he had a girl friend in Norway, Dagmar LAHLUM, to whom he had confided that he was in touch with the British Secret Service. He claimed that he could trust the girl implicitly; misguided or not, she loved him. Further questioning elicited the information that Dagmar lived on premises to which Abwehr personnel had free access, and she had social contact with several of them.

CHAPMAN hoped to continue his double-cross activities and then to return to Norway. But affection for a man and love of a woman had complicated what would otherwise have been a straight issue. CHAPMAN might be blown already in Norway; doubt would attend any new controlled transmissions. To send him back to Norway was to risk his life or, worse, to court disaffection.

In his final YP summarising the situation, the Commandant issued a note of warning:-

"The outstanding feature of the case is the courage of
CHAPMAN .... he has rendered, and may still render, his
country great service. For that, in return, CHAPMAN deserves
well of his country and pardon for his crimes.

"I make this point because I do not wish to be held wanting
in admiration of a brave man. It is, however, a duty to
focus attention on any weakness of the case, for otherwise
there would be little object in the investigation at all.
Thus it comes about that I must issue a warning about this
very strange character. In England he is wanted for crime.
In Germany he is admired and treated royally by the German
Secret Service. It is not unnatural, therefore, in the
years, that he has come to dislike the English in many
respects and like the Germans. Indeed, there is more than
admiration, there is genuine affection for his German
master, GROENING ....."

CHAPMAN was returned to the care of B.1.a on 5 July 1944.
Soon afterwards developments on the Continental fronts helped to
solve the problem of his further exploitation in England, for it had
already been agreed that he must not be allowed to return to Norway.
    In actual fact it is doubtful whether the Germans ever
suspected their "FRITZ" of ingrate duplicity, for after the war was
ended Kapitän-Leutnant Heinrich AHLRICHS, a knowledgeable Abwehr
personality who was held at Bad Nenndorf, said this of him:-

"A special radio operator had been sent from Domäne, the
Abwehr's master receiving station, to Paris to receive
'FRITZ's' transmissions. After he had been dropped in
England on this second mission, he announced his safe
arrival in that country. I happened to be in Paris at the
time, and GROENING celebrated the news in great style....."

CHAPMAN unemployed in the national interest could only
constitute a menace to national morality. M I 5 had done him proudly:
he received £6,000 and was allowed to keep £1,000 of the money given
him by the Germans; the outstanding convictions against him were
quashed. He was observed during off-duty hours by officers of Camp 020
in fashionable places in London, always in the company of beautiful
women of apparent culture. The drain on his banking account was watched
with some apprehension. Latterly he has been keeping the bad company of
some professional pugilist with whom he has been hitting the high
spots. He has been severely reprimanded once for giving an interview to
a French newspaper in which he disclosed a part of his story.

The Official Secrets Act allows of a hearing in camera; but what will happen when CHAPMAN, embroiled again in crime, as inevitably he will be, stands up in open court and pleads leniency on grounds of acknowledged, but highly secret, wartime service? The last chapter in a fascinating story remains to be written.

Jean SINDREU Cavatorta: Octavio SERRALLACH Garcia: José Rogelio STEVENS: Andrés BLAY Pigrau

The first fortnight of the year 1943 opened at Ham with the simultaneous arrival of the accumulated captures of the Trinidad Control over the later months of the last year. It would be invidious to single out from among the four men in this haul the least unpleasant individual, but each has his special interest, and to each was given the full attention of the establishment.

Jean SINDREU Cavatorta was a young Spanish-Argentine of good education but no persuasion for honest practice. He opted for the richer rewards of shady transactions; successively he was involved, in Argentina, El Salvador and Spain, in theft, fraud, black markets and blackmail. He was thus fair game for the German Secret Service in Spain. He was duly contacted by them in their numbers and, mildly protesting, followed the line of least resistance.

For his several German contacts and for the Falange too, he accepted at least five missions in Argentina. They ranged from reports on Spanish Republicans in South America and information on the British Security station in Trinidad to agent recruitment, general Intelligence work and platinum purchases in the Americas. His operational instructions produced interesting new sidelights on official Spanish connivance in German espionage, for he was given contacts among officers on board Spanish ships and advice to use for purposes of communication the Spanish diplomatic bag from Buenos Aires, this through the good services of the Police Attaché, Manuel PEREZ Garcia. (One of these officers, Joaquin RUIZ Goseascoechea, and PEREZ Garcia himself were to find themselves at Ham only a few months later, for the British Secret Service is not notoriously tolerant of hostile acts against Britain by her undeclared enemies).

SINDREU discovered on arrival in Trinidad in transit to Argentina that the local Security authorities knew more about him than he would ever have learned about them for transmission to the Germans. He was removed from the ship after preliminary questioning had confirmed his identity with an enemy agent on whom ISOS had much information.

SINDREU resisted interrogation in Trinidad and tried the same tactics at Ham, only to discover that nothing but disaster could be achieved thereby. He then hastened to unburden himself of much valuable Intelligence. If the man himself proved of little interest, the espionage implications of his case were great for its personalities were numerous, the ramifications widespread, the information generally provided a basis for counter-action .....

As a type, Octavio SERRALLACH Garcia offered little improvement on SINDREU, but the incidence of the Spanish war probably robbed him of opportunities for honesty which the other had despised. Jusuit-educated and the scion of a staunch conservative family, he preferred the joint cause of the heterogeneous and discordant forces of the Left in Barcelona. He began his military career as an air gunner and ended it as a Brigade Political Commissioner.

SERRALLACH was driven into France with the remnants of the Catalan Army and lived there in easy exile until the threat of deportation to Germany as a forced labourer decided him to return to Spain whatever the consequences. He was newly across the frontier when Spanish police seized him as a blacklisted milicaiano, but he was soon granted provisional liberty, only to discover that his family had disowned him.

Dabblings in the black market, his sole means of livelihood, attracted the attention of the police and military authorities. He decided that he must leave Spain urgently. No help was forthcoming from his parents. He turned to a cousin married to a German and long in sympathy with Nazi ideas. Financial and documentary help were promised, at a price: submission to "the suggestions of certain German friends".

SERRALLACH, just served with mobilisation papers for a penal battalion notorious in Spain as an instrument of liquidation, hastily agreed to meet the Germans. They were not much impressed by his military record and aero-technical knowledge, which they had hoped to put to good use by this employment as an agent in the Americas. It was probably in propitiation of the cousin, of whom they expected much in the future, that they agreed to finance and generally to facilitate SERRALLACH's flight from Európe to Argentina. He received no training or proper instructions, but was merely informed that he would be contacted in Buenos Aires and would receive his orders there.

With a false Spanish passport in the name of Oscar SANCHEZ Garcia, SERRALLACH reached Lisbon, there to await further contact by BRENDEL and other Germans before sailing for Argentina. He found that South American republics were not well disposed to Spanish émigrés, and at the suggestion of BRENDEL he was able to buy, from a corrupt consular official, a Bolivian passport in his assumed name. It cost him $1,000, and he charged the Germans $2,000, although they were still giving him a generous allowance.

Probably because they were a source of easy money which might be exploited over an indefinite period, SERRALLACH began to worry, after some months of carefree life in Lisbon, over BRENDEL's failure to show greater interest in himself, or at least to give him some more definite instructions. He made a plaintive entry in his notebook: "Dr BRENDEL - why have I no news of him?".

Shortly afterwards he sailed from Lisbon in a Spanish ship. Routine examination on shipboard in Trinidad established the falsity of his claim to Bolivian nationality even before he had been indicated to the interrogating FSP as a suspected enemy agent. He was removed from the vessel and eventually despatched to England for investigation at Camp 020.

The only evidence against him was derived from inviolable fragments of ISOS, but his literary indiscretion in Lisbon provided the lever which shifted him easily from his pose as an outraged innocent. His notebook was produced. Well, why didn't he have any news of Dr BRENDEL, that well-known German spymaster? SERRALLACH still didn't know the answer to that question, but at Ham he told everything else about his relations with the Germans.

Jose Rogelio Santiago STEVENS was a fortuitous Uruguayan of Belgian parentage who, having failed completely in a commercial career, became a ship's purser until displaced by the exigencies and chances of war. He returned peevishly to commerce in Belgium, but was cheered by the discovery that he had a certain aptitude for salesmanship.

Soon, however, restriction of markets and increasing currency difficulties decided STEVENS, by some tortuous process of thought, that he might be more profitably engaged in the potato growing industry in Uruguay, to which his dual nationality gave him unquestioned entry. Coincidence of this notion with the rupture of diplomatic relations between Uruguay and Germany suggested to him the attractive idea of travelling to South America as a repatriate at the expense of the Uruguayan exchequer.

STEVENS took his birth certificate and his big ideas about potatoes to the Uruguayan authorities in Belgium. They agreed to his free repatriation, not because of the potatoes, but because he had a legitimate claim to Uruguayan nationality. STEVENS spread the good news among his Belgian business friends. Inevitably, this being Belgium, one of them knew "a man who might be interested".

That man was a talent-scout of the German Secret Service in Brussels. STEVENS was interviewed and passed to another German, RADEMACHER, who had little difficulty in persuading him to accept an espionage mission for Germany as a sideline to his major agricultural purpose in Uruguay. He was to report regularly on Argentine and Uruguayan industries supplying the Allies. His spare time should be devoted to the propagation of Nazi ideas among the unconverted Uruguayans, who should also be persuaded to buy German goods. For all these services, STEVENS would be well paid.

After training in secret writing by two methods, one employing an aniline pencil, the other a specially prepared match, STEVENS was helped to cross the Franco-Spanish frontier and was then left to make his own way into Portugal, where he was to embark for South America. There was some contretemps on the Spanish-Portuguese border, and radio messages between Abwehrstellen carried the advice that the agent "STERN" had been unavoidably held up at Fuentes de Onoro on 7 June 1942.

That was interesting news to the British counter-espionage authorities when they read the ISOS intercept. The facts would facilitate the identification in Trinidad of "STERN", the Uruguayan repatriate of whom much had already been learned from earlier intercepts.

Examination at Trinidad of individual passports of the Uruguayan group revealed that STEVENS' alone bore the tell-tale date-stamp. He was at once removed from the ship, to the audible and visible distress of a wealthy young Venezuelan girl to whom he had just proposed. It had not worried STEVENS that both he and the girl were already married to other partners, for in these last days he had decided that there was less future in potatoes in Uruguay than in heiresses in Venezuela, especially if their fathers were Presidents of National Banks, in a country which could afford to tolerate neither national nor foreign debts.

STEVENS' moral fibre was on a par with his morals. A partial admission of contact with the Germans was obtained under brief interrogation in Trinidad, and at 11am the whole story was extracted from him with little difficulty.

Principal interest in the case centred on STEVENS' secret writing material, which showed a novel departure from established German technique, but a valuable list of contacts was also produced (One of them, SCHNEIDER in Lisbon, linked with SERRALLACH).

After his transfer from Ham to the Huntercombe oubliette, STEVENS made a half-hearted bid for freedom that only won him notoriety. With the help of fellow prisoners working in the gardens, he concealed himself under a false marrow bed. A check on the returning working party disclosed his absence. Bayonets were fixed and marrow beds were prodded. Before they had reached his, STEVENS surrendered.........

Last of the foursome from Trinidad was a corrupt, middle-aged Paraguayan consul de carrière, Andres BLAY Pigrau, who succumbed easily to German seduction. In Barcelona BLAY had made a fine competence in the sale of Paraguayan nationality and visas to

European refugees. In early 1942 there was trouble with some probably virtuous politico in faraway Asunción del Paraguay. BLAY began to feel uncomfortable and decided that he ought to visit Paraguay to talk his way out of his mischief.

His wife complicated uneasiness by contracting exanthematic typhus at the very moment when BLAY had counted up his black market dollars and found that he had the bare fare to Paraguay. Her husband, himself a qualified doctor, discovered that the serum which could save her was obtainable in Spain only from American or German officials. The American consulate was sympathetic, but could not help. BLAY turned to the German Consulate-General and was there received by one Horst MÜLLER, one of the most active of German spymasters in Spain. MÜLLER was sympathetic and helpful; within a few hours a consulate messenger had delivered several ampoules of the serum at BLAY's house.

There were further meetings between BLAY and MÜLLER, sometimes at the German Consulate, sometimes in BLAY's house. MÜLLER was unctuously solicitous for the welfare of Señora BLAY. His original helpfulness had won BLAY's gratitude; his further blandishments enticed the Paraguayan into confidences. BLAY spoke of his wish to return to South America on a brief visit and of financial and exchange difficulties........

This was the opening which MÜLLER awaited and he exploited it to the full. He told BLAY that he could and would arrange everything. So anxious was he to force the new obligations upon the Paraguayan that the latter's tainted dollars were credited to him by the Germans in Lisbon at many times their value. When BLAY pointed out the error, MÜLLER dismissed it as of little importance. "He did not appear unduly concerned", BLAY wrote many weeks later; "he said that it didn't matter if they had overpaid, for everything could now be fixed up and, in any case, they had done me this service as a special favour and with the greatest of pleasure."

Before he realised that he was irretrievably involved in an espionage conspiracy, BLAY was introduced to two more German Secret Service representatives, one of them the notorious Friedrich RUGGEBURG. It was not long before the special counter-favour was asked of BLAY. It was put to him suavely at first, then with ominous insistence. BLAY weakly agreed to report back from Buenos Aires items of naval interest to the Germans; but he qualified acceptance by pointing out that he would spend in that city only a few days both on the outward and return journey.

In Barcelona MÜLLER showed BLAY a typewritten espionage questionnaire which contained also coding notes and instructions on means of communication. BLAY, a congenital ditherer, looked at papers and handed them back with the alarmed haste of one who has burned his fingers. Twice in Madrid, when he went to regularise his passport and obtain his visas, a second German produced the same papers. Twice more he scanned them, twice more he thrust them back. He was scared, he told his contact, to carry them on his person. On at least seven further meetings with MÜLLER in Barcelona, the familiar documents were produced, read, handed back.

The Germans were patient with BLAY. They told him that they would have microphotographic copies taken of the papers. BLAY demurred; he wished to take with him through the British control nothing that was compromising, however small. The Germans agreed. They told him that the microphotographs would be handed to him by a steward on his ship after passing the British control; they hinted that he would receive money in the same way. Finally, MÜLLER told him that a letter of introduction to Señor VALLES, the Spanish Consul-General in Buenos Aires, would be delivered to him in Bilbao, before he embarked, by an "hombre de confianza".

That man of trust turned out to be a Spanish policeman. He called on BLAY at his hotel in Bilbao and produced the letter. BLAY read it and dithered about taking it. The policeman appeared to have come prepared to meet that situation. He produced needle, cotton and thimble. He asked BLAY whether he had anything else which he wished to conceal from the customs of the British. BLAY lamely produced a small gold coin. The policeman took it, neatly folded the letter, and deftly sewed both into the flies of the trousers which the astonished but unprotesting BLAY was wearing that morning. Before he left he named two members of the crew of the "CABO DE BUENA ESPERANZA", whom BLAY should contact during the voyage; Jesus AGUILAR, a steward, and Bernardino SOLANA, the pastrycook. BLAY obediently noted their names.

Shortly after embarking BLAY discovered that the Germans had indeed arranged everything. Jesus AGUILAR was his cabin steward; and although he had himself made every effort to secure privacy and comfort, it was significant that he had a cabin to himself on a very crowded ship.

Meanwhile his wife, convalescent, and their children remained in Spain.

The voyage as far as Trinidad was without special event. So far neither he nor AGUILAR had mentioned their common friends; their relations were those of passenger and steward. Not did BLAY make contact with "BERNARDINO the Pantryman". When his ship arrived in Trinidad he was free from the embarrassment of microphotographs or dollar notes.

Warning of BLAY's coming and orders for his arrest had preceded him at the Port of Spain. BLAY was subjected to routine examination and treated with simulated courtesy. His luggage was

plastered with printed claims to diplomatic status. He was cajoled
into acquiescing to examination of his papers. He fell asleep while
it was being done in his cabin, and the cabin was subjected to
minute search.

Nothing of an immediately incriminating nature was found and
it was decided that no useful purpose would be served by delaying
his removal from the ship. On arrival at the detention camp, BLAY
was separated from his clothes which he had been wearing and was
issued with a pair of shorts and a shirt. His clothing was carefully
searched. Industry and pains were rewarded with discovery of the
unexpected: the letter in the flies of his trousers.

It was indeed an embarrassing document for BLAY. It was
addressed to Sr VALLES, the Spanish Consul-General in Buenos Aires, a
known collaborator of the GIS: it begged courier facilities for the
bearer, "a man of complete trust"; it sent good wishes to Messrs PEÑA
and Manuel PEREZ Garcia, both tools of the Germans; and it was signed
with a flourish: "J. BATICON". That, too, was unfortunate for BLAY
because Joaquin BATICON, also on occasional steward in the service of
the Ybarra Line, was well known to M I 5 as a German agent.

Confronted with the evidence, BLAY, a complete neurotic,
staggered visibly and launched into a hysterical farrago of
untruths. These he contradicted and confused time without number
under extreme pressure, but the small lever of detail which might
have allowed of his breaking was not available in Trinidad; ISOS was
very properly not allowed to travel out of England.

Thus BLAY came to Ham after the passage of time, a bundle of
nerves but an unbroken spy. He proved a most troublesome Latin in
interrogation. Mendacity to him was first nature. His woolly-
mindedness complicated issues. Sustained pressure extracted details
piecemeal, and finally there was a rousing reception in the small
hours in the awesome privacy of the Commandant's office. It was a
lengthy session; an interpreting officer accelerated its end by
apologetic references to his increasing somnolence. But by that time
BLAY had discharged himself of most of the truth and all the clear
memory that was in him.

The case proved rich in Intelligence and had considerable
operational importance. It yielded much information about many
German spymasters in Spain; it focused attention on the impertinent
conduct of Spanish consular and diplomatic officials and underlined
the palpably unneutral employment of Spanish shipping and seaman in
the enemy service. There were practical results, too, for soon that
rash calligraphist, BATICON, and that unimaginative Police Attaché,
Manuel FEREZ Garcia, were to be brought to Ham. Jesús AGUILAR, whose
holiness was purely nominal, took fright later on his ship's arrival
in Buenos Aires.

[…]. And BERNARDINO forsook espionage for full time pastry cooking.

BLAY, with STEVENS, SERRALLACH and SINDREU, was held at Camps 020 and 020R until some months after the war was ended.

Homer SERAFIMIDES

Homer SERAFIMIDES, Greek seaman, added a new and sordid chapter to the odyssey of espionage. Homer was, however, given to much alteration and suppression, and the authorised and proper version of his sorry tale had perforce to await the Commandant's Yellow Peril edition.

"To swindle as a reinsurance against being swindled," he wrote, "appears a prime objective of Greeks, Smyrna born and bred. Once they have that taint they never seem to loose it. Homer SERAFIMIDES is no exception. Born in Smyrna, he passed from a primary school to a High School in Crete, and was thereafter trained at Hydra as an officer in the Greek Mercantile Marine. A stable and honourable career was open to him, but it held little appeal. Within two years of his first commission he interfered in the internecine strife of the Spanish war. He suffered many privations and gained nothing but disillusionment from his Republican sympathies. Next he was signalled as the leader of a dissident group of Greeks in Shanghai who were anti-German and anti-English at one and the same time.

"Then at Lourenço Marques he was found in close touch with CAMPINI, the Italian Consul. This official is known to be engaged not only in espionage in South Africa, but also in shipping movements in the Mozambique Channel where Allied losses have occurred.

"The sympathy of SERAFIMIDES for the Axis cause, however, is difficult to gauge for he, of all people, fell an easy victim to a British agent provocateur. The man was a fellow countryman named GOUMAS, the master of the Greek vessel "LEONIDAS". The story itself is an ugly deception, but quite pretty in war. GOUMAS, acting under instructions from the British Consul, interested SERAFIMIDES in a scheme whereby the "LEONIDAS" would be sold on the high seas to an Axis submarine. SERAFIMIDES was delighted at the prospect of such dirty business. First he approached the German Consul at Lourenço Marques, but he would have none of it. He persevered and contacted CAMPINI, the Italian Consul, who agreed to proceed with the plan.

"In return for the latitude and longitude for a rendezvous

at sea on three successive dates, CAMPINI satisfied
SERAFIMIDES on the all-important issue of money. He also
made arrangements, if the plan failed, for SERAFIMIDES to
meet an Italian agent for further instructions in Buenos
Aires. Finally, there is an indication that CAMPINI
detailed the scheme in code to the Italian naval
authorities in Rome.

"In pursuance of the plan SERAFIMIDES had signed on as Chief
Officer to GOUMAS. Together they left Lourenço Marques on 26
July 1942, but as soon as the harbour had been cleared
SERAFIMIDES was arrested by GOUMAS. Four days later he was
handed over to the British authorities in Durban. He was
admitted to Camp 020 on 16 January 1943, and his downfall
was then complete.

"Generally speaking, SERAFIMIDES has been difficult to
handle. He came here embittered, conscious that he had been
duped. At the same time it is typical of him that he was
oblivious of the enormity of a crime which entailed the
betrayal of his shipmates to an enemy at sea. He obstructed
his interrogation, but again it is typical of the man that,
finding obstruction availed him nothing, he attempted to
barter his tale for cigarettes.

"Real trouble arose, however, when he learned that the
removal of CAMPINI from Consular Office at Lourenço Marques
was the main objective of the contre-espionage plan and that
a signed statement from him was necessary to this end. There
was also the complication of the time factor, for the
Foreign Office were making representations in regard to
other Portuguese spies apprehended by us, so that it was of
importance to establish a case for the removal of CAMPINI
from Lourenço Marques before diplomatic pressure subsided.

"SERAFIMIDES at once saw a chance for a bargain, but
unfortunately he and I could not come to terms. SERAFIMIDES
on his part respectfully refused to produce a statement
unless he were released. I, on my part, said he must hang
unless he complied. A battle of wits ensued and was waged
for many desperate days.

"The first round went to us, as I obtained a statement in
English. SIS then felt the statement, in Greek manuscript,
would arouse less suspicion. They drafted a translation, but
SERAFIMIDES obligingly told us the syntax was hardly that of
a sailor and would arouse more suspicion than ever.
Thereupon he offered to translate the English document into
Greek.

"I was mistrustful, as SERAFIMIDES had much to gain. In fact there was an opportunity to get even with the British Secret Service and GOUMAS at one and the same time. I therefore warned SIS that a careful check was essential. SIS thanked me for my insistence on this precaution, for it transpired that SERAFIMIDES had altered the whole tenor of the statement in his favour.

"Then it was suggested that in any event GOUMAS, the agent provocateur, came too much into prominence and that a third statement should be obtained, this time in the inimitable English of SERAFIMIDES, a plan which ruled out the necessity of recheck. SERAFIMIDES not unnaturally felt in a strong position and would bargain once more. His case officer tried sweet reason. The position of SERAFIMIDES was so bad that it could not deteriorate. A satisfactory statement, therefore, could do no harm and might, if it succeeded in removing CAMPINI from office, react in his favour. Who could tell?

"SERAFIMIDES refused. He maintained he was on honourable man and should be released. Again SERAFIMIDES was sent to his cell. He was told that the matter was of no great importance after all and that it would be well to proceed with the prosecution in the customary manner. SERAFIMIDES, the self-styled honourable man, re-opened negotiations, saying he would sign anything, true or false, against CAMPINI - subject, of course, to release.

"It was then quite obvious that these negotiations, which appear such nonsense in retrospect but which are so exasperating when the time factor is involved, must come to an abrupt end. I therefore determined to see SERAFIMIDES myself once again. A statement was obtained from him. At that point I left the room as I anticipated he would haggle over the signature. The surmise was correct. SERAFIMIDES would not sign until he had seen the Colonel. The case officer rightly doubted whether the Colonel ever wished to see SERAFIMIDES again. SERAFIMIDES capitulated, and thus it came about that the statement was obtained without any promise whatsoever.

"Insofar as SERAFIMIDES is concerned, the question of victimisation arising out of the action of an agent provocateur deserves examination. The crucial point is that SERAFIMIDES was willing to betray a Greek ship and his shipmates to the enemy at sea ..... An honest man would have rejected the proposition out of hand, and the fact that the proposition was put to him by an agent provocateur does not, in my opinion, alter his position. Greek met Greek. SERAFIMIDES was willing to perpetrate a colossal swindle, and has been swindled instead. In the circumstances I consider SERAFIMIDES is well held."

Homer nodded wistfully at Camp 020R until August 1945.

Johannes de GRAAF

It is fortunate that Johannes De GRAAF, a young Canadian national of Dutch parentage, never exploited the capacity for mischief that was in him. The Germans certainly gave him the encouragement and the training, and the Allies the opportunity therefor.

De GRAAF has returned to Holland from Canada at the age of ten. There was no British essence in him but he clung, with lowland penchant for reinsurance, to his British passport. He regretted it when the Germans invaded Holland, for they thrust him into internment. After little deliberation he told them that he regarded himself as more Dutch than British. He wished to be liberated at once to resume a clerk's live.

The Germans were never slow to capitalise moral weakness. De GRAAF found himself free of the barbed wire but inextricably entangled in espionage, a situation that displeased him not at all. He was duly recruited as a saboteur and Intelligence agent and received unusually careful training in Belgium in a variety of espionage subjects and techniques. Finally he was informed that he was to leave on a mission in Britain, there to act not only as an operational agent, but to recruit and train other spies. Full instructions as to contacts and future activities would be communicated to him when he had advised his masters that his position in England was safely established.

De GRAAF, by German arrangement, was smuggled out of Belgium and though France into Spain along an Allied escape route penetrated at its eastern end by a traitorous young Belgian named Louis De BRAY. (It may be stated in parenthesis that De BRAY set many a bad man on the road to Ham before he, too, found himself there in 1945.)

The British Consular authorities in Barcelona, to whom he told his cover story, were most helpful. They gave him food, lodging and full protection until they could transfer him to Madrid. There the British Embassy were even more accommodating. The British Military Attaché gave the "refugee" full time employment in his office, and he kept it for nine months. At the end of that time the Military Attaché gave him a gratuity of £25 and since he had not bothered to communicate with his German masters since reaching Madrid, he probably felt that he had earned the reward.

De GRAAF was sent to England. To the immigration and Security officials at the port of disembarkation he told his cover

story. Fortunately it was not well received, and he was directed to
Brixton Prison for further examination. Officers of the London
Reception Centre visited him there, heard his story and were
inclined at first to recommend his immediate release.

After six long but unsuccessful interrogations, it was
decided to transfer De GRAFF to Camp 020. A phial of tablets was
found on examination of his property; glaring inconsistencies were
found in the statements which he had made during outside
interrogations. Confronted with the evidence and the will to break
him, De GRAFF surrendered his true story after only a brief
struggle.

Rogerio de Magalhaes Peixoto MENEZES

The exploitation by the Germans of Portugal and the Portuguese for
espionage purposes was fast becoming too much of a bad thing.
Effective counter-measures necessarily hinged on diplomatic action
at the highest level. The cases of De FREITAS, MESQUITA Dos Santos
and SIMOES, demonstrably grave as they were, had not provided the
Foreign Office with material of sufficient weight to force a gaily
tolerant Portuguese Government to take a serious view of the
situation and to remedy it by drastic action.

The instrument of disruption was provided with the
apprehension of a third-rate spy, Rogerio de Magalhaes Peixoto
MENEZES, a clerk at the Portuguese Embassy in London itself. The
repercussions of the case were of startling importance, and it
represented one of the major wartime triumphs of M I 5 and Camp 020,
for it led to the arrest by the Portuguese of no less than seventeen
spymasters and their agents.

The story of MENEZES was not without tragedy. He belonged to
a family which had been engaged in a respectable struggle abroad in
the Portuguese Colonial Service. There was difficulty in making ends
meet. Education of the children called for sacrifices that could not
adequately meet demands. Both he father and mother died before
MENEZES was fourteen, and the children lived on the scant capital
inherited from their parents, augmented by an official grant of £6
monthly. By scraping here and saving there, it was contrived that
MENEZES should study at the Faculty of Law in Lisbon.

He proved unstable and tired of his studies. He switched to
a clerkship at the Portuguese Foreign Office and sought
independence. His preposterous salary of £5 monthly hardly allowed
it, and certainly there was nothing left over for this sensuous
youth to expend on women, of whom he was abnormally fond. He
volunteered for service abroad, where conditions of pay were better.
Intrigue in his service was rife, and though MENEZES had recourse to

it to obtain a transfer to Washington, it was typical of him that he
resented a counter-intrigue which in due course was to land him in
London.

MENEZES gained nothing from those equally disaffected around
him. By January 1942 there was not even a sense of Service loyalty
to keep the dissolute youth in check, and it was then that he took
his first fatal step. He contacted an old school friend and
consented, at his request, to become a gutter informant for the
Germans. Petty sums of money passed between them.

By June 1942 arrangements for the transfer of MENEZES from
the Foreign Office in Lisbon to the Portuguese Embassy in London
were sufficiently advanced for the German Secret Service to take a
direct interest in him. MENEZES was introduced by his friend to
Amady KAES and Kurt FOERSTER, representatives, not of the Abwehr,
but of the then unfamiliar Sicherheitsdienst.

MENEZES agreed to work for the Germans in England as a spy
for £25 a month. He was taught to write in secret ink. He was
instructed to communicate through the diplomatic bag by means of
letters in a double envelope addressed to his sister, who remained
ignorant of his shame.

Including his official salary, MENEZES would have £60 a
month in London, but that was not enough for him. Again he intrigued
with his school friend. He slid even further down the slippery slope
of self destruction by making contact with the Italian Secret
Service. In this case a certain Arturo OMERTI was his master who,
knowing nothing of the German contact, also taught MENEZES to write
in secret ink and gave him instructions to communicate through the
diplomatic bag; but he, with Latin scepticism, undertook to pay only
on results. Thus the lugubrious position was reached that both Axis
partners had arranged to use the same agent and neither of them knew
it .....

The contre-espionage story was one of great success.
Information was available from ISOS that MENEZES was in the pay of
the Sicherheitsdienst. In consequence he was kept under close
supervision from the time he landed in England in July 1942. He fell
for attractive girls planted on him by M I 5, but disclosed nothing
to them beyond amorous disposition.

[...] an element of deceit entered into the case, for MENEZES'
correspondence was read. But all was fair in war and in due course
proof positive was obtained that MENEZES was communicating with the
enemy, to whom he had sent several items of Intelligence.

The detection of his messages in secret writing marked a
triumph for the M I 5 laboratories. The media were unusual and it
was essential that the correspondence should bear no trace of
interference. The solution of that problem, as reported later by

Professor Briscoe, was inspired. The letters were treated with ammonia gas to develop any [...] that might be present. This showed a bright fluorescence which rapidly faded away, but which could be, and was, easily photographed.

This was important, for in February 1943 it had been decided to terminate the agent's activities. To secure the co-operation of the Portuguese Ambassador, evidence of MENEZES' gross impropriety needed to be produced. A letter in secret writing which had not yet reached the traditionally inviolable diplomatic bag was intercepted. Development was successful. The Ambassador, in righteous indignation, proceeded to strip MENEZES of diplomatic privilege in order that he might be arrested as soon as he left the portals of the Embassy.

That same morning MENEZES made a partial confession in writing, for purposes of prosecution, before Colonel Hinchley-Cooke of M I 5. In it he refused to name the channel he employed for the despatch of his communications. That defect was quickly remedied at Camp 020 that very evening.

He had arrived at Ham within a matter of hours of arrest and preliminary interrogation. Through the time factor, the Commandant lacked both papers and exhibits, but as delay might have proved dangerous, he had determined to proceed at once with interrogation. Little was known of the man at the time, and he began to indulge in half truths. But it availed him nothing, and it was not long before it was discovered that he had been acting for both the German and Italian Secret Services. One contact led to another and quick reactions on traces by M I 5 were invaluable. Within two days of his arrival a tolerably comprehensive report had been submitted in the case.

Shortly afterwards the Portuguese Ambassador was presented by the Foreign Office with details of the case. Further strong diplomatic representations were supported by charts of Axis espionage activity in Portugal based on information obtained at Ham from other German agents, and soon the Portuguese Government was compelled to take drastic steps against the Germans and their collaborators.

MENEZES himself was tried under the Treachery Act at the Central Criminal Court on 9 April 1943. He was found guilty and sentenced to death, but as a gesture of appreciation of the tardy goodwill shown by the Portuguese authorities, he was reprieved in May 1943.

Frank Domien STEINER

The epitaph of Frank Domien STEINER, the Belgian spy who was executed by his compatriots after his postwar transfer to Belgium from Camp 020, was that he failed to live by his wits. The Yellow Peril which covered the report in his case was at once STEINER's death warrant and his obituary notice.

There was little wisdom in the bleary-eyed little man who at Ham won the sobriquet of The Red-Headed Owl. But the wits on which he tried to live were certainly there. His was one long history of retrogression, as dismal as it was instructive. Since 1929, when he could have been said to have reached his manhood, he had lived on his parents and a succession of women. Intermittently, owing no doubt to demurrers from those long-suffering people, he interested himself in a number of activities which included Kleen-Ezi brushes, cars, electrical appliances, hotel sculleries, night-club bars, cosmetics, tutorial establishments, enamel, mail order trade, smuggling, Black Marketing, translations and touting for brothels in Ostend. There had been much back-sliding since STEINER, a refugee, was a member of the 10th Croydon Wolf Cub Pack during World War I.

Now and then STEINER suffered from glandular trouble which was due, no doubt, to his failure to appreciate the paradox that it is much less exhausting to be honest than dishonest. Nowhere was there evidence of journalistic activities, but it was characteristic of the man, both when he fell under the influence of the GIS and later into the arms of the British Intelligence Service, that he described himself as a journalist. Yet withal he had a fine sense of values, for he could differentiate between himself who lived "seriously with a chambermaid", and his partner, who lived with a women of easy virtue.

It was only, therefore, a matter of patience in a history as long as STEINER's to arrive at the crucial entry, "First contact with the German Secret Service", and that appeared on 10 September 1941. STEINER had recently married a Jewess to suit his and her devious purposes and installed himself in a flat lent by his most recent mistress. At first the Jewess worked while STEINER idled, but some German friend suggested to her to suggest to her husband that the arrangement was not quite comme il faut.

Thus STEINER went reluctantly to work in an aircraft factory in Germany. He had not been there long when Moritz KÖCHLING, an Abwehr officer long active in Belgium and the Netherlands, claimed him on a talent-spotting visit as one who was wasting his time and his genius. For STEINER spoke many languages, among them English, and KÖCHLING was seeking a man to send to England.

The German Secret Service obviously regarded STEINER as in important find, for at fist sight he was a man of accomplishment. Moreover, he had a relative in England, a Mr HANNAN, Deputy Chief Constable of Blackpool; and his wife in Belgium would serve as collateral......

There is little doubt that KÖCHLING, whose protégé he became, spoilt STEINER. He was well trained and learned much. He was well equipped and well paid. It was only when the time came for action that STEINER failed. It was not so much the fact that he was twice arrested en route for Lisbon that irritated the German Secret Service, but rather his stupid conduct at the Spanish frontier and at Miranda Prison which made him at once suspect as a German agent.

His release from Miranda Prison was finally effected by the German Secret Service in September 1942, and STEINER reported to KÖCHLING at The Hague four days later. The position was considered so serious that issue was joined between Brussels and Paris as to whether he should be further employed. Berlin sided with KÖCHLING of Brussels, and steps were taken to retrieve the position. Further instruction took place and visits to Germany followed.

STEINER's final mission was to go to England, pass through various interrogation centres and upon release lie low for several months. He was to check facts, not persons, and the inference was that the Germans wished to check reports from other agents. STEINER was provided with secret inks and an unusually long list of cover addresses.

STEINER finally arrived in Lisbon in March 1943. After destroying his faked passport, he rang a German contact given to him in Paris, and left advice of his arrival in Portugal. On the same day he wrote two letters for KÖCHLING, one addressed to The Hague, the other to a Madrid cover address.

Next he called at the office of a Belgian firm under the impression that they assisted refugees, and was directed to the Belgian Legation. During the interrogations there he withheld all details of contact with the Germans. On redirection to the British Passport Control Office, STEINER disclosed only enough information about his espionage contacts to arouse their interest and provoke in them a wish to send him to England to give a full account of his relations with the enemy. This proposal STEINER accepted. But on the day before his departure for England, he decided to safeguard his interests and, if possible, his wife by again contacting the German Secret Service to advise them that he was at last en route for England, his final destination. Again he rang his Lisbon contact and gave him the news.

STEINER arrived at Camp 020 in early April 1943 and was at once seen by the Commandant. It was soon apparent that the man had much information to give, and it was decided to call off further interrogation until written statements had been completed. STEINER's output was phenomenal, and the material was not without value. But the Commandant issued a note of warning in view of suggestions that the man might be used for double cross purposes: it was quite obvious, he reported, that STEINER must be subjected to an extremely searching examination before he could be satisfied of his good faith.

A primary check on STEINER's good faith was whether he would divulge of his own account the fact that in Lisbon, after contacting the British authorities, he telephoned an Abwehr representative. This he did about a week after his arrival at Camp 020, but it was felt that only the atmosphere of the establishment had prompted him to disclose that vital information.

After the mass of written statements was completed, STEINER was subjected to interrogation. The view of him taken by the case officer became progressively unsatisfactory. In the end he stood revealed as the shabby type that he really was. Nor was that all, for a check on the Deputy Chief Constable of Blackpool proved highly unsatisfactory. That gentleman not only took an unduly optimistic view of his nephew's loyalties, but was good enough to forward a letter, dated October 1941, from his nephew. At the time when that letter was written STEINER had already been in the service of the Abwehr for a month. Charged with this new evidence, STEINER admitted he had written it at the instigation of KÖCHLING. Asked why he had withheld this information, he gave the sheepish answer that he presumed we would find it out!

STEINER, the Commandant commented in his YP, was no use to the German Secret Service, he was no use to the British Secret Service and he was no use to himself. He was treacherous to a degree and, were it not for the technical mischance that he was invited to England by the British authorities in Lisbon, he would most assuredly have been hanged in England. He died instead in Belgium, where technicalities are less apt to interfere with justice.

Jean Marie LALLART

A case as strange and as difficult as any which had been investigated at Ham was that of Jean Marie LALLART. He was a competent French artist who had served for over a year with a colonial regiment in Africa some years before the war. He belonged to Montmartre and he had fought for France until the collapse. The Germans, in their wisdom, believed him to be an anglophohe, and he was. What they did not know was that he was also a germanophobe and a true Frenchman. They landed him from a U-boat off the African coast on a mission that was to be specified to him by local contacts. LALLART neglected to meet these collaborators, and told his story to the French authorities at the fist opportunity, which was one of his own making. The French received him first as a hero, then threw him into a filthy African gaol as a traitor to France.

M I 5 received the dossier in the case and agreed that LALLART had considerable knowledge of the German Secret Service and its methods. They decided that his transfer to Ham on loan from the French might yield considerable Intelligence. The French agreed to the request, but insisted that LALLART be returned to them within twenty-eight days.

At Camp 020 it was decided, despite the time factor, to examine the entire case de novo. LALLART's good faith was not, in the terms of the arrangement, a primary issue, for this was an affair between Frenchmen. But it did condition the value of his information, and for that reason investigation dwelt with some insistence on this point.

It soon became apparent that the case of the French authorities had been pitched too high and that there was substance in the defence of LALLART himself. Under interrogation - and he was not spared - LALLART, who was delivered to the British long-haired, bearded and unkempt, as one who had come out of the most unfriendly wilderness, made a good impression. "None of the reactions of a guiltyman, so familiar to us, are present," wrote the Commandant in his preliminary assessment. "His replies are steady and to the point."

Scrupulous objectivity governed the conduct of the investigation. LALLART admitted that he had undertaken missions for the Deuxième Bureau before the war, and that one of them was in England. The admission, disquieting as it was, was not allowed to prejudice the current examination.

LALLART, the anglophobe, realised that the English were giving him a fair hearing. He responded by telling his story without equivocation and without omission.

It was a story of some fascination. LALLART had come to the attention of the Germans because, during a café discussion in Montmartre, he had vehemently defended French military conduct before the collapse and indicated 'British error and perfidy'. With Teutonic logic, they took this to mean that he would be willing to translate his smouldering contempt of the British into active collaboration against them. Because he was a good Frenchman, he accepted the Germans' money, their training and their decision to send him to Africa on a mission against the Allies. His determination from the outset was to cheat the Boche and betray his secrets to French authorities who still enjoyed liberty of action.

LALLART received careful training in radio transmission, secret writing, codes and preparation and use of sabotage material. The Germans were curiously reticent about his intended mission when he first enquired to what end all this business was intended. After the Allied invasion of French North Africa, his courses were intensified. Soon he learned that he would be expected to instruct other agents to be recruited in Africa, in the majority Arabs, in espionage, sabotage and political subversion.

In early January 1943 LALLART, who carried with him no money and no equipment, was placed in a U-boat at Lorient. He had no specific instructions from his spymasters. He was merely told that a rendezvous had been fixed with German and Arab agents at a point near Port Etienne where he would be landed. From these contacts he was to receive full support and instructions.

A fortnight later LALLART pushed off from the U-boat near the coast of Rio de Oro in a rubber dinghy manned by two German seamen. A succession of big waves swamped the dinghy and washed all three men ashore on their faces.

As signal received by the U-boat had warned LALLART that his rendezvous with the shore contacts had been put forward eleven days. When he took stock of his present situation, he decided that nothing more was to be gained by delaying his report to the French authorities. There was, in fact, no safe alternative. The German seamen were loth to return to the U-boat both on account of the treacherous seas running and because they had no love for their commander, who had been impatient to proceed about his unlawful occasions without delay. Moreover, one of them had lost his trousers and a boot. Between them, the three had five litres of water salvaged from the dinghy, and Port Etienne lay sixty miles across desert waste to the south.

LALLART's duty lay there. He could have shot the two Germans, for he had his own pistol and had persuaded the one German seaman who was armed to hand over his weapon. Such a step would have economised the meagre water supply. Instead he decided to take the Germans with him and hand them over as prisoners at the end of the long trek.

LALLART set out for the south, dogged by the bootless German and his exhausted colleague. They had no means of navigation save the stars by night. The heat was intense. Water began to run short. Finally they reached Port Etienne in a state of collapse. LALLART, who was well received at first, delivered his prisoners and then told his strange story.

At Port Etienne he was believed, but from faraway Dakar came a signal ordering that he be treated, not as a true patriot, but as a traitor to France. Treatment in a squalid African prison was inhuman for a European, but LALLART suffered it all during prolonged interrogation and in the silence and neglect which followed.

It was established later at Ham that suspicion against LALLART derived, not from the man's lack of good faith, but from the German failure properly to brief and equip him. There was no clear-cut mission. The fact that he was without real evidence of any kind defeated the investigation and the defence at one and the same time. LALLART realised the difficulty of the position, but he had confidence in British impartiality. He lent himself entirely to the investigation. In material facts there were no discrepancies between the story he had told at Port Etienne and that which he gave at Ham. He produced much new detail under fair treatment and threw in for good measure a series of excellent portraits of all his German contacts.

The Commandant came to the conclusion that LALLART had, in fact, acted in good faith when the first reported to the French authorities. What LALLART might or might not have done in different circumstances, he said, was speculation and should not minimise the value of the action he did in fact take.

"At Ham," he wrote, "LALLART told his story with candour. It was his only chance, for unless he was believed he would be shot by the French. When he left to be returned to Africa, he had no illusions and, oddly, no bitterness. He told me he had acted for France and that his fiancée would have wished it so. Lastly, if the truth of this case remains undetermined, at least one thing is certain: LALLART has not been without courage in this establishment."

Thus, while the French had rejected LALLART's story as improbable, it was accepted at Camp 020, not a notoriously credulous or simple centre. Justification came many years later at Bad Nenndorf, when Kapitän-Leutnant AHLRICHS, a member of the staff at Abwehr HQ who had seen LALLART board the submarine at Lorient, disclosed that Arab agents had reported shortly after LALLART's landing in Africa that they had observed his footsteps and those of his companions making for French territory. There was disquiet in Berlin, he said, because LALLART had always been suspected of being an agent of the Deuxième Bureau or at least a loyal Frenchman........

José Francisco Javier PACHECO Y CUESTA

José Francisco Javier PACHECO Y CUESTA was a Cuban Romeo who had danced his way to second-line stardom in South America and Europe. At his zenith he was billed at the Winter Garden in Berlin and the Piccadilly Hotel in London. Success was due as much to his wife, Viviana DIAZ, and publicity frauds as to his personal endeavours. Fundamentally he was a bad man. Insofar as his wife was concerned, he would have the world believe in a saga of devotion and affection. Actually he gave her syphilis and could not be certain that she had not given it to him in the first place, so that they never discussed that little problem.

Insofar as business was concerned, PACHECO later admitted that he had advertised his dancing turn as "DIAZ & PACHECO, Stars of Fox Films and Paramount," whereas, in fact, he had no connection whatever with these film companies. Insofar as PACHECO's personal endeavours were concerned, this son of a proud Cuban Army officer, this artist to his fingertips, was not above accepting a rake off the bottles of drink which were consumed at his wife's instance at night-clubs which might well have been brothels.

DIAZ and PACHECO thus appealed to the German Secret Service. They were Cubans. Cuba was at war with Germany. They had ample opportunity for travel in Allied countries. They were unscrupulous to a degree. In March 1942 PACHECO, with other South Americans, was interned by the Germans in Belgium.

PACHECO's wife was ill at the time, but left her bed to visit the various Kommandanturen to seek news of her husband. She was passed from one office to another and finally was sent to the Kommandantur at the Porte de Namurs, where, as she could not make herself understood, an official named KARSTEN acted as the interpreter. KARSTEN was a German Secret Service official. Through him she learned that her husband could come to no harm. PACHECO was interviewed in turn by KARSTEN, and to cut a long story short accepted service under the GIS.

The DIAZ-PACHECO mission was centred in Havana. There, by frequenting the various cafés and music halls, the couple were to contact British and Allied officers and men. They were given instructions to obtain information of naval, military and air force importance. Transmission was by secret ink, by the "matchstick" medium. An unusual number of cover addresses was supplied. Their immediate reward was $2000, which would include the cost of the two passages to Cuba.

PACHECO and his wife, who had already established relations of some intimacy with the Germans, were helped into Spain en route to Cuba. In Madrid they received further assistance from representatives of the Abwehr, among them one of BATICON's old friends, FOCK's deputy, STUBBS.

After arrest by the British authorities in Trinidad in March 1943, there were voluble disclaimers by PACHECO that he had any contact with the Germans. After one interview on board ship, PACHECO begged to be excused. A security NCO accompanied him to the excusado. PACHECO came back to the interrogation table. He wished to make a statement, he said, but he would like to be taken to the excusado again, because he had hidden something there some days earlier. He returned with the NCO and produced, from a hole in the panelling of the lavatory, three "matches" for secret writing.

He became voluble then about his German contacts. He

complained also that it had always been his intention to disclose the information, and feebly denied that the decision had been forced on him by his failure to dispose of the "matches" on his first escorted visit to the excusado.....

The subsequent investigation at Ham was not uninteresting. PACHECO, properly disciplined, could and did provide much valuable information, for he was not unintelligent. He realised at long last that a life of sham had come to an end. There was no dancing left in him, or in his consumptive wife, and certainly no desire to be involved again in espionage and its consequences.

He made a considerable effort in ingratiate himself with the authorities at Ham by becoming a romantically meticulous informer on other prisoners and by fawning virtuosity as an "assessor" in other cases. It availed him little. He won no preferment. When Ham was closed he was deported to Cuba there to live, no longer by his feet, but by his dulled wits.

Johannes Ignatius HUYSMANS

One of the most useful characters held at Ham was a Belgian who gave little promise of co-operation in the early days of his detention. He was Johannes Ignatius HUYSMANS, a Brussels businessman known from ISOS to have received careful training and alternative missions in Britain, the USA, Brazil and Mexico. In Lisbon the Belgian authorities were inclined at first to direct him to the Belgian Congo. That plan did not appeal to HUYSMANS, who had been specifically advised by his GIS masters that they were not interested in African intelligence. The plan had little appeal also to the British Secret Service, which wished to have words with HUYSMANS. A pretty plot was hatched between M I 5, the Belgian Legation in Lisbon, and the Portuguese International Police: HUYSMANS was virtually shanghaied onto a plane flying to Britain. The same procedure was applied to his wife a day or so later.

HUYSMANS, therefore, arrived at Camp 020 in May 1943 in a state of some bewilderment. He had been referred to the Commandant as an important agent of the German Secret Service. The Commandant determined on a policy of interrogation at high pressure with no respite.

HUYSMANS was a man of university training, travelled, experienced, and spoke five languages. He was also a man of composure, for he blandly maintained for over half an hour a defence of mistaken identity. His weakness, and at once his strength, lay in his affection for his wife: his weakness, because he feared repercussions from the Germans, for he had been compelled to leave her in Lisbon; his strength, because he lied astutely to protect her.

It became obvious that as he had been created a spy by blackmail, he could be broken by precisely the same means. He was told that the Commandant was in a position either to betray his wife to the Germans or to snatch her away from their clutches and bring her to England. The decision rested with HUYSMANS. The Commandant pointed to the telephone of the interrogation table and stated in terms that he had only to pick it up, put a call through to Lisbon, and order Mme HUYSMANS to be despatched to England forthwith. Such was the power of the British Secret Service. The Commandant was in a strong position. He knew that Mme HUYSMANS had been brought to England in the normal way; she was already lodged in Holloway; he had in his possession a letter which she had written to her husband. A partial break was duly effected, whereafter it became a battle of wits, for he weighed each question and lied whenever he could intelligently do so.

After six hours a story was obtained based upon his admission that he had first contacted the GIS in September 1942. The investigation continued day by day, but the Commandant was dissatisfied with progress: he issued a warning against HUYSMANS' employment as a double agent, pointing out that the man was not only under fear of blackmail, but was patently unreliable and a fluent liar.

Shortly thereafter an important reaction was received from M I 5 on reports submitted previously. In effect there was evidence that already in June 1942 HUYSMANS had been earmarked for a mission in Britain. A second offensive was launched forthwith. Among the points put to him in forcible terms was the disclosure that his wife had been saved from the German menace in Lisbon and now awaited the pleasure of the British authorities. His conduct henceforth would govern her treatment and her disposal.

Relieved of his anxiety for his wife, HUYSMANS broke completely. When he realised that he had also lost in disputation with his interrogators, he lost gracefully and had the intelligence to volunteer all manner of valuable information additional to his personal account.

There was nothing especially spectacular about HUYSMANS' espionage career. The threat of Gestapo persecution blackmailed him into the German service. Once recruited as a spy, he liked it. He was well treated by his master, SCHUMANN. The training which he received would have made him a dangerous spy at large. He received instruction in radio transmission and the adaptation of ordinary receivers from no less than four experts and he had spent two months at Ostend practising transmission at German expense. He received courses also in secret writing, and over a period of many months underwent frequent refresher courses on all subjects.

Already in May 1941 he was to have left Belgium for the

United States on a mission of economic espionage, but later it was proposed to send him to England to obtain economic and military intelligence. To this end he was despatched to Amsterdam to find for himself some Allied escape route leading to the UK. He failed. The prospect of reaching England by means legitimate or illegitimate seemed remote. The Germans groomed him for missions in either the United States, Mexico or Brazil, since his ultimate destination would be influenced by an uncertain visa outlook.

Under cover of a legitimate firm engaged in international business, HUYSMANS visited Spain to enquire into the possibility of obtaining visas for the UK or United States. The Belgian Consul in Barcelona was sympathetic by unhelpful. HUYSMANS returned to Belgium, reported to his master, and was again despatched to Barcelona, this time with instructions to contact the local Abwehr representatives. The entire gang which had aided and abetted LASKI surrounded HUYSMANS. The irrepressible PEDRO and PABLO and their acolytes placed themselves at his disposal, but all that he got out of them was a transparently bogus Mexican visa.

HUYSMANS hurried back to Amsterdam and Brussels and was severely reprimanded by SCHUMANN for doing so without instructions. He weathered the storm and even persuaded SCHUMANN to allow Mme HUYSMANS to accompany him to Spain on the next trip.

The couple travelled to Spain in October 1942. Both had much contact in Barcelona with PEDRO the Abwehrmann and other disreputable characters. It was not a profitable relationship, for the HUYSMANS got into difficulties over their Spanish residence permit, for foreign travel visas were still not to be got. SCHUMANN had to come down from Brussels to sort out the difficulties and precipitate the HUYSMANS' crossing into Portugal. Money and fresh instructions were handed to the agent from time to time by members of the Barcelona Stelle, and finally he was ready to leave Spain.

In Lisbon HUYSMANS found that the Belgian authorities insisted that he should go to the Belgian Congo, the wartime destination of all Belgians aged over forty. HUYSMANS reported to a local Abwehr contact, who advised him to avoid the Congo at all costs and make special efforts to reach Brazil.

A few days later the Belgians, under advice from MI5, informed HUYSMANS that he would need to go to England before being sent to the Congo. HUYSMANS took fright and appealed to be sent to the Congo direct. He reported his plight to the Germans, who could promise no more than that they would report to SCHUMANN.

HUYSMANS panicked completely when he was given a few hours' notice to leave for England by air. He told his wife, who collapsed, and was certified unfit to travel. He made frantic efforts to persuade the Germans to help him, but they appeared unimpressed, saying only that SCHUMANN's decision was still awaited.

HUYSMANS returned to his pension only to be arrested by the International Police because of his refusal to travel to England; he had outstayed his welcome in Portugal. After two days in prison, HUYSMANS was taken directly to the airport and put on the plane for England.

HUYSMANS certainly deserved the death penalty as a spy. Fortune, however, was on his side, for the Belgian authorities in Lisbon virtually kidnapped him and sent him to England before he had a chance to commit an overt act under the Treachery Act.

"Be all that as it may," the Commandant reports, "HUYSMANS was a doughty opponent and there is little doubt he will be of value in Camp 020 in assisting to unravel other cases on suitable occasions."

It was an accurate assessment. HUYSMANS was so impressed by the omnipotence of the British Secret Service, "which had even spirited his wife out of German harm by means of a simple telephone call," that he acted for almost three years as a counsellor of reason to the would-be tacit spies who passed through Ham. He became the grand stooge, the bell-wether who led the most reluctant sheep to the slippery slope of confession.

He needed no briefing. To every inmate introduced to his cell he would tell quietly and with sincerity the sad story of his own transgressions and end with a homily stressing the infallibility of the British Secret Service and the boot-less-ness of opposition to it. His climax came always with his highly romanticised version of the transfer of his wife from Lisbon to London, and it rarely failed to impress his listener. Although he rarely got a direct break from difficult cases, his earnest counsel was often an important factor in reducing the resistance of many a stubborn character. Nor did he lose his fellow-inmates' respect, for several of them requested of their case officers the valuable assistance of HUYSMANS in the preparation of their statements and the examination of detail no longer in the forefront of memory.

The value of HUYSMANS' services may be judged from the fact that the Commandant, whose view of spies could not be said to err on the side of leniency, recommended his release at the end of the war and reunion with his wife.....

Claud DE LA FERE

Claud DE LA FERE was a French innocent born out of wedlock. He fled from France to England in a canoe and tried to conceal his natural birth from the interrogating authorities. In his efforts to do so he became more and more involved. Sinister motives were read into his

contradictions. Finally he was sent to Camp 020 for detailed
investigation.

After four months of intensive interrogation during which he
clung stubbornly to his false claim to conventional birth, DE LA
FERE decided to acknowledge that he had been begotten in sin. The
Commandant dismissed his case in a Yellow Peril which began: "DE LA
FERE is a sensitive bastard who crossed the Channel in a canoe....."

He became a BBC announcer.

Claude Louis Albert POISSON

A poor French fish who swam happily into the German spy net was
Claude Louis Albert POISSON. If there had been no German Secret
Service he would have been good for nothing; as it was, he fitted
admirably into that foetid organisation.

A commercial artist, his war record prior to the
capitulation of France was confined to service in a French naval
vessel which never left port because any attempt to get up steam
resulted in her catching fire. This ludicrous denial of opportunity
for heroism irked POISSON not at all. He surrendered to the Germans
at the first opportunity, then made much play of his escape from
their clutches. He went to Paris and lived with a vast succession of
strumpets, on whom he sponged. Sometimes he robbed his tolerant
father in order to buy sweetening gifts for his equally tolerant
women.

By some monstrous mistake he came into contact with two
decent French people. They were arrested as sympathisers with De
Gaulle, and POISSON, against his honest protestations of innocence
of such a base charge, was gaoled with them. He emerged from this
proper confinement to resume his womanising. His success as a gigolo
eventually took him to unmanly service at the flat of a woman who,
herself in the German service, guided him into German hands.

POISSON, the facile traitor, fell in easily with their
plans, which allowed him women, money and movement in the free zone
of France against the provision of detailed information of naval and
military and aerial activity. He wallowed in the cess-pits of
Marseilles and served his German masters well. Appositely enough, he
was soon transferred to the control of a local spy-mistress. For her
he had to work with more than a semblance of enthusiasm, for she was
a Lesbian and a conscientious taskmistress. So well did he fulfil
the missions she had set him in southern France that she was moved
to engage him for more important work, in England. POISSON accepted
and with her connivance escaped to England via Spain and Gibraltar
to join the Free French Navy in order to cover his intended
espionage activities.

But POISSON was denounced to the British authorities by a loyal Frenchman who had not enjoyed his company at a Spanish refugee camp. Four opportunities were vouchsafed to POISSON to reveal his relations with the Germans and the real reason for his flight to England. They were not forthcoming until POISSON, the spoilt child and playboy, faced interrogators at Ham who greeted him with manifest displeasure. After much simpering and prevarication, he discovered that he was in real trouble for the first time in his outrageous life. He confessed with haste, but without shame.

Hendrik VAN DAM

A categorical denunciation by an informer believed to be reliable, brought to Ham a member of the Belgian Mission to Seamen in London, Hendrik VAN DAM. VAN DAM was said to have been in contact in Paris some months earlier with an officer of the GIS. For four months he was subjected at Ham to unrelenting pressure. Although he stoutly protested his innocence, the biting incredulity of his interrogating officer began to worry him. He began to see things in his cells, and the hear them. To HUYSMANS, the sympathiser, he reported the screams of a woman undergoing torture in a neighbouring cell; to PEEREBOOM, the irritant, he described the doings of ghoulies and ghosties and the things that went bump in the Ham night. He was especially convincing on Friday mornings, when he could describe supernatural noises from above. Thursday nights were Guest Nights in the Officers' Mess overhead.

He was not to be comforted until his release as an innocent man at a pass in his mental processes when he began to hear the welcoming bells of Hell.

Werner Alfred Waldemar JANOWSKI

Werner Alfred Waldemar JANOWSKI was typical of the filth bred by the Nazi creed. He joined the party in 1923 and became in turn a Lufthansa pilot, instructor of the secret German air arm, the keep of a Canadian wife many years his senior, a volunteer of the French Foreign Legion, and a pre-war recruit of the notorious Lehr Regiment zbV 800 Brandenburg. His espionage assignments began with a mission to Spanish Morocco in May 1939. In 1940 he was preparing agents on the Channel coast for the invasion of Britain. In 1942 he was preparing agents on the Channel coast to meet the invasion from Britain. Later that same year he was despatched to Canada by U-Boat on an espionage mission covering military, naval, aerial and economic interests.

It was clear later that JANOWSKI had been despatched to

Canada because he had made a nuisance of himself to the Abwehr, and they in turn had decided to off-load him to Canada. It seemed that, in their view, he was expendable. He was ill-equipped. His despatch by U-boat was incidental to the submarine's proper functions off the Canadian coast. Clearly his mission was foredoomed to failure for want of proper preparation.

JANOWSKI was duly landed and made for the township of New Carlisle. He attracted immediate attention by ordering a bath in his hotel, for in those northern regions no one bathed at that time of the year. So little did he know of war conditions in Canada that he went through some awkward moments wondering what he would do if he were asked for meal coupons. He had the best breakfast in years and then tendered in payment two dollar bills given him by his superiors in Germany. The manager was not slow to notice that they were of a type which had been withdrawn from circulation twenty years earlier. Suspicion was confirmed when, a few hours later, JANOWSKI carelessly dropped a matchbox which was picked up by the wife of the hotel proprietor: it was clearly marked, "Made in Belgium." The hotelier behaved with some intelligence. He contacted the Royal Canadian Mounted Police. They arrested JANOWSKI in the train en route for Montreal.

At first JANOWSKI posed as the reconnoitring officer of a U-boat which had failed to keep a rendezvous. The story was soon given the lie by an officer of the Royal Canadian Navy. JANOWSKI quickly confessed to his true identity and mission and miserably resigned himself to die as a spy. Offered the alternative of dying for the glorious Fatherland or ingloriously betraying it, JANOWSKI, proud holder of the Iron Cross First Class, had no scruple in accepting the double-cross offer.

His controlled transmissions to Germany over a long period proved negative, for all the ingenuity of his new masters. There were indications that he had been "blown." The last message which he received confirmed the fact. In reply to a personal message sent by him regarding his wife there came the cynical news that "PUTZI" (his wife) was sitting beside the German operator "having a good time." JANOWSKI burst into tears and explained to his RCMP controller that this was the usual soldier's farewell of the Abwehr to an agent in whom interest and confidence were lost.

JANOWSKI was brought to Ham because there was no further use for him in Canada and because it was felt that further information could be obtained from him which might be of operational interest. Moreover, since he could not be prosecuted in Canada, it was desirable that he should at least remain under the considerable discipline of Camp 020 for the duration of the war.

In the result much new information was obtained. Of especial value was the outline he gave of the contre-espionage arrangements made by the GIS in the event of an invasion of the Continent from Britain. For the rest, most of the personalities of the GIS disclosed in the investigation were found to be well-known at Ham from a variety of other cases, ranging from those of VAN DEN KIEBOOM in 1940 to that of a newcomer, PACHECO.

The Commandant took an extremely unfavourable view of JANOWSKI on sight. Not only was his record against him, but also his personality. "This creature," he wrote, "served the Nazis from 1923 until 1942, but neither that creed nor his country meant anything to him. Since November 1942, when he was caught, he has resolutely betrayed his country and his comrades. I think the depth of degradation was reached when he offered to betray ten other German agents who were to land in Canada on the condition that they would be executed upon arrest, so that he and his fair name should not be involved."

Comte Gabriel Billebault du CHAFFAULT

Nobility of spirit and espionage do not mix. That nobility of title, however shoddy, may do so, was well proved by Comte Gabriel Billebault du CHAFFAULT. He was a gentleman of France who epitomised the spirit of his country, which succombed to the Hun. He was a faithless, shiftless, spineless traitor of no moral fibre. Nor was he the first of his ancient lineage to foul it. His father had accepted a paltry seven thousand francs to spy on Laval himself, on behalf of the Germans.

On such infamy much could be conjured, but his was not all. Episode piled upon episode until the depth of degradation was surely reached. For example, Du CHAFFAULT, who had received as a youth the hospitality of a convent in Spain, though nothing of involving the unfortunate Mother Superior in espionage for purposes of a cover address. Again, when charged at Camp 020 with espionage, Du CHAFFAULT, a man of stature and age, had no compunction in laying the blame upon his treacherous if decrepit old father.

Du CHAFFAULT was arrested in Gibraltar as a result of information which had been received there before his arrival as a passenger in transit from France to Uruguay. His conduct after arrest ran true to form. As always it was despicable. He found himself in danger and there was an immediate volte face. And yet he had not the courage to make a clean breast of his activities in France and intent in Uruguay in the German Secret Service.

In the result the confession of espionage which he made in Gibraltar was a mere half truth. At Camp 020 the rest of his story had be extracted. It included additional cover addresses, an operational mission in the Americas, fresh details of monies received from the Germans, many important espionage contacts in France.

Proper investigations showed that Du CHAFFAULT was a willing tool of the Germans. Pressure was not exerted by them to secure his services; there were no mitigating circumstances whatsoever. The proposition of espionage suited his personal convenience, and he accepted it with no demur. The Germans had great hopes of him. He was well trained, well paid, well trusted.

To all these findings at Camp 020 Du CHAFFAULT agreed without pressure. He had no excuse to offer. The Commandant finally asked him whether he had any reason to advance against his deportation at the end of the war to France for trial as a traitor before a clean government. His answer was incoherent, and the impression was that he had come face to face with reality for the first time in his spoilt life.

To cover for Du CHAFFAULT's journey to South America was "the study of invertebrates." Introspection and association at Ham with other specimens of his breed afforded him more opportunity for it than all the Americas.

Artur VIANA DOS SANTOS

The Portuguese could not long be kept out of the espionage picture. The next such character in order of appearance was Artur VIANA DOS SANTOS, an uneducated young man with many dependants and few scruples. He was a trader on his own account; he was ready to buy or sell anything from potatoes and chestnuts to tin.

He was thus a natural for recruitment by the German Secret Service. With their customary flair for the inappropriate, they enlisted VIANA as a spy. He was invited to go to the Portuguese colonies in Africa to do further business on his own account and new espionage business on behalf of the Germans. He received a welcome payment in advance and was then put under instruction.

He was quite obviously to have been an agent of low grading. The sum total of his training and equipment consisted of two hours of instruction in secret writing with indifferent materials; one cover address; lessons in two codes which he was unable to master. His mission was to act as a courier on the outward journey from Lisbon to Lourenço Marques and thereafter to report on shipping and military movements.

VIANA was arrested by the security control authorities in Capetown in December 1942. They got little of his true story out of him, and he abused the tolerance shown him by communicating from his

place of detention with his master, CALDEIRA, who had featured in the
sad stories of MOREIRA and DOS SANTOS, through his family in Lisbon.

He did not arrive at Camp 020 until September 1943.
Preliminary papers indicated that it would assist relations with the
Foreign Office if a proper admission could be obtained on arrival.
VIANA proved a stubborn character. The first driving interrogation
lasted three hours, but shortly thereafter two signed confessions
were obtained from him, the first calculated for Foreign Office use,
the second ranging over the entire case.

With these as the structure within which interrogation could
proceed, the case was disposed of within a short period.

VIANA later brought trouble and disgust at Ham by twice
endeavouring to commit suicide. His technique was unusual,
especially in a Latin, for he tried to unman himself. He was sent to
hospital. Not long after the hospital authorities appealed for
assistance, as he was again attempting to destroy himself. A report
was made to the Home Office and his immediate transfer from the
hospital to the Banstead Lunatic Asylum was sanctioned.

It seemed that the disposal of this spy had been anticipated
by Providence. Not so, for a few weeks later he was returned to Ham
from the lunatic asylum with a report to the effect that his quaint
behaviour was a clear manifestation of sanity!

Alfredo MANNA

One of the most spectacular spy captures of the war was that of
Alfredo MANNA, manager of the Stefani News Agency branch in Lourenço
Marques. From a variety of sources it was known that this Italian had
much knowledge of Axis espionage activities in Portuguese East Africa,
even if his own intervention in them was not of great importance.

MANNA showed no disposition to move out of neutral territory
and so face capture and interrogation. It was decided to inveigle
him into British territory. Women were his weakness, and a casino
dancer named Anna Levy was used as bait to entice him in his car
across the Swaziland frontier. There he was seized, gagged and bound
by British agents, who took care to leave him on the right side of
the border. Shortly afterwards he was "found" by the local
authorities and arrested as an enemy alien who had sought illegally
to enter the country.

When he had overcome his righteous Italian indignation,
MANNA told part of his espionage story to the South Africans. Since
two further agents captured in South Africa, Lambertus ELFERINK and
Basil BATOS, were expected to arrive at Camp 020 shortly, it was
decided to transfer MANNA to the UK in order to obtain background
against their arrival.

At Ham MANNA, for all his protestations of good faith, did not make investigation of his case easy, for he was reticent in points of detail. He was aggrieved still by the manner of his abduction and he could never forget his loyalty to Italy. With the passage of time, however, he showed a greater willingness to talk, and much new information was obtained from it, most of it tending to confirm the deficiencies of the Italian Secret Service even as compared with that of the Germans.

Andre Alix Marie Jean POILS

Andre Alix Marie Jean POILS was a crooked Belgian stockbroker who found refuge from the law in the German Secret Service. They invested him with an importance and a mission far beyond his capability. The economics section of the Abwehr in Paris, working under direct instructions from its head office in Cologne, provided POILS with intensive courses in radio transmission and secret writing and despatched him to French Morocco to report on every aspect of local economic activity.

POILS, the spurious economist, left Belgium on a German passport and settled in North Africa as a Frenchman. For some weeks he was able to copy from the bulletins of African Chambers of Commerce enough material to satisfy his masters. When the bulletins ceased to include the data which he could lift and submit as the fruit of his own enterprise, his reports ceased abruptly. POILS, who had gone out to Africa with generous German offers of post-war employment, decided that there was little future for himself in espionage. He cast around for a more stable basis of future security. He thought he had found it in the stationery and tobacco business of a widow with an unattractive but no unmarriageable, daughter. POILS devoted all his time to serving behind the counter and fetching catsmeat for the family pets.

All his calculations were upset by the Allied invasion of North Africa. He sent urgent telegrams to his cover addresses demanding money and repatriation. There was no reply. He registered with the new French authorities as a Frenchman, using the name of LEGRAIN. When it seemed that he would be called up for military service, he betook himself to the Belgian consulate and re-registered himself as a Belgian in the name of PEKER.

The Belgian authorities began to make enquiries and decided that this man PEKER did not ring true. He was directed to England and commended to the British screening authorities as a subject deserving some attention. It was not until he had passed through two interrogation centres that he admitted his true identity and disclosed that he had originally been sent to North Africa by the Germans.

Inevitably he found himself at Ham, where he tried to speculate in rosy futures and found himself caught short. He was an aggravating blackguard, and his outstanding account was settled only after uncompromising insistence.

The irregular arrival in Iceland of [BEETLE] caused some perplexity to the local American security officers. [BEETLE] claimed to have been landed in his homeland, as a refugee from Scandinavia, from a Norwegian fishing boat. His story seemed plausible enough to the Americans. They accepted it with uneasy minor reservations imposed by the unsatisfactory result of immediate checks which they were able to apply. [BEETLE] then obliged by agreeing to be sent to England to give important information about Occupied Norway, but only after representations had been made to the security authorities in Iceland by the British Intelligence Service.

[BEETLE] had struck a bargain with the Americans before sailing for England. He would go, he said, on the understanding that he would be "treated like a gentleman." Not only was this concession granted, but he was promised a salary during his absence and a job on his return.

These were the terms under which [BEETLE] was to have been interrogated at Ham, as a privileged guest. The arrangement did not please M I 5, nor did it suit the convenience or the purpose of his interrogators. M I 5 intimated to the Commandant that their position vis-à-vis the "loaning parties" would be considerably strengthened if an admission of espionage could be obtained from [BEETLE] on the very day of his arrival.

On the face of things, it was no trivial task. The papers and the property which accompanied the body were examined without effect. There was, however, an indication, albeit slender, of an espionage flavour to a money transaction. There was a grudging admission that [BEETLE] had been contacted in Copenhagen by the German Intelligence Service, an approach which he virtuously claimed to have rejected out of hand. Lastly, there was the strong point that he story of his voyage to Norway was palpably false.

The Commandant decided to interrogate [BEETLE] at once. The interrogation began at 1230 hours and lasted for two hours. [BEETLE] must have wondered what constituted gentlemanly treatment in England, but by the end of that time a signed admission of espionage had been obtained.

He confessed that he had been blackmailed into the German service following his detection as a Black Marketeer. They had treated him as a spy of some importance. He had visited Abwehr centres in Copenhagen, Stettin, Hamburg, and Berlin itself; training in radio transmission and coding was thorough; payment was on an unusually generous scale. His mission had been given considerable importance; he was to report on shipping and troop movements in his native Iceland because the Germans feared a concentration there of Allied troops intended to invade Norway. To convey him to his operational area they had risked the use of a U-boat.

Once broken, [BEETLE] divulged every detail of his career as a spy with enthusiasm and sweet reasonableness. It seemed that he had never intended to work for the Germans, who had not only ruined his lucrative business in Norway, but had seduced his wife and threatened to do harm to his mother in Iceland if he should play them false or betray them. On landing in Iceland this last threat was no longer operative. He determined to carry out his mission. But he still wished to use the money which he had been given. Hence his earlier reticences.

The issue which arose out of the successful examination at Ham was whether [BEETLE] could be used for contre-espionage purposes. The outside authorities wished to double the profit which they had derived from their investment of him in Camp 020.

Now among the desiderata for a possible "agent double" are, firstly, that the whole story has been extracted; secondly, that the man will work under orders; and thirdly, that the menace under which the enemy demand service is no longer real. The Commandant found that the facts of the case were fully on record. He believed that [BEETLE] would work under orders; he was not unintelligent and certainly he had now learned on which side his bread was buttered. Lastly, it seemed that the security of his mother in Iceland would present no difficulty.

The recommendation, then, was that [BEETLE] should be used as a double agent. He was returned to Iceland within six weeks of his admission to Camp 020.

Nickolay Steen Marinius HANSEN

The case of a parachute agent never fails to capture the imagination: urgency, ingenuity, sometimes courage, are present; above all the case is alive. Even the most casehardened officers at Ham could find lively refreshment in the investigation of that Norwegian dullard, Nickolay Steen Marinius HANSEN. The manner of his arrival in Scotland on the night of September 30/October 1st 1943 was spectacular. He floated down from the skies with one radio transmitter strapped to his body and a second attached to an independent parachute. At 5 o'clock in the morning he surrendered to the drivers of two lorries laden with Aberdeen herrings. They fetched the police and HANSEN, who had considerable difficulty with the Scottish language, indicated the position of his transmitters and expressed the wish to tell his full story.

He contented himself with half-truths under police interrogation. He did not appreciate the dangers of such a course until he arrived at Ham on the following day, when he was startled to find himself as near the gallows as any man could wish.

HANSEN, a miner who properly belonged to the accommodating bowels of the Spitzbergen earth, was seduced into the German service as the alternative to discharging a sentence of imprisonment for theft from German Naval stores. He received careful training in secret writing and radio transmission and was intended to operate in the North of England or Scotland as a spy reporting on all matters of military interest.

Considerable ingenuity was displayed in his preparation for the mission by a number of Abwehr officers and their assistants. His cover stories were interesting. He was to be provided with two radio transmitters, one English and one German. The first he was to surrender to the British immediately on landing; the second he was to conceal until the British, in their gratitude, released him from further enquiry.

At Camp 020, under meticulous investigation, HANSEN confessed that the Germans had provided him with secret writing material also, and that it had been secreted in a small rubber bag inserted in the cavity of a hollow tooth. He professed to recall only one of the three cover addresses to which he was to address communications in this medium.

Now among the intelligence officers at Ham was one who in peacetime practised dentistry. HANSEN's permission for the surgical operation was obtained, and the officer pulled HANSEN's tooth in the interrogation room, thus retrieving the secret material.

Although a considerable amount of valuable information was also extracted from HANSEN, who showed himself slow-witted and quite incapable of speaking or understanding any language other than the lowest Norwegian, he proved reticent to a degree in many points of detail. The excuse which he gave later was that the Germans had menaced his family.

It was evident that HANSEN had undertaken espionage merely to escape imprisonment, and that he had surrendered in order to escape punishment. He was not actuated by any motives of loyalty. There was no real intention to work for the Germans, and there was no intention to be of use to the Allies. Indeed, his attitude was epitomised in his bland suggestion that the British should advertise his death so that his wife would be paid insurance money by the Germans.

HANSEN's unreliability and unsuitability for use as an double-agent was stressed in the first report submitted to M I 5.

That recommendation was soon reinforced by a voluntary admission by HANSEN that he could, in fact, supply his second and third cover addresses. Moreover, he confessed that he had almost swallowed a second secretion of secret writing material during his first meal at Ham. It had come adrift with a faulty stopping to a tooth. He had chewed it unconsciously in its rubber bag, and it had tasted bitter, which reminded him that the Germans, confident that it would defy analysis, had impressed on him the desirability, in the event of detection, of explaining it away as a suicide potion.

HANSEN, who was subject to periodic bouts of Nordic carfard, found his greatest happiness in detention at Camp 020 during the flying-bomb era, when he manufactured paper doodlebugs and scared his Latin companions with ominous noises.

Ernesto HOPPE

After the light Italian touch of BONZO, the heavy impact of the German Argentine Ernesto HOPPE. It was well said of him later that HOPPE's adventures would have run well in serial form in a servants' penny weekly. The highlights would have included espionage, loot, U-boats, clandestine landings, wireless transmitters, passwords, fast cars, pregnant wives, Spanish brothels, denunciations, forgeries, secret service prisons, escapes in hospital blue. All these things and more came under consideration during a difficult investigation at Ham of this one middle-aged man's story.

Ernesto HOPPE was arrested in Gibraltar when on his was to Argentina, of which he was a naturalised citizen, with a very pregnant wife. His arrest had followed a denunciation in categorical terms by a German living in Argentina; a letter allegedly written and signed by HOPPE was produced to confirm his Nazi fanaticism and subversive activities. That these charges were later found to be fabricated, was only one surprise in a long chain of happenings.

HOPPE in Gibraltar told a plausible story of haste to reach Argentina in order that his firstborn might have the advantage of Argentine citizenship. He could prove that all his interests, economic and emotional, were in Argentina. He hotly denied any mission on behalf of the Germans in Germany.

HOPPE at Ham was equally indignant over the first month of his investigation there. He would admit to no improper activity or intent at his journey's end. His denials were punctuated with hot tears shed in the name of his unborn scion.

He threatened to commit suicide by freezing to death. He removed all his clothing at every opportunity, but spoiled the effect by being twice discovered by the orderly officer sitting massively on a very hot radiator in his cell. He feigned a heart attack and collapsed at the feet of another officer, but erred by clutching at the right side of his breast, whereas even naturalised Argentines have their hearts on the left.

After a month of unfruitful examination, HOPPE was transferred to a military hospital for treatment of an old and unmentionable complaint. With commendable enterprise in one so clumsily built and lacking the agility of youth, he escaped from a private ward by prising away an iron bar and wire meshing. A grotesque red-haired figure in hospital blues, with over-long trousers turned up to his knees, without money or a word of English, HOPPE visited in turn a garage, a cinema and a vicarage in Woolwich in order to telephone the Argentine Ambassador and complain of his treatment. At the vicarage an ill advised priest helped him to telephone the Argentine Embassy; then decided that he might have sinned in aiding this grotesque, gibbering figure before him. He telephoned the police and soon a car from Special Branch arrived at the vicarage to collect the wayward HOPPE.

Developments on HOPPE's subsequent return to Ham were dramatic. In a history already complicated to the fantastic, it would be tedious to consider at any length the factors which led to his ensuing confession. He was certainly apprehensive to a degree as to his possible reception after his escape. He was under the impression that he would die; but he was nonplussed when, out of calculated policy, he was completely ignored.

His uneasiness grew. Maybe he thought it would be wise to volunteer a little information, but just how much and how true, no-one but HOPPE could ever say. For at this stage two quite fortuitous new circumstances were put to excellent account. In the first place a letter to "beloved HOPPELEIN" had arrived from his wife, now safely in Argentina. In the second place the Argentine Embassy in London had failed to react to HOPPE's desperate telephoned plea for intervention.

The Commandant sent for HOPPE. He showed the wife's letter, but refused to let HOPPE read it. His nerves, strained by his remarkable experiences, gave way and he broke into uncontrolled weeping. That angered him, but before he had time to recover, the Commandant told him that his Embassy had forsaken him. His reaction was complete, for he decided to help his captors in the hope, perhaps, of obtaining some corresponding advantage.

The first confession which he signed was the product of interrogation over a period of two hours. It told a remarkable story. HOPPE had been approached in Germany by the German technical expert for South American affairs attached to Wehrkreiskommando III and had been entrusted with a unique mission. On arrival in Argentina he was to direct and supervise the landing from a U-boat on a lonely stretch of the coast of some forty cases containing jewellery and other valuables, highly secret documents, radio transmitters, and other unspecified material. As proprietor of a motor-business in Buenos Aires HOPPE, who had also a good knowledge of Argentine waters, was to play the principal role in the safe reception of the clandestine shipment. Its further disposal would be the responsibility of other Germans in Buenos Aires who would have advice of his appointment and would approach him with a special password....

Their names were obtained, they tallied with MI 5 records of Germans known to be engaged in subversive activities in Argentina. The extraction from HOPPE of his covername allowed the story to be checked in part against ISOS intercepts. There it found confirmation.

HOPPE maintained always that he had no intention to carry out his mission. His real idea, he said, was to betray the whole scheme to the Argentine Government. He was not moved by patriotism, but out of consideration of the ten per cent commission which he would draw following the seizure of the contraband!

HOPPE, the unprincipled ruffian, had lost his last hopes of reward when the Argentine Embassy failed to react positively to his urgent appeal. Now he indicated his wish to serve England, at a price, by proceeding with the pre-arranged plan.

The Commandant had little good to say of HOPPE when it was all over. He acknowledged the soft spot in the fifty-two year old HOPPE - his pregnant wife. "Yet in his case," he wrote, "there is a long history of brothels, and his tongue is fouler than that of most of the prisoners in Camp 020, and that is saying much. Yet, withal, it would be unchivalrous to deny that he has been a doughty opponent, and it would be untrue to say he is devoid of courage and resource."

HOPPE returned to Buenos Aires to meet his Argentine baby, but no reward, in October 1945.

Lambertus ELFERINK

Much new information on the German espionage organisation in South Africa was expected on the arrival at Camp 020 of Lambertus ELFERINK, one of its more important members. ELFERINK, a Dutch journalist, had travelled to South Africa in 1940, then returned to spend several months in Portugal before sailing again for Capetown. During 1942 a series of ISOS intercepts showed that ELFERINK, who appeared in that material under the cover-name of "HAMLET," was an extremely active German agent and was in receipt of considerable sums of money from his masters. Towards the end of 1943 it was decided to put an end of his intrigues and to wrest from him his many secrets. Arrangements were made for him to be conscripted into the Dutch Army and arrested immediately on landing in England.

He arrived at Camp 020 in November 1943, a clear-eyed young blond with an air of injured innocence. The sole evidence against him at this time was vested in that irreproachable source, ISOS. Interrogation began in the knowledge that ELFERINK was a man of intelligence and that the ISOS material, ever treated with economy and delicacy in interrogation, must at all costs be protected.

There was much subtle play, at the first interrogation, with Shakespeare's King of Denmark. Quotation and taunt failed to shake the Dutch "HAMLET." He simulated mild and polite astonishment over the performance. Neither the harsh word nor the soft invitation could draw from him a single admission of espionage activities. There was weakness in his statement of financial affairs in South Africa, and on this point he was exhaustingly interrogated, but without profit.

Nothing could be more exasperating in an investigation than to have proof positive of a man's guilt and yet be unable to extract the admission from a man's own lips. About ELFERINK, ISOS was clear and positive enough. There was not, as could occasionally happen with the material, any question of misapplication, mistranslation or misinterpretation. It presented a solid case against the man. But one cannot catch custard with a hook, even when it is well covered, and ELFERINK was a slippery customer.....

Although the investigation proceeded for weeks and months, no admission of any kind was ever obtained from him. Towards the end of his stay at Ham fresh and usable evidence against him was obtained from other German agents, but by this time ELFERINK had hardened beyond impression. He was despatched to Holland in July 1945, still the jealous and defiant guardian of a heavy conscience.

José OLIVERA DEL RIO

A Spaniard who loved the Germans had hated the Allies with conviction, and was not afraid to say so, was José OLIVERA DEL RIO. He had fought in the Spanish war as a radio operator attached to a Junkers squadron of the German Condor Legion. Among his German colleagues was Otto HINRISCHEN, who was later to become one of the most active waterside spymasters in Spain. Inevitably, after the outbreak of the new and greater war engineered by the Reich, OLIVERA, now a ship's telgraphist, was invited through Otto's friend, Carlos IMAZ, to report on Allied shipping movements, to obtain newspapers and magazines at enemy ports of call, and to act as courier for the German Secret Service. He accepted with alacrity, for idealogical reasons: " I worked for the Germans," he wrote later, "because I thought I was doing a great service to Spain."

Now OLIVERA's activities on behalf of the Germans had become known to M I 5 very soon after he had embarked upon them in late 1941. Later, at Ham, confirmation of his illicit work was obtained from Joaquín BATICON. But it was not until OLIVERA was betrayed in Buenos Aires by Jesús AGUILAR, that opportunistic double agent, that arrangements were made to arrest him.

Hitherto OLIVERA had been engaged in acts and traffic of a relatively trifling nature, but now he was reported to be carrying on a considerable volume of GIS correspondence, code-books, and samples of some metal from Buenos Aires to Spain. On Admiralty orders his ship was intercepted on the high seas by a Dutch patrol vessel. OLIVERA quietly submitted to arrest and acknowledged responsibility for a number of incriminating letters and a packet of sample lead discs found behind a panel of his radio transmitter. Of the code-books and other correspondence there was no sign.....

OLIVERA was received at Camp 020 on 8th November 1943. At first he was inclined to meet interrogation with obduracy, but he got short shrift. Faced with incontestable evidence, he was intelligent enough to accept the usual Camp 020 proposition, that having gambled and lost, it was for him to pay his debts.

He faced the issue like a man. After announcing that he despised the British and would continue to do so, he agreed to disclose the full story of his work for the Germans. For good measure, he would volunteer the information that he had also served the Italian Secret Service. He was unrepentant and unashamed, but since so much was already known about him, he would like the case cleared at the first opportunity, and to that extent he would be helpful.

Later, when the investigation was over, OLIVERA had the courage to set out what he considered to be the true position. His words may be worth quoting, but it is proper to mention that he was never under the illusion that his notions were acceptable at Camp 020. He had been ordered to give any information in his possession about the radio operator of the SS "Monte Monjuich," Diego BELTRÁN LEIRO, who had been arrested and brought to Ham for investigation, a fact of which OLIVERA was unaware at the time.

He submitted a brief and innocuous acknowledgement of acquaintance with BELTRÁN. He had met him twice in German company. He had nothing to add:-

"In my own particular case," he wrote, "I did not hesitate to give you the facts accurately and without omission, so that the investigation might soon be concluded. For the rest, I wish to be regarded as your enemy. I can give you no further co-operation..... At my fist interrogation I was

told that I must realise, as a gentleman, that I had gambled
- and lost. I agreed that this was so, and I am taking the
consequences. Nevertheless, I refuse to be used as a source
of information on others. I remain at your orders."

Intelligence gains from the case of OLIVERA himself were
important. One of his earliest disclosures was the hiding place of
the correspondence and codes which he had been carrying; behind the
reflector of the starboard navigating light of his ship. This
material, which proved voluminous indeed, was duly recovered after
the information obtained at Ham had been broadcast to all British
shipping control stations.

Osmar Alberto HELLMUTH

The case of Osmar Alberto HELLMUTH, obscure insurance agent suddenly
risen to the dizzy eminence of diplomatic status with a secret
mission in Germany, had spectacular repercussions. The information
extracted from him at Ham was given practical and successful
application. Presented with a confession by HELLMUTH that his
mission had been sponsored in part by a section of the German Secret
Service in Argentina, the Foreign Office was able to take a strong
line. Concurrently certain of the facts were released to the Press.
Questions were asked in Parliament, and answered without
contradiction by the Secretary of State for Foreign Affairs. A
shaken Argentine President was compelled summarily to dismiss and
disown HELLMUTH. Cabinet Ministers resigned. A compromised Argentine
Government, which had long wavered over the step, was forced to
sever diplomatic relations with the Reich. Soon that Government
succumbed weakly to an opportunistic coup d'etat.....

In Germany, too, the blow was felt. Wildly RIBBENTROP blamed
the fracas on the Abwehr, which had been denied by the SD any say,
and as much knowledge, in the matter of HELLMUTH. HIMMLER promoted
the confused mutual recriminations that the commotion brought upon
the Abwehr, and in the final result its Chief, Admiral CANARIS, who
was already discredited, was dismissed.....

The whole fantastic chain of events was crowded into the
space of a few short weeks. In September 1943 the SIS
representatives in Buenos Aires learned of an intrigue between
members of the Argentine Government and the unknown representatives
of the SD in that country. In HELLMUTH they observed the
intermediary in the conspiracy and the chosen instrument of its
communication abroad. They saw him leap from merciful obscurity to
pretentious station. They observed how the German Embassy reacted
with disapproval to the whole secret business, because their

traditional functions were being flouted by the outsiders of the SD. These dissensions in the German camp were sweet music in British ears. But that interest was very subordinate to the curiosity felt over the major intrigue. Rapid exchanges between SIS and MI 5 ended with Foreign Office agreement to the arrest of HELLMUTH in Trinidad on his outward journey to Spain in October 1943. He was duly detained at Port of Spain, flown immediately to Bermuda, and there transferred to the waiting cruiser "Ajax," which brought him to England at all speed.

On arrival at Ham in early November HELLMUTH was very possessed, almost arrogant. He demanded at once an interview with the Argentine authorities. Now the case had been represented to the Commandant as one of outstanding importance and urgency, but he decided, in view of HELLMUTH's attitude, to ignore him for some days and thus undermine his ego.

In the meantime his documents were examined. Only one paper was immediately seen to be of use in the opening of the case. It was a letter of introduction addressed to one HOLM in Germany by a certain Hans HARNISCH in Buenos Aires, of which the salient passage was:-

"I also add a list of precision measuring instruments which I should be delighted to receive through a channel which my friend (HELLMUTH) will explain to you, together with the following machines....."

The list referred to precision machinery, and the inference was inescapable that HELLMUTH was implicated in contraband in war. The primary issue of secret diplomatic and espionage missions was unsupported by any clear documentary evidence, but suggestions of betrayal by the warring German factions in Buenos Aires could judiciously be hinted to HELLMUTH without revealing to him either the sources or the extent of the information against him.

HELLMUTH, chastened already by the official disregard in which he had been held since his arrival at Camp 020, was summoned to the interrogation room. Of interrogation, in the proper sense of the word, there was none. The Commandant did all the talking, and it was telling. HELLMUTH was told in loud and measured terms what the Commandant thought of him and of his friends the Germans. The HOLM letter was quoted. There was the insinuation of cynical betrayal by German masters and abandonment by his own Government. There was the warning that HELLMUTH found himself Walking In The Shadows of the Valley of Death. He looked as if he was beginning to sense it when he was curtly ordered out of the room.

He was allowed a few hours in which to meditate in the solitude of his cell upon the harsh and ominous words. Then he was given a sympathetic audience with officers who deplored his unhappy position, lamented the Commandant's implacable hatred of him, and gave him Good Advice. The reaction to the soft words after the morning's loud blast, was gratifying. A very deflated and apprehensive HELLMUTH made an immediate admission that implicated him irretrievably in German espionage. The weakness was at once exploited. HELLMUTH was duped into disclosing the names of his SD principals in Argentina.

This was an issue of primary importance. Before HELLMUTH's arrival at Camp 020, advance information was that the extent of the SD's influence in Argentina was unknown. It was represented that any information on the organisation would be welcome, in particular the identity of the chief. This was soon established, for HELLMUTH disclosed that on arrival in Spain he was to have been greeted by a certain individual with the password: "Saludos de parte del Señor Siegmund+ BECKER" ("Greetings from Herr Siegmund BECKER"). He was to have replied: "Ah, si, el Hauptsturmführer" ("Ah, yes, the Hauptsturmführer"). BECKER, he admitted, was the SD chief; Hans HARNISCH++ was one of his chief lieutenants.

Confirmation of BECKER's name and status was found shortly afterwards without reference to HELLMUTH. On the outside cover of a cardboard folder in his property were found five pencilled words in Spanish that at first sight appeared meaningless. One of the case officers had an idea: he translated the words into English and German. The result was pleasing:-

Spanish		English		German
Seguismundo	=	Sigismond	=	Siegmund
Panadero	=	Baker	=	Becker
Principal	=	Chief	=	Haupt
Temporal	=	Storm	=	Sturm
Conductor	=	Leader	=	Führer

HELLMUTH admitted later that although he was of German stock, his knowledge of the German language was slight and his memory was untrustworthy, so that he had resorted to the device as an aide-memoire.

+ "Siegmund" was one of several Christian names used by the capricious BECKER, who was actually christened "Johannes Siegfried."
++ Originally HARNISCH had been an agent of the Abwehr, controlled by the economics section of Ast Köln, but after a visit to Germany and a meeting with Walther SCHELLENBERG, head of Amt VI of the Reichssicherheitshauptamt, he became more active on behalf of the SD than for the Abwehr. It was this duality that caused the Abwehr to be dragged, quite innocently, into the splenetic RIBBENTROP's court of enquiry as the principal offender.

Not long afterwards the property of a new arrival at Ham, Diego BELTRÁN LEIRO, an SD courier, underwent the usual laborious check. Industry was rewarded: two of the many dozen photographs included in it were identified by HELLMUTH as portraying BECKER and HARNISCH.

Another interesting sidelight on the investigation of the case was that HELLMUTH was at pains to make drafts of his statements in pencil before proceeding on the typewriter with a fair copy. He was accordingly given a book rather than odd sheets of paper. During a nocturnal blitz in the Commandant's office, arrangements were made to intercept HELLMUTH's notebook. Among the facts which came to light on comparing the draft with the final statement was a note which dealt with the friendship which existed between HARNISCH and Walther SCHELLENBERG, the head of Amt VI of the RSHA. HELLMUTH, who confessed that he was ultimately to have been received in Germany by SCHELLENBERG and possibly even Himmler and Hitler, had apparently thought the reference to HARNISCH's relationship with SCHELLENBERG a dangerous thing. He had therefore crossed it out and did not allow it to appear in the final form.

Less of a trick, but even more irritating, was HELLMUTH's addiction to the adverb "probablemente." He was by vague Argentine nature incapable of giving a direct answer to any question. When it was not "probablemente," he would resort to "es logico suponer" ("it is logical to suppose,") and eventually he was sternly forbidden the use of either term in the Ham establishment!

After lengthy and difficult investigation, the whole fantastic story of HELLMUTH's adventure in the wonderland of secret diplomacy could be drawn up. It was not a long story, but it made up for that in complexity.

HELLMUTH, the insurance agent, had met one day in Buenos Aires his old business friend, Hans HARNISCH. The German was depressed and lamented the fall of the Castillo Government, for he had been left without any close contact with the new régime of General Ramirez. This was indeed regrettable, he said, for he had most influential friends in Germany, and his services could bring mutual profit to both Germany and Argentina.

HELLMUTH saw in this an opportunity for personal advancement. He recalled that he was on terms of personal friendship with the President's Secretary, Colonel Enrique V. GONZALEZ. Through him HELLMUTH learned that the Argentine Government was experiencing difficulty in persuading the Reich authorities to allow the tanker "Buenos Aires" to sail to Argentina from Gothenberg. HARNISCH seized on the opportunity to boast his influence with important German authorities. He agreed to meet GONZALEZ at the first opportunity, and HELLMUTH effected an introduction. GONZALEZ was much impressed

by the German's claims. He agreed that HARNISCH might open
negotiations with the German authorities in the matter of the tanker
and then enquired urgently whether HARNISCH might not be able to
arrange for the shipment of German arms to Argentina. HARNISCH
declared that this would be too easy and for good measure he would
arrange with his own Government for the freedom of the seas to be
allowed to Argentine shipping even in the event of a diplomatic
rupture between the two countries.

GONZALEZ undertook at once to introduce HARNISCH to
President Ramirez. Before this new meeting took place, HELLMUTH was
presented by his friend to Colonel Friedrich WOLF+, the German
Military and Naval Attaché, presumably in order to impress the
Argentine with his alleged influence in the German Embassy.

The meeting between HARNSICH and President Ramirez duly took
place. Ramirez was much interested in the affair of the tanker, the
offer of arms, and the German's account of the organisation and
power of the RSHA. From GONZALEZ's subsequent story of the
interview, it seemed that HARNISCH even tried to arrange with the
President for exchanges of information, political and military.
Ramirez had tactfully evaded that point. He felt that HARNISCH was
being premature. The President wanted proof positive of the German's
influence in the Reich before committing himself to full
collaboration.

HARNISCH now advised HELLMUTH that the release of the tanker
"Buenos Aires" was merely a matter of time. HELLMUTH reported the
news to GONZALEZ, who introduced him to the Foreign Minister,
Gilbert. The insurance agent was told that HARNISCH's good services
would be utilised. It had been decided to reward HELLMUTH by sending
him to Germany as the envoy of the Argentine Government in the final
negotiations over the tanker and other matters of interest. He would
receive a nominal consular appointment in Spain in order that he
might qualify for a diplomatic passport.

Events now moved fast. HELLMUTH, who had been misled by
HARNISCH into believing that his mission had the full support of the
German Embassy, received his final instructions from GONZALEZ and
his Minister of Marine. New items were added to his mission on
behalf of the Government: he was to obtain German official sanction
for the recruitment of German technicians for Argentine arms
factories. It was suggested that HELLMUTH might point out that owing
to diplomatic pressure from the Allies, President Ramirez foresaw

---

+ Later General-Major WOLF, a prisoner both at Camp 020 and CSDIC(WEA).
WOLF claimed to have no great liking for HARNISCH, the meddler in
diplomacy. He had reported him to the Chargé d'Affaires, Meynen, who
attempted, first to take the negotiations out of HARNISCH's hands, then
to oppose HELLMUTH's appointment as special envoy to Germany.

the probability of a severance of diplomatic relations between the Argentine Government and the Axis. HELLMUTH could advise the German officials whom he met that the true relations between the Argentine Government and Germany would not be affected thereby. Further orders might reach him in Europe.....

It was only at this stage that HARNISCH produced the power behind the scenes, Johannes Siegfried BECKER. The SD chief had been content to remain out of the limelight and still preferred not to enter into direct contact with the Argentine authorities. But he had insisted on meeting HELLMUTH, and this was arranged by HARNISCH. BECKER, who was said by the glib HARNISCH to enjoy the full confidence of Colonel WOLF and the Embassy, was to make all the arrangements for HELLMUTH's reception in Germany by SCHELLENBERG and possibly Hitler. At the first meeting, however, BECKER confined himself to a panegyric of SCHELLENBERG and an injunction to HELLMUTH that he must stress the very favourable attitude of the Argentine Government towards the Reich.

At an official dinner attended by HELLMUTH shortly afterwards, GONZALEZ enquired of him whether he knew what was going on among the Germans, for it seemed that the German Chargé d'Affaires, on the advice of an influential German businessman in Buenos Aires, had suggested to the Foreign Minister that the matter of the tanker might be negotiated, on the Argentine side, by Colonel Vélez, the new Military Attaché in Spain.

HELLMUTH reported the fact to HARNISCH, who muttered obscenely that the Chargé d'Affaires would pay for this gratuitous interference. HELLMUTH was taken to repeat the tale to BECKER, who instructed him to place the facts before SCHELLENBERG in Germany and agitate for the immediate destitution of Meynen,

At a new interview with GONZALEZ, HELLMUTH learned that the negotiations for arms from Germany were originally to have been entrusted to Colonel Vélez, but since HELLMUTH would have access to important German officials, Vélez was now to act as his assistant. In the event that the Germans raised any difficulties, HELLMUTH was authorised further to offer as an Argentine concession the recall of the Argentine Chargé d'affaires in Berlin, who had been described unofficially as persona non grata owning to his reluctance to think the German way, and his substitution by the Naval Attaché, CEBALLOS, whom the Germans obviously liked.+

Shortly before he was due to sail for Europe, HELLMUTH was approached by HARNISCH with a new request that he attempt to obtain for him a number of precision instruments which would be of great

+ And well they might, for CEBALLOS was known by MI 5 to be an active collaborator of the Abwehr.

use to Argentine war industries. Those instruments could be shipped to Buenos Aires clandestinely in the tanker "Buenos Aires," which was to be commanded by an Argentine Naval officer and might therefore be exempt from Allied examination. HELLMUTH agreed to take with him the letter addressed to HOLM, when HARNISCH suggested that it might be shown to GONZALEZ and approval obtained from him for its despatch to Spain through the diplomatic bag. From GONZALEZ later HELLMUTH learned that there was no official objection to this step.

A last meeting now took place between HELLMUTH, HARNISCH and BECKER, and HELLMUTH was shown a long and glowing letter of recommendation of himself and a list of the subjects which he was authorised and qualified to discuss. These papers would anticipate his arrival in Germany. He was given every assurance of resounding success in the Fatherland, where he could expect to receive further orders. Before the budding diplomat left his all-powerful friends, he agreed to carry on their behalf silk stockings and foodstuffs for their colleagues and relatives in almighty Germany.

HELLMUTH sailed from Buenos Aires with his head in woolly clouds. Financially he would not profit from this excursion into diplomacy and high intrigue. But his would be the glory, indeed, when he had discharged his mission, for the Germans would surely decorate him, and had not GONZALEZ promised that on his triumphant return he would be "one of us?"

The first inkling of impending disaster came in Trinidad, when the official Argentine courier reported to HELLMUTH that he had handed all the papers relating to the tanker to the British censorship, but had withheld the HARNISCH-HOLM letter as too compromising. GONZALEZ, he claimed, had not instructed him to place all the papers in the sacrosanct diplomatic bag.....

HELLMUTH always felt that the omission by GONZALEZ had "let him down," but in actual fact the British Security authorities were merely awaiting a more convenient hour to remove HELLMUTH from his ship. Their instructions to detain him had been in their hands for many days.

At Camp 020 later HELLMUTH was not surprisingly bitter. He had become the laughing stock of the diplomatic world. He knew that he had been sold by his President; he suspected that he had been sold by the German Secret Service. Certainly he had been fooled by his interrogating officers. He realised it much too late, for by the time that he had declared airily that he had no further wish to talk with them, there was nothing of intelligence interest left for him to say.

HELLMUTH spent two very unhappy years at Camp 020. There was not much of a future for anything save his disgruntlement when he finally sailed for Argentina, for his friends of the Government were fallen. There was no profit in being one of them now. The last straw came when he was arrested in error on the journey out to Buenos Aires, but by this time HELLMUTH is probablemente peddling insurance once again. It is logical to suppose that his clients do not include BECKER and HARNISCH, for both were imprisoned by the Argentines on strong representations of the Allies based on the information given by him.

Hans RUSER

A misinterpretation of instructions as to lodgment brought to Camp 020 a deserter from the Abwehr, Hans RUSER, an intelligent young man who had been very active indeed in Portugal and Spain. He was an adaptable person, and after expressing some disciplined surprise at finding himself in such surroundings he applied himself with such energy that within a matter of days he had produced a voluminous and detailed account of himself and of all the personalities and works of the Abwehr known to himself.

He had, in fact, written the report of his own case before the error of his imprisonment was rectified and he was transferred elsewhere for further exploitation.

Oswald John JOB

A British traitor of German parentage and French domicile was Oswald John JOB, who qualified for British nationality by the accident of birth at Poplar in 1885. JOB, an engineering salesman settled in Paris since 1911, was interned by the Germans in 1940. Three years later he was released conditionally on his undertaking to act as a German agent in England, whither he was prompted to return.

The mission first given to him was trivial. He was to report in secret writing on bomb damage in London and British morale. The true purpose of his recruitment became apparent later, when JOB was entrusted with a package of jewellery which he was to deliver to a Mrs May in London for onward transmission to one of the most active agents of the Paris Abwehrstelle in England, for he was urgently in need of money.

It seemed that the Germans were doubtful whether JOB had the courage to carry out this overt act, so that they had burdened him with the lesser mission to cover the primary courier service. They provided also for the eventuality that JOB might perchance prove reliable, realising that money would be an inducement to this shabby old man. To meet this possibility, they taught him a simple code which his low intelligence never mastered properly and told him that new instructions might follow.

JOB was helped out of France and eventually found himself in

Lisbon. At the British Repatriation Office there he told an unconvincing story of escape from Paris, and he was sent to England by air with a special endorsement to his visa.

MI 5 were already awaiting his arrival. The important and successful German agent in England who was to be the ultimate recipient of the jewellery was an important and successful double agent controlled by MI 5, "DRAGONFLY." Very obligingly the Germans in Paris had advised him by radio of the coming of the courier JOB and of the name and address of the woman who would be used for cover purposes.

At Poole Airport JOB explained away the jewellery found in his possession as personal property and said nothing of his contact with the German Secret Service. It was decided to give him some rope in the hope that he might lead to other, unknown contacts.

After a few days under observation, it was obvious that JOB was heading nowhere of intelligence interest, but only to the gallows. Nonetheless it was decided to give him a new opportunity to reveal his mission voluntarily. Two interviews in London with MI 5 officers elicited no admission; at a third he was taxed with lying and asked to explain possession of an address known to be that of a German agent. It was a hazardous move, for it imperilled both ISOS and "DRAGONFLY," but it shook JOB. In a complete volte face he made his first admission of contact with the Germans and a mission on their behalf.

Shortly afterwards he was admitted to Camp 020 for full investigation of his case. It was quite obvious that even at this stage he did not appreciate the enormity of his offence. MI 5 indicated that the case was not one in which B1(a) wished the man to be kept sweet. JOB was not greeted at Ham with open arms, but as the sottish traitor that he was.

Investigation proceeded with some difficulty, for JOB was unintelligent to a degree and constitutionally incapable of telling the truth unless under considerable pressure. When the case was completed, there was difficulty over the man's disposal. A coward and a traitor who had deserved the unutterable contempt of every British authority who had come into contact with him, JOB richly deserved the death penalty. Prosecution under the Treachery Act might involve "DRAGONFLY." As he enjoyed British nationality, he could not be held at Camp 020 under Defence Regulation 18B. There would be difficulty in operating him as an XX agent from any normal prison.

The Commandant recommended prosecution under the Treachery Act and offered a solution for the "DRAGONFLY" problem. The latter's radio traffic had shown that there was nothing conclusive in the opinion of the German Secret Service that JOB was reliable.

"DRAGONFLY" might safely complain that the jewellery had never reached him, then expostulate violently and demand further money at once. The Germans could then reasonably assume that JOB had in fact proved a crook, had obtained his liberty, had sold the jewellery and gone to ground. A subsequent prosecution could then be covered by the fact that the man had presented an unusual diamond ring to a pawnbroker and that enquiries indicated that the prospective vendor could not properly account for his possession of the ring from enemy territory.

JOB was duly prosecuted. Although hanging was too good a fate for him, he died a traitor's death in March 1944.

Guy Marie Joseph Julien WIJCKAERT

The fist boy spy in the German service to arrive at Camp 020 was Guy Marie Joseph Julien WIJCKAERT. He was a blue-eyed Belgian whose activities had been reported to the Belgian Secret Service from a variety of sources even before he left his native land for England. On arrival in Barcelona he reported to the Belgian Consulate and signed a statement in which he admitted his recruitment by the German Secret Service, but claimed to have done so only in order to reach England and there disclose all his information. Thus he arrived at Ham on Christmas Day 1943 in the guise of a patriot.

The spirit of realism was never subordinated at Ham to the spirit of goodwill towards all men. WIJCKAERT was not to be accepted at his face value, childlike and innocent as he looked in all his blond rosiness. The story of the patriot who used the German Secret Service as a means of escaping to England to join the Glorious Allies was wearing somewhat thin in the years. In the first place, the war was being won without the assistance of those dilatory patriots. In the second place, it might well be the story of an active agent who, seeing which way the wind was blowing, thought it high time to change sides. In the third place, the yarn had been used over and over again by the unimaginative German Secret Service for purposes of cover. Lastly, the problem was immeasurably complicated by the paramount necessity for security in time of offensive invasion.

At his first interrogation WIJCKAERT was warned, in his own interest, that it was necessary to make a complete confession. He produced a series of statements describing his recruitment and training for a sabotage mission in England, Canada or Africa. The statements showed traces of intelligence in him, but their apparent omissions showed even more traces of lack of intelligence. The Commandant reviewed the case generally as it then stood and found himself extremely dissatisfied with certain aspects of the case, ranging from mission to payments received.

He interrogated WIJCKAERT himself over a period of some days. He found the agent was inclined to be impertinent, stubborn, and reticent. A sidelight on his conduct was that after certain uproarious hearings he returned to his cell and broke up his utilitarian furniture. On one particular occasion he kicked the door of his cell with such violence that a fracture of his foot was feared and an X-ray was necessary.

In due course the inevitable change took place in WIJCKAERT's demeanour. He had come to the conclusion that it would be profitable to tell more, if not all of the truth. He broke on new details of his mission. He gave out three new cover addresses. He named new contacts. He admitted to receipt of relatively large sums of money from the Germans. He confessed that from Spain, after making contact with the Belgium Consulate, he had written several letters to persons Belgium, so that the Germans would eventually know that he was well on his way to England. In this way he felt that he could ensure his own safety with the Allies and a continuance of payment by the German Secret Service to his father in Belgium.

By all the normal tests of good faith, WIJCKAERT's claim to patriotic purpose failed to impress. He grew up many years at Ham, although he remained there for only two.

Diego BELTRÁN LEIRO

The case of Diego BELTRÁN LEIRO, youthful radio operator on the Spanish merchantman "Monte Monjuich," was as sordid in its personal aspect as it was rich in intelligence yield. He had cheerfully entered the German service in November 1941 at the instance of a fellow radio operator whom he had first met while serving in Franco's navy. Soon he was in blithe contact with all the familiar spy characters of the Spanish seaboard and the Buenos Aires waterfront. He reported enthusiastically on Allied shipping, he obtained valuable technical publications, he acted diligently as courier. His considerable service to the Germans over a period of two years brought him the shabby reward of £41.

MI 5 had first learned of his work as a courier in January 1942. In the intervening months evidence of his activities had accumulated in ISOS traces, from the reports of SIS and the FBI, and, finally, at Camp 020 from the case of OLIVERA DEL RIO. He was arrested on the high seas in December 1943 in possession of a considerable volume of German intelligence mail which he had collected in Buenos Aires for delivery in Spain.

At Ham BERTRÁN made no show of resistance to investigation. He was a very scared little roughneck when he arrived. He wept with

fright at the opening session and hastened to sign a brief
confession. Thereafter he became an irrepressibly cheerful prisoner
an a willing betrayer of his own and other people's sins. He had
never appreciated the gravity and the importance of his offences
under German direction; now that he realised that he had a big story
to tell, he revelled in its unfolding. For BELTRÁN found it
interesting to be considered interesting.

More than a dozen acts of espionage were established against
him out of his own garrulous mouth. His contacts were numerous and
for the most part well known already at Ham from earlier cases. They
included a few who had fallen into British hands already, or who
were to do so later. Among them were OLIVERA DEL RIO, PEREZ GARCIA
and MORENO REGO, on whom he would daily inflict cheerful reminders
of those happier days at large, and Krafft SIMMROSS, one of his
controlling officers in Spain, who came direct to Bad Nenndorf and
did not, therefore, have the pleasure of BELTRÁN's sprightly company
as a fellow prisoner.

The outstanding feature of BELTRÁN's case was the wealth of
new information and material extracted from his captured courier
mail. There were numerous new cover addresses and the addresses of
German Secret Service operators and their offices. There were many
photographs of Germans engaged in espionage and subversive
activities in Argentina, including Siegfried BECKER and Hans
HARNISCH of the HELLMUTH case. There was a report on a number of
agents and German diplomats signed by BECKER himself. It dealt in
part with the HELLMUTH affair, and it consigned the German Embassy
staff to the dung heap when they had finished doing other indecorous
things. A footnote described BELTRÁN, the bearer, as "one of our two
best and most trustworthy" couriers.

The summun bonum came out of a coded document. For when the
code was broken, the result was almost too fantastic to be true. The
document disclosed the names, cover-names and personal particulars
of no less than forty new German agents in Argentina.

It was not Germanic intuition that had inspired the loutish
and foul-lettered BECKER to close his note on BELTRÁN with the
comment: "It would be a great pity were we to lose 'DIEGO'". He had
reckoned to lose him, not to the British Intelligence Service, but
to the rival Abwehr. The loss thereby became the greater, and BECKER
must have felt more than pity when he heard the bad news.

Barone Filippo MANFREDI DE BLASIS

The case of the Barone Filippo MANFREDI DE BLASIS, shabby Italian
nobleman, had disastrous beginnings. A British Intelligence Officer
in Italy, having failed to extract a confession from a spy on

perfectly good evidence, went right out of his way to champion his innocence. He was backed by his Intelligence organisation in Italy. In the result, the authenticity of ISOS itself came into question and the evidence against fifty other suspected persons was held doubtful. SIS accordingly determined to have MANFREDI flown to England and lodged at Camp 020, not so much to prove the case against the agent himself, but to re-establish once and for all the incontestable nature of ISOS as a source of information.

The fact made plain by that source was that MANFREDI had been approached by the German Secret Service on the 29th August 1943 to work behind the 8th Army lines at Cerignola, Southern Italy. The advance papers in the case told a sorry tale on the one hand and stressed its importance on the other. The view held by the British Intelligence organisation in Italy was quoted in one letter from SIS:-

> "In summing up MANFREDI's character the interrogator says that in his opinion it was psychologically impossible for the man to have been a German agent; that he was neither fascist nor pro-German; that he was an impulsive and confiding child, for example, his servants held the keys to his safe; he was temperamentally incapable of keeping any important secret."

A second letter underlined the quandary in which SIS found themselves:-

> "...MANFREDI is the first alleged agent of the SD in Italy to fall into our hands; we regard him as providing us with a test case of the reality or the reverse of the SD's post-operational network... We have not far short of fifty names of non-Germans in Italy alleged to be involved in the SD. As we advance up Italy we may reasonably expect the question how far we can rely on evidence from ISOS unsupported from any outside source will become increasingly urgent. If only the question of MANFREDI's guilt or innocence can be finally settled, it will be of great assistance to us in dealing with similar cases."

MANFREDI was admitted to Camp 020 on 9th January 1944. At his first interrogation he proved to be highly indignant and recalcitrant. It then transpired that the Intelligence organisation in Italy were not only convinced of the innocence of MANFREDI, but had been good enough to acquaint him with the finding. Fortified with this knowledge, MANFREDI practised the tantrums of his race and hardly a word of sense could be extracted from him.

In this case of many tragedies came a new setback, for the Ham officer concerned with MANFREDI had to go on the sick list and the case had to be inherited all over again. The Commandant decided that it might be sound to use the self-styled co-belligerent Capitano BONZO in the case, both during interrogation and in association.

The first semblance of an admission from the agent came in a statement handed in on the night of 22/3 January. In it MANFREDI revealed that he had been in contact with a man named KOEHLER. After much consideration, the Commandant decided to bluff on KOEHLER. He told MANFREDI that KOEHLER was a known German Secret Service agent, and therefore he (MANFREDI) had admitted to contact with the German Secret Service.

He went on to inform MANFREDI that although he might not have committed acts of espionage on behalf of the Germans, he was possessed of much information, and the Commandant intended to have it. Many were the gesticulations that accompanied his prompt denials, and confusion became worse confounded when BONZO joined in the fray. They were both dismissed to the same cell. Pressure was maintained, either by interrogation or by the persistent arguments which resulted between MANFREDI and BONZO.

During the afternoon of 23rd January MANFREDI submitted a new statement which contained the following passage:-

"When I replied that I was ready to do anything to help my country, KOEHLER said that he would send someone down to me in Puglia to commit acts of sabotage according to plans which would be agreed upon later between us. I accepted the general idea in order to gain time, and KOEHLER told me that I was not to tell the Italian General Staff about the matter, nor would he inform anyone. The following day I immediately told Colonel De Carlo about the proposition made to me, and he told me to let the matter to drop."

At midnight on 23/4 January came a further statement, the significant passage of which read:-

"During the last quarter of an hour, just before I left, KOEHLER started talking about the political situation again and finished with the following words: 'As you came to ask me a favour, you might be able to do something for us.' I replied that I was always ready to do anything to help Italy. 'Would you be willing to look after a man who is a specialist in the art of sabotage and keep him in the country near your estate? At the moment he is not here, but he is due to arrive in a few days from Northern Italy. You could employ him as a watchman on the land, and as soon as he arrives I thought of sending him to you in Cerignola.' I replied that this might be arranged. But at this point KOEHLER asked me not to inform the Italian General Staff of what had been discussed..."

The Commandant saw MANFREDI again on the morning of 24th January. A monstrous argument took place between them, for an imperfect brief had stated in categorical terms that MANFREDI was himself to engage in bridge-blowing on his own estate in the gulf of Manfredonia. The charge was met by MANFREDI with frenzied eyes, wild ejaculations and intricate gesticulations. When he was allowed to say his piece, he almost sobbed out his logical apologia; "In my estate there is no water, there is no need of bridges. Where there are no bridges, they cannot be blown up."

By now the primary object of the investigation - the re-establishment of the incontestable accuracy of ISOS - had been achieved. The secondary object of the investigation - the espionage case against MANFREDI - had also been attained.

There was important by-products also, for it became clear in the course of the investigation that the Barone's wife, from whom he was estranged, was also a German agent in her own right. She had spent much time in travel abroad consulting specialists about her health. On one occasion she visited Berchtesgaden to recuperate. While dining out one evening, she collapsed and Heinrich Himmler, who was present, went to her assistance and put a car at her disposal.

MANFREDI made out at Ham that, to his knowledge, the choice of Berchtesgaden was fortuitous, and that the actions of Himmler were merely those of the chivalrous gentleman he was known to be. He may have been sincere in those beliefs, but they were not shared at Ham. Indeed, while MANFREDI was still at Camp 020 confirmation was received that the Baronessa was, in fact, a paid agent of the German Secret Service.

There was more of Poncinello in MANFREDI than of Machiavelli, but even BONZO, who co-belligerated the Barone in a bread raid on the prison pantry, found his company more nauseating in the ultimate than it was amusing. They left Ham on different dates to go their separate ways: BONZO to work for the Italian General Staff, MANFREDI to face its music.

Marcel Georges Armand DE RAPPARD

Marcel Georges Armand DE RAPPARD, a Belgian by birth but the legitimate holder of a Canadian passport, was a wretched traitor recruited by the Germans as a spy out of an Italian internment camp.

He was transferred to Stuttgart, Köln and Berlin successively for training and instruction for missions either in Britain or Canada. On completion of training he was returned to Italy to await the opportunity to "escape" to Spain. He reached Barcelona in November 1941, and it was not until November 1943 that he sailed from Gibraltar for England, on the direction of the Belgian authorities. In the intervening two years he had given much assistance to those old friends "PEDRO" and "PABLO" and their associates in Barcelona and Madrid, and for a time he was good enough to spend some weeks on their behalf at Figueras Prison as a stool-pigeon charged with obtaining information about Allied prisoners held there.

ISOS told a long story about him. As he had not troubled to tell it at the first opportunity, he found himself at Ham in an agitated position. It was there that he made his first admission to contact with the GIS, and it was there that the whole sordid story was dragged from him with much effort. It was there that every one regretted that DE RAPPARD could not die for his treachery. He was happily transferred to Dartmoor in December 1944.

Otto Emil Friedrich MAYER

Divide and rule is a sound principle for any occupying Power anywhere. In the Balkans, of course, it is merely a matter of taking existing divisions and sub-dividing them ad infinitum. The Germans tried it in Jugoslavia. One of their principal political advisers in the field was an Abwehr officer, Otto Emil Friedrich MAYER, a former refrigerator salesman in Belgrade with a good knowledge of the language and a sound grasp of the complex political scene. His several missions among the different factions provided the information on which the German Command could base its policy.

The skein was tangled indeed. In one area he found that the Albanians were warring with the Serbian Chetniks, while both parties were well disposed to the Germans. In another the Serbs and Moslems had combined under the slogan of "War Against the Intruders" to combat Albanians, Chetniks, Communists and Partisans alike; rather curiously, the Germans were not regarded as intruders at all, and relations with them were friendly. MAYER's finding was that the maximum profit would derive from German support of the Chetniks against the Partisans in actual warfare and an attempt to weld the other factions into some semblance of unity by the creation of small puppet states, as was his recommendation for Montenegro.

His reports were not always well received, and it was with some relief that MAYER was transferred for a time to Turkey, where he engaged in collecting operational intelligence by his own efforts and through sub-agents. He returned later to Jugoslavia and was despatched again on political missions among the warring factions. He was so engaged in November 1943 when he was captured in ambush by Partisans of Marshal Tito.

He claimed always to have been captured in uniform and insisted on his right to be treated as a Prisoner of War. The claim was never substantiated. Probably the uncompromising Partisans stripped him of his field grey. Certainly they interrogated him at pistol point, and drew from him information about the Abwehrstelle in Belgrade to which he belonged. By arrangement with the Allies, he was transferred to Italy for further interrogation. There he was cleverly finessed by British interrogators and induced to believe that British interests in the Balkans were bound up with those of Germany rather than with those of Russia. To them he gave much information of value. Finally he was admitted to Camp 020 in February 1944 for detailed examination.

Much new information was now obtained from him, but he also withheld much. He was disillusioned at Camp 020, where his claim to the status of an officer and Prisoner of War was summarily rejected. But the root trouble from an investigation point of view, the fact that he was a German patriot, remained. He was courageous enough to be indifferent to his fate; he was stubborn enough to withhold information, for at least thereby he could retain the only thing left him, his self-respect.

He was especially reticent about his activities in Turkey, making out always that he had acted there independently, whereas ISOS showed that he had been closely controlled by his Stelle and was in touch with other espionage directors.

It seemed that on arrival at Camp 020, or perhaps before, he had set himself a course. He would reveal information regarding Jugoslavia because the Allies could not effectively act upon it. He would not reveal information regarding Turkey which might prejudice German Secret Service activities in that important neutral country. His attitude, therefore, in interrogation was to confirm what was already known to his enemies, but to volunteer nothing. His fortunes did, however, fluctuate in the months of interrogation, and at times he found himself compelled wryly to admit to some detail previously denied or withheld.

The true position on the interrogator's side of the table was that further fresh information could only be obtained at the risk of exposing ISOS. MAYER temporised and finally reached the conclusion that the British had no further information on him relating to Turkey. In the result he proceeded to lie continuously and became impervious to pressure and, for that matter, to finesse.

It would, however, be wrong to write off the fruits of investigation at Ham as of little account. Information did, in fact, accumulate, admissions were obtained, and a general account became available of German activities in a locus previously unfamiliar.

Although Marshal Tito had demanded MAYER's return to Jugoslavia for trial as a war criminal, a fact of which the prisoner was aware, he has not transferred direct into the hands of the Partisans, but was sent to the Diest outpost in July 1945.

Pierre Richard Charles NEUKERMANS

Of all the spineless spies who ever had their spinal cords broken by the hangman's rope, Pierre Richard Charles NEUKERMANS was the most craven. He had been an officer of the Belgian Army. His career distinguished by espionage on behalf of the Germans from November 1939 until his arrest in England on 2nd February 1944. He was thus a traitor to his King six months before Belgium was overrun by the Germans. In addition, he communicated with the enemy eleven times since his arrival on 16th July 1943 in England, the country which was in the process of liberating Belgium from the Germans. A special feature of his detailed espionage mission, moreover, called for full and timely reports of any move from England to liberate the Continent. In fact, he was an invasion spy.

NEUKERMANS had arrived in England with a plausible story of escape from Brussels for service with the Belgian forces. He satisfied the Security officer at Poole Airport. He impressed the investigating officer at the London Reception Centre with his honesty. Re-interrogation on the subject of his escape resulted in an endorsement of that view by another examining officer. NEUKERMANS, then, was tolerably astute, for he was released on 8th August 1943 to the Belgian authorities in England.

On 29th December 1943, however, SIS received a statement from a certain Alphonse Coucke which had been given in Lisbon. Coucke admitted that he had left Belgium in the company of Guy WIJCKAERT, the sabotage agent lodged at Camp 020, whom he had known to be a German agent, and another person. He then stated that there was invariably a German agent in every group of refugees who followed the escape route from Belgium used by WIJCKAERT and himself. In support of this contention he quoted another group of three escapees consisting of Roger Louant, Omer Sevenans and a third man, the spy, whose name he could not recall.(+)

It was then to the lasting credit of SIS and MI 5 that the three men were traced and interrogated. From the interrogations it

---

(+) In actual fact, the attempt by NEUKERMANS to "escape" with his two companions proved abortive. The agent was taken into Spain by "PEDRO" of Barcelona.

emerged that NEUKERMANS, who had latterly been employed as a clerk in a Belgian Ministry in London, was the spy. A written confession was in due course obtained from him, and he was transferred to Camp 020 for further investigation.

The investigation at Ham may thus be described as the clearance of a broken spy. The new points established went far beyond the bare outline of espionage to which he had admitted outside. The story in its entirety revealed careful preparation of the treacherous blackguard for his work in England. Many of the characters were familiar: the spymasters ACKERMANN and UNVERSAGT in Brussels; the escape master Louis DE BRAY; the posture-master "PEDRO" in Barcelona.

NEUKERMANS did his best to serve them. In London he consorted with soldiers and prostitutes in the Victoria area, and from them and the newspapers he extracted items of military and naval information which he hastened to report to his masters in secret ink. ISOS showed later that they were very well received at the other end, but reconstruction of the reports indicated that the Germans were easily pleased.

NEUKERMANS, a low-voiced, snivelling creature under interrogation excused his treachery by claiming that it was only anxiety neurosis that had caused him to work for the Germans! No effort was made at Ham to relieve him of the affliction before he died on the gallows on 23rd June 1944.

Franciscus Josef Marie ABEN

Among spies bad is the best, but Franciscus Josef Marie ABEN, Dutch ship's captain, was worse. He was one of the most abominable characters who ever passed through Camp 020. He arrived at Ham with a button-hole badge proclaiming him a militant loyal Dutchman. He left Ham for Holland a year later without a button-hole badge proclaiming him a militant loyal Dutchman. Indeed, he was preceded by a dossier which showed him to have been an extremely disloyal Dutchman. In two years of service for the Sicherheitsdienst he had been responsible for the deliberate blowing to the enemy of at least two important Dutch resistance organisations and the arrest of practically all the members.

ABEN's background conditioned his base espionage career. He broke off a merchant navy career because advancement was slow. Successively he proved a failure as cigarette salesman, confectioner, radio technician, keeper of a low restaurant. Simultaneously he developed an infatuation with a child prostitute and with Nazi ideals.

After floundering unprofitably on land for several years,

ABEN returned to the sea in 1940. The invasion of Holland had him land-bound again for a year, but he found escape by stressing his membership of the Dutch Nazi Party (NSB) and obtaining a German endorsement to his Chief Mate's Ticket. In the process he was not surprisingly brought into contact with the Sicherheitsdienst. His protestations of full sympathy with Nazi ideals rang true; his offer to collaborate fully was accepted. Hauptsturm-führer MÜLLER, SD chief at The Hague, enlisted him as an agent without ado.

ABEN sailed to and fro between Holland and Sweden, the proud skipper of an almost unseaworthy lugger. On his first trip to Sweden he began enthusiastically to establish contacts who would serve him as sources of political intelligence. He conceived the idea of buying a ship chandler's business as the first step in the creation of a spy network in Sweden. MÜLLER gave his full support to the scheme and promised capital. By an act of sabotage ABEN contrived to have his ship laid up for some months in Swedish waters. During this period he effected cautionary links with the loyal Dutch authorities.

Soon ABEN came to be accepted by them as a good Dutchman, for he had brought news of would-be escapees to Sweden among members of a resistance movement. He was discouraged at first from accepting stowaways of minor importance. Instead he was entrusted with monies and letters for delivery to the chiefs of two major resistance groups in Holland. These he proceeded to betray at once to his German masters. They encouraged him to become a two-way courier for the Dutch, and they were able to control the valuable traffic. There was profit for ABEN, too, in the arrangement, for now he was drawing money from two sources.

After some useful play with the correspondence, the Germans proceeded to arrest the leaders of the resistance movements. In Sweden ABEN talked himself out of responsibility for the betrayals with such success that he was entrusted with instructions for the prospective leader of a new resistance group. This news, too, was soon in the hands of MÜLLER.

Further intrigues followed, and soon ABEN was taking SD agents to Sweden to act as agents provocateurs vis-a-vis the loyal Dutch and an occasional member of the resistance to act as cover for his more nefarious activities.

Such was his success that when MÜLLER was threatened from Berlin with dismissal following a quarrel with a senior member of the service, ABEN was able to intervene successfully on his behalf by direct appeal to Berlin. It seemed that the SD headquarters held ABEN's collaboration in high esteem, for not only did they confirm MÜLLER's appointment, but they began to take a direct interest in ABEN's services. Through MÜLLER they gave him, in the form of diamonds, capital for the ship chandler's scheme. Instructions followed to have him trained in radio transmission; a powerful transmitter was provided for installation in his ship that he might report on Allied shipping movements; he was taught the SD coding system utilising a circular disc. Authority was given him to recruit his First Mate, Gerhardus VAN DER MOOLEN, as an assistant, and to take to Sweden as a stowaway the leader designate of yet another Dutch resistance group..... ABEN, the buoyant Judas, was to be given further scope for his manifest espionage talents.

By this time suspicion had fastened on ABEN's good faith in Dutch circles in Sweden. When he arrived with a new resistance leader, arrangements were made for the despatch of both to England, ostensibly for consultations with the Dutch Government, but actually for investigation of ABEN.

ABEN thus arrived in England on 30th January 1944 in the fond expectation that new fruits of treachery would be put in his lap for future delivery to his German masters. He was disappointed. For twelve days he was subjected to close interrogation at the London Reception Centre. No admission of disloyal activity was to be extracted from him there. Then he was transferred to Camp 020.

By good fortune the Dutch authorities in Sweden had by this time discovered in the possession of Gerhardus VAN DER MOOLEN a letter of recommendation to all SD Dienststellen in the name of ABEN; it was signed by MÜLLER on notepaper of the SD office at The Hague. A circular disc code for ABEN's use was also found, and in turn this led to an admission by VAN DER MOOLEN that a special radio transmitter had been installed in the vessel.

The evidence was received at Ham shortly after ABEN's arrival there. It was displayed on the table when ABEN was summoned for his first interrogation by the Commandant. A gangling coward with a restless Adam's apple, he very rapidly came to the conclusion that opposition would be idle. He confessed his frightful sins over a period of some weeks, betrayed his Mate's complicity, and excused himself on the plea of misguided idealism. An opportunistic convert when he realised the magnitude of his crime, ABEN began to pose as a repentant sinner anxious to preach the gospel of Beautiful Truth to more stubborn characters in the prison. In that capacity he was used occasionally to lower the morale of the more inspirited recalcitrants.

It was much regretted at Ham that ABEN could not have been served summarily with his deserts. But his offences for the Germans had been committed against his own country. For the reason he could not incur the death penalty under English law. A recent amendment to the laws of Holland gave hope that the traitor might ultimately be hanged by his own people, and it was in this expectation that he was returned to Holland in July 1945.

Jean FRAVAL / Justin TOCABENS

In the scheme of German espionage, the Frenchman Jean FRAVAL, 27-year old Air Force pilot, was of no great importance. Here again was the dreary story of the spurious refugee who presented himself at the British Consulate in Barcelona and gave a cover story in which he had been versed by his masters. That cover was faulty, and in the result FRAVAL decided to admit that he had been recruited by the Germans for a mission in England. After a patient hearing in Barcelona, he was transferred to Britain and Ham for detailed investigation.

Perhaps the most interesting feature of the case as it then developed was that FRAVAL had originally been recruited as an agent by the so-called Anti-Bolshevist Legion, which was hoping to raise an Air Force to fight on the side of the Germans against the Russians and their Western Allies. In those tasks he signally failed, and after some weeks of fruitless effort he attempted to seek less dishonourable employment. In this, too, he failed, but soon he was summoned to the Legion HQ in Paris and was offered "interesting work of a nature similar to that of the Deuxieme Bureau." Further inducement was the glib argument of good service in the interests of France and the payment of considerable sums of money.

A few days later FRAVAL discovered that in his new work the interests of France did not so much coincide with those of Germany as they were subservient to them. His Legion bosses passed him to the care and attention of that persevering spymaster, Werner UNVERSAGT, of the Brussels Abwehrstelle, and FRAVAL offered no objection. A lengthy period of training followed, broken only by occasional excursions to France for Black Market produce for his master, whom he cheated outrageously in the matter of prices.

He was not alone in Brussels under instruction, for another Legion recruit, Justin TOCABENS, was also undergoing a course. FRAVAL was to operate in England as an invasion spy utilising secret inks; TOCABENS was to work in Barcelona as a radio operator relaying the reports of FRAVAL and other agents to Germany.

Eventually both reached Spain with the help of "PEDRO," and there conspired to report to the Germans the reception of their cover stories by the British authorities. FRAVAL broke down on his own and was sent to England; TOCABENS, a rogue male of the worst type, at once came under observation and at length found himself at Ham, too, on loan from the Free French authorities, to which he surrendered.

Between them they formed as unpretty a sample of the French collaborator with the Germans as could be. Faithful to the Germans while their comfort and their income derived from them, they had no compunction in protesting faithfulness to the Allies unto everything short of danger and death when they realised that they had been backing a lost cause.

In neither case was it possible to prosecute the men in England for treachery against the Allies. TOCABENS was returned to Africa for trial by the Free French authorities, while FRAVAL was made to bide his time at Ham prior to repatriation to a free France.

Lucien Alphonse Charles Victor ROMBAUT

The ways of the German Secret Service were at times surpassing quaint. The case of the Belgian research chemist Lucien Alphonse Charles Victor ROMBAUT, typified the division of the Abwehr mind in the year of decision, 1944. Abwehr officers stationed within easy call of each other neglected to compare notes or to co-ordinate effort. Thus while Werner UNVERSAGT was very properly concentrating on the immediate problem of an Allied invasion from Britain, a few miles away Kapitän KÖCHLING was congratulating himself on having despatched at last to the Congo an agent who should have arrived there two years earlier.

The man in question was ROMBAUT. His recruitment in 1941 was judicious to a degree. He was a defeatist; he had family commitments; intellectually he was no poltroon; he was ambitious; he knew the Congo well and was not averse to returning there in the German pay.

KÖCHLING, who had recruited him out of a German factory in Magdeburg, had excellent material in ROMBAUT. So much time did he take in making him word perfect for this task, however, that all the advantage was frittered away. Only KÖCHLING could explain what profit he and Germany could hope to derive from an agent with a Naval mission in darkest Africa in the year of German disgrace.

KÖCHLING, moreover, had been as careless with ROMBAUT as he had been careful. He had allowed him to enter into intimate contact at the early stages of his training with Frank Domien STEINER, who had betrayed the trainee many months earlier at Camp 020.

ROMBAUT was late in reaching Lisbon even after his final despatch from Belgium. The Germans had sealed him and all his paraphernalia in a goods waggon at Hendaye, with the result that the agent nearly died of thirst because the Spaniards were holding a three-day fiesta and took no interest in speeding the train from Irun. Seven and a half days after leaving Hendaye, ROMBAUT found himself parched, hungry and overheated on the Spanish side of the Portuguese frontier. He could stand it no more and hailed a small boy through an air vent with a request for water. The small boy betrayed him to the carabineros. There followed a spell of internment at several Spanish camps from which he succeeded in posting to KÖCHLING an appeal for help in a letter in secret writing. For this purpose he had used a "matchstick" pencil given him by KÖCHLING, and shortly afterwards he lost it. A fellow internee, borrowing a pipeful of tobacco, found the "match" between his fingers, tried to strike it, failed, and stamped it into the ground. ROMBAUT gritted his teeth and gave thanks that KÖCHLING had seen fit to place his more important espionage material, including a radio crystal and radio transmission instructions, in the heel of his shoe, safe from innocently praying hands.....

In course of time ROMBAUT found himself in Lisbon, where he had much traffic with new German espionage contacts before being directed by the Belgian authorities to travel to England before proceeding to the Congo. In his wisdom ROMBAUT was clever enough to hand his shoes, with the incriminating material, into German safekeeping pending his expected call at Lisbon in transit to the Congo.

ROMBAUT thus arrived in England without tangible evidence of his nefarious purpose. It had been decided by M I 5 that the case be allowed to take its normal course at the London Reception Centre, where the agent was allowed to tell his cover-story without cross-examination. It was a plausible story, too, for KÖCHLING had caused him to live some of its details. But there was the evidence of Frank Domien STEINER, and this had allowed of ROMBAUT's identification with an agent who had received much mention in ISOS despatches. ROMBAUT was transferred to Ham.

A break was obtained at the first interrogation, but not without a struggle. ROMBAUT fought the charges with obduracy, but succumbed when photographs of his wife and children were tacitly displayed before him. Even then he could not easily bring himself to write and sign a confession. Twice he picked up a pen, and twice he laid it down with a defiant "Non" before he realised that further resistance would be idle. His prognathous chin receded and tears streamed from his eyes as he wrote his first confession according to the time-honoured Camp 020 pro forma:-

1. "My first contact with the German Secret Service was in Magdeburg in September 1941 by Herr KÖCHLING.
2. My mission was to go in Congo (Belgian) and to try to give commercial informations. (+)
3. My means of communication with the German Secret Service was the radio.
4. My spy name was "NICO."
5. (Payment:) 10,000 fr. monthly in Belgium; he paid to my wife.
4,000 escudos in Portugal.
For expenses, $900.

(+) The admission of "military informations" came later.

6. I had to write to: Mr STRACHWITZ (++), 1 Parklaan,
Utrecht, when I arrived in Lisbon; and so I did.
(signed) L. ROMBAUT."

Detailed investigation thereafter yielded much profit.
Although ROMBAUT was contrarily upset by his "illegal detention"
while insisting that he had had every intention of carrying out his
mission, he was intelligent enough to surrender his information with
the meticulous attention to detail that one might expect of a
research chemist.

Josef Jan VAN HOVE

Josef Jan VAN HOVE, a Belgian waiter, aged 27, presented himself to
the British Consular authorities in Göteborg, Sweden, on 25th April
1943. There he recounted a story of forced labour in Germany and how
he had jumped a German ship in the harbour, with the object of going
to England to join the Belgian forces.

He spent roughly a year in Sweden, where he took a job as a
waiter, before his passage to Britain could be arranged by the
British and Belgian authorities in Stockholm. Finally he landed by
plane in Scotland in February 1944, and was sent from there, almost
immediately, to the London Reception Centre for the usual
investigation into his past history.

He held at first to the story which he had told in Sweden,
but under close interrogation he failed to account satisfactorily
for some of his movements in occupied territory, and suspicious were
aroused. Interrogations were continued, and finally, on 7th April
1944, he broke down and confessed to having been recruited as a
German agent in Antwerp by Werner UNVERSAGT, who had despatched him
to Sweden on the first leg of a mission to England to report on
invasion preparations and other military matters. He produced
"matches" for secret writing, one of them concealed in the handle of
his razor, and related how he had used them often in Sweden to
communicate with UNVERSAGT.

A statement was taken from VAN HOVE under caution, and on
9th April he was removed to Ham for a thorough investigation of his
story. No mitigating circumstance was to be found in the case. In
fact VAN HOVE damned himself for all time in a written statement at
Camp 020 which read as follows:-

(++) An alias of STRAUCH, an Abwehr officer active both in the Low
Countries and in Spain.

"I have no political opinion. The only reason to work for the Germans was money."

The luckless UNVERSAGT had certainly invested much Abwehr money in VAN HOVE. It was found at Camp 020 later that Justin TOCABENS, another of his recruits, had been employed for a time as the agent for UNVERSAGT's payments to VAN HOVE's wife and future widow. In fact, the links and cross links with other Belgian cases were many and illuminating of the general espionage picture in that country.

VAN HOVE himself was a curious character. Under interrogation he appeared somewhat stupid, and for a time it was thought that he was incapable of appreciating the danger of his position; but since he was giving information freely, there was no particular object to be gained by enlightening him on the subject. The original opinion required some modification later, for when a routine search of VAN HOVE's cell was carried out, the following poem was found:-

> "Le livre de la vie
> Est le livre suprême
> Que l'on ne peut ni ouvrir,
> Ni fermer sous choix.
> Le passage s'attachant
> Ne s'y lit qu'une fois;
> Et l'on voudrait revenir
> A la page ou l'on aime.
> Mais, déjà, la page ou l'on meurt
> Se trouve sous nos doigts..."

If those were the sentiments of VAN HOVE, then he must be given credit for a certain courage, for he did not falter during his incarceration at Camp 020. Whether he did so on the gallows on 12th July 1944, is not recorded in the obituary files of Ham.

Alejandro de URZAIZ Y GUZMAN

A new nigger in the woodpile of Ham successes was yet another Spaniard, Alejandro de URZAIZ Y GUZMAN. He had been an armchair soldier in the Spanish War, but had chosen the right side, for his inactive loyalty to the Cause won him appointment as Secretary-General of the Banco Exterior de España. He knew nothing about banking, but the defect was easily remedied by reading in bars and brothels the more easily assimilated paragraphs of a sixpenny pamphlet on orthodox financial practice.

Somehow and sometime this middle-aged student of Life and Banking came into contact with the German Secret Service in Madrid and was despatched by them on a mission to Mexico. ISOS picked up only a few references to him, and none of the cover-names which occurred in his connection appear ever to have been identified with members of the technical section of the Luftwaffe branch of the Abwehr, which was known to have recruited and controlled him.

Other known facts were that URZAIZ had at his disposal at least $10,000 in Cuba, that he had the appropriate cover-name of "VIENTO," meaning Wind, and that secret-writing pellets were to have been handed to him.

URZAIZ travelled out to Cuba and Mexico and was detained in Trinidad on the return trip for interrogation by a special investigator appointed by the FBI. That investigator appeared to have over-reached himself, for he obtained no admission from the Spaniard, and when the latter arrived at Camp 020 it was only too obvious that, as a consequence, he was spoiled as a subject for further interrogation.

URZAIZ, who combined all the qualities of Ananias, Uriah Heep, Don Quixote and a bewhiskered and toothless Lothario, was also a man of character and courage. Under the most severe pressure he admitted to no espionage contact in Spain; and when questioned about his activities in Cuba and Mexico, his reply was a bland reference to the FBI, "who told me that I was trailed and that everything was already known about me."

From that intransigent position he budged not one inch during his year's stay at Ham. The grand seigneur in him, however, asserted itself only when he was conveniently deported from Britain in a destroyer as an alien without visible means of support. The official ten shilling note given to him to correct his destitution was returned to a Special Branch escort with a courteous request that it be placed at the disposal of the British Secret Service.

Marcello MOCHI

Marcello MOCHI was the Italian Vice-Consul at Tangier at the time of the Italian surrender. ISOS traces and reports from other sources subsequently indicated that his loyalty was at issue. The attitude which he had adopted after BADOGLIOS's assumption of power seemed contrary to his protestation of allegiance. MOCHI was detained at Gibraltar when travelling from Madrid to Morocco and arrived at Camp 020 for investigation at the end of April 1944.

The simplest test of his good faith was, of course, to establish precisely how he had conducted himself after BADOGLIO took over the reins of office. But it was not so easy in practice to apply.

If, on the one hand, it was to be the sole test, then MOCHI must fail, for the traces after 8th September 1943 were against him. He was regarded by the Germans as a V-mann. He clearly intended to collaborate with them until he became quite certain that his interests lay on the side of the Allies. In addition there was the evil coincidence that in his property was found the name and address of a Spaniard which had occurred as an espionage link in the case of the self-centred German, Ernesto HOPPE. Furthermore, looking to his background, there were two other curious features. In the first place, MOCHI was a qualified doctor, and his deliberate change over to the Diplomatic Service was of his own volition. Indeed it was difficult for him to escape a charge of inherent Fascist sympathy and self-aggrandisement to the exclusion of his true profession. In the second place, there was an important journey across the Arabian peninsula during the war which might indicate that he was not petty official on a routine tour of duty to Jidda.

If on the other hand, not only the attitude adopted at a critical point of time, but the concomitant circumstances of the particular case, were to be taken into consideration, the problem became difficult indeed. The danger was that misplaced sympathy might become the order of the day.

The true picture in Tangier was that Italian consular officials had diligently worked for, and profited by, the Axis. Ambition came first and Mussolini came second. True patriotism was forgotten, though perhaps lip-service was paid to Italy and to the vacillating King. Officials no doubt allowed themselves to be pumped by the German Secret Service, but perhaps they did not descend quite so low as the average V-mann, who would betray so openly so much for money.

It was in these circumstances that the Italian officials, on the assumption of power by BADOGLIO, found themselves in a quandary. Some with a newly found love of country, changed sides within the hour. Others, more cautious, waited awhile to make perfectly certain that their personal interests were secure, and then plunged, Italian fashion, into protestations of eternal loyalty to Italy and her new Allies. Turncoats they were, and little to chose between them.

MOCHI's loyalties were as confused as anyone's, but it was in his favour that at a Fascist meeting shortly after the armistice he was accused of dumb insolence and hurled out of the hall through glass swing doors. With Italian duality, however, he seemed to have temporised later. At the same time as he paid lip-service to one side, he unwillingly assisted the other. Indeed, even in Madrid, which he visited in the hope of obtaining a visa for Northern Italy, he was not devoid of a German trace. Finally, distrusted by the Allies he found himself at Camp 020.

His indignation at the indignity knew no bounds but, paradoxically, he showed appreciation of the strength of the case against him. The fact was that he had gambled and lost, but did not like paying his debts.

The case was given much objective consideration. No undue importance was attached to the Arabian adventure, which was a considerable personal achievement. No undue weight could be attached to the coincidence of the cover address after MOCHI had given a reasonable explanation for his possession of it. When he had decided to collaborate less reluctantly in the investigation of his case, credit for that step was given him. But the adverse traces stood and collaboration with the Axis at a crucial time was proved. In the circumstances the finding was that MOCHI, like so many of his race, was wholly unreliable. At the best he would make an indifferent friend; at the worst he would prove an indifferent enemy. It was decided that he must remain in detention until the war was ended.

Magnus GUDBJORNSSON / Sverrir MATTHIASSON

German fear that the Allies planned to use Iceland as a base for the invasion of Northern Europe found expression in the recruitment and training of numerous agents intended to operate in the island. Two such invasion spies were Magnus GUDBJORNSSON and Sverrir MATTHIASSON, young Icelanders who had voluntarily gone to Germany to find work after the invasion of Denmark. Their different occupations separated them for a time: GUDBJORNSSON became successively a worker in a cigarette factory and a broadcaster in the Icelandic radio programme from Berlin; MATTHIASSON found profitable employment with a firm of Hamburg printers.

In the Spring of 1942 both men were approached simultaneously by officers of the Copenhagen Abwehrstelle with an invitation to return home at German expense in exchange for espionage service. Both accepted, and by the autumn of the same year they had begun an elaborate course of instruction in espionage, secret writing, radio transmission, construction and repair of transmitters, and the art of lying glibly under hostile interrogation. Delay in their despatch led to refresher courses, and before their training was complete both men had become well acquainted with training schools in Copenhagen, Hamburg and Lübeck.

It was not until April 1944 that they were despatched from Bergen in a U-boat and landed by rubber dinghy on the East coast of Iceland. Both men were soaked to the skin and their equipment was in no better condition. They repaired at once to a local farm and demanded to be put in touch with the Allied authorities. Shortly

afterwards both men had given a long account of their contact with
the Germans and the purpose of their present visit to the homeland.
After only the briefest delay, they were despatched to England for
investigation at Camp 020.

Here both men, who were abnormally intelligent for
Icelanders, but still not over-intelligent, gave in full detail
their personal histories and betrayed freely all facts known to them
about their German Secret Service contacts, their plans, activities
and technique. Valuable also was the disclosure by MATTHIASSON that
he had been promised a future contact in Iceland itself, one
Gudmundur HLIDAR, a German Secret Service agent at that time waiting
transportation from Sweden to Iceland, for later HLIDAR himself was
captured and brought to Camp 020.

Although both men had volunteered information at the first
available opportunity in Iceland, there were admissions of prior
willing service on behalf of the Germans outside the sphere of
espionage. Their reliability was thus necessarily in question, and
it was felt that their release might constitute a danger in view of
the impending invasion operations. Moreover, there was advance news
of further Icelandic agents who would be arriving at Camp 020, so
that the detention of MATTHIASSON and GUDBJORNSSON had justification
not only in prudence but in expediency. They stayed at Ham.

Knut Jørgen BRODERSEN

Knut Jørgen BRODERSEN held the rank of Lieutenant in the Norwegian
Army. He was also a professional tennis-player and an agent of
the German Secret Service. The Germans recruited him in Norway
after he had got into trouble over a Black Market deal in cognac,
and he bowed weakly to their wishes. These were that he should
travel to England, enlist in the Norwegian forces and then report in
secret inks on Allied military subjects. He was taught a code, too,
for his instructions were that he would receive further orders in
cypher over the German-controlled radio service for Norwegian
seamen.

Elaborate steps were taken to provide him with good cover.
Several months he spent in Southern France in the guise of an
impressed worker of the Todt organisation, and before his "escape"
into Spain he was made word-perfect in the additional details of his
cover-story. Further safety precautions were seen in the ingenuity
shown by his masters when concealing his secret writing material.
This was secreted in a hollow tooth, under a toe-nail, in the knee-
band of plus-fours, and under the stud of a boot.

BRODERSEN was thus able to face with confidence the closest
questioning by the uninstructed Allied authorities with whom he came

in contact. At Irun, Madrid and Leith, successively he lied
fluently, but at Ham, where ISOS traces had brought him, a halt was
called to his glib mendacity.

It was only at Camp 020 that his story was challenged, and
faced with the threat of death, BRODERSEN hastened to confess his
true tale. In the circumstances he could not be given much credit
for co-operation, and a reasonable conclusion was that his was an
outstanding case for prosecution under the Treachery Act. Conviction
was almost assured, for much of the secret writing material had been
recovered from his person and property.

Difficulties now arose because SIS had intercepted radio
messages in code from Norway which followed the form and times which
BRODERSEN had given as applying to the fresh instructions which he
and other agents in England might expect to receive. Although
BRODERSEN's code had been fully described by him at Ham, it was not
possible to make sense of the messages. BRODERSEN himself, in
frantic fear of death, could make nothing of them. Consideration was
given to the despatch by him of a letter in secret ink demanding
elucidation of the secret messages. Contact by secret message might,
in the ultimate, lead to an XX link which might assist in
apprehending other spies trained in the same, as yet undeciphered,
code. The proposition was, however, not a straightforward one and
was surrounded by difficulties.

This pretty problem was outside the province of resolution
at Ham, and BRODERSEN was put at the disposal of MI 5 in June 1944.

Inar Bjorn SIGVALDASON / Larus Sigurvin THORSTEINSSON

Nordic treachery has always a cold-blooded quality. The cases of
Inar Bjorn SIGVALDASON and Larus Sigurvin THORSTEINSSON ran true to
type. Both were recruited by the Sicherheitsdienst as meteorological
spies in Iceland without any semblance of resistance on their part.
In fact, they offered themselves willingly for any venture that
would bring them money and a sight of the dreary, old, geyser-pitted
homeland. SIGVALDASON, a knacker, plumber and champion accordion
player who had settled in Denmark before the war, was a man of no
scruples. THORSTEINSSON, an unemployed seaman with an amateurish
interest in radio, was little better, if slightly more intelligent.

The Germans had little difficulty in teaching them the
rudiments of coding and radio transmission over a long period of
schooling at the notorious Lehnitz school near Berlin. Eventually
they were despatched to Iceland via Norway in sole control of a two-
masted motor-vessel. SIGVALDASON was violently sea-sick throughout
the voyage, while THORSTEINSSON was feverish and suffering from
delusions, so that it was something in the nature of a dispensation
by Providence that allowed them to reach Iceland at all.

After lying sick off-shore for a day and being visited on board by at least three curious Icelanders, their vessel came under Allied notice. Haggard, unshaven and filthy the unhappy agents were escorted ashore by their callers, the Icelanders, and were handed to the Allied authorities. Both men told a story of escape from Denmark via Sweden and Norway that failed to ring true. They were placed under arrest. On the following day they were fortunate enough to see their boat founder in a gale, for in it there was much incriminating German material. In the course of time, after surviving further interrogations, they were shipped to England.

At the London Reception Centre both men lied monstrously. At Camp 001, the ante-room to Ham, THORSTEINSSON broke down and confessed to espionage. But it was only under a blitz interrogation at Camp 020 that SIGVALDASON confessed at all. Thereafter both told their stories without obstruction; but then, candour, after an interrogation break, is a matter of commonsense; the spy usually wishes to save his neck.

There were several new features in their joint story, for the SD personalities and the places and technique of training were novel. A link was established with the more recent Ham case of Icelandic espionage when both men admitted to knowledge of and contact with Gudbrandur HLIDAR.

It was quite plain after investigation of the cases that both spies had merely sought to suit their own convenience in accepting service for the Germans, and that they never had the slightest intention of assisting the Allies. Their detention for the duration of the war was thus a foregone conclusion.

Wladyslaw WILMAN

In May 1944 a young Pole arrived in Gibraltar from Lisbon in a party of refugee compatriots who had volunteered for service with the Polish Forces in England. He was Wladyslaw WILMAN, and immediately upon landing he reported that he was in possession of important information which he was anxious to divulge to the British Intelligence Service.

He was immediately given a hearing and disclosed the fact that he had been recruited and trained as a German espionage agent in 1942. The first contact had been made in Hamburg while he was employed as a forced labourer in an aircraft factory, and he had received training and instructions both there and in Bremen. His espionage schooling had included instruction in codes and radio transmission, and his mission was to proceed either to Britain or Canada and report on invasion preparations. His means of communication were to have been in secret writing and radio telegraphy; he had been shown in Hamburg and Bremen how to convert an ordinary household receiver into a transmitter.

From odd edgings of his clothing WILMAN then produced a number of micro-dot duffs containing his espionage instructions. From a pocket came a white handkerchief which reacted to treatment with cigarette ash and water by revealing the red traces the frequencies and wave-lengths which he was to use when transmitting.

WILMAN was hurried out of Gibraltar to England as a prospective double agent and arrived at Ham on 18th May 1944 for a thorough investigation into his background, knowledge, and reliability. He passed all the normal tests of good faith with signal ease and also added considerably to the MI 5 records on German espionage practice and its practitioners.

In view of the fact that he was still at Ham when the invasion of Normandy was launched, the idea of using him as a double-agent was dropped. He was released for work at a British aircraft factory towards the end of June 1944.

Ernst Christoph FRESENIUS: Hjalti BJORNSSON: Sigurdur Nordmann JULIUSSON

In the late evening of 5th May 1944 an Icelandic seal hunter reported to the American authorities in Iceland through his local Sheriff that he chanced upon three strangers whose appearance and activities seemed to him suspicious. Early the following morning a small American expedition into the wastelands apprehended a German, Ernst Christoph FRESENIUS, and two young Icelanders, Hjalti BJORNSSON and Sigurdur Nordmann JULIUSSON.

Interrogation in situ elicited from the Icelanders nothing but guttural protestations of innocent business. They were visibly upset when FRESENIUS proceeded calmly but haughtily to proclaim himself a German soldier and the leader of an expedition of three sent to Iceland to gather meteorological data on behalf of "a German shipping institute." He announced that it was not the first time that he had been taken a prisoner of war; he had spent the greater part of the last behind wire in England. When it was pointed out to him that his present capture in civilian clothing might not end so comfortably, he proudly declared that he was not unprepared for death. As leader of the party, he asked only one thing: that the two Icelanders be spared.

It was too cold and dark for further mountainside heroics. The Americans began to march the captives down to the prison cells of relative civilisation. On the way BJORNSSON, who had been shaken by FRESENIUS' seemingly casual betrayal, confessed that he had helped to conceal a radio transmitter, pedal-operated generator and other items of equipment at a spot some distance from their place of capture. Soon this incriminating material had been recovered. With it the three men were at once despatched to England for thorough investigation at Camp 020.

Somewhat remissly, no attempt was made either in Iceland or on board ship to segregate the men. The result was that they arrived at Ham agreed and word-perfect in a story that was modestly shy even of the half truth.

The situation called for careful handling. The case was one of outstanding operational importance, and it had to be resolved urgently and without defects. The solution lay in the old and tried device of proceeding through weakness into strength. FRESENIUS, the tough character, was ignored altogether while his two unsubtle retainers were played off against each other under separate investigation. Their resistance was short-lived: the main story emerged in its true version. Faced later with incontestable facts, FRESENIUS surrendered gracefully. Many, however were his reticences and stubborn his obstruction in material detail before the ultimate story could be set out in its complete form.

In particular FRESENIUS was ever insistent that although all three men had received training in secret writing, they had been given no cover addresses. This omission was not to the Commandant's liking. Again and again he returned to the subject in interrogation, and then, such is the luck of the game, FRESENIUS, defending still his specific argument on the absence of cover addresses, admitted that there was in Iceland a second radio transmitter which had not been surrendered. Directions were at once obtained for its recovery and the information was communicated to the Americans in Iceland.

FRESENIUS was most obdurate, however, in his refusal to disclose the control-sign which had been given to him by his superiors. He protested flatly that its betrayal would constitute an act of treason against the Fatherland. For reasons best known to himself he abandoned that stand later and gave the information quite spontaneously.

The story of the new Icelandic venture, in it final form, showed that the Germans had for once made an intelligent bid to establish an information post in the Allied camp. They were worried still about the possible use of Iceland as a base for Continental invasion, and it was with the object of enlightening themselves on this perplexing point that they had prepared the expedition.

The choice of FRESENIUS as leader was not without wisdom. He had lived for twelve years in Iceland, first as an agricultural labourer and later as the proprietor of a model farm which attracted visitors from many countries. Among these had been one Dr LOTZ, owner of a large estate in Pomerania.

With the outbreak of war LOTZ became an Abwehr officer. Entrusted with the recruitment of an espionage group to operate in Iceland, he recalled his meeting with FRESENIUS and traced him to a farm in Germany on which the latter was peacefully working. Although he had became a naturalised Icelander during his sojourn in the island, FRESENIUS responded promptly to an appeal to his native patriotism. He accepted his espionage mission and applied himself conscientiously to a long course of training and preparation at the Abwehr's new spy school at Schloss Schierensee.

He had been preceded there by BJORNSSON and JULIUSSON, both of whom had been picked up in Denmark by LOTZ through intermediaries who included the now familiar HLIDAR. The two Icelanders, who also received instruction in sabotage, had actually begun their training in radio transmission at a school in Oslo. One of their instructors there had been a young man called "FRITZ," who spoke German badly and English well. At Ham they described him, and he was at once identified as none other than Edward Arnold CHAPMAN. This was an interesting and valuable item of intelligence, for only a few days after it had been obtained CHAPMAN himself was back at Ham after parachuting into England with a new mission. A primary test of his constancy was whether he would mention his training of the Icelandic agents and name them. To his credit he did so without prompting.

After completion of its very careful education in espionage, the FRESENIUS group, equipped to the last detail with the latest implements of the trade, was ferried to Iceland by U-boat. For almost a week after landing they made their arrangements and dispositions to begin operations. For five days they made unsuccessful efforts to contact their radio control station at Hamburg, and it was while they were moving up to the mountains to find a new hideout at an altitude more favourable for radio communication that they were detected and captured.

Disposal of the three men after completion of the investigation at Camp 020 was not the prerogative of the British authorities, and in August 1944 they were returned to Iceland to answer to the will of their enlightened American captors.

A
DIGEST OF HAM

Volume Three

CASE HISTORIES
(Concluded)

HAM

HUNTERCOMBE

DIEST

BAD NENNDORF

Yves GUILCHER: André Louis Eugène GUY: Madeleine BERNARD

The projection of Ham into the field of military operations had been planned well in advance of D-Day. The establishment was to serve the counter-espionage and security needs not only of the British invading forces, but of the Americans and the French also. Arrangements had been made to provide the speediest possible processing of agents and suspects. Spies were to be flown from the field to England, and the commitment was that Camp 020 would return a report in the same manner within the week. A special pro-forma was drawn up to contain the personal history of each man and to classify the intelligence gained from his investigation.

The first arrivals were awaited with eager anticipation. Their calibre provided an early anti-climax.

Firstcomer was a 28-year-old former soldier of the French Regular Army, Yves GUILCHER, a German stay-behind agent arrested at Bayeux on 10th June following denunciation by a local Resistance leader. GUILCHER was categorically indicated as a German agent in possession of a radio transmitter. His house was searched: in an attic were found strips of torn paper which, on being pieced together, indicated that some object had been concealed in the garden of the house. Spades were obtained and digging operations began: in a matter of minutes a radio transmitter and documents relating to its operation and the use of codes were unearthed.

GUILCHER's first reaction was to deny responsibility for the embarrassing find. Without more ado he was marched to local FS headquarters and there, after a brief argument, he confessed to being a German agent. His despatch to Ham was arranged at once.

At Camp 020 GUILCHER, a quondam seller of lavender-water, and member of the Collaborationist LVF, had been suborned into service, but had not resented the fact when he began to receive generous payment for his treachery. The Germans had twice "suspended" him as indiscreet and unreliable, but in the ultimate they pinned their faith to him. GUILCHER may have had ideas of reinsurance in not betraying his masters voluntarily at the first opportunity, for the fortunes of the Normandy battle were not yet settled when he was arrested, but at Ham, he was voluble about them in his vain effort to please. He had no compunction, either, in naming his fellow-trainees and colleagues in German espionage, so that the Allies were able to open with his generous donation the long list of agents and suspects who were later to be arrested.

Misinterpretation in the field of orders for the grading of suspects led on occasion to the receipt at Camp 020 of shabby collaborationists who were not, however, of counter-intelligence interest. Such a one was André Louis Eugène GUY, an aged epileptic, who wasted much valuable time and effort before it could be reported with any certainty that he was free of any suspicion of espionage on behalf of the enemy.

The next arrival was a voluble, middle-aged Frenchwoman, Madeleine Gabriel Francine BERNARD, who had reported to the Americans in Calvados as an agent of the Deuxième Bureau who had allowed herself to be recruited by the German Secret Service. Mme BERNARD was received at Ham as a privileged visitor. She was available for interrogation for only five days, and within the time-limit a full report was issued in her case. She proved to be less important than she thought herself, but her patriotism was refreshing.

Michel SCOGNAMILLO: Henri Emile Jean MATHIEU: Henri Gaston ROGER

Perhaps one of the most important series of those early operational cases was that linking Michel SCOGNAMILLO, Henri Emile Jean MATHIEU and Henri Gaston ROGER. This prize packet of snivelling French oafs came from the American beachhead in the Carentan area.

French treachery is largely a matter of personal convenience and it is conditioned by French logic. SCOGNAMILLO, a 23-year-old grocer's boy from Toulon, had been in trouble with the police. He found security from the law by lending himself, first to the LVF and then to the Germans, as a common informant against the Maquis. He excelled in this dirty business and qualified for a course of instruction in sabotage at a special centre at La Montagnette. He was not bright enough to assimilate the simplest technicalities and he was transferred to the 8th Company of the notorious Brandenburg Regiment for minor espionage assignments. His first and last mission was to spy on a small village bakery suspected of supplying bread to local Maquis. Instead he returned to Toulon to comfort his Italian grandmother, who had been made bomb-happy by the RAF. When he came back to report the failure of his mission, the Germans clapped him in gaol, then packed him off to the Cherbourg area as an impressed worker under close supervision. SCOGNAMILLO realised that there was no future in German protection. He escaped to the Carentan area and there greeted the advancing American troops with Italo-French "vivas." An opportunity further to ingratiate himself with the Allies arose when he met in the street one Henri Jean MATHIEU, whom he recognised as a fellow-trainee at La Montagnette. He reported him to the Americans as a German agent.

MATHIEU, at the age of eighteen a seasoned collaborator with the Germans, was soon arrested. Promptly he returned SCOGNAMILLO's compliment by denouncing him as a German agent. Treachery being the order of the French day, he proceeded to denounce his companion en mission also, Henri Gaston ROGER. All three were interrogated in the field and a list of other agents was extracted from them. At Camp 020 a few days later, the list of German agents and German contacts grew prodigiously as a result of further, detailed investigation.

In the cases of MATHIEU and ROGER, dividends were particularly rich. Both had undergone an elaborate course in sabotage training at the Chateau Maulny under German and French instructors. Their fellow-trainees had been numerous: both agents proceeded to name and describe them with alacrity. ROGER, the veteran of the group at the mature age of thirty, had no compunction even in denouncing his own brother...

From the final story which MATHIEU and ROGER told it was obvious that the Germans had been caught short by the invasion. Their training had been on a long-term basis. ROGER's had been practically completed, MATHIEU's only just begun, when the Allies disgorged on the French coast. There was much confusion among their German masters as to their immediate employment, but finally they had been despatched together to the Carentan area as "Frontläufer" charged with the simplest espionage mission behind the Allied lines. They had no means of communication other than by personal contact, and by the time that the Allies had swept well past them, neither MATHIEUN nor ROGER had any intention of risking a return to the German lines. French logic told them that it would be safer to stay put and be silent.

Thanks to SCOGNAMILLO they did neither for long. They travelled to England and back and talked a lot before Free French logic was applied to them.

Claude COLLOMB: Daniel Jean Louis CROMBE

Claude COLLOMB, who came from Rouen, was the 21-year-old son of a deceased French hatter. Early in July 1944 he reported to FS headquarters at Caen and volunteered the information that he had been an agent of the Sicherheitsdienst and that he had much intelligence to impart. Preliminary interrogation suggested that COLLOMB, in a skin-saving act, was prepared to tell only as much as would make his change of heart acceptable to the Allies. He was promptly arrested and directed to Camp 020.

At Ham COLLOMB found it profitable to finesse. He was received without ceremony and was rapidly processed. His story was as sordid as any. He had joined a French collaborationist Party and almost simultaneously agreed to a fellow-member's suggestion that he work for the Germans of the SD. He had been entrusted with minor espionage missions at first, but later he had been despatched to the Franco-Spanish frontier to penetrate an Allied escape route. In this he failed, but later he had the satisfaction of betraying to probable death three "passeurs" in another zone.

He graduated to penetration of Resistance groups and effected many glorious coup on behalf of the SD before the Allied invasion prompted the Germans to despatch him to Caen as a "Frontläufer." He was to report on the morale of the population, civil administration, the activities of the Maquis, security controls, the food situation, and shelling of the area by British warships.

COLLOMB found the shelling so impressive that he decided the time was ripe to change sides. In the process of confession he decided that one of his companions in crime should also change sides, for good ideas are meant to be shared. Thus he named Daniel Jean Louis CROMBE, a 24-year-old student, as the companion sent with him to Caen by the SD.

CROMBE was duly arrested and joined his loyal friend at Ham. He, too, had originally been recruited for the SD through a French collaborationist Party. He got German francs and cigarettes and extra rations for betraying Maquis, and such was his enthusiasm that he even denounced burglars and hooligans to his masters for good measure.

The arrest of a Resistance leader on denunciation by two gamins rashly entrusted by a British officer with instructions for him, provided the Germans with the possibility of sound cover for CROMBE. The Resistance leader was forced to write a letter to the British officer commending CROMBE as "homme de confiance." Armed with this document, CROMBE presented himself to the British security authorities in Caen. They were inclined to accept him at first at his face value, but then CROMBE spoiled it all by splitting on him...

Hans Karl SCHARF (or SCHNEIDER)

Caught up in the dreary procession of petty invasion agents who were passing through Ham at his time was an experienced Abwehrmann with a colourful past. He had been captured in Algeria after being dropped by parachute to engage in military espionage and act as radio operator for other agents. He was loaned to MI 5 by his French captors for return to Africa within a month, but in actual fact he remained at Ham for some seven months.

The man in question insisted both in Africa and at Ham that he was a German, that his name was Hans Karl SCHARF, and that among his aliases was the name "SCHNEIDER." There was no reason at the time of his investigation to doubt these claims, for he showed himself willing indeed to impart the information in his possession, and it was considerable. Later, however, it transpired from a series of cases at Camp 020 that the agent's real name was SCHNEIDER, that he was a Lorrainer of German parentage and French nationality, and that he had deserted to the Germans during the first months of the war after recruitment into the French Army. He was not very hopeful when he left Ham for Africa that he would escape the death penalty as a spy, but it is clear now that he was determined not to force the issue by confessing to his true identity and his desertion.

He came to Ham as Hans Karl SCHARF, not for personal investigation, but as a prolific source of information, and for the purposes of this history, SCHARF he will remain.

His Abwehr history began in May 1940, when he joined the notorious Brandenburg Regiment. His first mission was in Lille, where he recruited Bretons for a new Separatist movement under German auspices, and later he was employed to interrogate and enlist members of other minority groups from among French soldiers in prison camps.

In August 1940 SCHARF received careful training in radio telegraphy, at which he showed himself an apt pupil. Soon afterwards came lessons in English, and it was obvious to him that his next task would have an element of adventure. He was not disappointed. In March 1941 Sonderführer HALLER (+), a leading light of Abt II of the Abwehr, informed him that he was to be despatched to South Africa to act as radio operator for two agents who would be operating there. One of them, Roby LEIBBRANDT, South African boxer trained in sabotage and espionage, would be travelling with him; the second, later identified by SCHARF as that mute Ham prisoner, ELFERINK, was already in Africa.

In the course of time LEIBBRANDT and SCHARF were despatched from Paimpol, in Britanny, in the well-found yacht "Kyloe," manned by an experienced German crew of six. The outward journey was uneventful until the point of proposed disembarkation was reached. Then LEIBBRANDT quarrelled with SCHARF over the latter's inadequate English, and in the upshot LEIBBRANDT (‡) went ashore alone and SCHARF decided to return to Europe.

Twice on the homeward journey the yacht was hailed by Allied patrol vessels, and twice she evaded close examination by running up the Stars and Stripes. The third time, the skipper decided, might not be so lucky: he decided to make for Villa Cisneros, in Rio de Oro, and thence report for further orders.

(+) In 1946, Prisoner at Bad Nenndorf.
(‡) LEIBBRANDT was subsequently captured by the South Africans and received a sentence of penal servitude for life.

Gradually the members of the crew were removed to Germany by air from Villa Cisneros. Only SCHARF remained when Sonderführer HALLER arrived from Berlin, not with reproaches for his failure to make land in Africa, but with instructions that he remain in the Spanish colony as assistant radio operator of the Abwehr group working there with the full collaboration and blessing of the local Spanish authorities.

SCHARF stayed in Rio de Oro until March 1942, when he was transferred to Paris. He found himself allocated to the Eins Marine section at the Hotel Lutetia for eventual service in Africa. For months he remained idle, then in October 1942 he was ordered to report to one Rittmeister Graf Joseph Von LEDEBUR, a liaison officer of Korvetten Kapitän Erich PHEIFFER, at this time Leiter III of Alst Frankreich. It seemed that he had been selected as one of the two Abwehr radio operators who were to accompany the collaborationist French industrialist, Charles BEDAUX, on some expedition to the Niger bend which had the full support of the Abwehr.

At Ham many months later both von LEDEBUR and PHEIFFER stated that neither they nor BEDAUX had any liking for the antipathetic SCHARF, whom they described as "the sick bird"; and when the irascible BEDAUX threatened that he would hurl SCHARF into the sea rather than take him to Africa, he was withdrawn from the expedition. SCHARF always preferred to believe that his exclusion from the BEDAUX caravan was due solely to more urgent need of his services in a more important mission.

Be that as it may, the next months he spent in relative idleness in France, and it was not until July 1943 that a new mission in Africa was mentioned. This proved abortive, but in November 1943 he received instructions to hold himself in readiness to leave France for Algeria.

His mission this time was indeed important. He was to be parachuted into Algeria to act as radio operator for an agent already collecting military intelligence there; he was to collaborate in this espionage work; and he was to carry with him funds totalling some 600,000 fcs.

SCHARF was successfully landed in Algeria at the second attempt. He was spotted in the sky coming down by a curious Arab who immediately challenged him as a German agent. Native honour was satisfied when SCHARF admitted that this was so, and the Arab went off happily to buy him a turban to top off the flowing djellaba with which he had been supplied in France.

The transmitter, which had been dropped by separate parachute, was nowhere to be found. SCHARF decided to make for Tangier and safety, since fulfilment of his mission was now out of

the question. On hot foot, by bicycle bought in outrageous bargain,
and by hitch-hiking he reached Montagnac. There he resumed the
djellaba that he had cast while cycling and riding beside car-owning
Arabs. But he forgot to remove his trousers and thereby outraged the
sense of propriety of a native who had watched him pass by. The
native hailed SCHARF: SCHARF took fright, tried to run, entangled
himself in his flowing djellaba, and fell headlong.

The inevitable crowd of natives gathered from nowhere to
watch the fun. SCHARF turned pleadingly on his tormenter, apologised
for his trousers, and offered a vast sum of money if he were allowed
to go his way in peace. The Arab sorrowfully pointed out that while
this was indeed nice talk, SCHARF should have kept it from the
public around them. Such bargains were to be struck only in private.
The Arab regretted that it was too late now...

Shortly afterwards SCHARF found himself under police arrest.
French interrogation processes are not squeamish, and the agent
confessed with little show of resistance. It was with chagrin that
he learned that his radio transmitter had been found by the police
not far from the point at which he had landed. There was bitterness
in his heart, too, when later he was taken to Algiers and made to
contact the agent with whom he was to have collaborated. Both were
thrown into gaol in Oran, and there SCHARF was kept until July 1944,
when he was flown to England for detailed interrogation.

Michel GIRKA: Roger BIANCHI: Gaston PIAT: Claude LOMBART: Roland BALL: Yvon MANCEAU

The trickle of invasion agents into Camp 020 had developed into a
steady stream. Out of nationality but in character with the precious
bane of French youth was Michel GIRKA, an 18-year-old Pole. He was a
grocer's boy and a member of the PPF in Vichy. In May 1944 he was
called to the local office of the party and invited, without
preamble, to offer himself to the Germans for service as a spy in
the event of an Allied invasion.

There was more money and more excitement in the proposition
than in the grocery business. His friend Roger BIANCHI, an errand
boy with a criminal record and police on his heels, agreed with him.
Together they travelled to Paris, where they received very sketchy
training in radio telegraphy and organisation and identification of
Allied units and their arms.

It was as "Frontläufer" that they were despatched, before
training was completed, to the Normandy bridgeheads. They parted
company to proceed to their respective assignments. GIRKA made for
Bayeux. The British are fond of feeding the hand that bites them,
and it was on rations cadged from soldiers of the front line that he

neared his journey's end. He didn't reach it, for his movements brought him under FS suspicion. He was too ingenuous to tell a plausible story about his front loafings and soon broke under interrogation. He betrayed a number of his fellow-spies, among them BIANCHI, who had told a cover story so convincingly that he was about to be enlisted into the Free French Army. They reached Camp 020 separately and much new and valuable intelligence was drawn from them.

Gaston Francis PIAT, a pimply bookbinder of twenty-one, arrived at Ham simultaneously with GIRKA. He had the sort of background that gladdens the heart of a German Secret Service recruiter. At eighteen he had manufactured a bomb which was set off at the entrance to the Vichy Synagogue; he was a member of the PPF; he had a prison record; he was a deserter from the Todt Organisation. Like GIRKA and BIANCHI, PIAT was trained in Paris before being despatched to the Calvados area to confirm reports of concentrations of armour and troops. He did not reach far into the Allied rear, for he was challenged by a British sentry, sent back for interrogation, and partially broken before being shipped across the Channel to Camp 020.

Claude LOMBART and Roland BALL followed. They, too, were PPF members who had been recruited into the German service through their political mentors. Training was at the Chateau de Maulny on normal infantry lines with elementary lessons in sabotage. They were despatched to an American bridgehead to ascertain morale of the population and reception of the invading forces. ROGER, MATHIEU and other agents at Camp 020 had described both LOMBART and BALL. The descriptions were circulated to all Allied units. So well did the two men answer to them that they were detected and detained almost immediately after crossing the Allied lines.

Yvon MANCEAU, an orphaned barber, gave himself up to the Canadians on 20th June 1944, but failed to tell the true story of his recruitment by the Germans. At Ham it was established that his service had been long and shabby. It had begun with enlistment in the Milice and operations against the Maquis in Haute Savoie. He transferred to full-time work for the German Secret Service out of monetary greed, and he was not ashamed to admit it. His training was at the Hotel Ambassador in Paris, and it was found that his case linked with GIRKA, ROGER and PIAT. His mission was to report verbally, within two days of crossing the line, on troop concentrations in the Douvres area.

Georges Gabriel LAURENGER: Bernard SEYS

A tenacious liar was Georges Gabriel LAURENGER, 24-year-old film extra, magazine-salesman and clerk, who was arrested in Bayeux after surviving many FS interrogations. He was a stay-behind agent with a relatively long German espionage history and much schooling in radio transmission, coding and identification of British units.

He came under suspicion shortly after British troops had occupied Bayeux, but it was not until a woman came forward to denounce him as a regular visitor to a house from which "suspicious tapping noises" had emanated over a long period, that he was trapped into a confession.

Even then he lied fluently. The Proces Verbal taken in the field and the First Interim Report issued from Camp 020 were ingeniously evasive of the greater and more incriminating truth. Sustained pressure at Camp 020 finally broke him.

Bernard SEYS was a very different type. He had been trained at the Chateau de Maulny as a saboteur. His mission was to place bombs disguised as horse-droppings along roads behind the Allied lines. At the first sight of an American tank he surrendered, bringing with him no sample of manure but a simple German soldier eager to desert. No difficulty was experienced in obtaining the full story from him.

Juan FRUTOS

Outstanding among the petty cases of the day was that of Juan FRUTOS, a Gallicised Spaniard settled in Cherbourg. For many years he had been an interpreter and baggage-master with the local branch of the American Express Company. From ISOS and other sources it was known that he had been recruited as a German agent and had operated a radio transmitter since August 1940 until after D-Day. His address in Cherbourg had been provided by another German agent, and following occupation of the port by the Americans search was made for him. Eventually he was discovered, acting as an interpreter in the American Army office responsible for reception and billeting of Allied units.

FRUTOS was discreetly arrested and taken to his flat for interrogation. Among his papers was found an envelope addressed to himself in his real name, but containing a letter which addresed him in his spy name of EIKINS. In the same breath FRUTOS made an admission of contact with the enemy and an offer to serve the Allies.

Somewhat recklessly his offer was accepted: for some weeks he was operated as a double-agent passing false information to his

masters by radio. A period of silence at the receiving end led to
suspicion that FRUTOS was "blown." He was sent to Camp 020 for
short-term investigation.

There, under sustained pressure, FRUTOS was compelled to
confess that his original admission of service for the Germans fell
far short of the truth. His original recruitment actually dated back
as far as 1936, when he had become involved in espionage on behalf
of a German steward of the liner "Bremen," Carl EITEL, who came to
Ham after him. His story was obtained in outline down to the time of
his arrest, and details were obtained of all the information which
he had communicated to his masters from Cherbourg since D-Day.

It was many weeks after FRUTOS had left Ham after his
hurried investigation that EITEL was forced to disclose the many
early acts of espionage which the Spaniard had withheld from his
investigators. Later still Korvetten Kapitän PHEIFFER, EITEL's
principal at the material time, contributed new evidence against
FRUTOS.

Patrick Pierre GUERIN

After a few more "Frontläufers" of stale and flat, if not wholly
unprofitable, interest, there appeared on the scene a new and more
dangerous type, the separatist fanatic with an unreasoning but
burning faith in disinterested German patronage.

First in this class to reach Camp 020 was Patrick Pierre
GUERIN, 30-year-old Breton Nationalist with a considerable pre-war
history of subversion. GUERIN, by profession an artist, was sent
to Paris by his parents in the hope that he would discontinue the
acts of political hooliganism that were becoming an embarrassment
at home. Rather contrarily, young Patrick Pierre intensified his
militant Bretonisme in the capital and fell in with a gang of
coreligionaries led by a hot-head named Guy Vissault de COETLEGON,
the evil genius who put him in touch with Germans of the
Sicherheitsdienst.

The German approach to GUERIN did not need to be subtle. He
was asked point-blank whether he would work for the SD against De
Gaullistes and Maquis as a common informer. He agreed with
enthusiasm, but was soon dropped by his first German master, who
made the cutting comment that "quite obviously, idealists and
dreamers and incompetent as spies."

Three years later, in September 1943, GUERIN was summoned
to Paris by de COETLEGON and again agreed to do his best by the
Germans. There was no question now of casual service as a gay
deceiver of patriots, but full-time occupation as a trained reporter
on political themes. GUERIN was carefully instructed in radio

telegraphy and codes at a Paris school of the SD and received also a short course of military training at an establishment in the country.

Towards the end of May 1944 GUERIN received urgent orders to return to his home town in Brittany and there deposit his transmitter. The Germans were nervous about the imminence of an Allied invasion and they wished him to be ready to begin his stay-behind assignment as soon as possible after the event. It was their belief that there would be friction between the French population and the Allied invaders, and this GUERIN was to promote to the best of his subversive ability. They had not neglected the possibility that GUERIN himself might be impressed into Partisan service on behalf of the Allies, and the agent was supplied with a box of pastilles calculated to induce heart attacks which would cause him to be rejected on medical grounds.

The actual invasion caught out GUERIN and de COETLEGON, for they were still in Paris in early June. Many were the abortive efforts they made to regain Brittany, but ultimately GUERIN succeeded in reaching his home town under German guidance.

Not long afterwards the first Americans troops marched in. For some days GUERIN was able to avoid them, but not an occasional challenge by FFI enthusiasts. Such was the zeal of the latter, that he was compelled to conceal his false documents, codes, and other compromising material in a riverside cache, while still keeping a transmitter in the imagined safety of a room he had rented for the purpose.

He was still playing nervously for time when he was stopped in the streets of Ancenis by a very small boy with an FFI brassard and a very determined manner. GUERIN could not satisfy him with his authentic identity papers. The boy took him to FFI headquarters, where he was told that GUERIN, as a civilian, could not be held by them. Doggedly the youthful rat smeller insisted on accompanying GUERIN to this room and searching it. The proud Breton was not prepared to argue the point, especially since the boy had now acquired formidable armed support from two colleagues of his age.

GUERIN's room was searched. Under a counterpane was found a radio transmitter in one case, a hand generator, accumulators and accessories in another. GUERIN went quietly to the local police station and FFI headquarters, where he made a confession. On transfer to Rennes for further interrogation and summary liquidation, he decided to disclose the fact that his documents were concealed near Ancenis and that a second transmitter had been hidden by him at Locminé, his home town.

The second transmitter was duly recovered by a party guided to the spot by GUERIN, but on the return to Rennes an ambush by an

isolated German patrol almost put an end to the sortie, so that
search for the documents was abandoned.

After further interrogation in France, GUERIN was
transferred under American auspices to Camp 020, where the full
details of his espionage history and contacts were extracted from
him. He was joined at Ham shortly afterwards by Vissault de
COETLEGON, and the mutual recriminations of the frustrated Bretons
were awful to hear. Neither of them saw the error of their political
ways, however, and both were unrepentant when they were returned to
united France.

Pierre Camille DUFFAU: Renée Marthe Eugènie DELOBEL

It was in the legitimate way of business that Pierre Camille DUFFAU,
a 24-year-old timber merchant, first came into contact with the
German Secret Service. He had been anxious to obtain a permit for
the purchase of some iron material, and someone how knew somebody
who had the right influence in the right quarters introduced him to
the Spanish mistress of a German Secret Service officer. Perhaps
because they wanted to make use of their man before making their
first approach, the Germans had DUFFAU arrested in Paris on trumped-
up charges. Blackmail followed: he could either face the music or
volunteer for services as a spy in North Africa, where he had served
as a French soldier.

DUFFAU offered no resistance. He received instruction in
radio telegraphy, codes and general espionage subjects. By the
beginning of 1944 he was ready to depart for Africa, where he was to
be dropped by parachute. But the African mission never matured;
instead he was given trifling missions in France itself. One such
was to check up on information that arms were to be landed from a
barge at Bagneaux. DUFFAU took his mistress, Renée Marthe Eugenie
DELOBEL, in whom he had confided in full, and spent a week-end
fishing in view of the barge. He was too busy at nights to continue
the watch, but he had no compunction later in submitting a negative
report.

By the early Spring of 1944 DUFFAU received orders to
establish himself in Caen as a stay-behind agent. It was agreed
that, for purposes of cover, he might buy and operate a cafe with
the help of his mistress. There was some argument about the
financing of the cafe project, but ultimately DUFFAU and Renee were
able to raise sufficient funds privately to supplement the meagre
resources put at their disposal by the Germans and buy their
business.

DUFFAU, who was being visited regularly by his masters,
fixed his radio aerials behind the wallpaper of the house and

installed one of his two transmitters in the most intimate corner of the edifice, a privy below stairs. From there he was successful in establishing contact with his control station.

When the Allies erupted in the area, DUFFAU buried his two transmitters in the yard of the café and stood by to await developments. They came soon enough. Both he and his mistress were denounced as collaborators with the Germans and as the possessors of ample funds of doubtful origin. The first charge was fair enough, the second galling to DUFFAU, who had made his café pay. He was truculent under preliminary interrogation, and the first admission of espionage was not obtained until a month after his arrest.

At Camp 020 he was not inclined to be overhelpful, while DELOBEL, who accompanied him, had the distressing habit of indulging in hysterics whenever faced with an awkward question. Parallel investigation, however, soon yielded a full and accurate account of DUFFAU's activities as a spy and DELOBEL's as a loyal accessory.

Guillaume Emile Auguste SANCIER: Emile Lucien MOUR

On 21st August 1944 a heavy American tank on reconnaissance on the outskirts of Bellegarde came upon a displaced German Army truck with four occupants, two of them in Wehrmacht uniform. The driver showed fight and the tank engaged the truck in unequal conflict. On of the Germans was killed, the second injured; out of the roadside ditch the tank crew hauled two hulking, shivering Frenchmen in civilian clothes, "Charles BAILLY" and Emile MOUR. Papers found on them did not allow of prolonged resistance to subsequent interrogation, and both men confessed to being German radio agents with missions behind the Allied lines. They explained that they were being brought up to their operational posts when captured and admitted that one of their espionage directors, Feldwebel DIETRICH, was the uniformed man who had been killed in the brush with the American tank.

"BAILLY" and MOUR arrived together at Camp 020, where the last details of their espionage adventures were dragged from them.

As was the case with many of the agents sent back from the field, no papers accompanied the bodies when the men arrived at Camp 020. "BAILLY," a broth of a man physically, had confessed that he was a certified paranoiac and blandly admitted that he was a congenital liar. There was reason to suspect that he had not told the whole truth even when comparison of his story with MOUR's showed that, where their espionage paths converged, his version of events was tolerably accurate. A strong note of caution was struck in the assessment of reliability attached to the first interim report on "BAILLY".

Weeks later "BAILLY's" diary and other documents arrived at

Ham. The writing differed appreciably from that adopted since his capture, but it was plain that he could not disown authorship. When challenged, "BAILLY" made a show of resistance, was coldly stared out and then confessed that his real name was Guillaume Emile Auguste SANCIER and that his first contact with the enemy had taken place some months earlier than he had hitherto admitted.

Interrogation was promptly broken off and SANCIER was delivered to the untender mercies of the Commandant. The upshot of a shattering interrogation was that SANCIER now confessed to a hideous criminal record. Tortuous processes of thought had led him to believe that the French authorities would view his deeds as a traitor more tolerantly than his crimes as a citizen, and he had therefore sought refuge in a pseudonym. It was only to cover his criminal record that he had post-dated his first contact with the Germans, for it had blackmail as its sole motivation.

The incident had its salutary effect at Ham. SANCIER's case officer was put in unforgettable remembrance of the maxim that the classical and prudent opening to any first interrogation is the simple question: "What is your name?"

Fernand SCHMITT

One of the most intelligent and best trained of stay-behind agents was a Frenchman born in Strasbourg, Fernand SCHMITT. He had been recruited as long ago as November 1940 and had undergone courses in radio telegraphy and codes in Brussels between February and August 1941. For reasons which he professed later not to know, he was then discarded by the Abwehr and allowed to return to Strasbourg. After a period of unemployment he joined the NSKK and served with that transport organisation in France until October 1943.

It was shortly after he had been imprisoned at La Rochelle on inexplicable charges of sabotage, defeatism and espionage that he was called to Brussels for fresh training in radio and codes. For many weeks again he underwent instruction, and soon his knowledge of the German's radio network controlled from Brussels and Lille was as intimate as his masters'. Many, too, were the other trainees with whom he rubbed shoulders in the Abwehr classrooms, for by this time he was a trusted agent, even though he had never yet been despatched on a mission.

It was late in August 1944 that SCHMITT was despatched to Lillebonne to establish himself as a stay-behind agent with instructions to report all Allied units and their movements, with the subsidiary assignment of making regular reports on civilian morale and conditions generally behind the Allied lines.

SCHMITT claimed later to have been soured by his unjust

imprisonment at La Rochelle and to have accepted his final mission merely because it would afford the opportunity of betraying the Germans and their secrets to the Allies. The fact, however, was that he was arrested by the FFI before he had made any voluntary admission to the Allied authorities. It was as a semi-broken spy, and not a willing informer, that he arrived at Camp 020.

Although he showed himself willing enough to disclose all the information in his possession about his German contacts and their technique and plans, he proved to be less voluble about his own share in their underhand affairs. The investigation proved most valuable, however, for he gave detailed descriptions of no less than 44 German spymasters and their agents, 16 of the addresses frequented by them, and 19 suspected agents. Especially valuable was his "croquis" of the German radio network in the Pas de Calais area.

Guy Louis Yves VISSAULT DE COETLEGON

The long and resentful memory of a member of the FFI led to the arrest in August 1944 of Guy Louis Yves VISSAULT DE COETLEGON, the adolescent political agitator responsible for the recruitment, among others, of the German agent Patrick GUERIN, who preceded him at Ham by some weeks.

VISSAULT DE COETLEGON was a very young man who took himself very seriously. His political ideas were above the level of his intelligence. Sometimes he was a fanatical Breton Separatist. At other times he was "a monarchist and traditionalist opposed to all materialistic Communist conceptions," which showed that he had mastered his jargon, at least. At all times he was an unmitigated nuisance to the forces of political order in France, for his acts of hooliganism could not be ignored.

Before the war, when he was in his early teens, he had met Sinn Feiners in Eire and had studied philology at Bonn University. The French authorities in Paris took a jaundiced view of him on the outbreak of war and lodged him out of harm's way in a civilian internment camp. After six months he was released; three months later he was in the service of Abteilung II of the Abwehr, for one of his mentors at Bonn and recommended him for service almost immediately after the collapse of France.

The Germans seem to have given him an importance as great as that which he gave himself. Soon he was talking ambitiously of subversion among minority movements in Ireland, Scotland, Wales and the St Lawrence Valley of Canada. Half-baked agitators from Eire in the German service encouraged him. There was talk of sending him to Ireland as a saboteur. He was trained at an Abwehr sabotage school and himself became a part-time instructor.

The Irish scheme was dropped. VISSAULT DE COETLEGON found himself entrusted with the less spectacular mission of finding Breton fishermen willing to ferry German agents to the United Kingdom. For all his persuasive talk, he could recruit only one, and he was a drunkard.

Perhaps his own inefficiency led him to resign from the Abwehr service. At all events he decided to join the Todt Organisation as an inspector of labour, but he soon tired of semi-respectability and he was back in Paris. He learned of a scheme to organise a French Waffen SS unit for service on the Eastern Front, underwent para-military training, and set himself up as a recruiter of volunteers. In this, too, he proved a dismal failure, so that later he presumed to have himself appointed a travelling inspector of LVF formations serving under German command on the Russian front.

In March 1943 the dampened young firebrand placed himself at the disposal of the SD section in Paris to train saboteurs on the lines set by the rival Abwehr. He gave practical and political instruction to five rather shabby young men intended to operate in Ireland, but never heard that they had been despatched en mission. After a brief tour of duty at the desk in the SD office, where he analysed political information from Ireland, the Breton autonomist organised a gang of thugs to combat the repressive Maquis in the Haute Savoie.

There were other unpleasant assignments carried out with a minimum of distaste before VISSAULT DE COETLEGON escorted a group of Breton espionage recruits, among them his copain and nominee GUERIN, to the military training school at Tavernay.

Soon afterwards he was summoned to Paris to be told that he had been appointed organiser of a network of stay-behind agents to operate in Brittany. VISSAULT DE COETLEGON objected that the members of his group, which included GUERIN, must be thoroughly "blown" to the French Resistance movement. Events proved him right. Although he ratted from the Germans at the last moment, he was recognised by an FFI member when hiding behind the uneasy skirts of his mistress at Sens.

At Camp 020 he soon realised that the British viewed him, not as a courageous champion of Breton liberty, but as a despicable little traitor. Bombast left him; he Told All with the meekness born of perplexity and cowardice.

Louis DEBRAY

Louis DEBRAY was one of the few agents of the German Secret Service who had the honour of worldwide publicity during the war. He was named by the BBC and the Press as one of several sinister figures behind the Belgian spy NEUKERMANS when news was released of the latter's execution in England.

DEBRAY had, in fact, been concerned as an exploiter of
Allied escape routes in the German espionage interest, in several
other cases investigated at Ham, among them those of DE GRAAF,
WIJCKAERT and LEJEUNE. Soon after the liberation of Brussels he was
in Allied hands. His interrogation in the field failed to extract
from him any admission of service for the Germans. He was
transferred to Camp 020 on 26th September 1944. Investigation there
was long and arduous, for DEBRAY was markedly uncooperative. He cut
a poor figure, but he had the desperate courage of the cornered rat.
Neither harsh words nor confinement in punishment cells could draw
from him a proper confession of his treachery.

To the end he maintained stubbornly that for the first
three years of his service as a passeur he had no actual knowledge
that he was helping the Germans; the first inkling that he was
himself a German agent was given to him when a prostitute
denounced one of his own principals as such. Thereafter, he claimed,
it had been impossible for him to withdraw from the filthy
business...

A puny little creature of 23, DEBRAY was not a bright
specimen. He was bottom of his class in school for two years. At
sixteen he was caught out in an act of immorality. At twenty the
best employment he could find was as a port butcher's boy. The
Germans could not fail to use such a type as a man of trust.

DEBRAY, in quest of youthful excitement, had once essayed to
escape to Spain. He had set out with another young rogue,
WASSILIEFF, who was innocent of espionage at all times in his
career, but ran into considerable trouble at Ham, before DEBRAY's
arrival there, due to his association with him. The escape failed
dismally. Its highlight was DEBRAY's appearance at a Lourdes court
on charges of having stolen jam from a local hotel.

The adventure appeared to have qualified DEBRAY as an
authority on escaped routes. Soon after his return to Brussels he
was approached by two men in German pay and was commissioned to
ascertain whether the escape route which he had himself used in his
abortive effort to reach Spain was still in operation.

It was. Thereafter many genuine refugees were set upon it to
cover the sprinkling of German spies sent out from Belgium for
England under the guidance of DEBRAY.

Pierre Marie Ernest SWEERTS

One of the most profitable of short-term cases investigated at Ham
was that of Pierre Marie Ernest SWEERTS, former Belgian officer who
had enjoyed a responsible position with the SD Dienststelle in
Brussels. SWEERTS actually crossed the British lines from Holland in

September 1944 and gave himself up to the 53rd Division. He made a full admission of his service for the Germans. He claimed to have volunteered for the Waffen SS on orders from Belgian Resistance leaders in order to obtain intelligence of value to the Allies. He was directed to Camp 020 with little delay.

At Ham SWEERTS, a slick young man, proved engagingly knowledgeable not only about the SD in Belgium, but about the RSHA in general. The Germans had taken to him with enthusiasm when he was invalided out of active service with the Waffen SS. They transferred him to the SD office in Brussels and later sent him on a course of instruction to Berlin. There he had been given access to records of RSHA history and organisation. Between April and September 1943 he attended schools of instruction in Berlin, and for a considerable period underwent instruction in radio transmission, codes and espionage at the notorious Afelinstitut at Wannsee. So implicitly was he trusted that he was even allowed to visit the spy-training school at Lehnitz, and there he noted the names and characteristics of a number of trainees.

In September 1943 SWEERTS was posted to a sub-section of Amt VI at the RSHA in Berlin. His immediate superior was a young braggart named Ramon GAMOTHA, but he was in touch also with the ambitious SCHELLENBERG and the swaggering SKORZENY.

The Germans intended to send him to Iran with the so-called "Norma" espionage and sabotage expedition at the beginning of 1944. Preparation for the venture was meticulous. There were courses in Oriental languages and customs, history and geography, sabotage and armaments, medicine, photography and cinephotography. GAMOTHA was to have led the party under the direction of SKORZENY, and in January 1944 he left for Istanbul to prepare the ground, leaving SWEERTS in charge of the military side of his Referat. GAMOTHA returned shortly afterwards to report difficulties in the path of the mission, and it was dropped.

Thereafter SWEERTS became a supernumerary at the RSHA. His friend GAMOTHA could find nothing better for him to do than to race him over occupied Europe and Spain in quest of Black Market coffee and cognac for the pot-bellied peacocks of Amt VI. He was so engaged in Spain, where he was an honoured guest of the Falange, during the early stages of the invasion. He returned by easy stages to Paris and reported finally at the SD office at The Hague, for he had a wife and child nearby. After transferring them to a place of comparative safety in the path of the advancing British Army, he crossed the British line and surrendered.

SWEERTS never deviated from his original claim that he had joined the Waffen SS and the SD only to gain knowledge of these German organisations in the Allied benefit. Certainly it seemed that he had memorised a vast amount of information on the RSHA with just that object in view: he named and described no less than 113 SD contacts; he provided 22 SD addresses; he disclosed everything that he knew of 61 SD agents training or in operation; he gave a comprehensive account of the organisation and personnel of the RSHA.

It was reasonable to doubt his good faith until independent evidence could be called to confirm his claim that he had acted under Resistance directions. Unfortunately for him, the principals whom he had named had either been killed by the Germans or deported to Germany, a fact that in itself heightened suspicions that his betrayal of his masters was less an act of patriotism than a bid to save his own skin.

He was kept in uneasy detention at Ham for many months, but eventually it was decided that he could be more profitably employed in the Allied service. He became a sergeant in an Allied intelligence unit.

Arthur GARITTE: René DELHAYE: André DE SMIDT

Out of the same school and stable as SWEERTS came Arthur GARITTE, a Belgian SD recruit of a very different type. He, too, surrendered to the British, and he was ingenious enough to approach them through a British agent who testified to the fact that GARITTE had saved his life. This step actually smacked of an attempt at infiltration of a British intelligence organisation. GARITTE arrived at Camp 020 in a state of nervousness and confusion, for he was left in no doubt during interrogation in the field that he was regarded, not as a hero, but as a particularly dangerous traitor.

Prolonged investigation at Ham reinforced the view that GARITTE was no patriot. Instead there was evidence from other prisoners, among them SWEERTS, that he was a trusted and willing agent of the Germans, whom he had served well. Finesse and confrontation with two of his former colleagues, René DELHAYE and André DE SMIDT, established that GARITTE had derived considerable financial profit from his association with the SD, that in a long term of service he had signally failed to embarrass his masters, and that he had deliberately withheld important information from the Allies at the first opportunity vouchsafed him.

All the evidence pointed to the fact that GARITTE was faithful to the Germans to the last. When, finally, the scales fell against him, he calculated to give just so much information to the Allies as would keep him out of trouble. That he failed was no fault of his own, for he withstood close interrogation for a prolonged period. He was returned to Belgium with the recommendation that he be treated as a dangerous enemy.

Shaken by the cold and dispassionate dissection of GARITTE's original claim to righteousness, his former colleagues DELHAYE and DE SMIDT hastened at Camp 020 to surrender many compromising details of their own treachery which they had judiciously withheld in the field.

Fritz Wilhelm LORENZ

The case of Fritz Wilhelm LORENZ, who was detained by members of the Belgian Resistance near Namur, presented many novel features. He was a young German of some intelligence and much experience who had served a variety of political, espionage and propaganda agencies since 1935. He was sagacious enough to realise in September 1944 that Deutschland was very much kaput, and he offered to change sides to make a good thing of it - for himself.

LORENZ was very much the eager collaborator at Camp 020. His case presented little difficulty, for his efforts to ingratiate himself helped the investigation.

He had started in life as a cadet in the German Merchant Navy, but was unable to save enough money to attend the school of navigation at which he could have qualified as an officer. At school and in his seven years at sea LORENZ had mastered English and French. He was well mannered and of presentable appearance. Through a passenger on one of the ships in which he was serving he was recommended, on his language qualifications, as a recruit for Ribbentrop's semi-official foreign relations office, the Dienststelle Ribbentrop.

It proved, in fact, to be the springboard for Ribbentrop's own political ambitions. LORENZ worked under Otto Abetz, another seeker after diplomatic power, in the press section of the office. When Ribbentrop began his advancement by engineering his appointment as Ambassador in London, LORENZ became one of his favourite couriers and advisers on foreign affairs.

In September 1939 he was called up for military service, but was released on the intervention of his chief to be put at the disposal of the head of Amt VI of the RSHA, for special services. His first mission had an element of adventure. He was to go to Paris to examine the possibilities of establishing an SD organisation in nominally warring France. With a false Italian passport and a legitimate French visa bought from a corrupt official of the French Embassy in Rome, LORENZ tripped through Switzerland to Paris as a salesman of shoes. He failed to make any contacts of profit from the espionage point of view but he was able to persuade the Commissaire de Police in Paris, for a cut in the profit, to make an offer for 300,000 pairs of non-existent boots for a French Army that never marched.

LORENZ enjoyed the joke so much that he celebrated it excessively when he got safely off French soil. In a drunken stupor he boasted mendaciously that in Paris he had intercepted a telephone conversation between Chamberlain and Reynaud in which mention had been made of an impending Allied attack on the Balkans. An over-zealous consular compatriot telephoned the story to Berlin as a fact. Goebbels broadcast it to the world as gospel. The Allies were sufficiently embarrassed by diplomatic reactions to issue an official denial.

The launching of the crushing attack on France in May 1940 prevented LORENZ from returning to Paris until after the occupation was firmly established. He found then that an SD unit was already posted in the city under a Dr Knochen and the sum of his endeavours on this visit was to interpret for Knochen and find him suitable billets. There were other missions in Southern France later, mainly with the object of tracing Jewish refugees from Germany, and an abortive plan to send him to Portugal to ascertain the whereabouts of Otto Strasser.

The work did not appeal to LORENZ, who quarrelled with Knochen and resigned from the SD, but remained at the disposal of the Dienststelle Ribbentrop even while engaged for a time as a broadcaster and compiler of propaganda programmes with a Berlin radio department.

Some time after his resignation from the SD LORENZ was called up again for military service as a humble soldier. He was posted to a special service unit and soon found himself attached to an SS division on the Russian front as a uniformed war reporter.

Ribbentrop still had a lien on him, however, and in 1943 he was withdrawn from the front and sent by the Foreign Minister to Madrid to report on the behaviour of the German Ambassador's wife and the alleged popularity of Sir Samuel Hoare. He discharged the duty to Ribbentrop's satisfaction, then returned to his war reporting duties before taking charge of a radio station at Trieste which was to combat Italian provocation of Slav elements in the area.

By the Spring of 1944 new employment had been found for him as Paris editor of copy produced by French war reporters. These duties took him into the battle areas during the early phases of the Allied invasion, and what he saw and heard then persuaded him that there was no future for the Nazi Party and little hope for Germany. When his office in Paris was closed he slunk away in independent retreat to sort out his defeatist ideas in a secluded corner of Belgium. He had not quite finished that introspective exercise when he was detained.

Peter SCHAGEN

Another rat who deserted the sinking German ship when it was well on
the rocks was Peter SCHAGEN, a lean and hungry type of sinister
appearance who had spent many years in Brazil before returning to the
Fatherland shortly before the war. Because of his language
qualifications, SCHAGEN was posted to the Abwehr on the outbreak of
war and failed in an exploratory sabotage mission to Portugal before
being transferred to the notorious Lehr Regiment Brandenburg zbV 800.

The Abwehr II missions which were entrusted to him
throughout his military career were of a trifling nature and
incompetently performed at that. He found more proper expression
with a combat unit of the Regiment on the Russian front, but
eventually he found himself attached to an Abwehrkommando of Abwehr
II-West in Southern France. There, in the tradition of the Abwehr,
he found himself about to do something on many occasions, but of
execution of plans there was none.

When the situation on the Western Front became alarming to
anyone in German uniform, SCHAGEN deserted across the Spanish
frontier with five of his men. After much delay in Madrid, where he
was in contact with a representative of Abwehr II, he was persuaded
by his mistress, a Frenchwoman whom he had brought with him, to
surrender to the American Embassy. He was promised transfer to the
United States after investigation in England, for he managed to
persuade the officials of the Embassy that he was now averse to the
Nazi regime. "The Allies," wrote this Nazi saboteur of twelve years'
standing, " need suitable Germans, willing and able to smooth the
way to a free Germany, to raise their voices now against the useless
shedding of blood and to lend their hand now to protect Central
Europe against Civil War, sabotage and guerrilla warfare."

He got less sympathy at Ham, where he failed to understand
the amusement caused by his description of a visit to Goering in
1938: "In an interview lasting 15 minutes, Goering discussed German
prospects in Brazil, for I had brought him some Brazilian cigars...
As I was leaving he shouted to a secretary at the end of his long
office: 'This man gets a picture.' Some months later an official
messenger brought me an autographed photo of Goering."

From Ham SCHAGEN went, not to the United States, but to
France.

Carl EITEL

Carl EITEL was a bad spy, a bad German, and a bad man. Nevertheless
he had a long run for his unearned Abwehr money, for his espionage
history was unusually long and crowded with incident.

He was a wine steward in the liner "Bremen" and joined the Abwehr in 1934 as a transatlantic courier for that veteran spy-master, Erich PHEIFFER of Nest Bremen. He began by buying technical magazines, graduated to carrying espionage mail between America and Germany, then became a contact man for agents active in the United States. Later he was induced to provide a few naval intelligence reports based on personal observation in Cherbourg and New York, and recruited another spy, that miserable wretch Juan FRUTOS, whose story has already been told.

EITEL was sacked from the "Bremen" in 1936 and retired forever from the sea and temporarily from espionage. The break was lucky for him, for in 1938 M I 5 had put the Americans wise to the existence of a considerable German spy network in the United States. Many were the arrests which followed on shore and on shipboard. EITEL, now harmlessly engaged in canning foodstuffs in Nürnberg, avoided apprehension, but not dishonourable mention in the ensuing American spy trials. His name was, in fact, writ large in many a volume of popular American literature produced after the event.

On the outbreak of war EITEL, in sweaty fear of active service, went to his old master, cap in hand and gifts in suitcase, and begged to be taken back into the non-combatant Abwehr. It was not only sentiment and the gifts that persuaded PHEIFFER to re-employ him: EITEL was at least an experienced doer of dirty work and he had a knowledge of several languages.

PHEIFFER sent him to Genoa early in 1940 with a naval intelligence mission that he was to fulfil by recruitment of local talent and contact with seamen off American ships. EITEL spent much money and little time on his assignment, but managed to cook enough reports to satisfy his superiors in Bremen. In cunning he had found the dark sanctuary of incapacity.

When PHEIFFER assumed command of the new Stelle in Brest, EITEL was attached to him as interpreter and factotum. His tasks ranged from contacting such agents as FRUTOS and attempting to establish a meteorological report system employing fishing boats, to cooking vast meals for his master and the latter's secretary-mistress, Hilde GERSDORF.

In the intelligence sphere he failed dismally, in the local Black Market he prospered exceedingly. He began to collect tainted money podgy hand over grasping fist, nor did he keep his dirty fingers out of intelligence tills. He took unto himself a fancy Brest woman, bought a hotel, and salted away much capital clandestinely won through judicious manipulation of a fishery fleet which was officially supposed to cover his espionage activities.

When PHEIFFER was posted away from Brest, EITEL remained

under a new chief to continue his immoral association and his moral
deception. In the course of time his inefficiency as an intelligence
agent became apparent to one of his superiors who had no sentimental
feelings about him. EITEL was recalled to Berlin for a new posting.
Although PHEIFFER was no longer able to help him, he was fortunate
in that two officers of Nest Bremen, Johannes BISCHOFF and Hans
BENDIXEN, were not only willing but anxious to attach him to their
outpost in Lisbon.

EITEL hated the idea of leaving his mistress, his hotel, and
his roomy niche in Brest's Black Market, but there was no gainsaying
orders at Abwehr HQ. In Lisbon his espionage work was so poor that
even his masters noticed it. Finally there came notice from Berlin
of his impending recall to face an enquiry. EITEL panicked and
offered himself to the American Intelligence authorities in Lisbon
as an informant. He told them nothing of his early espionage
activities against the United States, and they were not aware of it.
They liked EITEL and accepted him as a double agent. They persuaded
him to risk a return to Germany, for they were confident that he
could return to Portugal.

At Abwehr HQ EITEL was not well received: he was charged
with inefficiency, indiscipline and malicious scandal-mongering; it
had been decided to discharge him for military service. It says much
either for EITEL's powers of persuasion or little for the Abwehr's
sense of responsibility that he was then entrusted with a final
mission to redeem himself. He was charged with the delivery of radio
equipment, instructions and cash to agents in the South of France
threatened to be cut off by the Allied advance.

EITEL left Germany again with no intention of carrying out
his mission. The radio material he jettisoned; the cash he pocketed;
the instructions he kept for production to the Americans as evidence
of good faith, should he fall into their hands again. Then he
disappeared from the ken of the intelligence world. He reappeared
dramatically at Nancy after the Americans had swept through the city
on the heels of the retreating German armies. He had made no effort
to surrender to the Americans, and it was not until he was arrested
by French police as a moral delinquent and suspicious stranger that
he referred enquiries to his American contacts in Lisbon.

Under interrogation in France by American intelligence
officers, EITEL lied fluently. It was not his mendacity, much of
which passed unappreciated, which disturbed his interrogators, but
suspicion that EITEL might have triple-crossed during his German
visit.

It was decided to send EITEL to England for detailed
interrogation.

His American sponsors were ingenuously kindly. Their request to M I 5 was that he should be treated, not as a prisoner, but as a voluntary informant. Thus he came to Ham as a privileged daily visitor who had to be well fed and wined daily at the expense of British Security funds.

Patience with this servile, unprepossessing creature was soon exhausted, even though he was forced to admit at his first interrogation that his recruitment by the Abwehr dated, not from 1940, as he had told his American friends, but from 1934. Many times he was caught out lying or attempting to conceal compromising chapters out of his unhealthy slab of personal Abwehr history.

It was impossible thereafter to be polite to Carl EITEL, even to outward appearance. His protestations of "I tell you the true always" were washed away. M I 5 agreed that the farce of gentility with a rogue could not be allowed to continue. Arrangements were immediately made to have him properly lodged at Camp 020 as a very unprivileged resident.

It was then that EITEL, behind a curtain of hot tears that splashed on interrogation table and cell floor, was made to part with the full account of his activities and his treachery. Curiously enough, betrayal of FRUTOS and the Americans to the Abwehr was not included in his multiple wrongdoings.

It was a long and dolorous investigation, for EITEL had to be educated in the meaning of truth and the sorting of memories and facts before detailed examination could be properly pursued. When it was completed EITEL was a sorry figure for whom no one could feel sorry. He was very grateful indeed when he was granted the privileges, first of cleaning prison lavatories, and later of washing the dirty linen of his old friend PHEIFFER, when the latter came to Ham in 1945 with a broken heart and cardiac trouble.

EITEL fawned nauseatingly on PHEIFFER. Always he addressed him as Mein Kapitän. He would not sit at joint interrogations until his master was seated. He would not smoke in his presence, but at the same time never refused a charitable cigarette.

At times PHEIFFER bit the dog that showed him such devotion. On one occasion they were being questioned about FRUTOS. EITEL gave his version of a certain incident. PHEIFFER turned on him with a condescending smile and said, "Carlos, you were never much good at anything except cooking and scrounging, but do try to get your intelligence facts straight for once..."

EITEL winced and wept and whimpered a sycophantic "Jawohl, mein Kapitän". PHEIFFER could never be wrong.

Marcel Pierre Félix ALTAZIN

Money was the most important thing in the life of Marcel Pierre

Félix ALTAZIN, Parisian radio technician become German stay-behind spy. Indiscretions in its acquisition led him four times into French gaols. Happy surrender to its irresistible appeal took him into the German service. Money owing still for his treacherous activities induced him hopefully to continue to communicate with his masters long after they had been pushed unceremoniously out of France.

When the Americans captured him in Paris, he told a story, in part true, which resulted in his immediate employment as a double agent. It was not long, however, before his reliability came into doubt. He was sent to Camp 020 for further investigation.

At Ham ALTAZIN had nothing to gain by telling the whole truth. Indeed, he stood to lose if he deviated in any respect from the story which he had told in the field. He therefore proved troublesome under investigation. In due course however, he had to admit that a series of espionage messages which he had reconstructed for his captors in France represented only the half truth. In fact, ALTAZIN had actually sent important operational messages which might well have caused the Allied forces considerable losses in action.

His excuse for reticence was, firstly, faulty memory, and secondly, fear. He then undertook to tell the whole truth, but even then it was found that he was shy of many material facts. Right up to the end, ALTAZIN's case was one reeking of treachery and unrepentance. The recommendation which went out with him from the gates of Ham was that he should not be used further as a double agent; and that if this was agreed, the obvious disposal was death...

Christiaan Antonius LINDEMANS

One of the most grave cases brought to Ham during the operational phase was that of a former member of the Dutch Resistance Movement gone bad, Christiaan Antonius LINDEMANS. A hulking brute of a man, LINDEMANS had been well named "King-Kong" at the time when he was serving the Allied cause. (+)

LINDEMANS, a man of courage, had fought valiantly for the Dutch Resistance: up to the beginning of 1944 he had served with distinction as an Allied passeur. Germans had crossed his path, and he shot them. His tally was impressive, his enthusiasm unflagging.

Then he was caught by the enemy. There were threats, there was cajolery. LINDEMANS, grown weak when the Germans bargained release of a brother and sister if he would give information on the Resistance Movement, surrendered. Many were the names of former

---

(+) The Germans, with their special genius for the inappropriate, gave him the covername "Christian BRAND" when they took over his control.

colleagues of the Resistance whom he betrayed. A British officer, too, was sold by him with equal facility.

In May 1944 he was shot in the chest by the Gestapo, acting in all innocence of his present service to the German cause. He was taken to hospital. Two days later a German civilian called on him to warn him that he must continue to work for the Germans: "He told me," wrote LINDEMANS later in a confession at Camp 020, "he told me to get in touch with my friends of the Resistance through my nurses, so that they could help me to escape. I obeyed these instructions."

There was more treachery until the Allies over-ran Brussels. Then LINDEMANS, regarded still as a hero by many of the Resistance members whom he had so far failed to sell to the Germans, was given an appointment on the staff of Prince Bernhard of the Netherlands. In Liège and in Driebergen LINDEMANS had access to vital operational meetings and knowledge of the decisions taken. At Ham later there was every indication that he might have been responsible for the blowing of the vital Arnhem airborne operation. The suggestion brought little response when communicated to the field.

LINDEMANS was detected only on denunciation by another Dutchman, Cornel VERLOOP. He was rushed to Camp 020 as a priority case. The investigation fell into two distinct phases. The first consisted of two driving interrogations by the Commandant which produced damning admissions in writing. LINDEMANS then threw an epileptic fit and the investigation was suspended while he was under medical treatment. Demands from the field required further instant interrogation. Medical advice was sought, and although luminol had recently been administered it was decided to proceed forthwith with interrogation. The drug, it was found, had given LINDEMANS moral strength. He resisted forceful interrogation with unusual calmness; his denials were flat. Heavy interrogations without respite either for the prisoner or the case officers brought gradual success: partial breaks were consolidated, results were collated; back went the interrogators for more until all the vital issues had been made tolerably clear and the greater part of the awful story was laid bare.

A greater measure of cooperation in the field would have helped to clear important details of the case, but for one reason or another this was not forthcoming. LINDEMANS left Ham for Belgium in December 1944.

Thereafter much publicity was afforded him in the British Press, acting on leakages of information on the Continent. The officers at Ham who had conducted the investigation had to fall back on their newspapers for news of "King-Kong" after he had left the camp. It was at Bad Nenndorf that the Commandant, who had expended much spleen and patience and expectation of life upon LINDEMANS, had the satisfaction of knowing that the horrendous thug was dead in an Allied gaol, killed by his own hand.

Alfred NAUJOCKS

A typical thug of the New Order was Alfred NAUJOCKS, a killer without hate and without shame. He became a last-minute convert to the Old Order and tried hard to pose as the innocent dupe of vile masters. It was in this guise that he was arrested by Allied troops in October 1944, bent on a self-imposed, redeeming mission on behalf of an "Austrian Underground Movement." Interrogation in the field succeeded in obtaining from NAUJOCKS the bare outlines of a wicked history; at Camp 020 the full scope of his infamy was ferreted out of him.

At seventeen he had failed twice to keep a job. He blamed his incompetence on the Reds and joined the Partei. At twenty-one he married a woman of thirty-three, drifted from job to job and woman to woman and eventually became a driver at an SS Dienststelle. His wife made the mistake of having a child by him, and he instituted divorce proceedings.

NAUJOCKS saw a future for himself in the SD: he became a clerk in an Oberabschnitt and began his association with "Butcher" Heydrich, who saw rich promise of thuggery in him. It was not long after they first met that Heydrich sent him off to Prague with a friend, Werner Goettsch, to liquidate Otto Strasser. They failed in this mobster's mission and were roundly rated by their irate director.

In February 1935 Heydrich again summoned NAUJOCKS and despatched him to Czechoslovakia to destroy a clandestine anti-German radio transmitter and to kidnap the operator. NAUJOCKS located the station, then returned to Germany to persuade Goettsch to help him fulfil the task. Together they returned to Czechoslovakia. NAUJOCKS stormed the room in which the transmitter was installed, destroyed it, then killed the operator. In a fast car he and Goettsch recrossed the German frontier ahead of the Czech police and reported their success to Heydrich. The "Butcher" was ungrateful; for once he deplored a murder; he had wanted a live body... NAUJOCKS was in temporary disgrace.

NAUJOCKS switched to another department, the forerunner of Amt VI. He travelled over Europe on behalf of the SD, then settled in a Berlin office to help organise foreign intelligence activities. In 1937 he was transferred to a new section plotting mischief against Czechoslovakia, Austria and the Saar. A year later he became Sturmbannführer and head of a department dealing with South-Eastern Europe.

Early in 1939 Heydrich had new dirty work for him: he was to arrest or liquidate an official in the Propaganda Department. NAUJOCKS refused because the selected victim was one of his own friends. Heydrich, who may have been forgiven for failing to note any streak of sentimentality in the hired assassin, was again angry. When he had cooled down, he had a new proposition for NAUJOCKS: would he please organise a laboratory for the production of deadly bacteria for the subtle liquidation of persons whom he (Heydrich) regarded as dangerous? Even NAUJOCKS jibbed at this devilish scheme, but it seemed that Heydrich found a less squeamish hireling to satisfy his needs.

On 10th August 1939 Heydrich produced another pleasant task for NAUJOCKS. The dear Führer needed a pretext for attacking Poland within the month. Incidents must be staged to illustrate the provocation of the Poles which had finally exhausted the Führer's well-known patience. The idea was to take a number of lifers out of German concentration camps, kill or half-kill them by means of hypodermic injections, and dress them in Polish Army uniforms. The bodies would then be taken to selected positions in German frontier villages in boxes labelled "preserves." There they would be decanted and riddled with bullets. The Reich could then proclaim far and wide that Polish forces had made a determined but unsuccessful raid on sacred German territory.

NAUJOCKS' share in the grim proceedings was to lend colour to the frontier incidents be staging a raid on the Gleiwitz broadcasting station by "provocative Polish elements." With five other gangsters he proceeded to the scene. One of them, a Polish speaker, seized the microphone "by force" and began to broadcast a wild appeal to his countrymen to rise against the Germans. The broadcast was abruptly cut off, shots were fired, and a "preserved" body riddled with bullets was left on the studio floor as evidence of the unheard of incursion. A few days later the German armies were on the move...

The notorious Venlo incident which ended in the kidnapping of the British intelligence officers, STEVENS and BEST, provided further scope for NAUJOCKS' undoubted talent for violence. He was a principal in that affair and won much merit for its resounding success.

Towards the end of 1939 more refined employment was found for him. He was put in charge of a department engaged in the production of forged documents and other falsifications, including the printing of spurious Bank of England notes, a task which proved beyond him, but not beyond his successors in that particular office.

Later NAUJOCKS went to Holland to negotiate for the transfer to German ownership of a film company required to provide cover for

SD espionage activities. He took a colleague who could not resist
the temptation of making money on the side by selling exit permits
to Jewish directors. When his friend was arrested, NAUJOCKS decided
to have a nervous breakdown. The ruse did not save him from arrest
and charges of aiding and abetting his friend. Heydrich was
horrified by his lapse from Nazi morality and had him degraded and
directed to service with the Waffen SS. His stomach troubled him
when he found himself opposite bloody-minded Russians, and he got
himself invalided out of danger.

By May 1942 he had managed to have himself pronounced unfit
for further active service. He appealed to Heydrich for a new job and
was sent to Brussels to investigate Belgian Black Market activities.
There were breaks in this mission when he was despatched, first to
Jugoslavia and later to Denmark, on political and counter-espionage
and sabotage missions. He returned to Brussels to find himself
unpopular with the Wehrmacht because he had seen fit to arrest the
mistress of General Falkenhausen on Black Market charges.

The outlook was bad for NAUJOCKS. Belgium was unsafe;
Heydrich, his capricious protector, had died protecting
Czechoslovakia; the Allies were on the rapid march. It was high time
to change sides. NAUJOCKS hastened to Vienna and offered himself to
a group of Austrian malcontents as a link with the Allies. He was
accepted, then hastened to get himself arrested by American forces
in France.

At Ham NAUJOCKS told his nauseous tale with relish. He had
all the gangster's pride in his achievements. He eyed his
interrogators sardonically and their secretaries lecherously until
he was put in his low place by a deflatory blast from the
Commandant.

Towards the end of his long stay he began to lend [...]
devil's advocate. He was never accorded any privileges, and on more
than one occasion he remarked with tears in his eyes that he alone,
of all the prisoners, was unpopular with the Commandant. He
flattered himself.

Cornelis VERLOOP

A Dutchman with a remarkable record of treachery was Cornelis
VERLOOP. Once he had been a private detective; later he became a
convicted smuggler; later still he joined the French Foreign Legion
and fought against the Germans; ultimately he was recruited as a
counter-espionage agent of the Germans. For them he did excellent
work, betraying escape routes, escapees, and underground movements
with zest. He enjoyed his work, for he carried it on through the
many women with whom he carried on.

In May 1943 his industry was rewarded with the Gold Cross of the German Eagle and an illustrated address signed by Adolf Hitler himself for his betrayal from a sick-bed of a French Colonel working for an Allied organisation in Paris. When he was up and about again he spent a few months in honest employment, but it was distasteful to him and he resumed the role of Judas, not only among loyal Belgians but among the scum who had been employed by the Germans as informers. One of the German agents he was set to watch was "King-Kong" LINDEMANS, whose treachery was without reproach; another was DAMEN, whose loyalty to the Reich was equally clear; but a third agent who had the indecency to supply his masters with faked reports was immediately denounced to his death.

In the Spring of 1944 VERLOOP found a mistress who actually wanted to marry him. She promised to keep him if he would forswear his filthy business with the Germans. He married her and bought a cafe with funds she provided. His reluctant ideas of fulfilling his promise to end with the Abwehr were promoted when he fell into trouble with the SD because one of his Abwehr friends, whom he had accused of homosexual acts with another agent, denounced him as a suspicious character.

But later he decided that he ought to stick by the Abwehr in order that he might keep the document accompanying his German medal: he was convinced that he could sell it for a fortune to some American collector after the war. He continued his vile activities until arrested by an FSP serjeant when attempting to cross the Allied lines. He was handed to Dutch Security officials, and they were good enough to release him on parole. Later RAF police picked him up as he was travelling away from his oath as fast as his legs could carry him.

A cunning, treacherous and avaricious scoundrel, he was without shame, scruple or humanity. At Ham he told his story of betrayal and deceit with the air of a man modestly recounting heroic deeds. He was frank, at least, in saying that his main inducement to become an agent provocateur was that the work itself appealed to him, and he was evidently cut out for the job.

He was clearly disliked and distrusted even by his own colleagues of the Abwehr. He told the truth fully where he feared that the story could be corroborated, or where he felt that, according to his warped sense of values, a particular episode redounded to his credit. For the rest, it seemed that he was concealing many other meretricious acts which earned him the decoration he so much prized.

Throughout interrogation VERLOOP tried to impress his disgusted hearers with his importance in the service, his natural

astuteness and his intelligence, hoping by this means to be employed
as a double agent. Instead, the Ham recommendation was that he be
prosecuted to death.

Alfred Ignatz Maria KRAUS

Remarkable indeed even at Camp 020, where the sensational was
commonplace, was the case of Alfred Ignatz Maria KRAUS. He was a
bumptious young Austrian with business instincts who got himself
recruited for the Abwehr by a former colleague of the Siemens
combine, Theo SCHADE, an I/Tlw figure who enjoyed some notoriety at
Ham from a series of cases. In return for information on British
electrical firms which KRAUS had acquired during business visits to
England, KRAUS was given a posting in Paris as a representative of
Siemens.

Shortly after his arrival in the French capital, SCHADE
called on him. KRAUS was introduced to Major GEISSKES, a IIIF
officer of the Lutetia, who promptly enlisted the serious play-boy
as an informer and agent-provocateur. Through family connections and
new associations, KRAUS wormed himself into the upper strata of
Parisian society. He took up with an attractive girl who slept in
the half-world and lived in the high world, discovered that she had
a title of sorts and international social connections, and decided
to marry her. He succeeded in de-requisitioning her family home, and
himself moved in rent free with the rest of a glittering but shabby
menage.

As a German spy, KRAUS betrayed a British agent and
thereby disrupted a British organisation in France. He created a
cover address in Lisbon and handed over two others in Sweden for a
like purpose. He dined with a patriot, whose arrest was desired by
the Germans, and that patriot was arrested and shot by the Germans
immediately thereafter. At the instigation of a branch of his
family, he betrayed an American woman to the German Secret Service
for the all sufficient reason that they simply did not like her.
In addition he reported regularly on friends and acquaintances and
betrayed to the gentlemen of the Lutetia many persons connected with
the French Resistance Movement.

KRAUS turned his Abwehr connections to good business
account. He once successfully appealed to the German Secret
Service against a decision of his firm to transfer him from Paris
to Poland or Turkey. He successfully applied to the Abwehr for
facilities which enabled him to trade at great advantage against
his competitors. Visas were made available, free telephone calls
over Kriegsmarine lines were his for the asking. The Lutetia
provided him with traces on those with whom he would do business.

Commercial blackmail, Black Market activity and evasion of taxation were practised by KRAUS with impunity.

So highly valued were his services that his masters procured for him a decoration from the Führer. KRAUS buried it for safety at the bottom of his garden, which was a flower pot, and every day he watered it tenderly.

As a family man, the husband of Princess de Broglie and the son-in-law of the Hon Mrs Reginald Fellowes, KRAUS was used by his Anglo-French relatives, for the most part people of no patriotism, to get them out of trouble with the SD. To their lasting shame but content, he intervened successfully on their behalf. Indeed, in the result, his wife escaped internment and a brother-in-law was liberated therefrom.

When the Allies overran Paris, KRAUS had the crowning impertinence to arrogate to himself credit for assisting persons of French nationality against the Germans for whom he had worked so faithfully and for so long.

The next chapter of his story piled the Ossa of impudence on the Pelion of insolence. A British officer of the SAS Regiment who was enamoured with KRAUS' sister-in-law offered to enlist him in the British Army. KRAUS accepted the invitation with alacrity. He loaned the Englishman many francs, then agreed to travel to England in British battledress as his batman in order to play Cupid to the officer's married inamorata. He was smuggled through transit camps and onto a landing craft. On the trip across the Channel he was detailed to guard German prisoners of war, a duty not too smartly fulfilled as to drill and dress, wherefore he was reprimanded by OC troops.

On arrival in England KRAUS and his officer friend called on the married woman he loved. There were many meetings and much match-making by KRAUS. The woman went to hospital. The officer went to see her. He came back to KRAUS with a very black eye obtained of her very angry husband, who had chanced to visit the patient at the same hour.

There were more sordid incidents before KRAUS became worried about his officially unannounced visit to England. Enquiries were made by friends as to how he might call on the police "to comply with the usual formalities." Counter-enquiries were made by MI 5 as to how KRAUS had already got away with so much informality. He was arrested. Soon afterwards the British officer was dismissed the Service and simultaneously his wife resigned from a Government Appointment.

KRAUS arrived at Camp 020 in the course of time after withholding the more incriminating facts against himself. It was not until the gravity of the position was relentlessly borne upon him at

Ham that he slowly, over a period of six weeks, came forward with anything like his proper story.

No evidence was forthcoming to show that he had gone to England under orders of the German Secret Service or that they had even been aware of his intentions in that respect. The conclusion was that, like the rat that he was, he had merely deserted the sinking ship in order to prey elsewhere.

When the investigation was completed the resilient KRAUS laid claim to British nationality because of his marriage to a half-Englishwoman. When this piece of effrontery was thrown back at him, he returned unabashed with the claim that, as an Austrian monarchist, he was Anglophile anyway. Indeed, in proof of this attitude, it was his intention to negotiate a loan in the City of London on behalf of Austria through the kind offices of a relative who was formerly a director of Lloyds Bank.

KRAUS had brought much trouble on English friends through his association with them, yet, paradoxically, he, the principal in terms, went unpunished by law, for at Ham he received less than his due for the acts of espionage which he had committed in the first instance. In the fullness of time he was deported to Germany with a recommendation that he be excluded from Britain and the Empire for all time.

Even then it was his avowed intention to use his influential relations in England for his own ends on the termination of hostilities. He would wait until all was forgotten and then make another attempt to re-enter the country. It was whimsical at one time to speculate whether he might, in that case, be debarred on grounds of moral turpitude as well as espionage.

In the meantime his Princess also did some speculating. Without consulting KRAUS she divorced him, perhaps because she had no further use for an Austro-German husband in Free France.

Elie Gwodzdawo GOLENKO

Elie Gwodzdawo GOLENKO was once a Russian soldier. After the Revolution he moved with many more of his kind to Finland and Greece, and thence to Paris, where he lived by legal knowledge, journalism, and wits; mostly wits. He had worked for the Finnish and Greek Secret Services already: what more natural, on the outbreak of war, than he should join the French Secret Service, to monitor Russian radio stations? When the Germans came to Paris, he decided to switch to the German Secret Service. With a radio "poste" in his office in the "Paris-Soir" building, he received Russian operational messages and transmitted them to the Germans. When the Allies came back to Paris, he decided to join the American Secret Service.

Now the French police, a little belatedly, arrested GOLENKO and accused him of having collaborated with the enemy. On the intercession of the Americans, who were already using him as a double agent, he was released almost immediately. Some reasonable being then decided that perhaps it might be as well to check up on GOLENKO's association with the Germans in recent years.

So GOLENKO, black hat and cloak and all, came to England under the wing of the Americans. They lodged him at Claridges Hotel. MI 5 dislodged him from Claridges Hotel and sent him to Ham. There he was soon proved to be a traitor; but he had great faith in the friendship of the Americans and for a long time he planned to smuggle out of the Camp communications to them.

GOLENKO, a desiccated little courtier, was under the impression that the German code was unbroken by the British, and therefore assumed that there was little proof of treachery against him. His view was reinforced by the fact that no concrete evidence against him was produced, but naturally he did not appreciate that the reason was one of privilege.

The attitude he adopted was that, as a White Russian, he was only concerned in the fight against the Red Russians. Finding that the British at Ham were not unsympathetic towards their wartime Allies, he claimed that his politics changed in 1943, when the Germans perpetrated mass atrocities upon the Russians. He maintained that from that time onwards his sympathies were for Russia, the Fatherland, as distinct from the Russia of the White and the Red politicians.

He claimed that he began to give the Germans false operational information, and at the same time he denied that he ever indulged in espionage unconnected with Russia. And so he posed to his fellow-prisoners at Ham as a clever patriot victimised by British misunderstanding.

The fact was, however, that GOLENKO had been a well paid servant of the Germans over a number of years. He had given them a considerable amount of information detrimental to his own country, Russia. His betrayals might even have influenced the course of mighty battles in the East. He had, moreover, indulged in German espionage activities not connected with Russia, but with the West.

The finding at Ham was that GOLENKO was a dangerous German agent who had worked against his own country and against the Allies. He had obstructed his investigation. He had proved himself thoroughly unreliable. In strong terms it was recommended that the man should never again be used by the Americans.

Had GOLENKO learned of this check on his careering of international Secret Services, he would surely have applied to join the British Secret Service before leaving Ham.

Fred Hermann BRANDT

Fred Hermann BRANDT was a cross-eyed young man who collected nationalities and butterflies. Russian-born, he became successively an Esthonian, a Lett and a German. His interest in butterflies was less capricious: he had lived a hermit's life in Iran for $2\frac{1}{2}$ years in pursuit of lepidoptera, and later he became curator of a natural history museum in Germany.

He was a comic figure, but his subsequent employment by the Abwehr, with its notable genius for picking the wrong person for the job, had its serious implications. The Germans, in their bid for world domination, were ranging far: BRANDT was to spy against India from Afghanistan and to incite the tribes of Waziristan into revolt in the hope that all India might be brought into ferment.

He was hauled out of the SS, which he had been forced to join, and trained by Dr Wagner of Abwehr II for his mission. He was to be accompanied by a Herr Oberdoerffer, who was to pose as a doctor specialising in Leprosy, while BRANDT would be his assistant, but would continue lepidoptery as a hobby.

The two men boosted themselves so much on arrival in Afghanistan that the Customs officials queued up for spot treatment of their aches and pains. Oberdoerffer ladled out laxatives with generosity, so that the two agents were able to show that their baggage, consisting of surgical equipment and butterfly nets, was indeed innocent. In Kabul they picked up their sabotage equipment, which had preceded them under diplomatic seal.

For a time BRANDT enjoyed the gay whirl of Afghanistan society, which allowed him to wear for the first time in his life a boiled shirt and dress suit. The serious business began later. BRANDT was sent off to Paghman with his nets to catch butterflies and spy out the land. He was hardly settled when Oberdoerffer recalled him to Kabul: it seemed that the Italians, who were willing to pass on their findings, had already sent a political emissary to Waziristan, and the German invasion of Russia suggested that the German agents might be more profitably employed in the North.

It was for Waziristan, however, that BRANDT and Oberdoerffer set out eventually to fulfil their mission. They were ambushed by wild Afghans on the first day out and Oberdoerffer was mortally wounded. BRANDT himself came under official Afghan enquiry and was expelled from the country.

On repatriation to Germany he received an Iron Cross and was posted to the Brandenburg Regiment to prepare himself for a new mission in Iran. After a year and a half of staff employment as an interpreter for Tajik recruits, BRANDT learned that the SD had usurped the Iranian mission of the Abwehr. Shortly afterwards he was transferred to the new Kurfuerst Regiment and soon he was posted to an Abwehrtruppe which was to operate from Belgrade.

His new mission was to trace British officers known to be at large in Jugoslavia. Strangely enough, he succeeded in so doing, but decided to reinsure his butterfly-chasing future by changing sides. Instead of betraying the British officers, he offered himself as their willing servant. They got him out of Jugoslavia and into Italy. He was taken to Bari for detailed interrogation, lied clumsily in his own favour, and eventually found himself at Ham studying the flight of occasional cabbage butterflies from behind bars.

Charles WENDEL

Charles WENDEL was an Austro-Polish-German with residence in Paris. He became an active SD informant in France, contracted VD, and on discharge from hospital discovered that his spymaster was dead and the Germans about to leave Paris. He hurried out of the city and made for the township of Knutange. When the Americans arrived they appointed him local Resistance leader. Later someone in Paris decided that he ought to be arrested as a German agent, and he was.

While he was in his Paris gaol, he met an old boy from Ham, FIXEL, who had been returned to France on completion of investigation of his case. FIXEL was good enough to warn him of the conditions and treatment he might expect at Camp 020.

Forewarned, he tried to forearm himself by claiming that VD had effected his memory. At Ham he was cured free of all cost of the last traces of VD and of his loss of memory.

Rittmeister Graf Joseph von LEDEBUR

A walking "Who's Who" with an encyclopaedic knowledge of international Society and the Abwehr was Rittmeister Graf Joseph von LEDEBUR. He was a snob and had no time for the Nazis. Like KRAUS he was an Austrian; unlike him, he was no parvenu. He had intelligence, presence, social graces and something approaching the World Outlook beloved of internationalists.

His horizon became somewhat limited when war broke out. He was drafted into the Wehrmacht as a reserve officer of the old Austrian Army. He fought on the Western and Eastern fronts and was badly wounded. On discharge from hospital he was posted to Paris as liaison officer between the economic division of the German Military Administration and his old acquaintance, Charles Bedaux, friend of ex-kings and inventor and exploiter of the notorious B-hour industrial system.

LEDEBUR was to act as administrator of the sequestrated Bedaux companies, for he was a man of considerable business experience. Soon he discovered that he was also to act as intermediary between the Hotel Lutetia and Bedaux. The industrialist had become a German citizen by naturalisation. He had hawked around two grandiose schemes calculated to help the Germans in their struggle against the Allies. One concerned counter-sabotage measures in the Near Eastern oilfields to prevent their immobilisation by "the retreating British Armies;" the second referred to a trans-Saharan expedition to the Niger Bend to examine the possibilities of constructing a pipeline to carry vegetable oil from the region of Timbuktoo to Algeria.

That old friend of the British counter-espionage services, Erich PHEIFFER, at this time Leiter III in Paris, had agreed to sponsor both schemes, for he felt that the Abwehr, which could offer Bedaux many facilities, could profit from them. PHEIFFER commissioned LEDEBUR to act as intermediary between them, for the eccentric Bedaux was "as difficult to handle as raw eggs." LEDEBUR, a master of Anglo-American slang, told Bedaux often that he was 'nuts,' and their quarrels were frequent and violent.

The oil plan was dropped by the Germans on strategic considerations. They had not cared for it much since Bedaux had demanded General's rank and uniform in order that he might be parachuted in the East as a "soldier in broad striped pants," and not as a common agent. The Saharan scheme, in which the "sick bird" SCHARF was to have been employed, was frustrated by the Allied invasion of North Africa and the capture of Bedaux.

LEDEBUR continued to look after the international Bedaux interests, but was persuaded by PHEIFFER to become his personal adviser on international affairs and his personal agent in Parisian Society circles. LEDEBUR, who had been worried by the internment of many old friends in French and German concentration camps, entered the Abwehr game with zest to turn it to personal advantage. By bluff and sheer force of personality, he secured the release of many friends, often at grave personal risk. In fact he used his new Abwehr connections and influence purely to personal advantage. PHEIFFER, himself not a Nazi, had become a personal friend. He was tolerant to a degree. LEDEBUR even deceived him in recruiting as notional agents business acquaintances and friends whom he despatched out of danger into Spain. Many were the pleasure trips that he made with official sanction to "control" these agents; many too, were the reports which he had to concoct in their names in order to cover up his guile.

When PHEIFFER was transferred to Berlin as Abwehr Chief of Staff, he recommended LEDEBUR to the Amtschef, Oberst Hansen, as a personal and confidential agent. In that capacity he was used by Hansen even when the latter was engaged in the famous Hitler plot. Several of Hansen's other "gentlemen agents" were fully in the picture of that conspiracy. LEDEBUR was not: he was the innocent stooge. When he learned of Hansen's arrest after the 20th July, he decided that there was no future for him in Germany. Bitterly he resented Hansen's reticence. "It is the only grudge I have against him," he wrote later; "he never told me a thing about the plot, and there was I walking contentedly around with an unseen and unfelt noose around my neck..." He surrendered to the British Embassy in Madrid. For many weeks he was hidden away in a flat, for the Gestapo was on his trail, but in the course of time he was shipped out of Spain and sent to England for investigation at Ham.

His story, which had much comic relief, was one of fantastic proportions. His knowledge of the Abwehr and of personalities of that service was inexhaustible. He knew practically everything and everyone on the continent of Europe. He was the serious student of men and affairs and he was the blithe but informed scandalmonger.

At Ham he gave little trouble under investigation after he had been convinced that his belated defection from the Abwehr did not entitle him to any preferential treatment in Allied hands. He became philosophical and enjoyed himself hugely in producing volumes of invaluable information. Much of the intelligence which he gave read like fiction, but on check it was found that even in minute detail he had told nothing but the fantastic truth about his gay adventure in espionage.

His overweening curiosity induced LEDEBUR to take an active interest in other cases at Ham. Within a short time he had mastered the intricacies and technicalities of secret services other than the Abwehr. Indeed he became something of an authority on the SD and under direction helped to obtain much valuable information from such characters as Heinz JOST, Walther SCHELLENBERG and Ernst KALTENBRUNNER, all of whom were overawed into collaboration with this full-time prison agent.

Michel BOORTMAN

Grocer, dairyman, lightweight boxing champion of Holland, German agent, bigamist: that, in short, was the career of Michel BOORTMAN. He was left behind in Greece as a radio agent and gave himself up to the Allies when he had been left high and dry by the receding tide of German retreat. He was taken, first to Bari, then to Ham for interrogation. Investigation of his case gave no trouble, for he was as anxious to redeem himself as were the rest of his kidney.

BOORTMAN had first come into contact with the Abwehr as long ago as September 1940. He received radio instruction at Le Touquet and was to have been one of the pre-invasion spies in Britain. He was relieved when this notion was dropped, for the Germans, with supreme Teutonic tact, had mentioned to him the fact that one of his Dutch compatriots, VAN DEN KIEBOOM, had recently been hanged in England as a spy.

Thereafter BOORTMAN was dropped for a time by the Abwehr. He got into trouble and into prison. German officers of the Abwehr facilitated his release. He was sent to Berlin for a refresher course in radio. When training was completed he was prompted by his masters, who lamented their own inability to pay him handsomely, to marry a rich cousin.

The honeymoon was hardly over when BOORTMAN was despatched to Belgrade as a W/T agent under cover as a sports instructor of the Organisation Todt. He transferred later to Salonika, where he was to remain as a stay-behind agent. For reasons best known to themselves, his German masters again played marriage mongers; he was told that his wife in Holland was dead, and he was induced to wed a Greek called Fofo. It was doubtful indeed that the legal wife was dead, and it was significant that one of his Abwehr friends was for ever reminding him that his last marriage was valid only in Greece.

There was friction among the Germans shortly before Greece regained her liberty, and BOORTMAN was persuaded by Fofo to contact the Allies at the earliest opportunity. Like a model husband, he capitulated to her and surrendered to the Allies. He had the distinction of arriving at Ham on Christmas Day, 1944.

Gerhard NAGEL

Gerhard Ernst NAGEL was a fat German textiles merchant who preferred Belgium to Germany. He was a patriot, but a yellow-belly, too, for on the outbreak of war he hurried to volunteer his services as an interpreter in order to avoid conscription.

His first job was in the Abwehr holy of holies in Berlin. NAGEL was naif: "I had a feeling," he said later, "that I was in a department dealing with Secret Service matters because everywhere in the rooms and corridors there were posters urging silence and secrecy."

His initiation into Secret Service matters was not long delayed. The novitiate became a trained agent. He was sent on a mission to Marseilles to report on French adherence to the Armistice terms and on shipping movements. He picked up an assistant, Pierrette Lucas. NAGEL was naif about her, too: "She did very little work and only obtained scraps of shipping information from sailors whom she entertained when she was in financial difficulties."

For two years before D-Day NAGEL tapped his heels and a
practice morse key at Le Touquet, his post as a stay-behind agent.
When the Allies did land, he was withdrawn to Lille and despatched
to the Abbeville area to report on Allied troop movements from
behind the lines.

On arrival at his post NAGEL tried to contact his
controlling station by radio; he failed to do so and hastily
disposed of his set and all incriminating documents. He intended at
first to retreat to Aachen, but then set out for neutral Spain. He
was denounced in sight of that sanctuary and was arrested.

He lied to the French about his activities. For all his
inherent timidity, he tried hard to be a good German. It was not
until he was taken to Camp 020 that his true story was dragged from
him, and even then the impersonal intelligence which he gave was
limited.

Josef and Mathilde GOBIN

The vast majority of line-crossers and stay-behind agents were a
craven lot. They fell like ninepins to interrogation in the field
and at Ham. In a very different category were a Belgian husband and
wife, Josef and Mathilde GOBIN. It would be meiosis to say that they
were not easily bowled over. The full resources of Camp 020 had been
brought to bear before the break was obtained from the man and
confirmation from the woman.

Josef GOBIN was a rat-like little man and a dangerous spy.
KÖCHLING, that old Abwehr acquaintance, had first interested him in
the German Secret Service as far back as 1940. He was trained in
radio in 1941, but claimed that he was inactive until the Allied
occupation of Antwerp in September 1944. There was evidence from
ISOS, however, that he had sent operational information to the
Germans between September and October 1944, and that such
information warranted an increase in salary from 7,000 to 15,000
francs per month.

GOBIN's wife was involved in the espionage activities of her
husband. She was fully aware of the purport of the first contact
with the German Secret Service; she received, in toto, month by
month, the earnings of her husband from the Abwehr. She knew that
members of the German Secret Service had installed a radio apparatus
in her house; she was fully aware that her husband was transmitting
to the Germans after the occupation of Antwerp.

They came to England for investigation in the last days of
December 1944. The man came en pension to Camp 020; the woman was
lodged overnight at Holloway. They had been under arrest and
fruitless interrogation in the field since early October. Even

confrontation in Brussels with their German paymaster had failed to draw any admission of guilt.

Between them they gave considerable trouble at Ham. Their property included no incriminating evidence. GOBIN was determined not to commit himself out of his own mouth; he did nothing by whimper negatives. Mme GOBIN, a handsome woman and loyal withal, was determined to stick by her man; she would say nothing against him or herself.

Pressures was maintained, and the full resources of the camp were applied against them. In due course it became clear that GOBIN and his wife had lied in concert. It became apparent to the Commandant that no progress could be made until agreement had been reached between GOBIN and his wife that it was necessary to tell the truth.

Four days after his interrogation, GOBIN was persuaded to address the following note to his wife:-

"Ma très chère petite femme,
Ce serait mieux de dire la verité et de nous
fier aux autorités de justice anglaise.
Bons baisers,
Josef."

Later that day, after a stormy interview with the Commandant, Mme GOBIN agreed to reply to her husband's note in cautious terms:-

"Mon cher petit homme,
Si tu a fait quelque chose avoue.
Bons baisers,
ta Femme,
Mathilde."

Now the risk of using these documents was considerable, for there was an implication in both of them that the truth had not been told. Pressure was therefore maintained, and GOBIN, as usual, was allowed no peace: indeed his leisure hours up to midnight were spent in receiving Good Advice from a heterogeneous collection of fellow-countrymen.

GOBIN's morale was being sapped. An officer visited him in the "condemned cell" in the late hours of the night. For three hours he reasoned sympathetically or argued crossly with the prisoner. Several times the spy took up paper and pen to write a confession, then threw down the pen with a tight-lipped "Non." He was finally badgered into making a written confession at dictation speed.

One of the major issues in this case had been the identification of two "important agents" mentioned in ISOS. The brief received at Ham stressed the importance of identifying "Sophie" and "Bertha," who had received much mention in the traffic between GOBIN and his master. The officer told GOBIN that one of his German contacts had betrayed to the British Intelligence Service his connections with "Sophie" and "Bertha," and he had better explain them in his confession. GOBIN smirked: he had not only been an espionage agent of KÖCHLING, but his Black Market supplier too. For reasons of official discretion, KÖCHLING had suggested that goods despatched to him by GOBIN should be notified by radio under cover names: thus "Sophie" was butter, "Bertha" bacon.

He was made to write that down, too. When he had finished his confession and signed it, GOBIN made as if to destroy it, thought better of it and tearfully handed it over. Then he asked whether he might make a last request. He was told that it would be heard, but not necessarily granted. "Please, Captain," said the broken spy, "please can I have some bread and butter." The quick answer was "No."

In view of the difficulties of the case, the Commandant determined on the following morning to obtain further written confessions from GOBIN to confront Mme GOBIN with them. The woman proved more self-possessed than the man, and it was only with marked reluctance that she counter-signed the statements given by him. Nor would she add fresh information to them.

The couple were returned to Belgium in late January 1945 with a strong recommendation for their prosecution to death. That step should have offered no difficulty for interrogation at Ham had led to the discovery of "real evidence": GOBIN's transmitter, built into a desk specially bought for the purpose, had hitherto escaped detection in a series of searches of his flat.

Svend and Helene ANDERSEN

Svend ANDERSEN was a Dane born in Richmond, within sound of the Commandant's voice. He got full measure of it when he arrived at Camp 020 thirty-six years later with his wife Helene. They were both German agents of long standing. Their last mission was as stay-behind agents in Marseilles. The Allies overran them. ANDERSEN found employment with the Americans as an interpreter. He reported the fact to his masters along with valuable items of military information. Belatedly it was discovered that he was a German agent. It was then proposed to use the man and wife as double agents under American control. Ultimately reason imposed itself, and it was decided to send them to Camp 020 for proper investigation.

At Ham they gave almost as much trouble as the GOBINs. They were found to be equally guilty. ANDERSEN had been a German spy since May 1940. Helene was his assistant and his mistress from May 1941 until May 1942. In between spying on her countrymen and coding and encoding his radio messages, she aborted. This decided him to marry her in May 1942: thereafter she was his assistant and his wife.

A measure of their value to the enemy was that between them they received about three-quarter of a million francs. An indication of their treachery was that the woman claimed sympathy because her brother was a pilot in the Royal Air Force, and yet it was known that they betrayed the Allies up to the last possible moment.

In the field this loving but unloveable couple obstructed investigation at every turn. At Camp 020 it was soon seen that they intended to lie in concert, and this necessitated heavy interrogation of the man before any progress could be made with the woman. The one was finessed against the other until, finally, their stories tallied in the main.

Willem COPIER

On the evening of 23rd January 1945 an air-raid warning was sounded in the Antwerp area. A German plane sped across the sky, and a few minutes later two parachutists dropped out of the sky. One of them was found dead; the other, who was armed, aimed his pistol at the Belgian peasant who found him, then surrendered meekly. He was taken to the police, then to the Americans, later to the British Security office in Brussels, and ultimately to Camp 020. He was a German spy, and a radio transmitter attached still to a small parachute had been found not far from the spot where he had made landfall.

The man was Willem COPIER, a thickly bespectacled Dutch journalist of strong Nazi conviction. To the end, indeed, he was a fanatic and certainly proud of his conduct. His glory, in his esteem, was his faith. His undoing was the obstinacy of a weak man, for he was unable to see that he was a traitor to Holland. His tragedy was myopia; indeed, for practical purposes, in a fast moving world, he was blind. He must needs peer for enlightenment, but even this had become a heel-clicking drill.

Because of his disability, COPIER, the ardent volunteer, was rejected by the Waffen SS. Service then became the gnawing obsession even to the point of envy when a soldier came back from the front without an arm. His principles were unattainable, for he talked of "Honest National Socialism", which was a contradiction in terms. There had been brushes with the louts of the Party because he would not follow his tenets to the logical conclusion of barbarity.

After years of frustration, however, the Nazis made use of this man of ideals, but it was done with a sneer. In October 1944 they traded on his fanaticism to make him a spy, and they gave him as a covername the name of a buffoon of a pilot in a propaganda film.

They chose him for a parachute mission, but even then his conduct was odd. They offered him extra money for his wife, but this was rejected. They promised him employment after the war, but he was in no way impressed. "Pflicht" was the torch of this thwarted evangelist; but his character was such that he could never succeed, and the facts as they emerged at Ham were enough for a glittering farce.

The parachute release tapes of himself, of Beck, his companion, and of their respective equipments were crossed. He made a signal, probably the wrong one, but in any event it was misunderstood. COPIER was pushed out without further ado and lost his equipment; his companion fell to his death like a stone.

COPIER was hurt when he landed, but his intention was firm to carry out his mission: to report Allied troop movements and all other matters of military interest. That intent he freely admitted at Ham. Then came a peasant on the scene, and COPIER had a pistol. He levelled it at the man. Then the "Pflicht" of the day gave way to the chivalry of yore: the peasant was so old that COPIER just could not shoot. Instead the old man led him to captivity and, in the ultimate, to his death as a traitor.

Under interrogation at Camp 020 COPIER put up a good fight. In the field he had denied his companion until he knew that he was dead. He refused to give the names of his masters of the GIS. At Ham he tried to pursue the same course. He withheld information, but mainly to protect others rather than himself. But little by little he found that the Nazis, through their incompetence, had betrayed him. He listened to the counsel of another Dutchman who had also been betrayed. Soon he became disillusioned and his confession was complete. To his credit the man remained unafraid even when he was returned to Belgium to his certain death.

Karl REHBEIN

Ideological conflict within himself and a certain untidiness in his multifarious enterprises and meanderings made for difficulty in the investigation at Ham of a mousie little German, Karl REHBEIN. He had spent the years between the wars in Spain. He was anti-Nazi and anti-Fascist; he fought in the Spanish Republican Army eagerly but without distinction. In 1942 his German blood asserted itself. He offered his services at the German Consulate in Barcelona.

The fact that he had volunteered was not good enough for the local Abwehr chiefs. They told him he was a deserter from the German Army and blackmailed him into accepting a mission to infiltrate the British intelligence organisation in Barcelona. Procrastination by the British caused that mission to fail. He was sent to France to report on potential escapees and escape routes. Later he was to plant a woman spy on the Vichy War Ministry. He posed as a British agent, acquired a Russian doxy, and was soon involved in an organisation helping Russian prisoners of war to escape. His loyalties were divided: some times he would betray his new friends, at others he would shoulder grave risks to help them out.

In August 1944 he accepted a mission from Wehrmacht officers to contact the Allies with local peace offerings. At the same time he accepted a mission from the SD to report on the whereabouts and activities behind the Allied lines of senior Wehrmacht officers.

He made no effort to carry out either mission, but surrendered to the French as a British agent. He was evasive under French interrogation, but at Ham his drooling nonsense was given short shrift. In the end he seemed quite happy to have been delivered of the truth, perhaps because his mind had been made clear for him for the first time in his patchy life. He devoted his leisure hours to the modelling of Iberian figurines out of stale bread.

Helena BLITS

Helena BLITS was a widowed Dutch Jewess with a cast in her left eye and a bastard son in Lyons. Hers was indeed an unsavoury character. She was a crook who consorted with a criminal gang in Montmartre and was known to have been a principal in a bad case of extortion. She had been the mistress of a notorious German Secret Service agent named Van Poppel. She had an illegitimate child by another German Secret Service agent named Fosseux. She had received Black Market advantages and some money, on one pretext or another, from several members of the German Secret Service.

The only worthwhile thing that she tried in her life was to commit suicide and take Van Poppel with her. He was spending the night with her and had disclosed to her for the first time, in terms, the fact that he was a member of the German Secret Service. She turned on the gas-geyser in the bathroom adjoining the love nest and shut the flue of the coke-burning stove. In the result she was merely unconscious for two days and violently sick; Van Poppel slept quite happily through it all and did not miss breakfast in the morning.

It was on the extortion charge that BLITS was first arrested

by the French Police, but later the facts of her association with
German agents caused her to be held at the disposal of the
Americans. They passed her back to Camp 020 for detailed
interrogation.

BLITS maintained at Ham that, as a Jewess, she had suffered
so much at the hands of the Germans that she would never wittingly
have worked for them outside her boudoir. Her protestations of
innocence and ignorance in matters of espionage were not easy to
stomach. Indeed, so unsatisfactory was the position at the end of
investigation that a statement was taken from the woman for use at
her trial.

An interesting link in the case led to that Ham innocent,
VAN DAM, whose improbable account of contacts with Germans in Paris
now found full confirmation.

Firmin Emile Jean VERBIEST

Firmin Emile Jean VERBIEST was born out of wedlock in the Avenue de
la Joyeuse Entrée, Brussels. He could not keep a job or his wife. To
remedy these failings he found a well-to-do married couple and made
the woman, FLORETTE, his mistress. They moved triangularly from
house to house, with VERBIEST always as The Lodger. He did not get
in the way of the family, but the woman slipped and did. The husband
was an innocently obliging person and agreed that the child must be
his.

VERBIEST felt that the ménage à trois was nevertheless
endangered. He moved out and joined the Rexist Party as a musical
director. It did not worry him or his chiefs that he knew little
about music, but it may be significant that he was soon silenced by
drafting into the Walloon Legion. The idea of fighting on the
Russian Front appealed to him not at all, and by dint of sustained
malingering he managed a discharge. He went to Brussels and the
Black Market and FLORETTE, whom he shared with another lodger.
FLORETTE and the newer lodger then rid themselves of him by the
simple expedient of getting him recruited by the German Secret
Service and sent off to espionage schools at The Hague and in Paris.

On completion of radio training and practice he returned to
Brussels to discover that his fellow Rexists were cross with him
because of his defection. With the approval of his German masters he
transferred to Antwerp, where he picked up a café waitress as his
mistress while he waited to stay-behind as a radio agent.

In time she came to know of his espionage mission and the
Allies came to Antwerp. VERBIEST discovered that the Brigade Blanche
had his name on their blacklist as a wanted Rexist. He found that
his mistress was very unfaithfully leading a loose life with Allied

soldiers. He decided to surrender to the British Security authorities. He was arrested and learned that his fickle mistress had got there first.

Throughout lengthy and difficult investigation at Ham VERBIEST blamed the error of his treacherous ways on his own naïveté and the guile of FLORETTE. He admitted to sending two radio messages to his masters after the Allied landings, and naively sought to excuse himself by explaining that he had felt guilty about receiving money from the Germans for nothing...

Gudbrandur Einar HLIDAR

By reputation the Icelander Gudbrandur Einar HLIDAR was sinister indeed. He was the veterinary student who had featured in practically each and every Icelandic case handled at Camp 020. There was strong reason to suspect that he might be a principal in espionage, and he had certainly been very active at the recruiting stage. Indications were that he was being groomed for more important work on his return to Iceland on completion of his professional studies.

Quite obviously MI 5 were interested in interviewing the man. The odds were all against the opportunity presenting itself; and then, by the happiest chance, HLIDAR obliged by calling at the British Consulate in Stockholm with a request for a transit visa to enable him to return to Iceland via Britain. It was granted without demur. He arrived at air at Prestwick in February 1945. Neither there nor at the London Reception Centre was he subjected to close interrogation, although statements were taken from him.

When it became clear that he had no intention to disclose his espionage activities of his own volition, he was transferred to Camp 020. On arrival he tried hard to lie plausibly until he realised that that game was not worth the scandal with the Commandant, whereupon he began to talk ingenuous Icelandic truth.

The investigation had its value, but truth to tell, it yielded very little that had not already become known through the earlier cases. HLIDAR, it seemed, had been cast only for a minor role in the Icelandic spy-ring. His activities as a talent scout had been conducted with some innocence, for he was never fully informed of the real interest of his German friends in arranging the "repatriation" of fellow-countrymen. Later he was brought further into the picture. An espionage mission was mooted when it became known that he was himself returning home. He was taught secret writing and received vague instructions to report occasionally on matters of military interest. It seemed, however, that his real value was to be as contact man and possibly paymaster for other agents who would present themselves to him with a password arranged by the Germans.

HLIDAR made it clear to the Germans that he was more interested in practising artificial insemination, in which he was a specialist, than espionage, in which he was not. There was little intention in him to carry out his mission when he left for Iceland; but the certainty was there that the Germans would involve him willy-nilly in their murky doings. And yet he was never fully appreciative of the fact that the British had saved him from his friends and from himself...

Hermann Alois RAINER

There was nothing big or blond about Hermann Alois RAINER, who came from the Italian Tyrol; and yet he was even more fanatical than the representative Nazi from Germany proper. He was, moreover, an exceptional type. He was a German SS officer who had fought well in Russia and in Normandy. Because of difficulties with his CO, he volunteered for special duties with HIMMLER's resistance movement.

For all his fanatic Nazism, RAINER had certain scruples and a certain pride. Early in 1945, after casual involvement to a minor degree in the successful plot to murder the Mayor of Aachen, RAINER deserted to the Allies, holding that he was an officer and not a civilian saboteur.

RAINER's case, as it was revealed at Ham, was one of importance. It confirmed that at one time resistance sabotage within Germany was to have been on a wide scale and organised in depth. He had himself been put in charge of a group of saboteurs who were to have operated behind the Allied lines in the Kleve-Goch-Geldern area. Sabotage caches were arranged: plans were laid for reinforcements of men and material by air; communication was to have been by ground-air W/T; hopes were firm, as more than thirty groups would be operating in the south of the Vaterland itself. The case was examined in close detail and much information was obtained about sabotage schools and planned resistance headquarters in different parts of Germany.

RAINER was at first inclined to resist interrogation. In the field he had not broken because of his soldier's oath. His resolution was strengthened by a determination not to betray his comrades. At Camp 020 he proved a doughty colleague and gave a good deal of trouble before he was made to part with his story. In particular detail he often pleaded insufficient memory, lack of interest and overriding preoccupation with private affaires with a succession of mistresses. Even when the investigation was over, it was felt that both falsehood and reticence existed, but there was room for satisfaction in the results achieved.

Henri Edouard Eugène MORAEL: Jan HUYGENS:
Anne Marguèrite PRELOGAR

Three of a group of five saboteurs trained under the direction of
SKORZENY for a mission in Belgium arrived at Ham in March 1943. They
were an unprepossessing lot as to the two men involved, but the
third, a Jugoslav woman, had both courage and presence.

The ringleader of the entire group was a former chauffeur
and salesman, Henri Edouard MORAEL, a volunteer of the Allgemeine SS
who had acted as an SD informer. Anne Marguèrite PRELOGAR was a
pick-up from an Antwerp bar who became his concubine and secretary.
MORAEL failed in a course at Hildesheim in the theory of Nazism, and
PRELOGAR got herself arrested in Belgium as a suspected Allied
agent.

In August 1944, after the man had won a German decoration
for treachery in his own country, the couple were evacuated to
Germany and there agreed to undergo training in sabotage and to
undertake a mission in Belgium.

They were joined at Friedenthal spy school by another
treacherous recruit, Jan HUYGENS, former bank clerk and member of
the Waffen SS who had already received some instruction in sabotage
and radio transmission at The Hague and the notorious Seehof school.

With two other agents, the two men and the woman were
parachuted in error over France, 150 miles from their objective. The
descent was disastrous for PRELOGAR. She landed on an oak tree and
screamed for help. MORAEL, her lover, who had fallen nearby, urged
her to jump down into his arms; PRELOGAR countered by ordering him
to come up and fetch her. She screamed louder still when he pointed
out that the tree had no branches close to the ground. In a fit of
womanly pique she began to undo her harness, the whole thing came
apart, and down she fell. MORAEL tried to catch her before she hit
the ground, but it reached her before he did, and she fainted
noisily.

When she recovered she was volubly determined to surrender
to the nearest police authorities, and there was nothing that the
browbeaten MORAEL could do but follow meekly. HUYGENS, who had
landed separately but safely, made his way to Brussels, only to be
denounced by a former colleague.

All three were directed to Camp 020 in the course of time.
The investigation was relatively easy, for the prisoners were played
off against each other. The information obtained from them was of
considerable value both in volume and quality. Their training, it
was found, had indeed been careful and they had been in contact with
a remarkable number of GIS officers and other agents. Their
missions, too, were interesting, for they ranged from sabotage of

"PLUTO" to the smearing of door knobs with some particularly
virulent poison. SKORZENY evidently had ideas, but not the people to
carry them out.

Antonio Aristides MOGLIA

Antonio Aristides MOGLIA was a prematurely wizened Argentine
national of Italian parentage with precarious residence in France.
He was a thief and a whoremonger of the worst type, and the time
that he could spare from these rogueries was spent in evading a
deportation order made by the outraged French State on which he was
so tenaciously parasitic.

MOGLIA had all the low cunning of his kind; his wits were
sharpened by constant conflict with the law and the need to live
dangerously. He was thus made to measure as a low-grade SD agent. He
was recruited in Paris in 1942 and was soon active in the Lyons area
as an informer against the Maquis. The Germans had no difficulty in
1944 in persuading him to join them in the retreat to Germany,
beyond the immediate reach of re-established French justice.

It was not that they were interested in saving the skin of
MOGLIA; they intended to use him again, in France itself. MOGLIA
received a brief course of instruction at an emergency spy school.
His mission in France was considerable: he was to provide military
intelligence, act as paymaster to stay-behind agents, penetrate the
American Intelligence, try out a new spy route into France through
Italy, and report on the fate of several German agents who had been
lost in the retreat or had been ominously silent for some weeks.

MOGLIA accepted it all with glee when he learned that large
sums of money would be entrusted to him. He would pocket it all,
bargain his full espionage story with the Allies against a pardon in
France, and re-establish himself in the thieves' market.

His subsequent actions were not inconsistent with these
motives. In Italy he consorted with members of the Italian Secret
Service to please his German masters. In Switzerland he made
reinsurance doubly sure by telling a part of his story and betraying
other German agents to the Swiss counter-espionage authorities. In
France he contacted the Deuxième Bureau and re-told his tale, still
with its discreet reticences, especially in such delicate matters as
his betrayals of members of the Resistance movement. In
collaboration with American Intelligence, the French decided to use
MOGLIA as an agent-double.

The good faith of this bad man eventually fell in doubt when
he tried to save a former contact from arrest, for the woman in
question was in a position to betray his unconfessed frailties in
the German Service. Penetration was at once suspected, for on review

of the story which he had told glaring omissions and obvious lies were apparent. He was sent to Camp 020 for proper investigation in April 1945.

At Ham MOGLIA put up a good fight on the more compromising issues, but made a full confession in the end with the grace of the old lag who has at least tried to practice on judicial credulity.

There was a suggestion from American quarters that MOGLIA might be used again on his transfer out of Camp 020. Quite apart from the fact that he was already blown in France to several of his so-called friends and espionage contacts, there was nothing to commend the idea. He had had his chance, and he had chosen to ruin it by acts of bad faith. In espionage there can be no second chances.....

Julius HAGEMANN

Most valuable and voluminous information on that very active Abwehrstelle Wiesbaden, and different Abwehrkommandos and Truppen was obtained at Ham from a naturalised German of Belgian origin, Julius HAGEMANN. He was a shabby customer who had been recruited in Brussels in 1940 as a talent scout and was later promoted to the status of field manager of Ast Belgien agents.

Following the plot of 20th July, he was arrested as an associate of Dr WREDE, an Abwehr officer in Paris who was implicated in the abortive putsch. On release he was posted to a Frontaufklärungskommando, and with this mobile Abwehr unit and another to which he was transferred later, to a new base deep in Germany, where he was to continue his work as a talent scout.

The Allied advance cut him off from further retreat. He tried to escape arrest by remaining mum, but he had talked too much earlier and was arrested on denunciation by a German of German origin.

HAGEMANN, a grim character, was found at Ham more willing to betray his comrades and superiors than to talk of his own activities. His memory in the first instance was amazing: he provided a list of 250 descriptions that were found on check to be strictly reliable. His plea of forgetfulness on personal issues was therefore unacceptable, but investigation in this direction failed to given full satisfaction.

Karl Heinz KRÄMER

The last chapter in the history of Ham opened with the cessation of hostilities in Europe. Instead of the steady but shabby procession of stay-behind agents and occasional impressed spies there began to appear the van-guard of espionage directors and spymasters. It was the phase of historical research.

The first of the new genre was Karl Heinz KRÄMER, an assistant of Nikolaus RITTER at Hamburg in the days when the Germans were planning the invasion of England and were sending their go-before spies by parachute. KRÄMER had travelled throughout Europe as RITTER's intermediary with a number of agents, but later he had joined the German Legation in Sweden as Press Attaché and Eins Luft expert of KO Sweden.

As an intelligence officer he was certainly active, and by no means unsuccessful. At Hamburg he had suffered from uninspired direction. He was considered a useful recruit by his chiefs, for he handled a number of agents with apparent profit; but neither he nor his superiors were to know that many of them were double agents under the control of M I 5. In Sweden KRÄMER, enjoying greater independence and with some grounding in the business, proved a more real danger to the Allies. Within a short time of his establishment in Stockholm he had recruited his own agents and established valuable links and exchange arrangements with the Japanese, Finnish and Hungarian Secret Services. His sources of intelligence were varied and well placed: contacts were claimed in the Swedish Foreign Office, the French Military Attaché's office, and with a prominent Swedish businessman who was in a position to supply valuable intelligence on Swedish military and political affairs. It was through this man, too, that an espionage ring was set up in Spain and Portugal with links to Britain and the USA: through these channels much valuable information reached KRÄMER. Profitable, too, was KRÄMER's connection with a responsible official of the Swedish airlines whose sense of neutrality was more than irresponsible.

KRÄMER combined his military intelligence activities with work on behalf of the German Foreign Office, in which he had been employed for a short space of time before the war, and intervention in negotiations for the acquisition of Swedish ball-bearings for the German war machine.

The blowing of one of his agents in Sweden led to indignant representations by the Swedish Foreign Office, and in April 1945 KRÄMER was expelled from the country. He arrived at Flensburg on the day following the capitulation. For eight days he attached himself to a pathetic little office which called itself the German Foreign Office. On the ninth night he was arrested in his pyjamas in bed, and for weeks thereafter he complained that the timing was unfair, for otherwise he would have been wearing uniform and would have been entitled to POW status.

His reception at Ham a few days later was noisy and

shattering. Disillusioned but soured, he yielded his personal
history and knowledge only grudgingly. There were reticences and
there were half-truths. His attitude did not profit him, for months
later, after transfer from Ham to an L of C camp in Germany, he was
brought to CSDIC(WEA) at Bad Nenndorf to complete his story and
provide further information on the Abwehr.

At the moment of writing he is exercised in the
transcription and annotation of a formidable pile of teleprint
messages which passed between Sweden and Germany in the heydey of
his activities. He is not at home in his new surroundings, but
nearby, at Bückeburg, is his Alma Mater, and at Steinhuder Meer, not
far away, the scene of carefree agricultural activities as a member
of the Arbeitsdienst.

Wilhelm KUEBART

Wilhelm KUEBART was another interesting figure. He was a
professional soldier and had been head of Eins Heer and chief of
Abteilung B(West) of the Mil Amt of the RSHA when Himmler absorbed
the discredited Abwehr. He had been involved in very minor rôle in
the plot of 20th July as the protegé of Oberst Hansen, was
imprisoned and acquitted for lack of evidence, and the cashiered.
Embittered by his treatment at the hands of the Gestapo and by the
ascendancy of the Party over the Army, he bided his time in civilian
retirement until he could surrender himself and his story to the
Allies.

He arrived at Ham eager to disclose all the information in
his possession and quite prepared, in his spleen against the
Gestapo, to put up with any discomfort. Important information was
obtained from him about the structure of the RSHA and the events of
20th July in addition to a full account of his own activities both
as departmental head and controller of agents.

Later arrivals at Ham, including Erich PHEIFFER, were
inclined to despise KUEBART as a youngster who was not even an
infant prodigy, but had traded on the friendship of Hansen to win
his important position in the Abwehr and RSHA. They had nicknamed
him "MILCHBART" ("Milkbeard") because of his youth and much fun was
poked at the very broad, red General Staff stripe that had graced
his trousers in office.

Nonetheless KUEBART produced results no worse than those of
his critics, and it was to his credit that a weakness for overmuch
drinking and loose talk thereafter was acknowledged by him when no
hint of it had ever reached his detractors.

Hermann GISKES: Gerhard HUNTEMANN

One of the most intelligent and successful of Abwehr officers to pass through Camp 020 in the aftermath of crushing military defeat was Hermann GISKES, whose Secret Service career dated from 1938. He was a counter-intelligence expert who held appointments in Hamburg and Paris before being transferred to Holland as Leiter Referat III of Ast Niederlande.

Here his ability found full scope. Through and through he riddled Allied espionage organisations in that country, and many indeed were the SOE agents whom he turned and successfully played back through an assistant, Gerhard HUNTEMANN, a W/T expert who came with him to Camp 020. Both were willing to speak volubly at Ham. It was GISKES' boast that he had even governed senior SOE appointments in London. There was pride of achievement in them both, and well were they entitled to that attitude. Out of deference to a related Service, the Ham findings in the two cases were published with a certain discretion as to publication and distribution.

GISKES, as the principal in a rare case of Abwehr triumph, spent several months at Bad Nenndorf under an enforced vow of silence. There was something to be said both in his favour and HUNTEMANN's. Independent testimony from an SOE agent supported their claim to have done their utmost to spare the lives of captured Allied agents.

For all that, GISKES' outlook on the future was pessimistic. HUNTEMANN, on the other hand, was an optimist! He talked about a job now the war was over, and thrilled at the idea of marrying a girl 22 years his junior now that the kill-joy Nuremberg laws were invalid.

Heinz Maria Karl JOST

Heinz Maria Karl JOST had been the first boss of Amt VI of the RSHA. He had seen the department grow up from virtually nothing, and the fact was that he had done virtually nothing to help it grow up. He was an opportunistic early Nazi of legal training with no semblance of ability, but somehow he had impressed Heydrich and Himmler. He was well known to several characters at Camp 020, among them LORENZ and NAUJOCKS, both of whom held him in contemptuous esteem.

JOST was stupid enough to know no language except archaic, legal German, so that interrogation was attended by some difficulty until Joseph LEDEBUR, that prince of curiosity, was detailed to provoke in him an interest in the investigation of his own case and to translate his verbal and written statements into contemporary dialect.

The brighter spirits of the RSHA had dubbed JOST "Frau JOST" because of his weakness vis-à-vis both Heydrich and Himmler, and when the stigma was rubbed into him at Ham he summoned what little manliness there was in him to tell his resentful story of his superiors and to outline in meticulous detail the rise of the RSHA with particular reference to Amt VI, from leadership of which he had been ousted by the bumptious and competent Walther SCHELLENBERG.

Friedrich Wilhelm Hermann OLMES

Friedrich Wilhelm Hermann OLMES was a young German of 24 with bright inventive ideas and brighter ideas about himself. Nobody ever learned officially the circumstances of his delivery to the triumphant American forces in Germany, but the fact was that he arrived at Camp 020 with fancy notions that he would be allowed to go sight-seeing and frolicking in England in between interrogations. He was too young to have all the bounce taken out of him at Ham, but he sobered considerably after the first dampening interrogations. Even then he produced convincing and alarming accounts of the progress of atom research in Germany many weeks before the shattering die was cast at Hiroshima. His own claim to have invented a new anti-tank weapon found confirmation in the prisoner LORENZ, but OLMES' boast to have close and intimate relations with Hitler and Goebbels on technical issues was largely discounted by an admission that he had been in trouble with a CO of homosexual tendencies.

Generalmajor Friedrich WOLF

One of the most troublesome of post-surrender prisoners at Ham was Generalmajor Friedrich WOLF, who had spent the war in the unmilitary and unwarlike salons of Buenos Aires as German Military, Naval and Air Atttaché.

The case was important. The German diplomatic mission in Argentina, which had enjoyed its measure of success in South American espionage, had been expelled following the denouement of the HELLMUTH affair at Camp 020 and the subsequent representations of the Allied Governments. They had left a considerable stay-behind organisation to carry on the wicked work, and the onus was laid on M I 5 to ascertain its chiefs, its extent and its strength.

WOLF was, in many respects, the king-pin of the Abwehr side of the plot. There was evidence that he was aware of the SD contribution. He was certainly the one man in Allied hands who could supply the quick answers to quick questions, for the organisation had to be disrupted at the earliest opportunity.

He may have been a strutting soldier in peaceful avenues, but he was a good German. For days he refused to talk espionage turkey. He would have his interrogators believe that he was the complete innocent abroad. He was badgered into making two sorry attempts at suicide by plaiting typewriter ribbons of insufficient tensile strength and jumping off chairs that were too low. He was given no physical or spiritual rest. In the ultimate he began to surrender begrudgingly small but vital items of intelligence. At length he agreed to give direct answers to questions, and by laborious process of precise questioning sufficient information was dragged from him to allow of the disruption of the stay-behind gang in Argentina.

WOLF, by now a completely broken man, was brought out to Bad Nenndorf to act as regulator in the investigation of other German-Argentine cases. He proved useful. A team of American investigators had been unable to break a recent acquisition to Allied sources of intelligence, Ernst SCHLÜTER, chief of the executive of the stay-behind espionage organisation in Argentina. SCHLÜTER was brought to Ban Nenndorf from a Hamburg internment camp. He proved obdurate in the first minutes of interrogation. WOLF was summoned from his duties as a cleaner in the Officers' Mess and was given an order to instruct SCHLÜTER to disclose the full truth. There was a successful confrontation. SCHLÜTER told his story.

The intelligence obtained from WOLF, coupled with that tricked out of Osmar HELLMUTH at Camp 020, was acknowledged to have been the most accurate and comprehensive to have been obtained from any source on German espionage activities in South America.

Alois MÜLLNER

In the hope that the unsolved South African cases of Basil BATOS and Lambertus ELFERINK might be fully proved and exploited, there was brought to Ham a principal of the German Consulate-General at Lourenço Marques, Alois MÜLLNER, who was known from ISOS to have been a paymaster of agents in Moçambique.

MÜLLNER proved as difficult a customer as the rest from that part of the world. He admitted to contact with BATOS and to certain services on his behalf, but he was sufficiently desiccated to be dried up about intimate details of the spy-ring and its components. Points of confirmation but no new facts were extracted from him at Ham before he was sent to cool off in non-tropical Germany in the month of October 1945.

Bruno Friedrich WOLFF

From Turkey via Portugal there came to Ham a group of German Secret Service officers of both the SD and the Abwehr. Although on paper the services were now combined in the RSHA, distinction could still be made between the two. The leading Abwermann was almost invariably an officer and a German; the SD boss was always a Nazi.

Bruno Friedrich WOLFF had belonged to the NSDAP since March 1931. After losing a job in a furniture factory, and with it six months' arrears of pay, he joined the Gestapo. Thereafter he acted as liaison officer with the Italian police and received or visited representative police officials of other European countries. In 1941 he was despatched to Norway to establish a Sabotage Security Commission, but was made to abandon the plan owing to the non-cooperative attitude of local SD officials who resented the intrusion.

Shortly afterwards WOLFF applied for an SD vacancy in the Passport Control Office in Istanbul and got the appointment. Although a member of Amt IV still, he was to represent Amt VI under cover as Vice-Consul. His mission was to establish links with the Turkish police and Secret Service and to report on the attitude of neutral and Axis consular and diplomatic officials towards the Reich and the Western Powers. There were other tasks, too, and they included a watch on possible unofficial peace negotiations with the Allies.

WOLFF operated with more zeal than success. He recruited a number of agents and established exchange arrangements with representatives of other pro-Axis intelligence services. One of these, a Roumanian, was a persistent caller at WOLFF's office. The intelligence which he brought hardly justified his high frequency. At length WOLFF discovered that the man merely wanted an excuse to see his secretary. The secretary was packed off home to Germany; the agent's intelligence output declined in volume but increased in value.

Collaboration between the German Secret Service and the Turkish was well promoted by WOLFF. The Turks, it seemed, were especially appreciative of German plans to despatch agents to the Caucasus or to arm subversive groups there; there was coincidence of views on anti-Russian intelligence and security. German activities against the Western Allies, however, were almost invariably conducted without reference to the Turks, who were not to be trusted in this respect.

It was largely in an advisory capacity that WOLFF was involved in arrangements for a stay-behind espionage organisation in the event of a rupture of diplomatic relations between the Reich and

Turkey. When it did come and the German diplomats were interned, he
was himself able to maintain radio contact with Berlin through a
collaborator of the Turkish Secret Service who had access to him
under cover as buying agent for the German internees. The
arrangement was worked with profit until the Turkish Secret Service,
convinced of Germany's early collapse, refused to play further.

With the rest of the consular and diplomatic group, WOLFF
left Turkey for repatriation to Germany in a Swedish steamer. The
ship's call at Liverpool for control provided the British Secret
Service with the opportunity to off-ship him with several other
principals in espionage who would have an interesting story to tell.

He came to Ham under mild protest of violation of privilege.
He was a reluctant informer against his former associates in Turkey,
but told his own story readily enough.

Thomas LUDWIG

A pre-war clerk of the Abwehr, Thomas LUDWIG became one of the most
responsible and active German Secret Service men in Turkey. His
appointment was as a III F officer, and he arrived in Turkey with
neither training nor experience to help him. "I tried to master the
trade," he wrote, "uninspired by spy stories or films, but by sound,
serious and diligent application."

He certainly succeeded. He built up a network of informers
that might have served as an example to his Abwehr colleagues in
Turkey; but with them he was never popular, for he was viewed as the
master spy on spy-masters. He was one of the few German Secret
Service officers in Turkey whose loyalty was never in doubt in
Germany: he was confirmed in his appointment when the Abwehr was
merged in the RSHA and continued to enjoy full liberty of action.

He was a highly intelligent type, was LUDWIG, and at Ham he
showed it both by being fully co-operative and by writing his own
full report. In an appendix he listed no less than 64 agents in
Turkey with details of their several missions and their directing
officers.

Erich PHEIFFER

From Turkey, too, came that old friend, Fregatten-Kapitän Erich
PHEIFFER, whose last appointment had been that of Leiter of the Near
Eastern KO. The story of his career as an Abwehr officer of eleven
years' standing, as written at Ham in a report running to 195 packed
foolscap pages, had more colour than a work of fiction and contained
facts enough to delight the most serious of espionage historians.

His most successful years were his earliest. PHEIFFER loved

the game of active espionage. His happiest years were between 1934 and 1939, when he ran spies from Bremen to France and America with conspicuous talent and profit. Even when his activities in those countries were found out he could take pride, and M I 5 everlasting credit, for the fact that they were detected, not in the countries against which he was working, but from Britain. It was M I 5 that provided the warning that led to the disruption of his important organisation in the United States in 1938; and it was M I 5 again that helped the Deuxieme Bureau to apprehend a most dangerous French traitor who had for years served PHEIFFER's monstrous intelligence appetite with very meaty slices of military and naval information.

Thereafter M I 5 never lost sight of Master PHEIFFER. Paradoxically enough his threat lessened as his Abwehr status increased. PHEIFFER at a desk, surrounded by files and inept subordinates, was not the same menace as PHEIFFER in the espionage field. In Bremen, in Brest, in Paris, in Berlin, in Zossen and in Istanbul he was made to cope with the paper, and not the flesh-and-blood, of espionage. It bored him, but he did his best and, from the British point of view, worst.

PHEIFFER, a professional sailor before he became a professional spymaster, hated the Nazis, but he was a good German. He remained dutiful and loyal to his country to the end. In internment in Turkey he returned to direct espionage: he observed shipping in the Sea of Marmora and reported on it to headquarters in Germany by means of a radio transmitter clandestinely introduced into the camp. On arrival at Ham he ended the first statement outlining his career and contacts in the Abwehr with these lines:-

"I had a hard struggle before I could bring myself to write down the foregoing. I have only done it because most of the incidents are known already. Since the collapse, my country can suffer no further military defeats. And finally, the records are in the hands of the Allies. The officers who did all this carried out their duties where their military leaders placed them. It is all the same whether they fought with weapons or used their wits in 'the war in the dark.' They fought honourably and deserve to be honourably treated."

PHEIFFER was not dishonourably treated at Ham. He was philosophical about incarceration. He enjoyed interrogation and would ask for more at the end of each long session. His memory of the early years of his career had dimmed, but close questioning enlightened it and delighted him. He confessed that the British Secret Service knew more about him than he could remember without prompting. He was glad of it, for some day he planned to write his autobiography: "I would have missed many important chapters," he said, "because I had lost perspective as well as detail."

Below stairs PHEIFFER enjoyed the ministrations of his servant EITEL and the company of his friend LEDEBUR.

Werner UNVERSAGT

Werner UNVERSAGT was as well known to M I 5 as PHEIFFER, but his espionage history was shorter. He had joined the Abwehr in May 1940. For almost five years thereafter his name ran constantly through ISOS intercepts and dropped sourly from the mouths of a string of his agents at Ham.

From Brussels he had worked hard against England as an IH officer. Twenty at least of his recruits and spy contacts found their way to Camp 020: five of them died on the gallows. He suffered no twinges of conscience on that score; he lamented, not the men, but the time and the opportunities lost. He took his duties seriously and impersonally.

UNVERSAGT lost little time in surrendering to the Allies when he saw that the game and the battle were lost. He was intelligent: "I anticipated interrogation. Germany has lost the war; it is only right that I should surrender the information which is mine." He did it at Ham under strict and proper guidance.

His heavy losses in captured agents always puzzled UNVERSAGT, for he spent much time and care in training, grooming and equipping his men. He admitted that many of them were poor spy material, but he had great respect for the British Secret Service, which had caught even his "best boys." The Abwehr, he said, was pathetically ignorant of the organisation, activities and methods of British Intelligence: "Knowledge of the IS and its special wartime defence measures was incredibly scanty. For myself I can say that I knew only that a British Intelligence Service did exist; I never learned anything new about it throughout the war. It is true that there were courses for Abwehr officers which I didn't attend, but I don't believe that even the instructors knew much..."

UNVERSAGT had been conducting "the war in the dark" very much in the dark.

Karl Robert Johannes MEISNER

Another important Abwehr chief to surrender to the Allies for interrogation was Kapitän zur See Karl Robert Johannes MEISNER, who had a long run of success as a III officer in Kiel, Berlin, Oslo, Angers, and Paris and finally as KO Leiter in Switzerland.

He had seen active service in the Kriegsmarine in the 1914-1918 war and he carried out his Abwehr duties "with the sense of honour of a fighting man." To his credit he certainly intervened to prevent senseless cruelty and slaughter on the part of subordinates, but his other activities were not always as worthy of honour.

He spoke readily enough under interrogation about his colleagues and the agents known to him.

Ernst KALTENBRUNNER

Ernst KALTENBRUNNER had only to be seen and heard to realise what a power of evil was concentrated in the brute. His appeal to Hitler needed no further enquiry: he had brain, brawn, ruthlessness and a certain suavity to offset the overall impression of frightfulness.

He came to Ham from the American camp at Wiesbaden as a source of information on the RSHA as a whole and to answer specific questions, rather than to undergo full investigation of his personal history. He was a tough case. He had no wish to talk. But he had his weaknesses, and they were found and probed. The Commandant gave him a taste of his own medicine in fearsome interrogation, and the great KALTENBRUNNER shook. He was threatened with another of his own tricks: blackmail. He had neglected his wife and family and had twins by a mistress: it was put to him that the story of the sordid misalliance could ruin the lives of them all. KALTENBRUNNER talked cautiously for a time, then hardened.

Now, he was not without his enemies, and may of them were also resident at this time at Camp 020. They did not hesitate to provide all the material which they could to ensure that their late chief got all he deserved. In their uphill struggle with that mountain of a man the interrogators could count also on the willing and unflagging co-operation of such camp agents at LEDEBUR. When SCHELLENBERG arrived, he too was found anxious to indict his former chief. KALTENBRUNNER was advised of SCHELLENBERG's betrayals and responded with gratifying tu quoques.

The battle against KALTENBRUNNER was also a battle against time. He was wanted at Nuremberg as a war criminal. The case, moreover, was inherited by a succession of interrogators, for the staffing of CSDIC(WEA) was under way. Although important information had been extracted from him by the time that he was transferred back to Germany for trial, the investigation was by no means completed.

Hugo Ernst BLEICHER

Hugo Ernst BLEICHER was another relative minnow. He had played an astute III F game in Paris for three years and had been responsible

for the capture and turning of individual agents and the disruption
of larger Allied organisations. Later he served with a FAT and FAK
and was ultimately detailed to organise a stay-behind R-Netz of
agents in the Low Countries, in complete reversal of his Parisian
role. The hard winter of early 1945 conspired to frustrate his
knavish tricks and he was compelled to report the failure of his
mission. After brief service with a new FAT, he was ordered to bring
order out of the chaos into which the Amsterdam office had fallen.
It seemed that its previous chief had used it less for intelligence
purposes than to bed his mistress and conduct his Black Market
activities.

BLEICHER tried to run a few agents whom he had inherited,
but soon discovered that they were either double-crossers or idlers.
There was neither heart nor fight left in him when he was arrested
in Amsterdam by the NBS Dutch Resistance Movement.

Herbert Christian Oscar Otto WICHMANN

Herbert Christian Oscar Otto WICHMANN was as weak and woolly a
character as KALTENBRUNNER was strong and hard. He had been
Astleiter of Hamburg, where he had spent all but two years of his
Abwehr career. He had been in decay for years, but before the war he
had directed espionage against Britain, the United States and
France, and in the last stages of the war he had been nominally
responsible for the creation of a stay behind radio network in the
Hamburg area. M I 5 wanted to know about these doings, and so he
came to Ham.

WICHMANN was willing enough to talk, but the trouble was
that he had no memory. His many friends at Ham confirmed it; his few
enemies admitted it. Under patient handling such facts as he could
be made to remember were gradually drawn from him.

His espionage activities against Britain had not been
markedly successful: "All attempts to spy on England," he said,
"were disappointing; in spite of much effort, nothing of value was
ever achieved." The details which he gave revealed that it was he
who had been responsible of the control of Jessie Jordan in Scotland
and for many of the agents in the United States who had been blamed
on PHEIFFER.

Insofar as the Vi-Netz in Hamburg was concerned, he had
achieved nothing. Characteristically, he had delegated
responsibility to subordinates who had not known where to start in
the business of creating a sound stay-behind spy system.

Walther SCHELLENBERG

Walther Friedrich SCHELLENBERG is a blue-eyed German boy today, braving all the discomforts and the short rations of Washington, DC, as he sells his former friends and colleagues for his mess of American potage.

Walther Friedrich SCHELLENBERG had tried to bring the whole world to peace through Count Bernadotte, an amateur Swedish diplomat, when only lambasted Germany was in urgent need of it. Walther Friedrich SCHELLENBERG had ratted to the Americans after his failure in the opportunistic mission: he wanted to talk about the RSHA and his hated enemies, KALTENBRUNNER and HIMMLER. He had owed his job to them, it was true, and he had worked loyally for them because there was no other way; but the Allies would understand that Walther Friedrich SCHELLENBERG had really been working against nasty Nazi Germany all the time.....

Walther Friedrich SCHELLENBERG, a priggish little dandy, fetched up rakishly at Ham with an assurance born of extravagant promises in the field. He was shocked by his stern reception and sulked peevishly until he was brought face to face with the reality of British contempt for him and his evil works. He chose to be reticent in his personal detail, but there were reluctant admissions of espionage carnage and moral sins after the evidence against him, some of it KALTENBRUNNER's, was produced. The proud head of Amt VI had, among other indelicacies, a weakness for Swedish massage at the hands of a spy pervert.....

But he was an ambitious and an able young man withal. He had conducted the activities of Amt VI with ruthless efficiency. He was strong enough to have the ready ear of HIMMLER and KALTENBRUNNER. His bustle was young; his judgment was mature. His treason, in the ultimate, was studied. He played the skin-saving game with foppish elegance, but no one at Ham was deceived by his eloquence.

SCHELLENBERG was not as good an enemy as KALTENBRUNNER.

Martin Karl SANDBERGER

Martin Karl SANDBERGER was a sensuous type who had found happiness as Walther Friedrich SCHELLENBERG's principal aide in Amt VI of the RSHA. As such he played an important role in the RSHA's absorption of the Abwehr and eventually became head of the economics section of the new organisation. His considerable knowledge of the RSHA was discounted after SCHELLENBERG and KALTENBRUNNER had been made at Ham to disclose their more authoritative information of that institution. His chief value was as an informant against his former chiefs and as the source of more topical news on the movements of the extremely mobile RSHA personalities and departments in the closing stages of the war.

SANDBERGER was very anxious to please at Camp 020. His case officer reported him as being "polite, correct, co-operative." The report was dated October 1945.

Harald KIRFEL

Harald KIRFEL was a young psychologist, lawyer and student of Oriental languages. He was clever in these pursuits. The Oberkommando der Wehrmacht called him up for service with a censoring unit, then made him instructor in Japanese in the Army Interpreter Corps. In October 1944 he was transferred to the Lehrregiment Kurfürst and shortly afterwards took up an appointment with the Amt VI section dealing with the Far East.

His studies had made him knowledgeable about the East in an academic sort of way. He had never been in Japan or in China, but he became one of wartime Germany's supreme authorities on those countries. He impressed SCHELLENBERG.

It would be improper and churlish to dismiss KIRFEL as a man of no account. Even if his knowledge of the Far East was only bookish, the connections which he established with little yellow men in Germany and in Europe generally had their profit. His Japanese friends of the Secret Service were not fools. There was a ring of inspiration and a note of prophecy about one report which he received from such a source:-

> "Russia's aim is to seize as much of Germany as possibly, not because she is interested in territory which she must evacuate later, but exclusively because Russia lays great value on German specialists, technicians and engineers from the Ruhr and Magdeburg areas, as also Dessau and Kassel..... The task of the German specialists would be to develop inside Russia a specialised armaments industry. Russia had now plans to make war against the United States....."

Intelligence obtained months later at CSDIC(WEA) showed that the Russians had indeed carried out the first part of that plan. The ultimate Russian plans, as read in Bad Nenndorf, did not limit warlike intentions to the Untied States.....

Reverting to KIRFEL: he claimed at Ham to be anti-Japanese at heart. He said that unblushingly. He was captured by Italian partisans in Milan in the company of Japanese diplomats for whom he was buying food, on 26th April 1945. He was obviously pro-Japanese at stomach.

Appendix

The statistics below come from Lieutenant-Colonel Sampson's draft history of Camp 020 (KV 4/8, pp.25-7). They show the variety of nationalities employed by the Nazis as agents, many of whom worked under duress. Also included are the names of fourteen of the 'Unlucky Sixteen' who were executed (the names of Armstrong and Estella Key were added in handwriting) and details of the agents who landed clandestinely in Britain.

THE INTELLIGENCE WORK AT CAMP 020

STATISTICS

Before summarising the actual intelligence work carried out at Camp 020, some statistics may be given.

Intake of Prisoners

Up to September 14th 1945, the intake of internees at Camp 020 was as follows:-

1940............	107
1941............	55
1942............	67
1943............	65
1944............	119
1945............	57 (up to 14.9.45.)
	480

Nationalities

Thirty four nationalities have been represented, namely:-

Belgian	68		Italian	12
German	77		Portuguese	9
French	64		Polish	9
Norwegian	35		Danish	8
Dutch	31		South & Central	
British	29	(mostly before	Americans	16
Spanish	25	Oct. 1940)	Swiss	5
Icelandic	16		Swedish	5

The other nationalities include Austrian, Hungarian, Russian, Roumanian, Czechoslovak, Greek, Irish, Canadian, Yugoslav, Lithuanian, Egyptian, Japanese and stateless persons.

Interrogations took place in English, French, German, Dutch, Flemish, Norwegian, Swedish, Danish, Spanish, Portuguese and Italian.

A considerable number of women were interrogated, either at Camp 020 or by officers sent to Holloway Gaol. No women were detained at Camp 020.

Disposal

The following fourteen spies from Camp 020 were executed in England during the War:-

Van den KIEBOOM	Dutch	December 1940
Karl Heinrich MEIER	Dutch	"
Jose WALDBERG	German	"
DRUECKE @ DE DEEKER	German	August 1941
Werner WAELTI	Swiss	"
Josef JAKOBS	German	August 15, 1941
Karl P. RICHTER	Czech.	December 1941
A.L.E. TIMMERMAN	Belgian	July 1942
Johannes DRONKERS	Dutch	January 1943
Johannes WINTER	Belgian	November 1942
Duncan SCOTT-FORD	British	November 1942
Oswald JOB	British	March 16, 1944
P.R.C. NEUKERMANS	Belgian	June 23, 1944
Josef Van HOVE	Belgian	July 12, 1944

55 prisoners were released. These included five of the temporary internees examined in the early days of the Camp and 50 of those admitted since October 1940. These cases often called for more work than straightforward spy cases, since no prisoner was admitted to the Camp without strong prima facie evidence against him.

During the entire period, 11 agents were released to B.I.A.

Of the remaining cases, few were at all doubtful and in almost all cases confessions were obtained.

The peak figure for internees held at the Camp was 168, which was reached in November 1944.

Staff

The final joint intelligence establishment of Camp 020 and 020 R, was:-

    1 Commandant
    1 Assistant Commandant
    25 Intelligence Officers including Administrative Officers

Since the inception of Camp 020, forty four M.I. Officers have been engaged. The peak was reached early in 1945, at twenty-five, plus two on attachment. The figure also included four officers on detachment at Diest and four permanent Administrative officers.

The peak figure for secretaries was 52.

PHASES OF THE WORK

It will be necessary to give some details of the more important cases dealt with at Camp 020 in order to show the varying methods employed by the enemy.

Of the total number of 480 cases investigated at Camp 020, about a 100 were agents intended to spy in this country. The others consist of some 70 persons examined in the early days of the camp, very few of whom could be classified as spies, and later agents intended for America, Africa and other parts of the world. The total also includes the fifty agents later released as innocent, and finally, the 140 odd prisoners sent from the continent for investigation after D-Day.

It is somewhat surprising that of all the cases handled at the Camp since its inception, only 19 were sent to this country and one to Ireland clandestinely, i.e. by parachute, small boat or rubber dinghy, and of these, 13 arrived in September and October 1940, when the Germans were contemplating invasion. To these must be added the enemy agent J. Willem Ter BRAAK who arrived by parachute at the beginning of November 1940 and remained undiscovered until April 9th 1941 when he shot himself in an air raid shelter in Cambridge.

For convenience of reference, the details of these landings are given below:-

Date of Landing	Name	Method of Landing
Sept. 3rd 1940	WALDBERG	Small boat
	MEIER	"
	PONS	"
	Van Den KIEBOOM	"
Sept. 5/6th 1940		Parachute
Sept. 19/20th 1940		"
Sept. 30th 1940	DRUECKE	Seaplane and dinghy
	ERICHSEN	"
	WAELTI	"
Oct. 3/4th 1940	GOOSE	Parachute
Oct. 25th 1940	EDVARDSEN	Seaplane and dinghy
	LUND	"
	JOOST	"
Jan 31st 1941	JAKOBS	Parachute
Apl. 7/8th 1941		Seaplane and dinghy
		"
May 12th 1941	RICHTER	Parachute
July 18th 1941	LENIHAN	Parachute in Ireland
Dec. 16th 1942	CHAPMAN (1st landing)	Parachute
Sept. 30/Oct.1st 1943.	Nikolay HANSEN	"
June 27/28 1944	CHAPMAN (2nd landing)	"

Eight agents were landed clandestinely in Iceland from U-boats, or small motor boats from Norway, namely:-

September 1943	
April 17th 1944	Einar SIGVALDSON
	Larus THORSTEINSSON
April 25th 1944	Magnus GUDBJORNSSON
	Sverir MATTHIASON
April 30th 1944	Ernst FRESENIUS
	Hjalti BJORNSSON
	Sigurdur JULIUSSON

One agent, Werner JANOWSKI, was landed from a German submarine in Canada in September 1942.

For the most part, the agents sent to this country by the Germans from November 1940 came in the guise of refugees from Nazi oppression either direct from occupied territory or through neutral countries, in many cases in company with genuine refugees.

Index

Bold page numbers refer to photographs.

Aben, F.J.M. 51, 284–6
Abetz, Otto 321
Abwehr 13–14, 27
    Argentina 266–7, 268n, 277, 357–8
    Belgium 149, 240–1, 288–91, 342–4
    Boortman 340–1
    Brandt 337–8
    Canada 252–3
    Chapman 218–26
    Denmark 294
    Egypt 202
    Eitel 323–6
    France 154, 167, 305–8, 315–17, 341–2
    Hamburg 137–8
    Iceland 299–300
    Invasion Spies 14–15
    Jugoslavia 281–3
    July Plot 353
    Krämer 353–5
    Lahousen 93
    Ledebur 339–40
    LRC 15, 17, 22
    Pheiffer 73, 360–2
    Portugal 187
    Schagen 323
    Spain 249, 292, 347
    Turkey 359, 360
    Verloop 332
Ackermann 284
Afghanistan 337–8
Africa 242–5
    see also individual countries
Aguilar, Jesús 231, 232, 265
Ahlrichs, Heinrich 52, 92, 225, 245
Albrecht 97, 99
Alcazar de Velasco 52, 178–80
Algeria 305, 307–8
Alseth, Sigurd Edvard 175–6
Altazin, M.P.F. 326–7
Amsterdam 137
Amt VI of the RSHA 48, 81, 268, 319, 321, 329, 356–7, 359, 365
Andersen, Helene 65, **66**, 344–5
Andersen, Karl 152, 163, 175
Andersen, Svend 65, **66**, 344–5
Anderson, Sir John 39
Anti-Bolshevist Legion 287
Argentina
    German agents in 78, 226–7, 230–2, 261–3, 276–7, 357–8
    Hellmuth 48, 115, 266–73
Arnhem 328
arrests 114
assessors 57, 125–6, 182, 207, 247
associations 144, 147, 192, 279
atom bomb 2, 34, 77, 104, 357
Attlee, Clement 39
Austria 338

B.1.A 25, 27, 138, 140, 162, 221–6, 368
B.8 35
Bad Nenndorf 7–8, 22, 58, 72, 82–102, 328–9, 355, 358
Bailly, Charles *see* Sancier
Ball, Roland 308–9
Balsam, Edward 168–70
Barcelona 249, 281, 287, 347
BASKET 166–8
Baticon, Joaquín 48, 55, 232, 265
Batos, Basil 79, 256, 358
Becker, Johannes Siegfried (SIEGMUND) 115, 268, 271–3, 277
Bedaux, Charles 77, 307, 338–9
BEETLE 258–9
Belgian Congo 187–8, 210, 249, 288
Belgium
    Abwehr 288–91, 290–1, 342–4
    Belgians working for the Germans 194–5, 275–6, 283–4, 317–18
    German agents in 210–11, 239–41, 247–8, 317–22
Below, Nicolaus von 83, 84–7, **86**
Beltran, Basilio 176–7
Beltrán Leiro, Diego 115, 265–6, 269, 276–7
Bendixen 325
Bernadotte, Count 81, 365
Bernard, Madeleine 302–3
Bernhard, Prince 328
Best 51, 330
Bianchi, Roger 63, 308–9
Bischoff, Johannes 325
Bissel, Major-General 59
Bjornsson, Hjalti 61, **62**, 124, 298–300, 369
blackmail 106
Blay Pigrau, Andrés 114, 226, 229–33
Bleicher, Hugo Ernst 363–4
Bletchley Park *see* Intelligence Service Oliver Strachey
Blits, Helena 347–8
blow hot, blow cold 21, 127–8, 214
Boeckel, Hauptmann 165, 166n
Boes 110, 111
Bohle 34
Bonzo 55, **56**, 279–80
Boortman, Michel 340–1
Boreas 145–6, 152, 163
Bormann, Martin 83, 84, 87
Boyd, Charles Olivier 214–15
Brand, Christian *see* Lindemans
Brandenburg Lehr-Regiment zbV 800 43, 149, 252, 303, 306, 323, 337–8
Brandt, Fred Hermann 67, 337–8
Braun, Eva 84
Brazil 199–201, 211
Bremen 187, 297–8, 324
Bremen 73, 324
Brendel, Dr 227–8
Brest 154, 324–5

Breton Nationalists 68, 306, 311–13, 316–17
Briscoe, Professor 239
British Union of Fascists (BUF) 14
Brodersen, Knut Jørgen 60, 295–6
Broglie, Princess de 334, 335
Broschinski, Sonja 99, **100**
Bruening, Eleanora von 93
Brugada 183
BRUHNS 156
Brussels 149, 284, 315, 318–20
Buenos Aires 269–71
Buenos Aires 357–8
BUF *see* British Union of Fascists
"bugging" *see* "M" cover
bunker agents 59, 70–1

Caldeira 255
Calvo Andaluz, Luis 52–4, **53**, 178–82, 199
Camp 020R (Huntercombe) 46–7
Camp WX (Stafford) 151
Campini 78–9, 233–4
Canada 200, 252–3
Canaris, Admiral 93
CARLOS *see* Eitel, Carl
CARMEN 210
Caroli, Gösta *see* SUMMER
Casabayo, Fernando 176–7
Ceballos 271
Cell Fourteen, legend of 21, 126–7
Chapman, Edward Arnold (FRITZ/ZIG-ZAG) 51, 61, 217–26, 300, 369
Chateau de Maulny 309, 310
Chateau-Thierry, Sonia, Duchesse de 141, 143, 146–7, 148
China 78
Ciano 55–7
SS *City of Lancaster* 223
Coll, Axel 151–3
Collomb, Claude 61–3, 304–5
Combined Services Detailed Interrogation Centre (CSDIC) 7–8, 22, 71–2, 82–102, 113, 355
  see also Bad Nenndorf; Diest
Comintern 97–9
Commandante Affonso de Carvalho 192
confessions 109, 118
confrontations 124–5, 144, 146, 159, 320
Copier, Willem (QUAX) 109–12, 345–6
Costa, Jose *see* Salamon, Janos
Costenza, Countess 37, 146–7
Coucke, Alphonse 283
cover story 128–9
Creedy, Sir Herbert 40
Crombe, Daniel Jean Louis 304–5
cross-ruff 124
CSDIC *see* Combined Services Detailed Interrogation Centre
Cuba 245–7, 291–2
Curry, John 3, 5, 12, 23, 27
Czechoslovakia 329

D-Day 22, 25, 60–1, 124, 302–10
Dalberg, Hallgrimur 186
Damen 332
De Bray, Louis 236, 284, 317–18
De Deeker, François *see* Drueke (Drüke), Karl Theo
De Jonge, Jan Roelof 160–1

De Rappard, Marcel Georges Armand 280–1
De Smidt, André 320–1
Dearden, Dr Harold **18**, 19
Del Campo y Palaez, José Antonio 162
Delhaye, René 320–1
Delobel, R.M.E. 313–14
Denmark 294
Deuxième Bureau 161, 198, 243–5, 303, 361
Diaz, Viviana 245–6
DIEGO *see* Beltrán
Dienststelle Ribbentrop 321–2
Dierks, Hauptmann 143
Diest 22, 55, 58, 71–2
Dietrich, Feldwebel 314
documents 114–17
Doenitz, Karl 83, 84, 85
Dos Santos, Maria 156–8, 255
double agents 22–6
  Altazin 327
  anonymous 42–3, 138–41, 162, 166
  British 15, 51, 178–82, 217–26, 273–5
  Frutos 310–11
  Golenko 335–6
  Goose 149–50
  Iceland 258–9
  Janowski 253
Double Cross system 2, 14, 15, 19, 22–6
  see also double agents
DRAGONFLY 273–5
Dronkers, Johannes Marinus 191–2, 368
drugs 21, 328
Drueke (Drüke), Karl Theo (François de Deeker) 43, **45**, 125, 137, 141–9, 368, 369
Du Chaffault, Comte Gabriel Billebault 254–5
Duffau, Pierre Camille 313–14
Dulag Luft 82n
Durbayllo 101

Edvardsen, Gunnar 43, 125, 141–9, 152, 369
Eeman 67
Egypt 67, 196, 201–2
EIKINS *see* Frutos, Juan
Eitel, Carl (CARLOS) 73, **74**, 106–7, 311, 323–6, 362
Ejsymont, Edward 168–70
Elferink, Lambertus (HAMLET) 79, 256, 263–4, 306, 358
England, German agents landing in 134–51, 153–66, 177–8, 183–4, 191–2, 216–17, 283–4
Erichsen, Vera (Schalburg) 43, **45**, 125, 141–9, 152, 369
escape attempts 21, 54, 92, 138–9, 229, 262
Evertsen, Cornelius 43, 153–4
executions 20, 156, 195, 198, 275, 284, 291, 367–8

fake newspapers 130, 223
Federal Bureau of Investigation (FBI) 58, 292
Fegelein, Hermann 83
Fellowes, Hon Mrs Reginald 334
FFI 65, 312, 316
Fidrmuc, Paul Georg (OSTRO) 24
Field for Ops 113
Fifth Column 11–13, 14, 34–5, 40
Finckenstein **45**, 46
Finland 97
Fixel 338
Florette 348–9

Foerster, Kurt 237
Fosseux 347
France
see also Deuxième Bureau;
Free French
Abwehr 316–17, 341–2
Breton Nationalists 68, 306, 311–13, 316–17
cooperation with Ham 242–5
double agents 52
German agents in 61–5, 67, 203, 251, 254–5, 287–8, 302–17, 327, 333–6, 344–5, 352
Fraval, Jean 78, 287–8
Free French 182, 198–9
see also Deuxième Bureau
Freitas Ferraz, Gastão Crawford de 54, 213–14, 237
Fresenius, Ernst Christoph 61, **62**, 124, 298–300, 369
Friedenthal espionage school 351
FRITZ see Chapman, Edward
FRITZCHIEN see Chapman, Edward
Frontläufer (line runners) 22, 61–7, 304, 305, 308–9
Frutos, Juan (EIKINS) 310–11, 324, 326
Fukken, Englebertus see Ter Braak, Willem

Gambia 189–91
Gamotha, Ramon 319
GARBO 25
Garcia Tirador, Onofré 182–3
Garitte, Arthur 320–1
Gartenfeld, Oblt Karl 15, 137, 139, 164–8
Geisskes, Major 333
Germany
agent network 60–71
Allied invasion of France 59–72, 60–1
Allied occupation 33–4, 95–102
invasion of Britain 11, 12, 15, 78, 134–7
post-war subversive movements 95–102
resistance 350
saboteur agents within 70–1
Gersdorf, Hilde 324
Gestapo 184–5
Gibraltar 160–1, 195, 254, 297
Gil Eannes 213
Gilinsky, Oscar 55, **56**, 114, 173–4
Girka, Michel 63, **64**, 308–9
Giskes, Hermann 126, 356
Gisvold, Sverre 175–6
Glad, Tör see JEFF
Gleich 99–101
Gleiwitz raid 330
HMS Gloucester 196
go-before spies 354
Gobin, Josef 2, 65–7, **66**, 124, 342–4
Gobin, Mathilde 2, 65–7, **66**, 124, 342–4
Goebbels, Joseph 83, 84, 322
Goering, Hermann 83, 85, 94, 114
Goettsch, Werner 329
Golenikov, Col 101
Golenko, Elie Gwodzdawo 75, **76**, 106, 335–6
Gonzalez, Colonel Enrique V. 269–72
Goodacre, Captain E. 20

Goose, Kurt 43, 140, 149–50, 369
Goumas 233–4
Graaf, Johannes de 236–7, 318
Great Britain
British prisoners 40–1
double agents 15, 51, 178–82, 217–26, 273–5
Invasion Spies 14–15, 78, 137–41
parachute agents 15, 43, 137–9, 149–50, 163, 164–8, 219–20, 259–61, 369
traitors 192–3, 195–8, 273–5
Greece 233–6, 341
Greenland 151–2
Greenwood 39
Greese, Irma 72
Greim 87
Grobben 52
Groening, Hauptmann 218–19, 221, 223–5
Grothmann 72
Gudbjornsson, Magnus 224, 294–5, 369
Guerin, Patrick Pierre 67, 68, 311–13, 316–17
Guilcher, Yves 302–3
Guy, André Louis Eugène 302–3
G.W. 178–9

Hagemann, Julius 353
Halfkath 101
Haller, Sonderführer 306, 307
Hamburg 75, 78, 137, 138, 142–3, 156, 165, 297–8, 354
HAMLET see Elferink, Lambertus
Hankey, Lord 13
Hanna, Sobhy 50, 51, 67, 116, 201–2, 212
Hansen, Bjarne 163–4
Hansen, Hans 163
Hansen, K.C. 46
Hansen, Nickolay 114, 129, 259–61, 369
Hansen, Oberst 77, 339–40, 355
Harker, O.A. 4–5
Harnisch, Hans (Juan) 115, 267–73, 277
Hau **100**, 101
Hellmuth, Osmar Alberto **44**, 48, 115, 266–73, 277, 357, 358
Henry, Lee Vaughan 41
Hernie 170–1
Heydrich, Reinhard 329–30, 331
Himmler, Heinrich 350
and agents 48, 81, 115, 266, 280, 365
arrest 72, 114
last days in bunker 83, 85
Hinchley-Cooke, Colonel 239
Hinrischen, Otto 264
Hirsch, Leopold 173–4
Hitler, Adolf 79, 83–7
Hitler Jugend 95–7
Hlidar, Gudmundur (Gudbrandur) 295, 297, 300, 349–50
Hoare, Sir Samuel 322
Hoffman 125, 150, 158, 177
Holland 184, 284–6, 327–8
Holloway 38
Holm 267, 272
Hoppe, Ernesto 48, **49**, 108, 261–3, 293
Hotel Ambassador, Paris 309
Hotel Lutetia, Paris 167, 307, 333, 339
HUMINT 26–7
Hungary 199–201

hunger strikes 54–5
Huntemann, Gerhard 356
Huygens, Jan 351–2
Huysmans, Johannes Ignatius 123–4, 247–50, 252

Iceland 60, 61, 185–6, 258–9, 294–5, 296–7, 298–300, 349–50, 369
identity papers 114–17
Imaz, Carlos 264
Information Index 16–17
Iniesta Pozos, Mercedes 204, 206
intelligence officers 41–2, 57–8
Intelligence Service Knox 14
Intelligence Service Oliver Strachey (ISOS) 13–14, 20–1, 27
    Coll 151
    De Freitas 213
    Elferink 263–4
    Gobin 344
    Manfredi 277–80
    Mochi 292
    OSTRO 24
    Wallem 170
internment 9, 12–13, 14, 16, 34–9
interrogations 9, 17–21, 57–8, 70, 105–12, 117–31
interrogators 7, 18, 41–2, 107–9, 117–19
Invasion Spies 14–15, 42–6, 134–50, 369
investigations 113–17
Ireland 67, 166–8, 316
ISOS see Intelligence Service Oliver Strachey
Italy 47–8, 55–7, 238–9, 257, 277–80, 292–4

Jakobs, Joachim 51
Jakobs, Josef 105, 155–6, 164–5, 368, 369
Jan Mayen Island 46, 151
Janowski, W.A.W. 252–4, 369
Japan 180, 366
JEFF 26, 162
Jersey 218
Job, Oswald John 43, 51, 273–5, 368
Jodl 85
Johansen, Ingvald 175
Jonasson 43, 153
Jonsson, Sigurjon 185–6
Joost, Otto 43, 141–9, 369
Joppe 191–2
Jordan, Jessie 364
M/V Josephine 46, 153–4
Jost, Heinz Maria Karl 340, 356–7
Jude, Leon Ernest 193–4
Jugoslavia 67, 281–3, 338
Juliusson, Sigurdur 61, 124, 298–300, 369
July plot 353, 355

Kaes, Amady 237
Kalkowski 99, 100, 101
Kaltenbrunner, Ernst 22, 23, 78, 79–81, 80, 106, 340, 363, 365
Kaminski 101
Karsten 210, 246
Keitel 85
Kell, Vernon 13, 22
Kieboom, Charles Albert Van den 15, 42, 44, 134–7, 147, 163, 341, 368, 369
Kirfel, Harald 366
Knochen, Dr 322
Köchling, Kapitän (Moritz) 65, 240–1, 288–9, 342, 344

Koehler 279–80
Kopkow, Horst 92
Kraemer (Krämer), Karl Heinz 72, 74, 75, 145, 353–5
Krag 54, 154
Kraus, Alfred Ignatz Maria 75–7, 76, 333–5
Krebs, General 84, 85
Kuebart, Wilhelm 355
Kyloe 306

La Fere, Claud de 52, 250–1
La Montagnette 303
M/V La Part Bien 153
Lahlum, Dagmar 224
Lahousen, Erwin 93–4
Lallart, Jean Marie 51–2, 53, 92, 105–6, 242–5
Landfried 94
Langen, Jan Bruno De 191–2
Latchmere House, Ham 10
    bombing of 46, 147
    creation of Camp 020 4, 6, 9–11, 14, 40–2
Laurenger, Georges Gabriel 310
Laureyssens, Joseph Auguste 124–5, 156–60, 177
Le Touquet 341, 342
Lecoq, Lucien Jules François 216–17
Lecube, Juan Gómez de 54, 126, 205–7
Ledebur, Rittmeister Graf Joseph von 77, 307, 338–40, 356, 362, 363
Lehnitz training school 319
Leibrandt, Roby 92, 306
Lejeune 318
LENA, Operation 15, 137–41
Lenihan 369
Leonidas 233–4
Levy, Anna 256
Lindemans, Christiaan Antonius ("King-Kong") 22, 69, 70, 327–9, 332
line runners 22, 59, 61–7
Lipkau 126, 207
Llanstephan Castle 195
Lojendio 180
Lombart, Claude 308–9
London Reception Centre (LRC) 15–17, 27, 113, 175, 192, 210, 217, 289
Lorenz, Fritz Wilhelm 321–2, 356, 357
Lorenz, Heinz 83–4
Lotz, Dr 299
Louant, Roger 283
Lourenço Marques 78–9, 202, 211, 233–4, 255, 256, 358
LRC see London Reception Centre
Lucas, Pierrette 341
Ludwig, Thomas 360
LUND 170
Lund, Legwald 43, 141–9, 369
Lunde, George 170–1

"M" (microphone) cover 11, 119–22, 129, 130, 147, 179
Macher 72
Madrid 162
Magnusson, Marel 186
HMS Malaya 48
Manceau, Yvon 308–9
Manet 63–5
Manfredi de Blasis, Barone Filippo 56, 57, 277–80
Manna, Alfredo 256–7
Marshall Group 182–3

MARTINEZ *see* Morales Serrano, Luis
Masterman, J.C. 23, 26
Mathieu, Henri Emile Jean 303–4, 309
Matthiasson, Sverrir 223, 294–5, 369
Mayer, Otto Emil Friedrich 54, 67, 281–3
Meier, Karl Heinrich 42, 134–7, 147, 368, 369
Meisner, Karl Robert Johannes 362–3
Meiss-Teuffen, H.J.O. von 54, 189–91
Menezes, Rogerio de Magalhaes Peixoto 24, **44**, 47–8, 237–9
MERCATOR 92
Mesquita dos Santos, Manoel (TOME) 116–17, 211–13
Metzger 97
Mexico 291–2
MI6 (SIS) 185, 266–7, 278, 283, 295–6
MI9 13
MI19 22, 42, 58, 71, 113, 119
Mochi, Marcello 57, 292–4
Mocsan, Sandor 54, 199–201
Moe, John *see* MUTT
Moglia, Antonio Aristides 352–3
SS *Monte Monjuich* 265, 276–7
Moolen, Gerhardus van der 286
Morael, Henri Edouard Eugène 351–2
Morales Serrano, Luís 203–5, 206, 215
Moreira 256
Morel, Pierre Henri 203, 216
Moreno Rego 277
Mour, Emile Lucien 314–15
Mueller, Gruppenführer Heinrich 92
Muellner 79
Muhlstein, Jan 168–9
Mulder, John Alphonsus 191–2
Müller, Huptsturm-führer (Horst) 230, 285
Müllner, Alois 358
Mussolini, Benito 79, 87–92
MUTT 26, 162

Nagel, Gerhard 341–2
Nantes 218–19
nationalist organisations *see* separatist movements
Naujocks, Alfred **50**, 51, 329–31, 356
Neukermans, Pierre Richard Charles 60, **62**, 78, 283–4, 317, 368
newspapers, fake 130, 223
NICO *see* Rombaut, Lucien
NIGHTCAP, Operation 219
Nilsen, Ingard Westerlid 170–1
Nilsen, Olaf *see* Wallem, Helmik
NORMA expedition 319
Normandy landings *see* D-Day
Norway 151–2, 163–4, 170–1, 172–3, 175–6, 223–4, 295–6
Nuremberg trials 22, 79, 81, 93, 363
NURSERY 95

Oberdoerffer, Herr 337
Olivera del Rio, José 48, 264–6, 276
Olmes, F.W.H. 77, 357
Omerti, Arturo 238
Operational Intelligence 59–72
Oratory Schools 9, 38–9
OSTRO 24
Otto, Margarete **37**
Owens, Arthur *see* SNOW
PABLO 249, 281

Pacheco y Cuesta, José Francisco Javier 48, **49**, 245–7
Palsson, Jens 185–6
parachute agents 15, 43, 137–9, 149–50, 163, 164–8, 219–20, 259–61, 369
Paraguay 229–32
Paris 167, 307, 309, 312, 317, 333, 339
Parti Populaire Français (PPF) 22, 308, 309
Pazos-Diaz 153–4
PEDRO 249, 281, 284, 287
Peereboom 51, 252
Pelletier, Jean Charles 184–5
Perez Garcia, Manuel 48, 226, 232, 277
Petin, Robert Charles Roger 198–9
Petrie, Sir David 3, 5, 13, 20
Pheiffer, Erich 73, **74**, 307, 311, 324–5, 326, 339–40, 355, 360–2
Phoney War 12, 35–9
Piat, Gaston 63, **64**, 308–9
Piernavieja Del Pozo 178–80
Pohl 93
Poils, Andre Alix Marie Jean 257–8
Poisson, Claude Louis Albert 251–2
Poland 51, 168–9, 188–9, 297, 330
Pons, Sjoerd 15, 42, 134–7, 369
Portugal
    African colonies 255–6
    German agents in 192–3, 196–7, 207–9, 213–14, 237–9, 247
    Hoffman 177–8
    London Embassy 23–4, 47–8, 237–9
PPF *see* Parti Populaire Français
Praetorius, Hauptmann 72, 165–6, 218–19, 221
Prelogar, Anne Marguèrite 351–2
Price, John Henry Watkin 192–3
Prieur 65
prisoners of war 119–22, 129–31
Pruetzmann, General 55
Pry, Gabriel Jules Emanuel 210–11
Pujol, Juan *see* GARBO

QUAX *see* Copier

Rademacher 228
Rainer, Hermann Alois 70–1, 350
Ramirez, President 269–70
RANTZAU *see* Ritter
Reemtsma, Phillip 94
refugees 15–17, 22, 153–6, 160–1, 183–4, 192, 236–7, 250–1, 283–4, 369
Rehbein, Karl 346–7
Reichssicherheitshauptamt (RSHA) 22
    Argentina 269–70
    Belgium 319
    Hellmuth 48
    Jost 356–7
    Kaltenbrunner 363
    Kuebart 355
    Lorenz 321
    Naujocks 329
    Olmes 77
    Sandberger 365–6
    Schellenberg 81, 268, 365
    Turkey 359
Reitsch, Hanna 83, 87
Renault, Marie 65
Reserve Camp, Huntercombe (Camp 020R) 46–7

Resistance 59, 68–70, 327–8, 333, 350
Ribbentrop, Joachim von 34, 266, 321–2
Richter, Karl **20**, 156, 164–6, 368, 369
Rithman 196–7
Ritter, Major Nikolaus Fritz Adolf 15, 43, 75, 92,
    137, 140, 142–3, 146, 148n, 354
Robertson, Colonel Tommy 25
Robles 154
Robr, Eigil Dag 172–3
Roger, Henri Gaston 303–4, 309
Rombaut, Lucien A.C.V. (NICO) 288–90
RSHA see Reichssicherheitshauptamt
Ruggeburg, Friedrich 230
Ruiz Goseascoechea, Joaquin 48, 226
Rundstedt, von 79
Ruser, Hans 273
RUTHERFORD see Scott-Ford
Rymer, James see Jakobs, Josef

saboteurs 59, 70–1, 310
Saetrang 21, 55
Salamon, Janos 54, 199–201
SALO see Jude, Leon Ernest
Sampson, Lt-Col G. 3–5, 3, 11, **20**
Sanchez Garcia, O. see Serrallach Garcia
Sancier, G.E.A. 314–15
Sandberger, Martin Karl 365–6
Sander, Erika 97
Schade, Theo 75, 333
Schagen, Peter 323
Scharf, H.K. (Schneider) 305–8, 339
Schellenberg, Walther **80**
    arrest and interrogation 22, 78, 81, 340,
        365
    Hellmuth 48, 115, 269, 271
    Jost 357
    Kaltenbrunner 363
    Sweerts 319
Schiffer 35, 38
Schipper, Pieter Jan 183–4
Schloss Schierensee 300
Schlüter, Ernst 358
Schmidt 203
Schmidt, Wulf see TATE
Schmitt, Fernand 67, 315–16
Schneider 229
Schneider, Hans Karl see Scharf, Hans Karl
Schreider, Josef 72
Schumann 248–9
Schwerdt **86**
scientific information 94
Scognamillo, Michel 303–4
Scotland 163–4, 170–1, 175, 259–60, 364
Scott-Ford, Duncan Alexander Croall
    (RUTHERFORD) 48, **49**, 195–8, 368
Screening Establishments 113
SD see Sicherheitsdienst
SEA LION, Operation 11, 12, 15, 78, 134–7
Sebold 200
secret writing 19, 156–7, 208, 229, 238–9, 259–60,
    288–9, 295
Security Executive 13
Seehof school 351
separatist movements 59, 67–8, 178–9, 306,
    311–13, 316–17
Serafimides, Homer 54, 79, 233–6
Serrallach Garcia, Octavio 226–8, 229, 232

Serrano Suñer 54, 178, 180, 182
Sevenans, Omer 283
Seys, Bernard 310
Short, Major R. 3–4, **4**, 5, **20**
Sibert, Brigadier-General 59
Sicherheitsdienst (SD) 22
    Argentina 266–8, 271–3, 277, 357–8
    Belgium 318–20, 351
    France 305, 311, 317, 321–2, 338, 352
    Holland 284–6
    Iceland 296–7
    Iran 338
    Italy 279
    Menezes 237–9
    Naujocks 329–31
    Turkey 359
    Verloop 332
Siemssen, Nina 75
SIGINT 26–7
Sigvaldason, Inar Bjorn 296–7, 369
Silberman **99**
Simmross, Krafft 93, 277
Simoes, Ernesto 207–9
Sindreu Cavatorta, Jean 226–7, 233
SIS (MI6) 11, 16–17, 24, 185, 266–7, 278, 283,
    295–6
Skorzeny, Otto 79, 87–92, 319, 351–2
Skorzisko 46, 150–1
Slovenes 67
SNOW 11, 15
SNUFFBOX, Operation 34–5, 40
SOE see Special Operations Executive
Solana, Bernardino 231, 233
Solem, Thorleif 175–6
South Africa 211, 214–15, 256, 263–4, 306
South America 226–32
    see also individual countries
Soviet Union 75, 97–102
Spain
    see also Barcelona; Madrid
    German agents in 48, 171–2, 195,
        203–7, 226–8, 264–6, 281, 291–2
    London Embassy 23–4, 52–4, 176–7,
        178–82, 204–5
    Marshall Group 182–3
    Poles 188
Special Operations Executive (SOE) 17, 356
SPITZENBERG 147
stay-behind agents 22, 59, 61, 67
    Argentina 357–8
    Belgium 342–4
    France 65, 67, 302, 310, 313–17, 327,
        344–5, 352
    Greece 341
    Turkey 359–60
Steiner, Florent Sylvestre 177–8
Steiner, Frank Domien 48, 239–42, 288, 289
Stephens, Lt-Col R.W.G. 1–2, 4–11, **9**, 17–19, **20**,
    22, 25, 27–8
STERN see Stevens, José Rogelio
Stevens (British Intelligence Officer) 51, 330
Stevens (South American) 54
Stevens, José Rogelio (STERN) 226, 228–9, 233
Stiege, Korvetten Kapitän 72
Stimson, Lieutenant-Colonel D.B. **20**
Stockholm 354
stool pigeons 21, 57, 119, 122–4, 159, 214

STRACHWITZ *see* Straugh
Strandmoen, Johan 137, 163
Strasser, Otto 322, 329
Strauch, Fritz (STRACHWITZ) 184, 290n
Stubbs 246
Student, Kurt 88
suicide 21, 55, 70, 139, 205, 256, 261–2, 358
Sukiennik, Jakob 168–70
SUMMER 15, 26, 137–40
Swaziland 256
Sweden 285–6, 354
Sweert, Otto 87–92
Sweerts, Pierre Marie Ernest 71, 318–20
Swinton Committee 13, 14
Swinton, Lord 13, 40–1
"Sympathy Men" 21, 129
Szumlicz, Tadeusz 188–9

M/V *Taanevik* 163–4
Tangier 57, 161, 292–4
TATE 26, 138–41, 149, 166
Ter Braak, J. Willem 15, 23, **24**, 162–3, 369
Thorsteinsson, Larus 296–7, 369
Thysville 187
Tikhmenev 60, **62**
Timmerman, A.L.E. 171–2, 368
Titford, Margarete *see* Otto, Margarete
Tito, Marshal 281–2, 283
Tocabens, Justin 287–8, 291
Todt Organisation 63, 317, 341
TOME *see* Mesquita dos Santos
Torgersen, Henry 163
Trinidad 48, 174, 203–4, 205–6, 226–32
Turkey 281–2, 359–60
Twenty Committee 23, 24–5

Uhe 101
Ullring, Captain 151–3
Ulrich, Karl 195
United States 59, 71, 79, 82n, 95–7, 335–6
    German agents 193–4, 325–6, 361, 364
Unversagt, Werner 78, 136n, 284, 287, 288, 290,
    362
Uruguay 228–9
Urzaiz y Guzman, Alejandro de (VIENTO) 291–2

Vae Victis 157
Vageler 94
Valles 231, 232
Van Ackere, E.J.C. 52, 185
Van Dam, Hendrik 97, 252, 348
Van Gils, Karel Hendrik 159–60
Van Hove, Josef Jan 60, 290–1, 368

Van Poppel 347
Vélez, Colonel 271
Venlo affair 51
Verbiest, Firmin Emile Jean 348–9
Verlinden, Jack 124–5, 150, 156–60, 177, 187
Verloop, Cornelis 328, 331–3
SS *Vesle Kari* 151–2
Viana dos Santos, Artur 55, 255–6
VIENTO *see* Urzaiz y Guzman
Villaverde 180
Ville de Namur 171
Vishinsky 97–9
Vissault de Coetlegon, G.L.Y. 67, 68, **69**, 311, 312,
    313, 316–17
Volpi 55–7
Vuolijoki, Hella 97–9

Waelti, Werner Heinrich 43, 125, 142–9, 368, 369
Waldberg, Josef Rudolf 15, 42, **44**, 78, 134–7, 147,
    368, 369
Wallem, Helmik 170–1
Wassilieff 318
Waziristan 337
Wehran, Pastor 36
Wehrkreisdommando III 262–3
Weidemann 78
Welsh Nationalists 178–9
Weltzien, Kuno 193, 198, 209, 214
Wendel, Charles 338
WERNER *see* Unversagt, Werner
Werz, Luitpold 78–9
Westerlinck, Hilaire Anton 186–8
White, Dick 9, 16
Wichmann, Herbert C.O.O. 364
Wichmann, Korvetten Kapitän 78
Wijckaert, Guy M.J.J. 275–6, 283, 318
Wilheim 99–101
Williams, Gwilym *see* G.W
Wilman, Wladyslaw 60–1, 297–8
Wings, Raymond 39
Winter, Johannes Franciscus 194–5, 368
Wolf, General Friedrich 78, 270, 271, 357–8
Wolff, Bruno Friedrich 359–60
Wrede, Dr 353

XX *see* Double Cross

Yellow Perils 5–6, 109, 115, 207–9, 220–5, 233–6,
    242
Yugoslavia *see* Jugoslavia

Zebralla, Uffz (ZEBRA) 156
ZIG-ZAG *see* Chapman, Edward